A Cause for our Times

Oxfam
the first 50 years

Maggie Black

Oxfam

D0235031

A catalogue record for this book is available from the British Library

Cover photo: Labourers at a lime kiln in Bihar, India. (CLAUDE SAUVAGEOT)

ISBN 0 85598 172 5
ISBN 0 85598 173 3 pbk

Produced by Oxfam UK and Ireland
274 Banbury Road, Oxford OX2 7DZ

Typeset in 10 pt Palatino by Oxfam Design
Printed by Hartnolls Ltd

OX:729/DH/92
Oxfam is a registered charity no.202918

CONTENTS

LIST OF ILLUSTRATIONS

We are grateful to the British Red Cross Museum and Archives for supplying the photographs 4 and 5 of relief work in Greece in 1942, and to the International Committee of the Red Cross for permission to use them in this book.

ACKNOWLEDGEMENTS

Exactly 21 years ago, I joined the staff of Oxfam. Although I stayed only for four years, those years shaped my world view more than any other passage in my adult life.

Oxfam has its quota of self-critics at any given moment, chastising its shape, its size, its pretensions, and its failure to deliver on a dizzying number of agendas, including that of transforming the world. But there is no doubt in my mind that it has transformed the lives of thousands of people, and brought a speck of gold – hope, opportunity, material help, a new self-confidence – into millions of others. No-one will ever convince me that this organisation is anything less than extraordinary, possessing a concentration of calibre, energy, and dedication which would be the envy of any organisation in the world.

Having confessed to an outrageous degree of bias, how can my account of Oxfam's history claim to be independent? First, it is independent in the sense that it does not assume that Oxfam is all-important in its own story. The centre of gravity of this book is not Oxfam and its many works, but ideas in the wider society of which it is a reflection and, at its most inspirational, a goad. Second, it is able to be independent because there is no need for an essay in self-congratulation; Oxfam at 50 has a sufficient record of achievement not to waste resources on a 'vanity book'. Third, Oxfam's penchant for self-criticism means that most Oxfamers – including my own ex-Oxfamer self – would be antagonised by an account which belonged to the genre of artificially untroubled self-advertisement.

If this book can justifiably claim to be independent, it should also admit to being idiosyncratic. There is almost no subject in the international pantheon of causes that Oxfam can bear to leave alone, nor a geographical corner of the Third World that it abjures. To try to write, authoritatively, on such a plethora of subjects and vicinities from a historical perspective, and to do so in such a constricted space, leads inevitably to arbitrary decisions about what to cover and what to leave out. The requirements of narrative and chronology as well as personal predisposition have also narrowed my choices, which are not the choices another author would have made.

There are those who will search in vain for their pet project or their personal heroes; who will look for a dissertation on certain areas of Oxfam concern – AIDS, disabilities, urban health, paravets, Gujarati dairy co-operatives, cholera control in Bangladesh, Bolivian tin-miners, disaster housing, genetic seed-banks, Turkana fishermen, the travails of fundraisers, the modern role of the charitable trustee – and who will be disappointed. Many people and organisations have played a vital part in the Oxfam story whose praises remain unsung, a feature of this account I readily acknowledge and regret.

So many people have contributed in their different ways to the perspectives which find expression in these pages that it is impossible to apportion credit or blame. They include many at Oxfam in whose company I first discovered the Pandora's Box of 'World Development' back in the early 1970s; those at the *New Internationalist*, where I served as an editor in 1976-77; and also many staff members of UNICEF, both in East Africa and in New York, where I worked from 1977-1987. Most of all, they include innumerable people in what is called 'the field', people in villages, in health centres, in slum settlements, in refugee camps, in hot and dusty offices, who said something or did something which told me as much about this inexact science of 'development' as all the experts' treatises combined.

Many people have given valuable help during the preparation of this book. These include Bill Acworth, Annie Allsebrook, Mary Allsebrook, Ferdinand Ali II, Odhiambo Anacleti, Phil Baker, Chris Barber, Philip Barron, Tim Brierly, Audrey Bronstein, Peter Burns, Mary Cherry, Sam Clarke, Peter Coleridge, Bruce Coles, Paddy Coulter, Pat Davidson, Leslie Durham, Richard Exley, Henry Fletcher, Brendan Gormley, Hugh Goyder, Frankie Hamilton, Malcolm Harper, Jim Howard, John Isherwood, Bill Jackson, Philip Jackson, Joel Joffe, Frank Judd, Mary Kirkley, Robin Langdon-Davies, Alan Leather, Tim Lusty, Joan McCartney, Bill McGuire, Gordon MacMillan, Nick Maurice, Ed Millard, Amanda Milligan, Joe Mitty, Richard Moseley-Williams, Adrian Moyes, Roger Newton, Reggie Norton, Mike Parkinson, Timothy Raison, Andrew Phillips, Bruce Ronaldson, Joan Rough, Michael Rowntree, Gordon Rudlin, John Saunders, Charles and Jane Skinner, Susanna Smith, Nicolas Stacey, Tigger Stack, John Staley, Peter Stalker, Richard Stanley, Jonathon Stockland, Mary Stringer, Harold Sumption, Og Thomas, Marcus Thompson, Matty Townsend, Pramod Unia, Tony Vaux, Brian Walker, Peter Wiles, Suzanne Williams, Carole Wills, Elizabeth Wilson, and Bill Yates. For comments and encouragement well beyond the call of duty I am especially indebted to Raymond Andrews, David Bryer, Michael Harris, Bernard Llewellyn, and Guy Stringer.

Thanks are also due to those who helped with research in the Oxfam archives, especially Paresh Motla and Niel Wigan; also to staff of the Friends' House Library, the Bodleian Library (especially for access to the Gilbert Murray Papers), Rhodes House Library, the libraries of the British Refugee Council and the Refugees Studies Programme (QEH, Oxford), the archive of the Manchester and Salford Committee for Famine Relief (lent by Lionel Cowan), and the curators of the Philip Argenti collection in the Greek Island of Chios.

Finally, there are two people who have made a unique contribution. One is Elizabeth Stamp, whose encyclopaedic knowledge of Oxfam's world has been laid generously at my disposal and without whose guidance and research I would have been frequently at a loss. The other is Ann Cullen, whose patience and editorial support have never flagged.

Maggie Black
Oxford, June 1992

1

'FANATICS, SOFT-HEADS, AND SENTIMENTAL IDEALISTS'

On a war-time evening in October 1942, a small group of people met in the Old Library of the Church of St. Mary-the-Virgin in Oxford. Their concern was the misery and starvation pervading Europe as an outcome of the war.

One of them was an Anglican cleric. One, a retired Indian Colonial Service officer. Another, a Jewish refugee from Germany. The most prestigious was a Greek scholar and a leading figure of his time in the field of international social endeavour. All were people whose outlook had been strongly influenced by the ideals of international understanding to which the carnage of the first World War had given birth. The 'internationalist' ideology to which they all subscribed had launched the League of Nations and, in Britain in the 1920s and 1930s, a ferment of movements and societies dedicated to brotherhood and peace.

When Hitler's armies tramped through Europe, such ideas were overwhelmed by a new dark age of hatreds and antagonisms, national suspicions and distrust. Britain was far from immune from this contagion. In the sudden reversal of public mood, doctrines recently seen as brave and visionary – Gandhi's espousal of non-violent protest, for example – were discredited. Pacifism, until 1939 a highly respectable creed, became tainted with overtones of cowardice and treachery; its followers deserted in droves. The call to arms against the Nazis became compelling. To resist the forces of spiritual and political darkness, a chilling doctrine was proclaimed: 'total war'. But for those committed to the ideal of international fellowship, this policy ran against deepest conviction.

The group of Oxford citizens who met at the University Church on that October evening were not only concerned about the hunger and suffering inflicted upon innocent civilians by Hitler's armies of occupation. Along with a network of other like-minded groups throughout the country, they stood for a principle not yet enshrined in international law, a principle then too frail to stand the shock of international conflagration: humanitarian neutrality. This principle states that the needs of innocent men, women, and children involuntarily caught up in war transcend the political divide. The group in Oxford felt anguished about the impact of 'total war' on helpless civilians. They were, at least in thought, part of an incipient protest movement about the ruthless conduct of the war, not only by Germany but by Britain.

The elements of the debate that evening were recorded in a school exercise book. The tone was tentative and exploratory, the outcome inconclusive. But before the participants bade each other good-night and set off into the black-out, they made a decision: to call themselves the Oxford Committee for Famine Relief.

From this hesitant beginning grew in time an organisation which, as Oxfam, has changed the face of British charitable activity. Not only in its genesis, but in its adoption of the multiplying causes of distress among peoples in other lands, Oxfam's mission has reflected major evolutions of 20th century thinking. This is true not only of its work among victims of war and other disasters, but among victims of poverty in what the post-colonial world came to call the developing countries.

A voluntary aid organisation such as Oxfam is, ultimately, of historical interest as a barometer of the way people in Britain and elsewhere have viewed other societies over time, especially the fortunes of their least privileged members. The story of Oxfam is primarily the story of what happened to the doctrine of 'internationalism' over the course of half a century. That, anyway, is the starting point for this particular historical voyage of enquiry.

On 20 August 1940 at the height of the Battle of Britain, Winston Churchill made one of his great war-time speeches in the House of Commons. His salute to British airmen went ringing down the years: 'Never in the history of human conflict was so much owed by so many to so few.'

The tribute was contained in a speech of much broader purpose addressed to a beleaguered people. Churchill told the chamber that this was a new kind of war, not like the war of 1914-1918. This was a conflict not only of men·versus guns, but 'of strategy, of organisation, of technical apparatus, of science, mathematics and morale'. This was total war, in which everyone – not just those who fought, but entire populations – were involved. He stiffened his audience for the single-mindedness which must characterise the conduct of the war, not only for the defence of one island realm, but for the counter-attack which Britain must mount, alone, to rid Europe of Nazi aggression.

'It is our intention', Churchill stated, 'to maintain and enforce a strict blockade not only of Germany, but of Italy, France and all other countries that have fallen into the German power.' He made it clear that the blockade extended to all relief, including food, for the people of friendly countries now overrun. To let food through must nourish the Nazis and prolong the agony of the conquered. 'There have been many proposals, founded on the highest motives, that food should be allowed to pass the blockade for the relief of these populations. I regret that we must refuse these requests.'

He went further. It was the responsibility of the Nazis to feed the peoples they had conquered. If they did not, and famine prevailed, this would encourage the hungry to bring forward the day when their yoke would finally be broken. 'We will organise food immediately an area is liberated. We will build up reserves of food all over the world so that these will always be held up before the eyes of the people of Europe – I say it deliberately – the German and Austrian peoples, the certainty that the shattering of the Nazi power will bring to them all immediate food, freedom and peace.'

In the debate that followed, many speakers rose to applaud Churchill's call for unconditional commitment. With the battle for the skies still far from won and the threat of German invasion still imminent, this was not a time for equivocation. Churchill refused point-blank to provide any statement of his eventual peace aims, which was a way of saying that he refused any dialogue with those who still had a toe in the anti-war lobby. Only one voice, that of Dick Stokes, the Member for Ipswich, expressed a reservation about the impact of total blockade. 'Surely you can hold out some hope to our own friends in Europe who, according to the Ministry of Economic Warfare, will suffer the most appalling privation of famine and plague during this coming winter?'

No, the Prime Minister could not.

Encirclement and siege, with their corollary, the gradual starvation of a blockaded people, are weapons of war as old as warfare itself. The policy of Britain in the second World War, as laid down by Churchill in this speech and re-confirmed on many later occasions, was to use these ancient weapons to the limit of their applicability. Not only were all goods traded with the enemy declared contraband; so were all goods destined for the relief of friendly countries now under occupation by the enemy.

In August 1940 these countries included Poland, Czechoslovakia, Belgium, Holland, Norway, and France. Germany had announced that it would introduce a unified economic system in Europe, and was clearly going to draw upon the resources of all the countries in its power to fuel its war machine. Industrial workers, labour of all kinds, would produce on behalf of the Third Reich. To cut off German supply lines therefore entailed cutting off all supply lines, even where allies in the fight against Hitler, including civilians – women, children, the sick and elderly, the bombed, interned, and refugees – might suffer cruelly as a result.

As modern weaponry had pushed out the frontiers of warfare until its theatre became all-embracing, it had become much harder to wage war in a way that distinguished between combatants and civilians, enemies and subjugated peoples. Parleying relief across enemy lines to distribute among civilians under neutral supervision was first undertaken during the first World War, but the procedure was not yet coded or articulated in any internationally binding legal instrument.

In the 1920s and 1930s the International Committee of the Red Cross managed to achieve ratification of improvements in the Geneva Conventions dealing with the wounded in battle and treatment for prisoners-of-war. But similar proposals put forward to limit the bombing of civilians and protect people in countries under occupation proved stillborn. When war began in 1939 there were, therefore, agreed international rules for sending food parcels to prisoners-of-war; but none for the delivery of food and medical relief to suffering civilians, even where they might be living in the same country, even community, as combatant internees.

The Hague Conventions of 1907 maintained that it was the responsibility of the occupying power to feed those people under its authority, or to allow them to feed themselves from their own resources. It was this which provided Britain with legal respectability for the total ban on relief for those now subject to Nazi rule. In other contexts the Hague Conventions were not conspicuously honoured: Article 25, for example, prohibited the attack or bombardment of undefended towns and villages. The Conventions also stated: 'The Laws of War do not concede to belligerents unlimited power with reference to the choice of means of injuring the enemy.' Britain never trusted Nazi Germany to honour any such 'Laws of War'. The arguments in favour of a watertight blockade included the accusation that the Nazis would certainly pillage anything allowed through. On the one hand, the British insisted that the Germans were most unlikely to act in the interests of their conquered peoples; on the other, they asserted that Germany alone must come to their relief. Public debate of any such inconsistency was, however, for the future.

In the first World War a different precedent had been set. In the autumn of 1914, the people of Belgium had faced starvation as a result of the British blockade of North Sea ports. While the US was still a neutral party, a private philanthropic body, the Commission for Relief in Belgium, was set up in London at the initiative of an American magnate, Herbert Hoover. Hoover, whose exploits as Europe's unofficial 'Food Czar' eventually led him up the ladder of US power and into the White House, managed to obtain agreement from the warring parties to take food through the blockade, and distribute it to civilian committees under the supervision of American and other neutral nationals. Drawing on Belgian government deposits abroad, as well as British, French and US loans and private contributions, the relief operation dispensed supplies worth $1 billion in Belgium and German-occupied northern France during the war and immediately afterwards.

In May 1940, with the US similarly neutral, ex-President Hoover put together a similar proposal for relief of civilians in Belgium. His Commission for Polish Relief had already delivered supplies through the blockade in 1939 with British consent. But by May 1940, with Churchill in power, the atmosphere had altered. In early August, Hoover laid a fuller proposal before the warring powers for relief to Norway, Holland, Belgium, and France. The Germans did not rebuff his initiative but were reluctant to concede its necessity. The British dismissed it out of hand. It can not have helped his case that Herbert Hoover, whatever his humanitarian credentials, was an isolationist and President Roosevelt's most bitter political foe.

Hoover's proposals were uppermost in Churchill's mind when he issued a blanket refusal to all such requests. At a time when the German armies had rolled all before them, when 'Battle of Britain Day' – 15 September – was still three weeks away, and every last fibre of effort was needed to harden British resolve to fight on, let alone to believe in victory, total war was an understandable policy. Its implications, however, were extremely harsh, if not immediately, then for the future. For the moment no-one could tell how fully the Germans would shoulder the obligation to act as quartermaster to their subject peoples. In the autumn of 1940, there was some food scarcity everywhere on the continent, and there was hunger in southern France, Norway, and Poland. But there was no evidence of disaster. Not yet.

Deep civilian distress would only come with the changing tide of war – the change envisaged by Churchill in his address to the House of Commons in late August 1940, which the hardening of the blockade was itself designed to hasten.

In September 1941, the International Red Cross delegate inAthens cabled an SOS to headquarters in Geneva. 'Food situation in Greece extremely grave. Mortality increased sixfold in the last two months. Catastrophe inevitable unless outside help arrives quickly.' The cable proved prophetic.

After a heroic campaign against Italian forces during the winter of 1940-41, the exhausted Greeks – assisted by British troops – had been unable to withstand the German invasion of the spring. On 27 April 1941, the Greek government capitulated and went into exile. The Germans initially offered friendship to their latest subject people. When it was repudiated, retaliation was severe.

The Germans needed provisions for the campaign in North Africa, so they requisitioned all Greek public and private stocks of food, clothing, and medical supplies. The 1941 harvest, planted in the midst of war, had been meagre; but the Bulgarian occupation in the north and the Germans' disruption of the transport system cut off all access from Athens and the south to whatever wheat there was. Greece, mountainous and stony, was a poor food producer at the best of times, importing 60 per cent of food requirements in a normal year. During the Italian campaign, British naval convoys brought in supplies. With defeat came something quite different: British naval enforcement of the blockade against all such shipments. Within weeks, food became desperately scarce.

In July, the Greek Ambassador to (neutral) Turkey began to try and organise cargoes from Istanbul. Through the mediation of the Turkish Red Crescent, the Turks agreed to the use of a ship and to the purchase of food, but insisted on permission from the adversaries. Since Turkey was within the blockade area, Britain had no technical objection to food purchases there or their shipment through the Dardanelles. Italian and German agreement was also needed: their planes controlled the air. After lengthy diplomatic negotiations in Ankara, the parties agreed that both shipment and distribution should be put in the hands of the International Red Cross.

The Turkish ship S.S. *Kurtulus* – painted brilliant white with a huge Red Crescent on each of her sides – was finally loaded and left for Athens in late October.

The *Kurtulus* was greeted by haggard crowds. The Master reported: 'Barefooted children almost stormed the vessel crying pitifully for food.' Marcel Junod, a senior Swiss Red Cross delegate, arrived from Istanbul. He found a city full of refugees and desolation. 'In the streets were walking spectres. Here and there old men, and sometimes young ones, sat on the pavement. Their lips were moving as if in prayer but no sound came. They stretched out their hands for alms and let them fall back weakly. Pedestrians passed backwards and forwards before them without paying the least attention. Each one was asking himself when his own turn would come.'

The *Kurtulus* made five voyages between Istanbul and Piraeus before January 1942, each cargo bringing enough to give half a pound of food to around 12,000 people for ten days. Junod and his staff set up kitchens which ladled out hundreds of thousands of bowls of soup, feeding stations for 100,000 children over seven, and 130 nursery centres; but only in Athens, and without firm guarantee of more supplies. By the end of the year, nearly 8,000 metric tons had been sent from Turkey. Many of the supplies were paid for by the Greek War Relief Association of America, a voluntary body which was extremely active throughout the next two years.

In January 1942 came disaster: the *Kurtulus* struck a rock and was wrecked in the Sea of Marmara. A few provisions arrived from Italy, Switzerland, and Germany, but very, very few. Pressure built up in Britain for something to be done and on 27 January, the Minister of Economic Warfare announced that a cargo of British wheat stored in Egypt would be sent. It took until late March for the ship to arrive. Meanwhile two other Swedish ships carrying flour were mobbed by small boats when they arrived in Piraeus. One was bombed by Italian planes and lost at sea after discharging its cargo. During March and April, Athens continued to be the scene of terrible suffering.

At the height of the famine, the death toll from starvation and exposure in Athens and Piraeus alone reached over 1,600 a day; towards the end of January 1942, it was reported to exceed 2,000. The authorities issued ration cards to the Greek population. They were useless: there was no food to be distributed. More than half the townspeople were trying to survive on 250 calories a day, one-tenth of a normal diet.

Whatever food there was vanished onto the black market, flourishing to the benefit of members of the German occupying forces and their collaborators. Inflation was astronomic and the currency lost all value. Only those with gold sovereigns could buy provisions. Thousands of children in Athens were described as 'living skeletons' and infant mortality rose to over 50 per cent. Every morning found more dead bodies in the street, left there anonymously by families frantic to retain their ration cards. In other parts of the country the situation was as desperate. 'Send bread or coffins' was the message received in Athens from the half-starved population of one Aegean island. In the Peloponnese and some of the islands, neither wheat nor flour had been seen for months.

Not until 16 April 1942, after pressure from the International Red Cross, Sweden, Canada, and finally the US, did the British government accept that to allow in a few shipfuls was not enough. In Parliament, Dingle Foot announced on behalf of the Minister of Economic Warfare that Britain had agreed to let regular relief for Greece go through the blockade. Monthly cargoes of 15,000 tons of Canadian wheat were to be loaded in Swedish ships, carried under the Red Cross flag, and distributed under the supervision of a joint Swiss and Swedish Red Cross Commission. Some dried milk for children as well as dried vegetables and vitamins were to be included. The quantity of basic food amounted only to a quarter of estimated need, but it was still significant.

The system of regular shipments took some months to establish. In July 1942, news came from a Swiss Red Cross delegate that the first cargo in the Aegean had arrived in the island of Chios. With starving children scouring the streets and thousands of famished islanders fleeing in small boats to Asia Minor, food had arrived just in time. By August, eight Swedish ships were in commission for Greece and by October, the relief programme was relatively well organised.

Around 200,000 Greek people died of starvation during the terrible winter of 1941-42, proportionately far more than in any recent Ethiopian famine. 'Catastrophe inevitable' had proved correct. And catastrophe continued on a less drastic scale until liberation in late 1944 and beyond. Starvation, exposure and disease took up to 500,000 Greek lives between 1941 and 1944 out of a population of seven million. Without the relief operation, at least a quarter – maybe more – of the population would have perished.

The severity of the famine in Greece was exceptional. Elsewhere the blockade held firm. From France, Norway, Poland, Belgium came further reports of serious food shortage. To pleas on behalf of people other than the Greeks, the British government remained unmoved.

When news about the starvation in Greece began to filter through to London in the autumn of 1941, prominent individuals had begun quietly to use their influence on behalf of the Greeks. Among these were Lord Robert Cecil (Viscount Chelwood), and Professor Gilbert Murray, leading figures in the League of Nations Union, a citizen support group for international peace and understanding.

Chelwood and Murray believed that the Germans were using starvation as a deliberate instrument of war, and that this required the British government to reconsider the morality of their position on relief. On 6 November, they set up a small committee to consider what should be done for the people of friendly countries, and began to press for a meeting with Hugh Dalton, the Minister of Economic Warfare. Dalton was implacably committed to the policy of total blockade. Early in January, Chelwood finally managed to see Dingle Foot, Dalton's Parliamentary Secretary. His attitude was not encouraging.

It was in January 1942 that the *Kurtulus* foundered and the famine in

Athens reached its height. There were reports in the British press from correspondents based in Turkey, and pacifists began raising their voices about Greek starvation. The Peace Pledge Union had already set up a 'Food Relief Campaign' with the author, Vera Brittain, as Chairman. Local committees began to petition their MPs. But, as Vera Brittain lamented, a campaign by pacifists could easily be dismissed as the work of 'fanatics, soft-heads, and sentimental idealists'.

On 27 January, George Bell, Bishop of Chichester, a churchman known for his outspoken defence of humanity, spoke in the House of Lords in support of an appeal for Greek relief. This appeal was successful: on the same day, Dalton made the announcement about the cargo of British wheat from Egypt. Vera Brittain then suggested to Bishop Bell that he establish a weightier group of churchmen, academics, and public figures than the pacifists could muster, to lead protest against British policy on relief and the blockade.

On 29 May 1942, the creation of a national Famine Relief Committee was publicly announced. The active spirit behind what was to become a nation-wide campaign was the redoubtable Edith Pye, a Quaker then in her late sixties. Pye had devoted a long professional life 'to the margins of chaos', to refugees and the war-torn in countries all over the world, through the relief services of the Society of Friends. As honorary secretary of the Famine Relief Committee, she was its chief strategist and organiser. Like Vera Brittain, Edith Pye devoted herself to dispelling British indifference towards hungry women and children in occupied countries.

Apart from its Chairman, Bishop Bell, the Committee boasted three Bishops and a number of other leading clerics. Members included Gilbert Murray, the Master of Balliol, the Master of Selwyn, Julian Huxley, Douglas Woodruff, editor of the Catholic journal *The Tablet*, and other figures whose titles and honorifics placed them squarely in establishment circles. The Archbishop of Canterbury, the Cardinal Archbishop of Westminster, the Moderator of the Free Church Council, and the Chief Rabbi, all lent public support.

The Famine Relief Committee's aims were very carefully phrased. 'Objects: To obtain authentic information as to food conditions in German-controlled or invaded countries; to promote schemes for the sending of food, vitamins and medical aid into such countries, wherever control is possible, in co-operation with existing organisations.' The Committee also opened a Famine Relief Fund, to pay for such relief 'as soon as permission is obtained to use it'. In 1942, there was no way to spend such money because that, too, would breach the blockade.

Throughout the summer of 1942, Edith Pye began to develop a network of support committees all over Britain. She organised speakers for meetings, and attended many in person. On 20 July she travelled to Oxford for a gathering at the Friends' Meeting House, prompting a handful of citizens led by the Rev. T.R. Milford, Vicar of the University Church, to become actively concerned. The same pattern was repeated in towns throughout the country.

Information about the condition of people in occupied Europe was difficult to come by. What little there was came from refugees or those who managed to get reports through to friends and relatives. Occasional short despatches from newspaper correspondents based in Ankara, Cairo, Geneva, Stockholm and other neutral capitals were printed, notably in *The Times* and the *Manchester Guardian*, both of which tended to be strongly sympathetic towards relief. Other reports were circulated by governments-in-exile or Red Cross representatives in London. But full statistics, which could only have been collected and provided by the German-controlled authorities, were unobtainable.

The lack of information and the question marks which hovered over the accuracy of many reports – particularly if circulated by anyone with well-known pacifist leanings – dogged the efforts of the Famine Relief Committee and the food campaign groups throughout the next 18 months. The lack of pictures and graphic accounts and the shortage of evidence made it very easy for the government to advance the virtues of the blockade while omitting to dwell on its negative aspects. For these reasons Edith Pye did her best to cull from all sources information of unimpeachable veracity and circulate it as dispassionately as possible.

Political overtones were unavoidable. To suggest, however circumspectly, that Britain's war policy was causing starvation among women and children in friendly countries was, at best, unpatriotic; their sufferings were essentially Nazi-induced. The question remained whether Nazi responsibility exonerated Britain's refusal to allow any help to be sent. Gilbert Murray believed passionately that it did not, and he also believed that assistance to the enemy was unproven: 'Does all this famine and misery injure the Germans? On the contrary, it helps them,' he wrote. His case: decent rations were given to industrial workers, therefore the able-bodied co-operated with their conqueror; the rest – children, the sick, the elderly and infirm – were expendable.

The problem faced by those who took such a line was that all positions which were equivocal about total war, even on moral grounds, were out of tune with the times. George Bell, who vigorously protested against both the blockade and mass civilian bombing, was expected to become Archbishop of Canterbury until he publicly opposed the evil of all-out war. Sentiments about our membership of 'one humanity', the idea of a new world order based on common understanding between peoples, had become unpopular to a degree unthinkable a few years earlier. Their advocates, so recently in the philosophical mainstream, now needed courage to stand up for their principles against the blacker side of the bulldog spirit Churchill had so successfully conjured among his compatriots.

Although there was no hard data on hunger from Europe, the level of official rations was known. This in itself provided some benchmark of shortage, even though entitlement – as in Greece – did not necessarily mean that the rations were available. The content of rations and the calorific needs of children and mothers were a constant focus of enquiry.

According to the Ministry of Economic Warfare, in spring 1942, rations were lowest in Norway, Belgium, Poland, and Greece. In Poland, the food allowance was not much higher than in Greece: per week, 39 ounces of bread, one-and-a-half ounces of meat and one ounce of fat; and rations were not evenly distributed, with native Germans receiving more than Poles, and Jews receiving almost nothing. But Poland could not be supplied by neutral shipping from the sea. Belgium and Norway could.

Belgium was the most likely next candidate for special status. Like Greece, Belgium never fed itself in normal times, depending on imports for up to 70 per cent of food supplies. Since Herbert Hoover's first proposal in May 1940, efforts had been made to open up the blockade for Belgium, as had been done in the first World War. Hoover never stopped trying: a third proposal was turned down in January 1941. Thereafter, the Belgian government in London put forward its own proposal for 'controlled relief'.

Professor Emile Cammaerts, a Belgian intellectual living in London, campaigned persistently on behalf of his compatriots. He described the situation, in *The Tablet* on 1 August 1942. 'Only bread and sugar can be purchased regularly at the fixed price. Potatoes have been unobtainable after the exhaustion of last year's crop in April. The black market only supplies the wealthy, about five per cent of the population, and this last resource is waning fast. The vast majority are reduced to a diet providing 900 calories.'

The situation of children was poor. 'The mortality among children under six has trebled in the large hospitals. There is a fall of 80 per cent in the growth rate of the young. Attendance at school has considerably decreased. ... In hospitals and sanitaria, the number of cases of tuberculosis has trebled. ... The only efficient remedy is a healthy diet and doctors stand helpless, since they cannot obtain the means of curing their patients.'

By July 1942, the Famine Relief Committee, with eminent nutritional and medical advice, had developed a scheme for 'controlled food relief' for children, mothers, and the sick in Belgium and Greece. In the case of Greece, the scheme was intended to supplement the existing imports; no relaxation of the blockade for large-scale food imports into any other country was proposed. Bishop Bell went to see Lord Selborne, now Minister of Economic Warfare, and Anthony Eden, the Foreign Secretary. He was told that no further exceptions to the blockade were likely to be admitted. Undaunted, the Committee set out its proposal in a pamphlet called 'Hunger in Europe' in October 1942. Every care was taken not to criticise government policy. Indeed, the Committee applauded the existing relaxation in the blockade, and argued that this experience could be built upon for a modest, medicinal, injection of dried milk and vitamins which could have no impact on the German war effort.

An amount of 2,000 tons a month for a daily nutritional 'tonic' for six million recipients in Greece and Belgium would be sent from the US, paid for by the countries concerned, and shipped in neutral vessels. Distribution would be supervised by International Red Cross personnel, and if any diversion occurred, the pipeline could be instantly closed. All the British needed to give was navicerts – permission to pass the blockade.

The Famine Relief Committee believed that existing evidence showed that the practical obstacles of controlling relief could be overcome. Not only was there the Red Cross operation in Greece, but the American Friends' Service Committee were still running a relief programme in southern France. From neither was there evidence that feeding schemes were disrupted by the Germans, or were made the pretext for a reduction in rations. The Committee also believed the moral case for trying to help was unanswerable. On 15 October 1942, the Archbishop of Canterbury, William Temple, addressed the Upper House of the Convocation: 'It is intolerable that Christian people should be forced to acquiesce in the slow starvation of their fellows, and particularly of children and nursing or expectant mothers. ... Neither can we justify, from a purely humanitarian point of view, the mental and physical mutilation of a whole generation of European peoples. True peace will be harder to win if this is allowed, and many Christians will feel impelled to do their utmost to prevent it.'

In November 1942, under pressure from Britain, the American Friends' Service Committee feeding scheme for 100,000 seriously malnourished children in southern France found its sources of supply closed off. Its Director, Howard Kershner, visited London to protest. He argued for controlled relief in terms diametrically opposed to those employed by Churchill against it in August 1940. A starving people did not rise against their oppressor; on the contrary, their predicament reinforced their powerlessness. He put it strongly: 'The proud boast of the Nazis that they are a superior race is coming true. Those that have enough to eat are indeed superior to the tuberculosis-ridden, under-sized, misshapen bodies of the starving inhabitants of the occupied countries.'

Kershner undertook public meetings and newspaper interviews to boost the cause of food relief. He also did the rounds of government offices and representatives of the occupied countries. The latter were all in favour; but the former, however sympathetic some might privately feel, were obdurate. Kershner was disappointed: 'I won all the arguments but I certainly lost the decision.' He went on to Washington in February 1943 to campaign from there alongside Hoover and others, believing that US pressure on Britain was the only way to obtain a change. In time the 'Kershner Plan' for limited relief became well-known in the US, and his appeal to American citizens began to bear fruit.

Meanwhile, Edith Pye was succeeding in building up a network of support in Britain. By October 1942, there were over 100 groups on the list of correspondents for her newsletter. The Derby Food Relief Committee had held a Greek Relief Week, with special church services, entertainments, and a flag-day, and raised £5,000 against the day when a way could be found to send the money on. Gradually, public opinion was beginning to stir.

On 5 October 1942, a support group for the Famine Relief Committee was formed in Oxford. At the invitation of the Rev. T.R. Milford, those who had expressed concern about starvation in Europe at Edith Pye's visit on 20 July met in the Old Library of St. Mary-the-Virgin, and constituted themselves the 'Oxford Committee for Famine Relief'.

Gilbert Murray, who lived just outside Oxford and had been Regius Professor of Greek at Oxford until his retirement in 1936, was one of their number. Murray's links with the Greek Royal Family in London, as well as his membership of Bishop Bell's Committee, meant that he was particularly well-informed. Another present was a colleague of his in the Oxford branch of the League of Nations Union, Nowell Smith. The Friends were also represented; Dr. Henry Gillett, a well-known Oxford figure, was a strong supporter. Other founder members whose relation-ship lasted over many years were Dr. Leo Liepmann, a refugee from Nazi Germany, and Sir Alan Pim, ex-Indian Civil Service, who became Honorary Treasurer.

Murray described the food situation in occupied countries, and explained to the group how difficult it was to advocate relief without invalidating the policy of blockade. The fourth minute of the meeting, entered in a school notebook, reads: 'Several speakers urged caution in planning effort lest controversy be aroused.' Whatever light years of purpose and organisational effort separate this nucleus of well-meaning citizens from the charity which much later emerged, engagement with political controversy is stamped in Oxfam's genes.

Milford's meeting in the Old Library of his church, mindful of the black-out and other exigencies of war-time Britain, did discuss what they could do immediately to relieve the suffering of those infinitely worse off in Europe. They talked of raising money to spend on supplies for famine victims. But at this point the Famine Relief Committee in London had not been able to come up with any way of spending donations on food relief. It had not been able to obtain permission to transfer funds outside the sterling area, to contribute to operations being run by the Swedish, Swiss, and International Red Cross. Pressing for a government change of heart on the hermetic seal of the blockade, an exclusively political activity, was still the only avenue for effort.

During the next few months the Oxford Committee for Famine Relief did some modest lobbying. A letter to the press was organised, signed by heads of various colleges and distinguished academics. So were two meetings: in late November the Greek Ambassador's son addressed an Oxford audience about the famine, and in early February 1943, Emile Cammaerts spoke at a public meeting held at New College presided over by the Bishop of Oxford. A shopkeeper in Queen Street made available some space in his window for a display of photos from Greece. A pamphlet put out by Edith Pye was sent to all Oxford churches with a request that they commend controlled food relief as a subject for prayer. Milford wrote to the Minister of Economic Warfare, and received the standard negative reply.

In spring 1943, when the Committee was running out of steam, a letter was received from Dr. Cawadias, President of the Greek Red Cross 'in Foreign Countries', based in London. It was now possible for people in Britain to support the International Red Cross relief operation via this route. Edith Pye encouraged Cawadias to make his own connections with local Committees; it was her policy from the outset that Committees should act independently rather than be co-ordinated under a central umbrella.

Oxford, with its intellectual connections both to Greece and to liberal dissent, was a natural target for Dr. Cawadias' appeal. His request that the Oxford Committee raise funds for famine relief in Greece had the effect of galvanising the Committee. Or rather, it galvanised one very special member: Cecil Jackson-Cole.

This eccentric philanthropist had decided to take up the Oxford Committee for Famine Relief as the forum in which he would find expression for his particular sense of mission. If he had not done so, the Committee would probably have sunk without a trace, if not in 1943 or 1944, then certainly after the immediate postwar period. Jackson-Cole originally heard of its formation from Quaker contacts in London, and offered his services as its Honorary Secretary in December 1942. He brought to it a businessman's zeal to succeed and a Christian humanitarian's zeal to do good. A political pressure campaign adorned with the signatures of prominent liberals was not enough for him. People in Europe were praying for food and he wanted to help put food in front of them.

Jackson-Cole had been born in the East End of London at the turn of the century, and he certainly knew what hardship felt like. At 13, he left school, and at 19 he bought his father out of his flat-letting and furnishing business. He was a hard worker and consummate trader, and drove himself forward relentlessly – so relentlessly that in his thirties his health collapsed. He spent most of the next two years in bed, a time of inactivity which caused him to think deeply of God's purpose in his life, and how his ability to make money could be harnessed to help the helpless. He sought a new combination of business and charitable principle, something akin to Quaker good works. He was himself not a Friend, although he was powerfully influenced by the Quaker spirit.

It was purely fortuitous that Jackson-Cole surfaced from his illness living on Boar's Hill, opposite the gates of Gilbert Murray's large house, and that it was the Oxford Committee for Famine Relief which supplied his need for a vehicle in which to put his ideas to the test. On Jackson-Cole's initiative the Committee was registered as a charity in March 1943 under the War Charities Act and began to appeal for funds. This cantankerous yet self-effacing figure in a crumpled suit did not always elicit more than pained forbearance from some of the more conventional types on the Oxford Committee. He also expected those he employed in his business to go house-to-house canvassing for the Committee at his whim. But no-one could be other than impressed by his results, both commercial and charitable.

In the first place, financial support for a Greek Famine Relief Appeal was sought from members of the University. Over the summer months, this appeal raised more than £3,000, which was promptly despatched to the Greek Red Cross in London.

Jackson-Cole now proposed to extend the Appeal to the city. Milford gave him the go-ahead. Following the pattern of other recent successful war-time charity drives, Jackson-Cole opted for a special week of fundraising in Oxford to take place during mid-October. He was an excellent organiser, and recruited the necessary dignitaries for ceremonies and endorsements, and an army of volunteers to run events, address envelopes, and hold collections. The Mayor, the Sheriff, the Vice-

Chancellor, the Editor of the *Oxford Mail*, local churches and educational associations, Lady Beveridge, Frank Pakenham, the Warden of All Souls, leading department stores, Quintin Hogg MP, the Presidents of the District Trades Council and the Chamber of Trade, lent their names, their energies, or both. It was a remarkable achievement for a cause not widely known and a committee almost no-one had previously heard of.

A gift shop on the most conspicuous corner of the city's shopping area managed to raise £3,000 in 11 days. The opening event of the week saw the Mayor officiating and Gilbert Murray introducing the Greek Ambassador. There were lunch-time concerts, a variety show in the Town Hall, an evening of Greek folksongs and dance performed by children in national costume, talks on Greek history and lantern-slide shows, and a celebration in St. Mary-the-Virgin by the Archbishop of Thyateria of the Holy Liturgy according to the Greek Orthodox rite. Even Vera Brittain came down to Oxford, to speak out for controlled relief in tones which Milford found a little too contentious.

Above all, there were repeated appeals for churches, groups and individuals to donate. Every few days, Jackson-Cole advertised a list of donors in the Oxford press: even those who had contributed two shillings were fastidiously enumerated. When all the donations were counted, £12,700 had been raised. Dr. Cawadias came down from London for a ceremony at which Gilbert Murray presented the cheque. Jackson-Cole was delighted with the results, crediting Oxford's 'altruistic spirit'. The effect on him was profound; he had sought and found his own path of missionary endeavour.

He had done something else. He had begun to put the Oxford Committee for Famine Relief on the philanthropic map.

Throughout 1943, as the tide of war turned and the German armies were pushed increasingly onto the defensive, conditions in occupied Europe deteriorated.

Although the death rate in Greece had dropped, it still hovered at horrendous levels. In the first two weeks of October, there were 500 hunger deaths in Athens. The weakening effect of persistent under-nutrition allowed epidemics of malaria, typhus and diphtheria to play havoc. Relief stations were reasonably organised over most of the country; but the Swedish ships brought in just over a quarter of what was needed and very few protective foods for children. As Dr. Cawadias pointed out: 'Babies cannot live on wheat alone.' Most of the newborn perished. Thousands of other small children, whose parents were in detention or dead, appeared at the soup kitchens on their own, homeless and uncared for.

From other parts of Europe, the picture was almost equally grim. Serbia reported 400,000 orphans and there were 20,000 cases of typhus in Sarajevo. In France, the basic ration was down to 884 calories, with extra distribution bringing it to 1,100. In Belgium, the Germans continued to feed workers adequately, but women and children had to survive on 900 calories, one-third of pre-war consumption. Emile Cammaerts continued to write and campaign: 'People used their savings in the first two years, but by 1943 they had nothing left and the years of privation are telling.' One-third of children under 18 were tubercular; in some cities, 80 per cent had rickets from vitamin D deficiency.

By mid-1943, Edith Pye could report that the groundswell of support for 'controlled relief' was growing. Famine Relief Committees had been set up in 109 localities, many chaired by the Mayor, the Bishop, or some other local figure. Most were in the north, and pacifists and Friends played leading roles. Another 78 organisations had lent Bishop Bell's Committee their public support, among them the British Red Cross and the British Council of Churches.

Press coverage had been generous; 20 petitions had been delivered to MPs. The Committee now had a Council of Supporters, a Medical Committee and a Political Committee. The Archbishop of Canterbury had addressed a special meeting in the House of Commons, as had M. Hubert Pierlot, Prime Minister of Belgium. There had been two Parliamentary debates, with MPs thoroughly briefed by the Food Campaign and the Famine Relief Committee. But still the government refused to budge.

The Committee did not change its proposal: it still sought monthly cargoes of 2,000 tons of dried milk and vitamins for Greece and Belgium only. The case in international law was based on the two countries' normal reliance on imports. Vera Brittain put it best: 'We all know that the Nazis have plundered the occupied countries but even they cannot remove food which never went there. There appears to be no dictum of international law which requires an occupying power to make good the shortages resulting from a blockade imposed by its enemy.' The case for relief had on its side the continued lack of any evidence of German diversion of food relief in Greece. Dingle Foot admitted this while insisting that the operation still helped the Germans and could not be emulated elsewhere.

Harold Nicholson MP, speaking in an adjournment debate called on 27 October 1943 by Stokes, the tenacious Member for Ipswich, echoed the views of many when he described the government's counter arguments to relief proposals as utterly insubstantial. He had found himself deeply embarrassed when, in Stockholm, he tried to articulate the British government's opposition to a plan to send Belgium a modest amount of food and medicine in sealed trains from Lisbon. 'I racked my brains to think of the arguments Ministers have in the past given me, hoping I would find in them some armour-piercing javelins which would confound my Swedish critics. I searched, and what did I find in the palm of my hand? Not a javelin, not even a pointed dart, but just a handful of dust. I had not come to Sweden to throw dust in the face of the Swedish Red Cross.'

With a growing body of public and parliamentary opinion moving its way, the Famine Relief Committee held a delegate conference on 3 January 1944 at Caxton Hall in London. Over 120 delegates came from support groups all over the British Isles. Famine Relief Committees in 82 towns and districts were represented. Among the delegates were a number of Bishops and leading churchmen, as well as Mayors, Councillors, and local notables. The representative of Leeds FRC was a certain H. Leslie Kirkley.

While they listened to speakers from the stricken countries – Cawadias, Cammaerts, and a representative of the Free French – a deputation went simultaneously to see Lord Selbourne, Minister of Economic Warfare. The Bishop of Wakefield led the deputation, which included representatives of many of the strongest local Famine Relief Committees: Birmingham, Derby, Manchester and Salford, Newcastle-on-Tyne, Swansea, Peterborough, and Coventry, as well as Professor James Young, Vice-Chairman of the FRC Medical Committee, Hugh Lyon, Headmaster of Rugby School, the Master of Selwyn from Cambridge, and Dr. Henry Gillett from Oxford.

The deputation came back to the conference to report on the outcome of their meeting. Keen frustration was felt at having yet again to listen to the Minister's familiar recitation of what had become a tired, tattered, and defensive stance. His manner indicated that even he did not agree with it. Martin Parr, Chairman of the conference, closed the proceedings on as upbeat a note as he could manage: the discovery that the Minister of Economic Warfare had no secret weapon up his sleeve to counter their case. 'If there had been some secret weapon he would have let it off on this occasion. He has not got one, and I am more convinced than I was yesterday that our right policy is to go on hammering away until the British public can convince sufficient Members of Parliament that something has got to be done.'

An announcement came some days later that the amount of food for Greece was to be significantly increased. On the basis of a gift of 20,000 tons of wheat from the Argentine, food deliveries gradually rose to 32,000 tons per month. When Antony Eden, the Foreign Secretary, went to Athens after the liberation in October and saw the situation for himself, supplies were finally increased to 60,000 tons a month.

For Belgium, nothing. The only concession was Vitamin D, a shortage of which was afflicting Belgian children with rickets. Vitamin D was removed from the contraband list in spring 1944, and the South African Red Cross began to send in supplies. Cases of advanced tuberculosis had reached 109,500; but for TB, the antidote was a good diet, and no food went in.

On 16 February 1944 good news came from across the Atlantic. The US Senate approved a resolution of its Foreign Relations Sub-Committee calling for the US, British, Swedish and Swiss governments to formulate a relief scheme for Belgium, Norway, Poland, Netherlands, Greece, Yugoslavia, and Czechoslovakia. This, surely, must embarrass Whitehall. All statements in the House of Commons had referred to the blockade policy as that of both the British and US governments; this common front – in which the British bulldog had always barked the louder – was beginning to split. US support for controlled relief was now used with good effect in Famine Relief Committees' local campaigns.

Edith Pye's next newsletter repeated the need to keep up the pressure on local MPs. She was a clever lobby strategist, advising Committees first to gain evidence of widespread local support before petitioning Westminster. A series of deputations and Parliamentary questions would, she believed, prove more effective than one co-ordinated onslaught.

On 17 January 1944, Henry Gillett and Leo Liepmann, back from the Famine Relief Conference in Caxton Hall, described the day's disappointing results to their colleagues on the Oxford Committee. In an effort to put pressure on the Member for Oxford City, Milford had already paid a visit to an unresponsive Quintin Hogg. Hogg stuck to the line: 'the government has secret information about how this would help the Germans', which by this stage had little credibility. It was agreed that a petition should be got up: this might be somewhat more persuasive than Milford's call to conscience.

Jackson-Cole opened the bid for signatures in the correspondence columns of the *Oxford Times*. 'Oxford people have already subscribed generously for Greece,' he wrote. 'In the case of Belgium it is not money which is needed. Belgium wants to be given the right to buy their own supplies from their own money and transport them in their own ship from the USA for their starving children. The US is openly in favour, but our own government is not.' He asked those in favour to send a postcard to the Committee to that effect. By June, Jackson-Cole had collected over 7,000 signatures. Even Quintin Hogg was impressed.

On 7 July 1944 a deputation from Oxford went up to London to visit Dingle Foot at the Ministry of Economic Warfare. Hogg introduced the members, while careful to disassociate himself from their cause. Milford was present, together with the Chairman of the Oxford Trades Council, the President of the Oxford Rotarians, and two members of the University. Familiar arguments were produced – the thin end of the wedge argument, the argument that any relief helped the German war effort; but Foot did admit 'the intolerable dilemma of total war'. The Committee was not best pleased with this response, but was at a loss about what to do next.

Events overtook the Oxford Committee and others. As summer gave way to autumn, the issue of breaching the blockade to send in relief became out-dated. In September 1944, Paris was liberated. Greece and Belgium were close to freedom. Although the worst fears of famine on the continent turned out not to be realised, the dimensions of relief needs in the formerly occupied countries were enormous. Churchill had promised that the Allies – now called the 'United Nations' – would organise food for civilians the minute an area was liberated. The instrument for so doing, and for trying to put ruined economies and infrastructures back on their feet, had been launched in November 1943. This was the first experiment in post-war co-operation between the nations: UNRRA, the United Nations Relief and Rehabilitation Administration.

Voluntary organisations – Friends' Relief Service, the Red Cross, Save the Children Fund, and many others – were to play an important part in the post-war relief operations alongside UNRRA and under its umbrella. There were now, therefore, a variety of channels through which aid could be given to help relieve what was to be two more years of bitter hardship throughout continental Europe. But to ship in and distribute food was a task of such monumental size that it was left to governments and UNRRA. In the new circumstances the Famine Relief Committee in Brook Street, London, gradually wound itself down and handed its assets over to the Friends' Relief Service: the cause that had brought it into being had thankfully disappeared.

Many of the support committees out in the provinces swiftly followed suit. Others, such as those in Manchester and Salford, Huddersfield and quite a few others, felt that the misery now exposed in Europe demanded their efforts as never before. In February 1945, the Oxford Committee for Famine Relief closed down its Greek Relief Fund, with the proceeds standing at £13,517 14s 10d. At the same time, it decided by resolution to enlarge the objects of charity 'to the relief of suffering in consequence of the war'. A new phase was about to begin.

Over a period of nearly two years, and with the active support of senior churchmen and eminent individuals in all walks of public life, the

Famine Relief Committees' campaign to breach the blockade for humanitarian relief was a failure. Whatever they may have achieved in support of the Red Cross operation in Greece, not one navicert for one meagre cargo of milk and nutritional supplements was ever granted for Belgium or elsewhere. It is very doubtful that the British government's dogged refusal to allow aid through did anything to shorten the war. The iron-clad nature of the blockade was entrenched as an article of war-policy faith, and no quarter – except for Greece – was to be given. Many who officially defended it, especially towards the end when Germany was collapsing and conditions across the continent were rapidly deteriorating, found it upsetting to have to do so.

Vera Brittain drew comfort from the ashes of defeat. She wrote in late 1944 that, for all its disappointments and the lives lost that might have been saved, the campaign had been worth it. At a time of despair for those entering their fourth, fifth, even sixth, winter of occupation, the campaign offered moral encouragement and a sense of solidarity: 'The concern of a few bore witness to the oneness of humanity.'

The war-time famine relief campaign, quickly forgotten in the turmoil of the post-war scene, left one other important legacy: Oxfam.

2

WINNING THE PEACE:
THE MORAL AFTERMATH OF WAR

Few bonfires were lit in Britain on 8 May 1946, the first anniversary of VE (Victory in Europe) Day. A year after the end of the war, the mood was far from festive. Two months later, bread rationing was introduced. Even at the hardest time of the war when bread was rationed everywhere else in Europe, it was Britain's boast that this step had never been necessary. A storm of protest arose from shortage-weary house-wives. But however unwelcome, the 'bread unit' was to be a part of their lives for the next two years.

Far from ushering in an era of 'food, freedom and peace', the end of the war had brought prolonged hardship and, across Europe, continuing upheaval. In Britain, 'austerity' was to become the watchword of the next few years. But Britain's austerity was well-heeled compared to others'.

In the countries UNRRA (the UN Relief and Rehabilitation Administration) was supplying – Greece, Italy, Yugoslavia, Albania, Austria, Poland, Czechoslovakia – food had only reached 60 per cent of pre-war levels by mid-1946. The long disruption of farming, trading, and factory life had reduced the supply of basic necessities – coal, cloth, thread, leather, wool, paper, wood, fruit, vegetables, cows, chickens, pots, pans – to the point of universal scarcity.

Everywhere, fuel was desperately short during those bleak post-war winters. The bitterness of the continental climate exacerbated hardship in Central Europe. Lack of warm clothes and bedding, shoes disinte-grating from years of wear, made the cold and wet yet harder to bear, specially for those living in bombed and burned-out dwellings. Holland endured a 'famine.winter' in 1944-45, and there was much sympathy in Britain. The Oxford Committee for Famine Relief was one of many groups to run clothing appeals in spring 1945, moved by the condition of the Dutch people at liberation.

But nowhere was need more severe than in Germany. Attitudes towards this need were perceived by some as a test of the civilisation the war had been fought to retain. A world informed by crude, nationalist antagonism could not be a safe world. It could only be a world in which the moral cause – the only possible justification for such a war – had been betrayed, a war whose battles were won but whose peace was lost. The need now was to build bridges with hearts and minds in a Europe grateful to be free, but liberated at terrible cost to its physical, economic, and spiritual fabric.

Germany was now divided into four parts, administered separately by the British, French, Russians, and Americans. The Allies had determined on Germany's unconditional surrender, with all its implications of annihilating destruction and humiliation. They had brought Germany and the German people to their knees, and as victors they were now obliged to shoulder the responsibilities of occupation in a blasted land. Among these was the responsibility to feed, clothe, and care for civilians; a principle they had insisted upon when Germany was itself an occupying power.

But there were serious problems in contending with the extraordinary destruction and chaos wrought by war until the bitter end. Bombing had created widespread homelessness. Over 12 million people displaced during the war needed repatriation. The re-drawing of boundaries in the East led to a spate of expulsions in the second half of 1945, bringing an influx of millions of refugees westwards.

Meanwhile, major German wheat-growing lands had been ceded to Poland, and industrial plant in Germany itself was being deliberately wrecked and jobs closed down as a part of 'denazification'. It was impossible for the area administered by the British, the country's urban and industrial heartland, to feed itself. On top of this, there was a serious shortage of food grains worldwide and the US was reluctant to export its surplus.

By the time bread rationing was introduced in Britain – so that cargoes of wheat on the high seas could be diverted to Germany – the government had decided it had no option but to import some food into the part of Germany for which it was responsible. At the end of June 1946, people in Hamburg were losing weight at an average of one kilo a week. *The Economist* wrote: 'The threat of starvation in the Ruhr – of real starvation with men, women and children dying of hunger in their thousands – has been hanging over the world for so long that many people have ceased to take it seriously.' This journal and others had been sounding the alarm for months.

UNRRA's Food Committee had laid down that the minimum for a healthy diet was 2,650 calories a day. In March 1946, rations in the British Zone had been reduced from 1,500 calories a day to 1,014. For many townspeople, even this minimum was not available. The idea that most could somehow make up their food needs adequately from the black market or elsewhere did not hold up to inspection. The amount they were getting, as *The Economist* and others pointed out, was the amount provided in Belsen up to a few weeks before the final collapse.

The comparison was not casually made. In Britain at this time, the ration was 2,800 calories – nearly 95 per cent of pre-war food consumption levels – and the British were better fed than other Europeans. But there was an ugly mood in the country. People were not only disgruntled by shortage, queuing, and the endless constraining regulations, but still influenced by the hatred whipped up against the foe by war-time propaganda. The revelations of concentration camp atrocities and the Nuremburg trials only hardened anti-German feeling.

Xenophobia was fanned by the popular press which demanded a rise in rations on the grounds of the nutritional damage being done to British health. People tired of plain fare and limited menus willingly believed this. As a result there was great resistance by Attlee's government to any action which could remotely be seen as removing a morsel of food off a British plate and putting it into a German mouth. Sir Stafford Cripps, austerity's father figure, talked of there being no question of 'depriving John to help Hans or Gretel'. Many felt that indefinite helpings of humble pie were the only way to quench the German instinct for aggression.

On 3 March 1946, a few days before German rations in the British Zone were reduced to a third of British rations, George Bell, Bishop of Chichester, gave a well-publicised sermon with a text from *Romans*: 'If thine enemy hunger, feed him; if he thirst, give him to drink ... Be not overcome of evil, but overcome evil with good.'

Another voice, the most resonant in this cause, was that of Victor Gollancz, the left-wing publisher and forceful polemicist: 'The plain fact is that ... we are starving the German people. And we are starving them, not deliberately in the sense that we definitely want them to die, but wilfully in the sense that we prefer their death to our own inconvenience.'

For the next two and a half years, many of those who throughout the war held fast to their faith in 'one humanity' gave their energies to the relief of suffering in Europe, irrespective of nationality. Their keynote was reconciliation, not vengeance. Among them were many of the same people who had opposed the iron-clad blockade against relief from 1942 until the liberation. One of the active local groups was the Oxford Committee for Famine Relief.

Victor Gollancz' campaign to 'Save Europe Now' began in September 1945. In a letter published in the *Manchester Guardian*, *News Chronicle*, and the *Daily Herald*, jointly signed by Bishop Bell, Gilbert Murray,

Bertrand Russell and others, he described the appalling misery in Berlin and wrote: 'It is not in accordance with the traditions of this country to allow children – even the children of ex-enemies – to starve.' Gollancz, who was Jewish and had spoken out during the war against the concentration camps and Nazi terrors, could hardly be accused of softness towards the Germans. He appealed to people to send him a postcard if they agreed to forego some of their own ration entitlement so that 'men, women and children of whatever nationality may be saved from intolerable suffering'.

He received over 75,000 postcards. Here was Gollancz' ammunition: he could show the government that there was strong popular disfavour with an attitude of vindictiveness towards the vanquished. In early November, a 'Save Europe Now' delegation laid a series of proposals before the Minister of Food. They suggested that people in Britain be allowed to make voluntary contributions to help the needy in Germany through a national scheme for giving up ration points, and that the ban on sending food parcels to Germany be lifted. The Minister, Sir Ben Smith, was anti-German and unenthusiastic, but agreed to have his department examine these ideas.

Before Gollancz had received any reply, he was horrified by an announcement that British rations would be increased at Christmas. Immediately, he rushed out a booklet – 'Is It Nothing to You?' showing photos of starving German children – and planned a mass meeting in the Albert Hall. By the time it took place, Smith had turned down all proposals except one: the Ministry agreed to sell – not donate – £100,000 worth of food to British relief agencies acting under the umbrella of the Council of British Relief Societies Abroad (COBSRA).

On 26 November 1945, the Albert Hall was packed to overflowing. The Archbishop of York took the chair, and among the speakers were MPs Dick Stokes, Michael Foot, Bob Boothby, and Sir Arthur Salter, as well as Victor Gollancz himself. Gollancz set about the government's position with his verbal truncheon, attacking Smith's refusal to let anyone voluntarily give up anything for relief purposes. 'This is intolerable. We are free citizens of a free country and ... how we balance our obligation to ourselves against our obligation to our neighbours is a matter for our own conscience.'

The demand to be allowed to give relief for Europe, especially for Germany, had become a moral crusade.

That same day, the Oxford Committee for Famine Relief met and discussed the issues to be brought before the Albert Hall rally. They were in no doubt where they stood on 'Save Europe Now': in favour.

In September, they had passed a resolution supporting voluntary food relief. They wanted people to be able to surrender food points from their ration books at Food Offices, on the understanding that the government would send equivalent supplies to help those 'most in need' on the continent. They were willing to run depots in Oxford either for food point surrender, or – if this was refused – for food collection. They had sent their resolution to Gollancz' London headquarters, and circulated it locally.

Now they were told that all such proposals had been turned down. Meanwhile children in Germany were starving. 'Save Europe Now' was about to launch a £100,000 fund to buy the food offered by the Ministry for relief distribution via COBSRA, whose members included the Red Cross, Save the Children, the Friends' Relief Service, the Salvation Army, and Catholic and Jewish relief organisations.

The Committee wanted to run an appeal in Oxford, but were not sure of its advisability. So before going ahead they decided to seek the advice of Sir Arthur Salter, MP for Oxford University. Salter, who had been prominent in international relief after the first World War and spent the second negotiating supplies in Washington, was knowledgeable about food stocks and shipping. He had spoken out strongly in the House of Commons, claiming that if millions froze and starved in Europe during the winter it could not be excused by overall shortages either of food or transport worldwide.

Salter outlined his understanding of the position to key members of the Oxford Committee on 2 December. His immediate concern was to have military reserves of food released, and to mobilise imports from the US, and he was calling for a White Paper on European requirements. He advised the Committee in favour of supporting the COBSRA relief agencies; their work in Europe could, he said, in no way let the authorities off the hook from the main responsibility of providing rations. In view of sensitivities, he felt that there was no particular need to emphasise Germany.

After this reassurance, the Committee went ahead forcefully. The appeal was to be mounted for 'Europe'; funds would be spent on food distributed by the Friends' Relief Service 'wherever needs are greatest'. Milford wrote to the *Oxford Times* on 21 December: 'Many people this Christmas will be troubled in conscience by the knowledge that winter in Europe means cold, hunger, misery and death.' He explained that the voluntary surrender of food points had been refused by the government, and that Sir Arthur Salter and others were still urging 'large-scale action'. Meanwhile: 'The Friends are working in the liberated countries; need is however very acute in certain parts of the defeated countries also. ... Eventually, it is hoped, supplies will be directed where need is greatest, without distinction of nationality. Personally, I am convinced this is the right principle, but those who wish may earmark their gifts "for liberated Europe only".'

Milford was a gentle, almost a saintly, figure. It was his voice that thus established on behalf of the Oxford Committee the principle of impartiality governing its aid; that relief should be given purely on the basis of need, without reference to nationality or religion. This principle governed the work of the Friends, and was also to be adopted by the new international humanitarian organisations set up within the United Nations family.

Sir Arthur Salter led a panel of MPs at a meeting held on 23 January 1946 in the Oxford Town Hall to launch 'European Relief Week'. The Mayor spoke eloquently: 'It may have been a necessity of war to bomb villages, bridges and factories, but peace entails responsibility and gives us the opportunity to relieve suffering wherever the need is greatest.' The Rev. Henry Moxley, Congregationalist Minister in Summertown, was in charge of the appeal. Volunteers sent out an appeal letter signed by civic and university luminaries. The Oxford newspapers gave excellent support. Over the next weeks, as more and grimmer information about hunger in Europe appeared in the national press, the appeal gained momentum.

In February, the Ministry of Food finally admitted to a serious world shortage of wheat. The tone of government statements was, however: 'We in Britain are comparatively lucky, so don't complain', rather than: 'We in Britain may have to do more for others in need.' Not all reactions in Oxford were positive towards the Committee's appeal. A Flag Day was turned down by the Oxford City Council when four councillors refused to sanction a collection whose proceeds might feed the ex-enemy.

There was great ignorance about what serious food scarcity meant, both in its effect on an individual person and among a population at large. As Victor Gollancz complained, many people refused to believe in a problem of hunger unless those on the scene found streets full of wraith-like people collapsing and dying at their feet. Fifty years later, his words would still be valid.

Within two months the Oxford Committee raised £6,000. They channelled their support to the Friends' Relief Service (FRS), the special war-time relief organisation set up by the British Quakers. FRS, as part of COBSRA, was also appealing for funds to buy food from the government. Its teams were based in Austria, France, Germany, Greece, and Poland. Altogether, 'Save Europe Now' raised £56,083; with the appeals by COBSRA members, the target of £100,000 was easily surpassed.

This was only a first stage of the campaign for European relief, a campaign which was to continue until Marshall Aid was introduced in

1948. By July 1946, several of the measures urged by crusaders in Westminster and Whitehall had been put into effect in the face of deepening disaster. But rations in the British Zone of Germany were still at starvation level: 1,014 calories amounted to two slices of bread a day spread thinly with margarine, a spoonful of porridge, and two potatoes – except that the potatoes were often unavailable.

The ban on sending food parcels abroad was still in force. But the installation of a new Minister of Food, John Strachey, gave Gollancz cause for optimism. In meetings at the Ministry, a parcels scheme was painstakingly worked out. Committees around the country were geared up to accept parcels and run depots. But the imposition of bread rationing cut the ground away. In so grave a national crisis, said the Minister, no food could be allowed to leave the country.

The battle for a better peace was far from won.

During the next few months, public pressure was kept up. Famine Relief Committees wrote to the press and to their MPs. But it took a six-week visit to the British Zone by Victor Gollancz, and a barrage of letters to *The Times* and other newspapers describing the realities of food supplies and German misery, to break down Attlee's resistance.

Gollancz set off on his mission on 2 October 1946. Eighteen months after the end of the war, he found cities still in total ruin, families living in crowded cellars and squalid boltholes. In Hamburg, 100,000 people were suffering from 'hunger oedema'. A bunker without light or air was used as a school for 800 children, many of whom had skin sores and protruding ribs beneath their shirts. They came to school without breakfast, and at 2.30pm were given their meal: half a litre of 'biscuit' soup with no bread. TB cases had multiplied by five, perhaps ten, times in Germany since 1939. Gollancz saw the effect on morale when the Salvation Army handed out a few sweets and goodies. How could the ban on parcels be justified? Gollancz railed in copious detail and forthright prose in every newspaper that would print him. Photos appeared of his bulky figure, heftily coated, in ruined buildings surrounded by skimpy children pathetically shod and clad.

Gollancz and the Minister fought out the issue in the correspondence columns of the *News Chronicle*. The newspaper's mountainous postbag was two to one in Gollancz' favour. On 25 November, the government gave in. Replying to MPs' questions in the House of Commons, John Strachey announced that food parcels could now be sent. No-one should send more than one parcel a month; contents should be limited to 7lb, with no more than 2lb of any commodity, and only rationed foods and soap could be included. Although food parcels alone could only touch the misery, this was an important moral victory, and it symbolised a spirit of goodwill.

The immediate problem was how to ship the thousands of parcels that poured into 'Save Europe Now' and depots set up around the country. The parcel post to Germany did not open for another six weeks, so 'Save Europe Now' had temporarily to take on this function, using private carriers. Over the next two months, in spite of snow, floods, and all the administrative difficulties at both ends, over 100,000 parcels of food were successfully delivered to Germany. For three weeks, the Air Ministry provided 1,000lb of freight, free, every day. Those parcels not addressed to any specific individual were given to the churches for distribution to the neediest.

Famine and European Relief Committees up and down the country played an important part. In Oxford, premises above a toyshop were lent, volunteers were organised, and children from local schools spent their Saturday mornings wrapping up parcels of tinned soup, coffee and sugar. All packages were sent to a named German family, marked with the name of the sender. A well-known local figure, the Stationmaster, F.C.Price, sent a parcel to an opposite number in Berlin, railway inspector Albert Wurl-Rothweil. He received a touching letter of thanks: 'You would have been overjoyed if you had seen the shining eyes of my wife and children. At last we lived like human beings again, and hunger and worry vanished for a time from our faces. Dear Mr. Price, it tasted so good to us. We had not eaten such good things for so long.'

Food relief answered only one element of need. The winter of 1946-47 was one of the harshest on record, in Britain as well as in Europe. In February, icefields were reported off the Norfolk coast and on the continent railways were inoperable and vehicles froze in their tracks.

Fuel was still in short supply. So was clothing. On 6 January 1947, the *Manchester Guardian* reported: 'Hamburg has two needs of desperate urgency; hope, and immediate physical help in shoes and clothing. A ragged people may be able to endure hardship if they have hope. Hamburg today is cold, in rags, and hopeless.'

Since the end of the war, the Friends' Relief Service had been appealing for 'warm clothing, menswear, underclothing, overcoats, shoes and boots, napkins, and blankets in clean, mended condition'.

On 11 November 1946, the Mayor and the Sheriff of Oxford, Lord Lindsay the Master of Balliol, and two Reverends, Milford and Moxley, stood outside a modest shop premises owned by the Oxford and District Co-operative Society. A presentation was made of its key to the Mayor, who then declared open the Oxford Committee for Famine Relief's first clothes collection depot. The European Relief Fund had raised £15,000 and the response to their clothing appeals was generous; they needed a proper address for receiving goods. In their borrowed premises, they set up a tiny office and took on a paid part-time organiser, Robert Castle. He organised publicity, while rotas of helpers sorted, mended, and packaged clothes and shoes to send to the Friends in London.

By this time, the FRS clothing operation was well-established: on 11 January, their special newsletter, *Clothing News*, recorded that the 10,000th bale of garments was on its way to Europe. The provision of these clothes met real survival needs in a way difficult to picture today, when images of mass deprivation are almost always associated with people in tropical climates.

In Dortmund, 160 of the 1,737 children enrolled in a feeding scheme could not attend because they had no shoes. In Normandy, German prisoners of war were clearing mines off beaches in mid-winter, clad in rags. Thousands of children took daily turns to go to school, sharing one set of clothes and shoes with brothers or sisters. People went to work in unheated offices, shops, and factories through the blizzard, wearing threadbare summer garments. Mothers of newly-born infants sought despairingly for layettes and napkins. A *Times* leader observed at the height of the cold: 'It is better to hunger than freeze.'

By May 1947, the European Relief Appeal in Oxford had raised £20,000, and £8,000 worth – 800 sacks – of clothing had been forwarded to the FRS depot in London. The Friends expressed appreciation for 'a most remarkable success that far outshines the efforts of any other city in the country'. By this time, FRS had sent to Germany over 1,100 tons of food, clothing, and medical and other supplies since mid-1945.

The situation had still failed to improve significantly. On 10 May 1947, the *Manchester Guardian* reported a hunger strike by 150,000 people in Hamburg. In the Ruhr, food administration had collapsed and things were even worse. In the town of Wuppertal, the week's ration came to 627 calories a day. People were so busy scouring the countryside for food that offices and factories were empty. The lesson was clear: the Germans could not rebuild their economy if they did not have enough to eat. The crisis of austerity and hardship in Britain and Europe endlessly continued.

In November 1947, the Oxford Committee took up more permanent abode in a shop at 17 Broad Street, leased for £325 a year from the City Council. This original Oxfam Giftshop is still at 17 Broad Street today. Initially it was primarily a clothing receiving point and an office, although some gifts were accepted and sold. A part-time worker, Frank Buckingham, was recruited to help, and Committee members organised rotas of volunteers. Through the intervention of Michael Rowntree,

Manager of the *Oxford Mail* and later a key Oxfam trustee, free transport for the clothing to London was provided by a weekly Rowntree's van. In the year up to February 1948, the Committee brought in clothing worth £25,000; funds raised for two years came to £26,000.

In the winter of 1947-48, the third winter after the war, misery again pervaded Europe. In tones weary with repetition, the *Manchester Guardian* repeated the stories of calories promised and not available in the British Zone of Germany: 'Almost opposite the British Military Government headquarters in Dusseldorf the walls of the building are inscribed with the words: "Bizonesia Verhungert" (Bizonesia is starving). These writings are three weeks old but nobody has troubled to rub them out. In the Ruhr, the next food crisis is always just around the corner.' Michael Foot wrote in the *Daily Herald* of Germany's cry of hunger, and of 'millions of people facing the imminent collapse of the whole fabric of society'.

Why was the agony so prolonged? One reason was the premature demise of UNRRA early in 1947. The joint effort of United Nations governments to expedite post-war relief and rehabilitation was an early casualty of the frost entering East-West relations. It was also symptomatic of US failure to grasp the depth of need and desolation on a continent in ruins. In spite of bitter protests from Norway and elsewhere, in the autumn of 1946 at the UNRRA Council meeting in Geneva, the US representative declared that 'the gravy-train has gone round for the last time'. Desperate for a major US loan, the British government followed the US lead, and the UNRRA Council voted its programme of aid out of existence.

Until the Marshall Plan began to fuel a proper economic recovery, voluntary organisations, many working in close liaison with UNRRA, shouldered more responsibility for relief than had earlier been envisaged. Their work required, and won, support from fundraisers from all over the world on a continuing basis. 'Save Europe Now' carried on until 1948, as did the FRS teams, until such time as European recovery was assured. Not until the end of 1948, when governments' own welfare and social services had been rebuilt to the point where they could cope, was misery reduced to pockets.

In a valedictory on 'Save Europe Now', Peggy Duff, its chief organiser, recognised the modest scale of the effort in proportion to need, but recorded the following: 'The value of these gifts and of this work has been tremendous because they have been to Europe a token in tangible form of the sympathy and human understanding which exists in Great Britain for suffering wherever it may be.'

A letter received by the Oxford Committee for Famine Relief from a refugee schoolmaster in the North Frisian Islands off the German coast illustrates the point: 'When I returned with my daily load of dry heather everyone was up. That is rare, because for weeks now an icy east wind has been sweeping across the island and we stay in bed as long as possible, wearing the few clothes we possess or covering ourselves with them to keep ourselves warm. The rooms are never really warm, as only coal would be of use against this icy blast and that we have not got. Cabbage soup doesn't warm one's inside much either and few have enough winter clothing.

'I enter. The room looks quite different, all are up, all are talking at the same time, happy faces, bright eyes, children laugh and stare. I am just going to ask what has happened when my eyes fall on the table. Am I seeing aright? Things are lying there, lovely warm things, suits, clothes, underclothing, shoes. A little girl can't stop admiring the brightly coloured pullover which her mother has put on her. A white-bearded man over there has tears in his eyes as, with trembling hand, he strokes a woollen waistcoat.

'You unknown friends in England, you have brought warmth to our hearts. May the fire you have lit grow till it burns up everything that divides us.'

1948 marked the watershed in post-war relief. As Marshall Aid took effect and life in Europe began to hum again, organisations active in post-war relief began to close down their programmes or adjust to better times.

The FRS wound up its operations, passing on a much reduced programme to the Friends' Service Council, the Quakers' permanent body for overseas relief. Many of the Famine Relief Committees felt that, like the emergency, their life had come to its logical conclusion. But not the Oxford Committee; nor a few others.

The driving force behind the continued existence of the Oxford Committee was Cecil Jackson-Cole. Milford had by now left Oxford, handing over his chairmanship to Henry Moxley. Jackson-Cole took a simple view of the Committee's mission. Despite the improvements in European conditions, there was throughout the world great suffering and need, and as long as this was so – and surely it would indefinitely be so – 'the work' must go on. An efficient if modest vehicle had been developed. It should grow. There were no heights of charitable enterprise, in his view, to which it could not climb.

Jackson-Cole was not entirely sure, and with justification, that other members of the Committee would see things in the same light. To some, his aspirations for this citizens' group and its clothing appeals must have seemed grandiose indeed. When the Committee met in September

1948 to discuss whether to close down, Jackson-Cole had laid the groundwork for a decision in favour of widening the scope of its activities. Letters strongly endorsing this choice had been received from two founder members who attended rarely, but whose moral backing was tremendously esteemed: Professor Gilbert Murray and Dr. Henry Gillett. Their voices and that of Leo Liepmann swayed the Committee in favour of going on, for which in the end the decision was unanimous.

Jackson-Cole had also developed plans for putting the Committee's management onto a more regular basis. He was prepared to lend an 'Interim Administrator' from his own business company, an estate agency called Andrews and Partners. In the past few years, Jackson-Cole had considerably advanced his mission to couple entrepreneurship with Christian service. Andrews and Partners, established in London in 1946, was a business with an ulterior purpose: the development of charities. Jackson-Cole did not intend to do this primarily by ploughing company profits into good works: his enterprises rarely had many profits since these were all ploughed back into their development. He wanted to attract a team of committed Christians who would use their skills to make Andrews flourish, and would also spend some of both the company's and their own time on charitable activity. He appointed as its General Manager Raymond Andrews, a Methodist and a businessman to whom Jackson-Cole's ideas had strong appeal. The guinea-pig organisation that Andrews and his team would set about building up was the Oxford Committee for Famine Relief.

At this time, the idea of charitable organisations employing professional or business people was strange. Charity was still almost exclusively an affair of the churches, of vocational activity; or an affair of the shires, with admirable and titled patrons leading drives and collecting subscriptions. Jackson-Cole's idea that charities should follow the path of business practice was extremely radical, even subversive; charities were by definition run by amateurs so as to keep costs to a minimum. And the notion that they should plough back part of their receipts into growth, as did commercial concerns, was almost indecent; like gambling with the Sunday collection. When Robert Castle had been appointed to run the clothing drives, the Committee had agreed to pay him a part-time salary, and Jackson-Cole made up the rest. But by 1948, he felt the Committee needed someone more experienced to build it into a larger, more permanent body. So he borrowed from Andrews and Partners one of his best managers, Leslie Swain. The Committee paid Swain a modest income, and Andrews topped it up. Jackson-Cole wanted to establish with the Committee the principle that a permanent organisation, even a small charity, needed qualified and remunerated direction.

Swain was a success. He had drive, flair, and efficiency. He was also able to cope with Jackson-Cole's idiosyncrasies and restless ambitions for his Oxford cause. The appointment lasted into the 1950s, but in 1951 Swain began to redevote his energies to his business career. At that time, Jackson-Cole set up a branch of Andrews and Partners in Oxford so that Swain could remain closely involved with the Committee's affairs.

One of Leslie Swain's earliest proposals to the Committee was to do up the premises at 17 Broad Street and make the Gift Shop into a going concern. Although charities often used temporary shop premises during fundraising campaigns, the use of a permanent site to sell donated items of value was a novelty.

In November 1949, a full-time manager – Joe Mitty – was appointed. Mitty had faith in the maxim that people would happily give away something they no longer needed if it could be turned into help for someone in distress. He loved a deal for items great and small in value or in size, and had a knack for mining a speck of gold out of the most unpromising contents of somebody's attic. In his hands the shop at 17 Broad Street became a thriving concern, turning over anything from candlesticks to fur coats, false teeth to feather boas. Gift Shop appeals broadened and Gift Shop income rapidly grew. Within a short time, income doubled to £3,000 a year, and climbed to over £10,000 by 1953.

Meanwhile the Committee had begun to develop a new source of income for clothes, cash, and gifts: advertisements.

Curious as it nowadays seems, at that time the sustained marketing of a charitable organisation by placing advertisements in newspapers and journals was uncharted water. Ads for worthy causes could be seen in local newspapers, but they were of the demure, 'here we are' variety.

Jackson-Cole, a self-made man, had a natural enthusiasm for advertising, and regarded as axiomatic in the growth of any enterprise that certain financial risks would have to be taken. But for charities, risk was a most uneasy, even unrespectable, partner. Charities were still clad in their Victorian uniform of gentility, probity, and earnest good works. Although Oxfam's patrons were known rather for their commitment to ideals of international peace and understanding than for their social connections, when it came to the day-to-day running of affairs, they adhered to the conventions of the time. These included utmost financial caution.

Jackson-Cole's most important contribution to Oxfam, and to the charitable movement in Britain generally, was to discard this conceptual straitjacket. In doing so, he trod on toes, and ruffled feathers, but his vision and persistence, backed by his reliance on his own company to provide risk capital, eventually changed the face of charitable activity in the UK. It may also inadvertently have sowed the seeds of ambivalence towards Oxfam, an anti-establishment upstart brat among the dignified ranks of the ineffably correct – charities such as Dr. Barnardo's, the Red Cross, and Save the Children – an ambivalence which continued down the years.

In January 1946, with the misery on the continent daily in the press and the European Relief Appeal at full spate, Jackson-Cole purchased in *The Times* the maximum amount of space permitted under newsprint rationing for an Oxford Committee advertisement. If the charity's own funds had been involved, the Committee would certainly have prevented this venture, but they had little choice in the matter. Headed 'European Relief', the ad sought funds to purchase food offered to COBSRA by the government. At its foot was the legend: 'Space presented by Andrews and Partners'. It cost £55; it raised £1,200. After this result, the Committee found it hard to maintain that national advertising was an inappropriate use of charitable money.

The Committee then agreed that part of the proceeds could be ploughed back into further advertising. Robert Castle wrote the copy, and Fougasse, a famous *Punch* cartoonist, donated a drawing of a scarecrow for clothing appeals. Raymond Andrews ran the campaign on behalf of Jackson-Cole, trying Christian and special interest journals, taking the risk on Andrews' account for experiments in unproven outlets. Newsprint was still rationed, and there were long waits for space. *The Times* and the Sunday qualities were the most fruitful. The *Manchester Guardian* was also used on a monthly basis. The Manchester and Salford Famine Relief Committee regularly contributed £5 to the cost of the space and, in return, their own address was included.

The advertisement – a squarish upright across two columns – was standard. Alongside the scarecrow motif, the caption read 'No clothes are too old'. Codes were used as part of the appeal address to identify the source of response: 'Manrelief' for the *Manchester Guardian*, 'Telrelief' for the *Daily Telegraph*. 'Oxfam', originally contracted from the Committee's full name for telegraphic purposes, was a useful shortform for cramped advertising spaces. A registry was kept of all contributors. Thank-you letters went out under a well-known signature, for many years that of Dame Sybil Thorndike; responses from the religious press were acknowledged by a Reverend.

In 1949, a new partnership began which dramatically affected the evolution of the Committee's advertising and the role it played in Oxfam's future fundraising success. Like so many of Jackson-Cole's 'finds', Harold Sumption came into contact with him through the Society of Friends. During the war, Sumption nearly lost his life to TB. His case was so bad that, as a last hope, he was sent in 1947 with charitable help to a Swiss sanatorium. Many of his fellow patients were concentration camp victims and churchmen persecuted under Hitler. This exposure to his own near death and that of a very special group of others had a profound effect upon him.

In 1949 when he returned to England still in a frail condition, Sumption wanted to resume his career in advertising. A correspondence in the Quaker journal *The Friend* led to contact with Jackson-Cole, who employed him for a few hours a day writing advertising copy. When he was sufficiently recovered to join an agency, Sumption took the Oxford Committee advertising with him, remaining its manager for the next 20 years. He became fascinated by the application of marketing and advertising to the whole charitable field, and over his career has influenced its development profoundly.

Sumption soon proved his effectiveness by turning £5,000 worth of advertising space into £25,000 for one of Jackson-Cole's pet causes. This gave him confidence that advertising was a sure path to a charity's growth and to gaining public visibility. Sumption went for a dramatic expression of human need, making the message sing. Out with the scarecrow, in with a photo of a child in distress, in with the punchy message, away with long sentences in small print. The theme was still the detritus of war and emergency: refugees, the sick, the destitute. The appeal was for clothing, or for a specific sum of money – 'Send 10s. to help one stricken family' – to cover the costs of transport.

It was newspaper advertising, using increasingly striking images as the 1950s progressed, which did most to familiarise the British public with the name of the Oxford Committee for Famine Relief. Between 1950 and 1961, Oxfam had five appeals on BBC radio's 'The Week's Good Cause'. The increase in response, from under £10,000 to Gilbert Murray's appeal in 1950, to £105,000 to Richard Dimbleby's in 1961, was not a matter left to chance or divine intervention. The key to success was an increasingly intense promotional effort for each appeal, with ads placed around the broadcast to encourage people to listen and respond. The increase in national recognition the appeals gained for Oxfam's name were closely associated with this achievement: another Jackson-Cole inspiration.

In the late 1940s and early 1950s, disasters overtook one another in different parts of the world and the map of overseas relief began to fill in.

The Oxford Committee's first grant to a specific project overseas went, appropriately, to Greece. In spring 1948, £200 was given to the Friends' Service Council for the Domestic Training College for Girls in

Salonika. This was a pioneering educational venture for young Greek women, set up in 1945 by Sydney and Joice Loch, a Quaker couple deeply committed to Greece and involved in war-time and post-war relief.

Support to the school paved the way for help to other projects connected to the Lochs and to Salonika. Piping was given so that the mountain springs which constituted the water supply for many Northern Greek communities could be trapped and brought to a standpipe in the village. Greece thus became the first country in which there was a group of defined projects with which the Committee had a direct relationship. Other special grants were also made to orphanages and individuals running schemes in Europe known personally to Committee members such as Leo Liepmann; but most help went in bulk form – mostly clothing – to the FSC or other welfare organisations for use at their discretion, primarily among refugees and displaced people in Europe.

In early 1949, the Oxford Committee broadened the stated objects of its work to: 'The relief of suffering arising as a result of wars or of other causes in any part of the world'. This was designed to cover both geographical expansion beyond Europe, and the relief of distress caused by emergencies other than war. The situation then commanding the attention of organised compassion was the human fall-out from the creation of Israel in May 1948: war and a mass exodus of Palestinian refugees. 'Arab Relief' was made the subject of advertising appeals; but met with much less success than those highlighting need among displaced people in Germany and Austria.

The winding down of the post-war programmes run by the Friends, as well as expanded income, encouraged the Oxford Committee to broaden its links with societies, groups, institutions, missions – organisations of any kind which ran operations on the ground to help those in distress. The framework of Oxfam's work overseas has, throughout its history, been defined by this continuing quest. There was never any idea of a special 'Oxfam' recipient pre-selected by age, faith, or sex; nor of employing its own workers at the front-line to fulfill among such recipients an 'Oxfam' mission. It was from the beginning a 'donor' body. Its ideology held that the giver of money, goods or of time, fulfilled a mission as spiritually significant as that of the relief worker. The quest was always for sound and reliable practitioners to use money and relief goods on the donors' behalf, to provide the essential link between the funds Oxfam could raise and the suffering it wanted to alleviate.

In the late 1940s and early 1950s, the range of possibilities was not overwhelming. Relief work and the relief worker belonged to a relatively new sub-branch of social welfare, inspired by compassion for unfortunates beset by some cataclysmic crisis outside their control, whose needs were not met by existing public or private social services. As an activity of the fledgling international civil service, relief management was still in its infancy. Most relief work was carried out by missionaries and representatives of proselytising faiths, when a crisis beset their flock or the human family around their physical and institutional presence.

Thus the Oxford Committee looked for partners among the array of religious societies at work in all corners of the world; age-related welfare groups such as the Save the Children Fund and YM- and YWCAs; in emergencies, the Red Cross and Red Crescent Societies; and whatever else it might happen upon in the way of local initiatives overseas. It excluded no partner on the grounds of faith, nor sought any special pre-qualification. The main inhibition to developing the network was the need for Committee members – or staff – to travel to distant overseas destinations. In the meantime, some members visited Europe; and each different disaster situation – Palestine, Korea, India – produced a new crop of partnerships as the Committee sought the best route for response.

In 1951, when the combined value of clothing, gifts, and donations had reached around £80,000 annually, the Oxford Famine Relief Committee was ready to open a new chapter. A General Secretary was appointed. Jackson-Cole undertook the most careful search, and made his best-ever 'find'. He picked the man who would stay in the Committee's driving seat for 24 years and turn it into Oxfam: Howard Leslie Kirkley.

Leslie Kirkley was born in Manchester in 1911. His father, a schoolteacher, encouraged his interest in social and political affairs. As a young man he was much moved by the damaging poverty of the Depression; and he was also inspired by the idealism then widely current which, until the rise of Nazi aggression, envisaged a new world order built on justice and peace. Kirkley became close to the Society of Friends, and more importantly, active in that part of the peace movement which held that all war was evil and armed violence morally unacceptable. He joined the Peace Pledge Union, and helped pack Manchester's Free Trade Hall for speakers such as Bertrand Russell.

In 1936, Kirkley qualified as an Associate of the Chartered Institute of Secretaries. By this time he was employed by Manchester Corporation. As war loomed and Hitler's aggression appeared unstoppable, many pacifists dropped their opposition to all war. Not Kirkley. In 1939, at the age of 28, he registered as a conscientious objector. At the tribunal, he chose not to become a member of the Society of Friends to claim exemption from military service on religious grounds, but based his case purely on his convictions as a pacifist. He won the exemption, at a price: he was fired by the Manchester Corporation.

During the war years, Kirkley moved to Leeds and remained active in the pacifist network. He helped found and run the Leeds Famine Relief Committee, and as its Honorary Secretary, attended the national Famine Relief Conference in Caxton Hall in January 1944. The Committees in the North of England worked closely together, and were particularly active in trying to protest against the impact of the blockade on civilians under German occupation. After the war, the Leeds Committee – like the Oxford Committee – took up the cause of European Relief, raising funds and collecting parcels of food for 'Save Europe Now'. It was during the course of joint meetings and delegations that Kirkley first had contact with Jackson-Cole.

In 1950, the Leeds Committee for European Relief decided to follow the example of other similar committees around the country and close down. Jackson-Cole invited Kirkley to come and be interviewed by the honorary officers of the Oxford Committee, then looking for a Secretary to back up Swain and ultimately replace him. Kirkley was appointed, and took up his new job early in 1951. For the next several years Swain formally remained Administrator, later becoming an influential trustee; but day-to-day responsibility passed to Kirkley.

Leslie Kirkley was a man cut in solid cloth, not a person who visibly trailed his charisma. He was not by any means a simple man. But his manner was simple and direct, he had great charm of the quiet kind, and a persuasive tenaciousness which worked its leaven slowly but effectively. His Lancashire doggedness was belied by an outwardly easygoing style, which might frustrate but rarely angered. He inspired respect, and great affection, among people from many different cultures and walks of life. He gave his friendship freely, usually with a twinkle in his eye, although he remained an essentially private man.

Kirkley was not an intellectual, but neither was he anybody's fool. He had a canny instinct for people, admired those with strong ideas forcefully expressed, and never felt threatened or overshadowed by them. He liked to stay in the background, quietly steering and encouraging those more inclined to take the limelight. He brought the ideal combination of personal qualities to a task at Oxfam into which – and in which – he grew as if it was a tailored garment.

Like Jackson-Cole, Kirkley had a deep-rooted sense of service and a long-term commitment to a vision of a better world. It was not an apocalyptic vision. There was no imminent dawning of a great tomorrow. Building this world would require as many tortoises as hares. When he joined Joe Mitty and the volunteers in the premises at 17 Broad

Street, life went on as normal. He got to know the Committee, visited refugee camps and orphanages in Europe, consolidated links with like-minded organisations, cultivated useful public figures, and in his spare time he wrote out appeal receipts with other volunteers.

From this very early period of Kirkley's involvement, two milestones stand out. One was the first effort to respond to a natural disaster in what would later be known as a 'developing country': famine in Bihar, India. This took place in 1951, and confronted Kirkley with the difficulty of finding the right partner to whom to entrust funds donated for relief in a place thousands of miles away. Eventually, mission routes were found; much of the £3,500 raised over the course of 1951 went to a Famine Relief Committee run by the wife of the Bishop of Bhagalpur. The appeal was a landmark, for it gained the Oxford Committee its first, approving, mention in the House of Commons.

The second milestone had, once more, to do with Greece. In August 1953, a devastating earthquake struck the Ionian Islands. The Rev. Henry Moxley happened to be in Greece at the time, checking up on village water projects helped by a national 'Help for Greece' committee, on which he was the Oxford Committee's representative. Moxley cabled Kirkley after the earthquake struck. He flew out and attached himself to a Greek Red Cross team on one of the worst-hit islands. He took a money order in his pocket, and used the funds to purchase supplies – utensils, bedding – on the spot.

This was the start of Oxfam's direct involvement in disaster relief. It was also the start of something that became Kirkley's hallmark: his own immediate arrival at the scene of catastrophe. In Hungary, Algeria, Morocco, and the Congo, his presence among the first emissaries of aid would help to put Oxfam definitively on the map.

3

ASYLUM IS AN AFFAIR OF THE HEART

On the night of 23 October 1956, students in Budapest staged a demonstration. They demanded a change of regime, liberalisation, and the departure of Soviet troops from Hungarian soil. In the early hours, police and troops opened fire. Thus began the Hungarian uprising, a patriotic insurrection which engulfed the country and horrified the Western world.

In the confusion of the days that followed it seemed for a time that the revolution would succeed. With Hungarian troops fighting alongside them, the reformists won control. Political concessions came thick and fast and Moscow promised military withdrawal. But on 4 November, while Budapest was celebrating, the Red Army struck back. Tanks rolled down the streets reducing to rubble any building where there was resistance. Citizens smeared the streets with soap to slow them down, tore up cobblestones for barricades, and cut out the Communist emblem from the centre of their flags.

Their bravery was futile. While UN and Western attention was caught up with the simultaneous Suez crisis, tens of thousands of Hungarians were killed. By 12 November the uprising had been crushed, blamed on 'Fascists and counter-revolutionaries'. A shocked world looked on as a stream of refugees, many wounded, some frost-bitten, began to pour across the Austrian border. They carried suitcases, balanced bundles on their bicycles, pushed farm-wagons and baby-carriages. They hurried their children through the cold and snow, hiding by night, risking the bullets of the secret police.

By 23 November, 48,000 people had crossed the Austrian frontier; on one day, the exodus reached 8,537. By the end of the year, 171,000 refugees had taken flight. Many who witnessed this thin stream of humanity plodding its way to freedom, faces bleak with cold and desperation, found its image indelibly imprinted in their minds. The sight encapsulated the agony of the refugee: sudden forced departure, arrival at a strange destination, and the loss of nearly everything – personal identity included – in between.

Among those witnesses were members of the world's press and an armada of sympathisers, people with or without organisational affiliation from all over Western Europe. Leslie Kirkley of the Oxford Committee for Famine Relief was one of their number. He reached the border on the bitterly cold night of 26 November, helping a Friends' Service Council team deliver supplies to temporary shelters. Voluntary agencies ran mobile canteens at border towns, ferried people across canals by boat, took exhausted women and children to sleep overnight in monasteries, schools and churches. Many arrived hungry and wretched with only the clothes they stood up in, feet blistered and poking through their shoes.

The Oxford Committee had been providing help to refugees in Austria through the Friends' Service Council for many years. Early in the crisis, a lorry was loaded with five tons of warm clothes and sent off post-haste to Vienna. Other consignments by train soon followed, as did Leslie Kirkley. At Oxford's request, he had cut short a visit to the Far East to fly back to Europe, and as he listened to the stories of the newly arrived, he was sobered to discover that their foot-slogging journey had taken the same four days it had taken him to come from Hong Kong.

The Hungarian uprising and the mass exodus it prompted made a profound impression on the world. There had been the expulsions and, later, the flight, of Germans from Eastern into Western zones of Germany; but their migration was perceived as an intrinsically German problem, a wash from the human ebb and flow set in motion by the Third Reich and still eddying about the continent. What happened in Hungary was a symptom of the new threat to freedom posed by the Cold War. The revolt had happened suddenly, with terrifying and unexpected consequences.

The care of the uprooted was traditionally regarded as a charge upon the authorities of the country where they sought refuge. But in the case of Hungary, the usual view was thrust aside. The problem of the refugees could not just be left to Austria simply because it happened to be next door. The armies of occupation had only withdrawn in 1955, and Austria's national government was neither administratively nor economically in a position to cope with such an influx.

Austria declared her borders open, offering sanctuary to all those who wanted it. Almost in the same breath, she appealed to the United Nations High Commissioner for Refugees – then Dr. Auguste Lindt of Switzerland – to open up every possible channel for international assistance. With co-operation from the battalions of the Red Cross and help from voluntary organisations great and small, the UNHCR proceeded to co-ordinate a relief and resettlement programme for the thousands of men, women, and children who had abandoned their fate to Western hospitality.

UNHCR launched an appeal to the member nations of the UN Refugee Fund (UNREF). The response was immediate and generous. The League of Red Cross Societies recruited 650 volunteers from member societies to run reception centres. Non-governmental appeals were launched all over Europe – the Lord Mayor of London's Appeal for Hungarian Refugees raised several million pounds – to support the voluntary organisations providing hot meals, clothes, health care, and comforts. The Oxford Committee opened a Hungarian Relief account to receive special donations, and clothing poured into their depots.

Contemplating the machinery of the Red Cross with partners and resources all over the world, and the seasoned know-how of social workers from long established church and voluntary networks, the one-man band of Kirkley might well have felt daunted. He trod warily, looking for nooks and crannies into which he could insert modest but useful amounts of on-the-spot assistance. He was beginning to develop a style of response to mass human crisis. He searched for unforeseen or unforeseeable shortages, sometimes petty but often critical: shelter materials, blankets, utensils, fuel, babyfood, water equipment.

Kirkley stayed in Vienna for most of a week. He tried, unsuccessfully, to get into Hungary itself to see how those left behind were faring. He used £2,750 to plug some immediate relief gaps, and made contact with those organisations – the YMCA, the Friends, Save the Children, and Austrian and Hungarian agencies – who would continue to be in action over the coming months. Inevitably, there would be special casualties: the sick and elderly, young and orphaned. Teenagers were singled out as a particular focus for the Oxford Committee's ongoing concern.

The camps in Austria were only the first stage of the refugees' journey. Every new arrival was screened with a view to onward passage to a new country of residence. Strict conventions governing refugee status were waived. Several countries offered immediate homes for large numbers of refugees, so strong was the flow of public sympathy. In November, an airlift brought 7,500 Hungarians to Britain. By the end of January 1957 over 100,000 had departed, nearly half for countries in Europe, the rest for North America and Australia. Among them were many problem cases, handicapped and elderly, on whose behalf a special appeal was made by Oscar Helmer, Austrian Minister of the Interior: 'Asylum,' he said, 'is an affair of the heart.'

This operation of unprecedented size and effectiveness to handle a sudden mass migration and resettlement cost $14 million, to which the Austrian government and the voluntary agencies contributed around $10 million. In comparison to the whole, the £20,000 for feeding and medical supplies and the 125 tons of clothes, bedding, and shoes sent from Oxford appears insignificant. But voluntary effort depends on carers who are not diverted by the size of the whole problem, and are content to do something for a few of its myriad human parts.

Of those who fled from Soviet bullets and shells on the streets of Hungary, only some 19,000 remained in Austrian camps by early 1958. The Western world and its charitable fellowship had made a supreme effort to pick up the human pieces of Hungary's blow for freedom. But while for the broken heroes of Budapest, asylum might well be 'an affair of the heart', the fate of thousands of other refugees inspired no such feeling.

Among the 42,000 European exiles still languishing in Austrian camps 11 years after the end of the war were many refugees of Hungarian nationality who had repeatedly sought, and been refused, a home and prospects elsewhere. This process mortified their self-esteem: they were being constantly put in a human auction where they failed to find bidders. At the time of the uprising, they watched their compatriots set off with their new passports for their new lives, and understandably they felt great bitterness. Some even slipped across the frontier to re-arrive and enjoy the special privileges, the waiving of strict immigration tests, that would enable them finally to leave camp life behind.

The gross unfairness in the world's behaviour did not go unnoticed. Hungary dramatised anew the heartbreaking plight of refugees everywhere and raised their status as a preoccupation of international concern. It showed that, in a volatile world, the refugee problem required a special commitment from the forces of the new internationalism. And it led, in time, to a special crusade on their behalf.

The story of each refugee is an individual story. It is a story of fear, in which flight and exile, material loss, the abandonment of home, kin, country, personal status, job and profession, even of birthright and identity, seems preferable to the fate involved in staying put.

During the war, around 30 million people in Europe were uprooted by one cause or another from the land where they belonged. The task of wholesale repatriation was given to UNRRA, but it was a difficult task to complete. At the end of 1945, 750,000 displaced people who refused to go home were still living in camps in Austria, Germany and Italy. Most came from countries absorbed into the Soviet bloc; many had ethnic or other associations which led them to fear persecution if they returned. New waves of refugees soon joined them. All these people, rich and poor, young and old, skilled and illiterate, wanted a new start in life. Many set their sights on emigration to North America.

When the United Nations General Assembly discussed what to do about these refugees early in 1946, the debate was long and heated. The idea that, under certain circumstances, the citizen of a country might claim as a right protection against being made to belong to it was a relatively novel concept, and by no means universally agreed. Finally, against opposition from the Eastern European countries, the principle of no forcible repatriation – first upheld by Fridtjof Nansen, Refugee Commissioner for the League of Nations after the first World War – was accepted. This advance for human rights gained ground when a UN Convention set out as the criterion for refugee status 'a well-founded fear of persecution' in the home country. It was many years, however, before the 1951 Convention was fully recognised in international law.

In the meantime, the UN set up an International Refugee Organisation (IRO) with a set life-span of five years to deal with the remaining refugees, the lingering human scar of war. The IRO managed to find new homes, mostly in North America, for over one million. But there were still 130,000 'hard core' refugees lingering in German and Austrian camps when the IRO's mandate expired in 1951. Its successor, the United Nations High Commissioner for Refugees (UNHCR), was brought into being with the greatest international reluctance for a period of three years to make these hard-core cases disappear.

No-one wanted the remaining refugees. They had a tubercular patch on the lung, or their eyesight was poor; they were too old to earn, or learn a new language; there were whispers about communist leanings and more sinister disabilities. Likewise, no-one wanted to help pay for their upkeep, or invest in their retraining or rehousing. Their right not to go home was respected, but not their right to leave the decrepit limbo of the camps, to live in a way that showed respect for them as human beings. The US refused to make any contribution to the UNHCR's $3 million appeal, their UN delegate, Eleanor Roosevelt, declaring that the 'refugee problem is over'. Somehow, without funds and with no place for them to go, the UN High Commissioner, Dr. G.J. van Heuven Goedhart of the Netherlands, was expected to sort out 130,000 reject people's future existence within three years.

Since governments were so unhelpful, Goedhart turned to the voluntary sector. If countries of asylum would not accept the refugees, they might be integrated into the communities where they were already living. In August 1952, the Ford Foundation came up with a grant of $2.9 million, to be administered by UNHCR and utilised in programmes run by voluntary agencies. These included the YMCA, the World Council of Churches, and the international Lutheran, Friends, Jewish, and Catholic networks. Many of the projects were for youth centres and vocational training: the problem of delinquency, the camps as breeding grounds for youthful anger and political extremism, were common worries of the time.

Other prospects improved when Sweden, in 1952, showed a willingness to provide 'asylum from the heart': places specifically for active TB cases. Since a shadow on the lung disqualified entrants from the US, there were tragic stories of suicide and break-up within refugee families because one member had TB. Often it was the squalor and overcrowding in the camp itself which spread the infection, especially to children whose parents had then to choose between abandoning a sick child or refusing a long-awaited exit visa.

For the Oxford Committee for Famine Relief, the plight of the residual camp residents in Germany and Austria was a natural focus of concern. During the late 1940s and the 1950s, the notion of overseas charity was virtually synonymous with relief for destitute refugees. The official attitude of neglect, even discrimination, towards those debilitated in body or in mind – marginals among the already marginal – reinforced the compassionate feelings of the charitable donor.

Leslie Kirkley and Leslie Swain travelled often to Germany and Austria to visit projects and make contact with partner organisations during the 1950s, as did Dr. Leo Liepmann and other members of the Committee who had a special interest in Europe. As the Committee's cash income increased, more grants were made to rehousing schemes, handicraft workshops, scholarship and vacation funds, on top of the usual consignments of clothing, shoes, and bedding for camp inmates.

Most refugee camps were miserable places. They had their own special smell: old cooking, sour sweatiness, and cheap tobacco. It was redolent of the demoralisation suffered by people whose rotting surroundings reflected the world's valuation of them as human beings; who were bitter and quarrelsome in quarters too communal for the preservation of personal dignity; whose sorrows had pushed their wills and minds into a place from which it was hard to recover them. Many struggled to maintain the precious atmosphere of family life. 'Oh yes, we have a lovely home,' explained a child to a visitor, 'it's just that we have no house to put it in.'

In the wake of the Hungarian crisis, Kirkley was put in touch through the UNA with a Dutch social worker, Frankie Hamilton, working with refugees in the market town of Enns in Upper Austria. Camp 106 had been set up in a cavalry barracks from imperial times; the building was dark, humid and depressing. Enns camp was a headache to all voluntary organisations trying to resolve refugee predicaments. The authorities had made it a dumping ground for problem cases from other camps, and its 400 inmates included a high proportion of prostitutes, alcoholics, and social misfits. There were Poles, Yugoslavians, Hungarians, Russians, and Rumanians, of all ages and social status, some very old, some with criminal records. The task of rehabilitation seemed truly daunting.

When almost every organisation had given up, the Netherlands Federation for Aid to Refugees sent Frankie Hamilton, courageous, competent, and warm-hearted, to Enns. She set out single-mindedly to close Enns down. While she sought permanent solutions for the residents – immigration, integration into local communities – she organised temporary help for the sick, elderly, and those with special problems. Her work – building small apartment houses for problem families, running handicrafts classes, finding hospital places and funds for TB treatment, helping unmarried mothers find jobs, scraping small pensions together from obscure sources – was wholeheartedly supported by several voluntary agencies; for the latter part of her time in Enns, Oxfam met her salary and costs.

In November 1958, the last of the hard-core cases left Enns; as a camp, the building was closed. But not before it had been totally rehabilitated, and some refugee as well as Austrian families given apartments. Frankie Hamilton had achieved a goal no-one had thought possible. Kirkley was so impressed that, when she went off to Greece and settled among the northern villages, the Committee paid for her to promote the kind of health and water supply schemes they had long supported there. She also set up a number of social schemes for women and their families. Frankie Hamilton was one of those very special people whose humanitarian work in various parts of the world was infinitely worth backing.

When Leslie Kirkley hastened back from Hong Kong to Hungary in November 1956, he had been on his first ever visit to the Far East. His itinerary was long: Pakistan, India, Vietnam, Hong Kong, and Korea. Most of the projects he visited were also for the human casualties scattered far and wide by regional conflict and its accompanying upheavals.

By the mid 1950s, a large share of the Committee's relief assistance was going to Korea, where the after-effects of war required painful years of recovery. Hostilities had broken out in June 1950 with the North Koreans' offensive across the 38th Parallel. The war was protracted, sweeping up and down the peninsula as first General MacArthur's troops counter-attacked from the south, and then the Chinese army counter-attacked from the north. Not until mid-1951 did the war become relatively static and the vast movements of population cease; the war itself did not formally end until political settlement divided Korea in July 1953.

The damage inflicted by the war on the civilian population was tremendous. The total death toll was estimated at around three and a half million. Nine million people in the South lost their homes or possessions. The economy was completely disrupted, plunging living standards below subsistence level and consigning war widows and their families to destitution. Until peace negotiations bore fruit, all relief work was carried out by the unified military command, and voluntary agencies were effectively banned. With no FSC or Save the Children teams on the ground, the Oxford Committee had no channel for clothes or other relief goods. By November 1951, the only supplies they had managed to send were reels of cotton thread, despatched to an orphanage in South Korea via the small packets service of the GPO, 'the parcels service being suspended'.

During 1952, the Committee became so bothered by the blockade against voluntary agency relief to Korea they considered protesting to *The Times*. The long stalemate which no-one could agree to end deepened the tragedy in Korea, exacerbating food shortages and inflation, and delaying prospects of economic repair. Finally it was decided that UNKRA, the United Nations Korean Reconstruction Agency, set up in preparation for the peace, should start its operations early in 1953 even without a cease-fire. This opened the way for the Friends to send a team to Kunsan, under UNKRA's umbrella. Save the Children also managed to gain permission for a relief team to establish itself further south, at Pusan.

A major concern of all the agencies was the condition of the children. The estimated number of those orphaned or made fatherless was 100,000. The first representatives from the Friends to go to Korea late in 1952 were told by the military authorities that 30,000 orphans were being cared for in 300 orphanages set up since the war. Some were run by missions, some even by groups of soldiers who had taken compassion on the hungry mites surviving on leftovers on the outskirts of their camps. Some of these places were terrible, barely providing a roof and some food. Most of their charges were dull and apathetic, showing every sign of neglect and expressing 'neither joy, interest, nor fear'.

Outside the orphanages were at least as many waifs and strays. Quite small children could be seen walking the streets, sleeping rough in a sheltered corner, begging for food. Some were not orphans but had become separated from their parents and had no way of finding their way home or discovering where their parents had gone. Many fetched up in a wretchedly malnourished condition in hospital wards. Older children were better able to look after themselves, forming gangs and living wild by thieving. Bringing such children into care, rehabilitating them, giving them some skills and education, was a major preoccupation, as was the rebuilding of health care facilities.

Between 1954 and 1956, more financial grants from Oxfam went to Korean orphanages and welfare schemes than to any other part of the world.

Clothing was also sent. That refugees and indigent war victims were in need of clothing was an article of faith with the Oxford Committee; in fact, most British cast-offs – particularly women's, which were much more commonly given than men's – were not the kind of garments that Koreans would wear. One enterprising missionary set up war-widows with sewing machines to adapt the less suitable items, using part of the clothing as currency to pay them in. If the contents of some bales fetched up in the market, sensible helpers looked the other way. Needs were so great among the poor that if unusable relief goods could bolster a petty trader's livelihood, so much the better for his or her family.

By October 1956, the Oxford Committee had spent £60,000 on projects in Korea, and the need to check up on this expenditure was the primary justification for Kirkley's Far Eastern tour. What touched him most was, however, not the Koreans' plight but that of the refugees in Hong Kong.

In the years following the Communist takeover on the Chinese mainland, over a million people fled to Hong Kong. With an existing population of two million crammed into the usable 62 square miles of Hong Kong's territory, this was already the most crowded space on earth. Half the refugees had no resources and nowhere to go. They set up flimsy packing-case and tin-sheet shacks, a piece of rag serving for a front door, on any piece of ground they could find. They spilled over pavements, stairways, and rooftops; they erected plank and basketwork dwellings on steep hillsides and ravines.

Accommodation was not counted in 'rooms' or 'huts', but in 'bedspace', an area three or four planks wide within which every possession had to be stored, every activity carried out. When rehousing was provided in special new apartment blocks, a family of five refugees moved into comparative luxury: one room, twelve feet by ten. Smaller families had to share.

A number of church-related organisations ran welfare programmes for children, the elderly, and other specially needy categories of refugees. One of these was a mission with the unlikely name of the West China Evangelistic Band, whose leading light, Mrs. Gladys Donnithorne, was the wife of an Archdeacon. Mrs. Donnithorne did not exactly run a project; whatever she did was the project. A ministering angel by method and instinct, she unearthed pockets of misery on rooftops and in alleyways of the kind the authorities were loath to admit existed. She was prepared to go anywhere, however distressing, moving around among the most pitiful 'bedspace' cases to bring a little extra in food or cash, to pass around warm garments or blankets, to arrange for an invalid to be taken to hospital. Her activity was not particularly orderly or planned; but its sincerity could not be doubted nor that it brought solace into some poverty-stricken lives.

Mrs. Donnithorne's work became a special concern of the Oxford Committee. If she wanted to buy some sewing machines to help some girls use their bedspace as a trouser-making venture; if she wanted to set up an old people's home; if she wanted to find a dwelling place for a family flooded out by Hong Kong's notorious downpours, she would write to Leslie Kirkley, and the Committee could be counted upon to help. Her personality and the quintessentially charitable nature of her work were in themselves sufficient guarantee; as yet questions about the method and conduct of programmes were exclusively confined to financial queries. Occasionally a formal statement of accounts was sought; but Oxford's requests for information were more typically for the little human stories of suffering relieved and tears replaced with joy that could be put in an advertisement or otherwise used for fundraising.

One of Oxfam's handful of staff members took a very particular, almost proprietary, interest in Mrs. Donnithorne's work among the Hong Kong refugees. This somewhat eccentric individual was Frank Carter, appointed in 1953 as Oxfam's first organiser of local appeals. Carter was an evangelical Anglican lay preacher, an Old Testament figure with a flowing patriarchal beard. He ran clothing and gift drives in towns and cities all over the country, recruiting local dignitaries, churches, and voluntary groups according to Jackson-Cole's 'Appeals Week' formula. He was also a determined publicist.

Frank Carter took on the plight of the Hong Kong refugees as his personal crusade. He studied Hong Kong until he knew it like the back of his hand, although he did not go there until 1961. His descriptions in local newspapers sounded as if they came from the very pavements of the colony, elbow to elbow with the tin-shack dwellers. More than once he hit the correspondence columns of the *Daily Telegraph*, and managed almost a regular 'Hong Kong Notes' in the religious press, often raising hundred of pounds at a time for Mrs. Donnithorne's good works.

Carter conducted a personal correspondence with Mrs. Donnithorne, asking by name after her many families' tribulations and sending her blankets knitted by his pet supporters. Carter was a law unto himself. Over the years he raised amounts running into four figures for her projects independently of the Oxford Committee. By 1960, nearly £20,000 had been provided to Mrs. Donnithorne altogether. When she came home on leave, Frank Carter managed to collect an audience of 450 in Westminster Central Hall to hear her; Sir Alexander Grantham, ex-

Governor of Hong Kong and an Oxfam trustee, introduced Mrs. Donnithorne. She spoke movingly of the 'grannies', women of over 80 living on pieces of rain-soaked matting, now moved to her old people's home in Kowloon. She epitomised the simplicity of the Oxfam ethos of those days.

The Oxford Committee also channelled funds through more conventional channels than the West China Evangelistic Band, notably the much more organised and professional programme run by the Lutheran World Service under the well-known figure of Pastor Ludwig Stumpf. Clothing distribution, vocational training for teenagers, roof-top schools, medical care, flood relief, and community services for the inhabitants of the new refugee apartment blocks, were among the activities of this and similar Christian bodies. By 1960, the Oxfam cash and clothing total to Hong Kong had reached nearly £125,000. Pastor Stumpf deeply impressed Leslie Kirkley, and his programme continued to receive Oxfam aid for many years.

Until 1957, the colonial government regarded the refugee influx as a matter solely concerning the British and Chinese. But as numbers mounted beyond one million, the scale of need grew well beyond the authorities' capacity. In the wake of the Hungarian uprising and the international response it elicited, the Governor, then Sir Alexander Grantham, sought United Nations assistance both for relief and for possible resettlement of refugees elsewhere. UNHCR was glad to have the Hong Kong refugee problem internationally recognised and brought within its remit; but, as always, it was short of money. As in so many parts of the world, private philanthropy did what it could while the machinery of international assistance slowly took on a definitive shape.

There was one part of the world where the needs of a large refugee population were accepted as an international responsibility from its inception: the Middle East. After the war which followed the creation in May 1948 of the new state of Israel, the United Nations Relief and Works Agency (UNRWA) was set up to care for the 982,000 Palestinians who lost their homes and livelihoods. This most intransigent of refugee situations, whose victims were scattered between UNRWA camps in Jordan, Gaza, and Lebanon, was perceived in Britain as a running sore. During the 1950s, it was the most well-known of refugee predicaments outside the European camps.

UNRWA was persistently underfunded. UN member states might recognise their responsibility for problems caused by the creation of Israel; but were parsimonious in helping pay for repairs to the many lives it shattered. UNRWA provided rudimentary services: a ration of 1,500 calories; basic medical care; shelter, first in the form of tents and later more solid huts; and schooling for refugee children. But the Palestinians rejected anything which carried even a whiff of permanency concerning a future outside their homeland. The UNRWA mandate was limited; even the 'works' of its title – supposed to provide refugee employment on resettlement schemes – never came into existence. In spite of the large numbers it cared for, UNRWA existed from hand to mouth and some of its programmes depended heavily on philanthropic support.

Outside Europe, UNRWA refugee camps were the largest recipient of clothing from the Oxford Committee. UNRWA – like UNKRA – met the costs of freight; this contribution to the costs of exporting cast-off British clothing to distant locations made it a just practicable form of relief. Reports from the Middle East were reassuring. In late 1956, a vivid account of a clothing hand-out arrived from the Lutheran World Service, whose Committee in Jerusalem had been invited by UNRWA to give out winter clothes to 6,500 needy families.

'When we started, the central hall and four surrounding rooms were stacked to the ceiling with bales, bags, and boxes of shoes. UNRWA provided the families' ration numbers, and their members' ages and sexes. All day long for five weeks we could hear a voice calling out: 'Man, 50 (or 40); woman, 45; boy, 15; girl, 12', and so on. The women took down suitable warm garments for each member of the family, and placed them in the centre of a coat. When neckties, blouses, socks, underwear, had been added to the bundle, it was tied securely. We were not prodigal at any time. But the mass of bales which had appalled us at the start now appalled us by the speed with which it seemed to melt, with thousands yet to care for and winter coming fast.

'The UNRWA team were efficient and courteous. At all times a member of our Committee was present so that the refugees would understand that the clothing was an expression of the loving concern of Christian people in the West.'

Grants were also made to health projects among the Palestinian refugees, especially in Jordan, mainly through the usual network of Christian organisations. Not entirely, however. One early recipient was Musa Alami, a charismatic Palestinian who set up a home and vocational training school for 160 orphaned refugee boys in the Jordan Valley under the aegis of an organisation he called the Arab Development Society, essentially consisting of himself.

Ignoring the advice of experts, Musa Alami drilled for water in a stony wasteland near Jericho, and went on to 'make the desert bloom' with grains, fruit, and vegetables. He then established an imported herd of Friesian dairy cattle in the wonders-of-the-world tradition beloved of Middle Eastern potentates. This farm was supposed to cover the costs of the boys' training, and Oxfam supporters were invited to 'buy a cow' – £250 including passage from Holland – to graze in his miraculous pastures.

Musa Alami was a brilliant fundraiser, and by the late 1950s had become a recipient of Ford Foundation money on a scale which made grants from Oxfam look like pocket money. Oxfam continued to support his home for boys, however, only finally concluding in 1971 that the four-star standard of accommodation – for boys and cattle – and other showpiece characteristics of Musa Alami's farm disqualified his Arab Development Society from receiving further aid. He represented a type of heroic charitable entrepreneur that Oxfam often fell for. He was a dedicated visionary, but his schemes were touched by a grandiosity which unfitted them for the environment they were supposed to serve. Donors from the foundation and government world might not object to elaborate buildings and agricultural high tech, but charity ultimately did.

News of Musa Alami's water drilling success spread to Zerqa, a small town in a stony desert 20 miles north of Amman. This was a home of last resort to a refugee community, and to the chunky and determined figure of a retired headmistress turned relief worker: Miss Winifred Coate. Since 1948, the elderly Miss Coate had set up a small sewing factory, given loans to tinsmiths and carpenters, and done what she could in a most unpromising setting. Throughout the 1950s, Oxfam was a regular supporter of her centre for 'Refugee Industries'.

Pondering the ruined medieval castles just across the ridge, Miss Coate deduced that the courts and garrisons they had once contained must have had access to water. All the experts assured her that the land around Zerqa was totally dry. In the early 1960s, one of her Palestinian workers said he had a knack as a water diviner. When they went out into the desert, his stick moved. Miss Coate thereupon bought 500 acres of stony waste. She was regarded as crazy. All her attempts to gain the necessary £5,000 to sink a well and install a pump were greeted with derision. Except by Oxfam. At 400ft, water was struck, and the source turned out to be abundant.

Miss Coate was a shrewd businesswoman. Her deep regret was not to have bought a much larger chunk of the landscape, whose value swiftly multiplied by 40 times. She set up irrigation works, and carved up the land into five-acre smallholder plots. With water, two crops a year were possible, as well as citrus trees and vegetables. By the end of 1964, the first nine farmers had received title deeds: Miss Coate believed strongly in incentive and self-sufficiency. This was the first land to pass into peasant ownership in Jordan for as long as anyone could remember. The settlers were soon renowned for the biggest cauliflowers in the vicinity of Amman, and became a flourishing community.

The civil war in Algeria produced yet another 1950s refugee emergency. Fighting broke out in 1954, and by 1956 had engulfed the country, driving refugees across the borders into Tunisia and Morocco.

International action was severely hampered by the insistence of the French government that the refugees were technically French citizens and therefore not entitled to international protection. Alternative mechanisms for relief assistance were few. Until 1958, there were no properly established Red Crescent Societies in Tunisia or Morocco. The Tunisian government appealed to the UNHCR for help, but significant assistance had to wait until the UN General Assembly adopted a resolution for full-scale action in November 1958. The war, and the outflow of refugees, continued until 1962.

When the Oxford Committee first became exercised on the Algerians' behalf, there was virtually no private philanthropic channel for assistance to the Algerian refugees except the embryonic Red Crescents. Late in 1957, a Commander Fox-Pitt of the Anti-Slavery Society visited Oujda, a Northern Moroccan border district. He described conditions as the worst he had ever seen: 'The ration is calculated at 300 to 400 calories. Starvation has already begun.' Oxfam gave Fox-Pitt some drugs, and money to help 500 families buy sugar and olive oil. They then began to send out relief goods via Red Cross channels.

By March 1958, the Committee had already despatched 37 tons of clothing and footwear, thousands of blankets, and two tons of milk powder – by now a standard relief item. Leslie Kirkley decided to visit Tunisia to see what could be done for the 70,000 refugees crowded in makeshift border camps, and for 60,000 more inside Morocco, half of whom were children. He was horrified to discover the appalling conditions they endured. 'Some had not had proper food for days and the children showed every sign of prolonged malnutrition – babies with big stomachs, large eyes and unhealthy skins, ragged and inadequate clothing, shivering in the cold wind. The mother of one family of ten had died from eating a poisonous root.'

Throughout 1958, while a full-scale relief operation was yet to be mounted, the Algerian refugees suffered quite agonising hunger. Food distribution was sporadic and inadequate. Many were reduced to eating grass and prickly pear. Each eye-witness report was a terrible repetition of the last. 'I have never seen hunger as I saw it in those refugees,' reported an Oxfam correspondent. 'Not only were they thin, but their nervous, drawn, cadaverous faces had pits where their cheeks should have been. They looked like victims from some fearful concentration camp.'

Oxfam was still one of only a tiny handful of voluntary agencies trying to do something. One modest venture was organised by Sheila Bagnall, a London schoolteacher who spent her holiday in Morocco

MARGARTE TOMLINSON

ROBERT CASTLE

1 *Edith Pye, a veteran of Quaker relief work, prompted the formation of a Famine Relief Committee in Oxford in 1942.*

2 *The Committee's most distinguished member, Professor Gilbert Murray OM, with Lady Mary Murray, at their Boar's Hill home.*

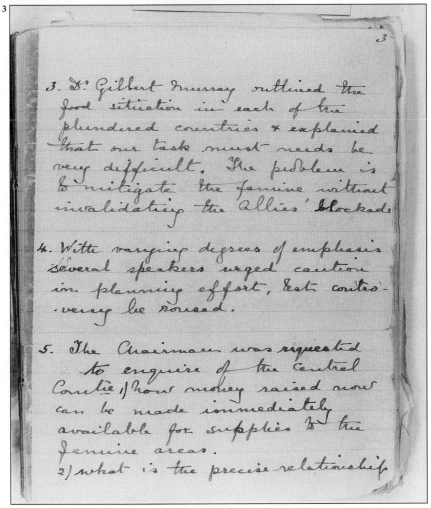

3. Dr Gilbert Murray outlined the food situation in each of the plundered countries & explained that our task must needs be very difficult. The problem is to mitigate the famine without invalidating the allies' blockade

4. With varying degrees of emphasis several speakers urged caution in planning effort, lest contro-versy be roused.

5. The Chairman was requested to enquire of the central Comtee 1) how money raised now can be made immediately available for supplies to the famine areas.
2) what is the precise relationship

3 *The minutes of the first meeting of the Oxford Committee for Famine Relief were recorded in a school exercise book.*

4 *Famine in Greece, 1941-44: 500,000 Greeks lost their lives in the war years. International Red Cross soup kitchen for children in Athens.*

INTERNATIONAL RED CROSS

5 *Queue for relief provisions in the Greek island of Chios, June 1942. The islanders telegraphed Athens: 'Send bread or coffins'.*

INTERNATIONAL RED CROSS

6 Left to right, *Leslie Swain (Administrator), Cecil Jackson-Cole (Hon.Sec.), and Robert Castle (Organiser): Oxfam's 'three musketeers' of 1948.*

ROBERT CASTLE

7

7 The severe post-war distress in continental Europe touched many hearts in Britain, in spite of shortages at home.

OXFAM ARCHIVE

8

OXFAM ARCHIVE

8 Post-war relief in Holland: the Oxford Committee held a clothing appeal in Spring 1945 to help survivors of the Dutch 'hunger winter'.

9

Times 4/3/47 Top right M/M. 7

As Lord Halifax says:—

"No cause can appeal more strongly to our sympathy and to our conscience than the cause of trying to bring relief to the stricken countries of Europe." "I wish all success to your Committee in their work."

OXFORD RELIEF is entrusted to Friends Relief Service whose voluntary workers act with economy, care and a personal touch, regardless of frontiers, race, politics, class or creed. Many countries have benefited and now the peoples of Austria, Poland and the British Zone of Germany are getting most attention, but France, Greece, Hungary, Italy, Norway, etc., are not neglected.

from Oxford to Europe

Gifts as below will be welcome (if no local body is collecting for Europe) :—
MONEY FOR FOOD, MEDICAL SUPPLIES, BLANKETS, ETC., for children, the aged, and special cases. (This does not reduce our rations.) Please make cheques payable to "European Relief," cross and post to Barclays Old Bank, High Street, Oxford. Sir Alan Pim will acknowledge.
CLOTHING, FOOTWEAR, UNIFORMS, TOWELS, BEDDING, BLACKOUTS, MENDING MATERIALS, Etc. (including clean, mendable articles for repair, by Displaced Persons sadly needing work); to :—"Oxford," c/o Messrs. Taphouse's, 3, Magdalen St., Oxford. Lady Franks will acknowledge (if address supplied).
BOOKS & PERIODICALS (any language; for Reading Rooms) to "OXFORD," c/o C.O.B.S.R.A., 75, Victoria St., London, S.W.1.

OXFORD · FOR FAMINE RELIEF

COMMITTEE (Reg'd War Charities Act, 1940) **FOR THE FRIENDLESS**
N.B.—We cannot accept food or coupons nor send parcels to individuals.

Cost £55
Donations 67
Value £374/5/8
Average £5/11/8

Clothing
Parcels 86
Est. Value £258

Books etc.
Gifts ———

Est'd Total Proceeds
£632
or 11½ times cost.

9 Helping to win the peace: the Oxford Committee advertised in the national, religious, and local press, keeping a careful tally on financial results. From Robert Castle's scrapbook.

10 *Rowntrees vans detoured to Broad Street weekly to collect sacks of donated clothing and deliver them free to London.*

11 and **12** *In 1949, the premises at 17 Broad Street became a Giftshop selling anything from candlesticks to fur coats, false teeth to feather boas.*

THOMPSON NEWSPAPERS LTD

13 *Receipting donations, circa 1960: Canon T.R. Milford, Oxfam's first Chairman* left, *and H. Leslie Kirkley, Director of Oxfam 1951-74.*

OXFAM ARCHIVE

14 *Clothing drives and fund-raising appeals in towns all over Britain were the fundraising style for the late 1950s. Organiser Gordon MacMillan* right.

15 *Winifred Coate* (centre), *a retired headmistress from Jerusalem, became a legend by striking water with money from Oxfam in the 'waterless' east Jordan desert (1962).*

16 *Oxfam's oldest ever supporter: Mrs. Roe, 110, of Lowestoft, gives a donation to Organiser Frank Carter.*

17 *The Pimlico warehouse: clothing donated to Oxfam was stored and baled here for despatch abroad.*

18 *Camps like Enns in Austria remained home for many years to 'hard core' war-time refugees. World Refugee Year 1959 tried to close the camps for good.*

19 *Clothing distributions gave each family member one good garment: Algerian refugees, 1958.*

20 *Refugee living, Hong Kong style, in the 1950s: a family of seven manages to eat a meal in one 'bedspace'.*

21 *Bernard Llewellyn, Oxfam's first Overseas Aid Officer, and later its Field Director in the Far East, visits a hospital in Hong Kong.*

setting up a milk distribution scheme for 1,200 children. 'When all is ready, we call 'Ajee, ajee' ('come, come'), and in less than 20 minutes 600 pints of milk have disappeared into tins, bottles, cupped hands and down throats, and supper time is over.' Sheila Bagnall was to be another forceful figure in the network of people involved in many pioneering projects, later working at Swaneng School in Botswana, and becoming an Oxfam trustee.

Victims of the Algerian Civil War, at first in the refugee camps, inside the country once peace was declared, continued to receive Oxfam help throughout the 1960s.

As the relief emphasis moved ever further afield throughout the 1950s, it became obvious that the future of any serious overseas aid programme did not lie in clothing. Many voluntary agencies already felt that garments had had their day: they cost a lot to ship and, unless people were desperate, climate, culture and pride inhibited their usefulness. In 1956 the Friends' Relief Council – to whose Bourne Street depot in Pimlico most of the 'men's heavy', 'women's light', and other categories collected by the Oxford Committee had long been consigned – announced its intention of closing down its clothing operation.

This precipitated some soul-searching in Oxford, particularly as the volume of clothing coming in was rising: in 1954-55, 472 tons, in 1955-56, 546 tons. Clothing appeals were deeply entrenched in the Oxford Committee's *modus operandi*, even its identity; the idea of dropping them overnight was impracticable. So Oxfam decided to take over the FSC depot and continue the operation themselves. But Kirkley used the opportunity to give the clothing issue a thorough airing. He did not want to see the growing list of grant-aided projects foreshortened because a high proportion of cash income had to be spent on shipping to destinations such as India cast-off clothing which no Indian woman would want to wear.

Over the clothing issue, Kirkley was at odds with Cecil Jackson-Cole, still the hyperactive 'Hon. Sec.'. Jackson-Cole was a great enthusiast for clothing, partly because he genuinely wanted to wrap up every refugee in a woollie. But also because clothing was a card he could play to fulfill his expansionist ambitions for Oxfam. All clothing donated was valued, and this value was expressed in the accounts by a money equivalent. In this way, the Oxford Committee's overhead expenses appeared very low: under 10 per cent. This was useful at a time when all charities were supposed to run if not on air, at least on a shoe-string. But it was also a liability because aid in the form of grants instead of clothing – as grants grew in proportion – looked extravagant.

After Frank Carter's appointment in 1953, Jackson-Cole wanted to take on more people like him and expand Oxfam's local branch network. Clothing drives were still the key local activity. Jackson-Cole convinced himself that spending money – employing people – to bring in clothing would also help boost appeals for cash. It would also, incidentally, be represented by money in the balance sheet and thus contribute to the charity's overall growth. Although he was a great schemer, Jackson-Cole's motives were of the best. He simply wanted Oxfam to become well-known and thereby widely supported. A network of local organisers would provide a set of building blocks for a financially solid future. These considerations, in his mind, overruled Kirkley's desire to reduce the role of clothing in Oxfam's overseas allocations.

Jackson-Cole's instinct about Oxfam's growth and visibility was correct. But he was constantly thwarted by the much more cautious Committee. With something close to sleight of hand, Jackson-Cole found a way around his colleagues' objections. He had set up a philanthropic organisation called Voluntary and Christian Service in 1953, and he began to use it to run local clothing appeals on Oxfam's behalf. This created considerable friction. Not only was Kirkley trying to diminish clothing's predominance in the aid programme; he also disliked the fact that helpers were operating in the Committee's name without Oxfam having any control over their actions. It was, however, unthinkable to tell them to stop. Suggesting this course to Jackson-Cole was almost as difficult; hints were invariably ignored.

In 1958, the status of the Oxford Committee was changed, a move which Kirkley justified to Jackson-Cole by saying that it would make Oxfam 'more settled' – a prospect which did not appeal to Jackson-Cole at all. But the Committee had outgrown the temporary character implied by its original registration as a 'War Charity'. It was now registered as a non-profit-making company, a step which indicated its permanent nature and its seriousness of intent. This, it was hoped, would encourage trusts, industry, and wealthy patrons to give long-term support. It would also, incidentally, make it more difficult for Jackson-Cole to apply his mastery of the art of bending 'his' organisation to his will.

From this point on, the 'Hon. Sec.' became a less potent figure. Jackson-Cole resigned his formal position in 1966, but stayed in close touch as the 'Hon. Sec. Emeritus' for many years. Whatever the extraordinary quirks of his personality, for the first 12 years of its life, Oxfam owed more to Jackson-Cole than to any other individual.

The legal and administrative consolidation of the Oxford Committee for Famine Relief was an important landmark. Physically the Committee had become more dispersed, occupying several office locations in central Oxford as well as the premises above the Gift Shop at 17 Broad Street.

Income expanded steadily: in the financial year 1958-59, the total topped £500,000, of which just over half was cash, the rest representing the value of clothing. Cash donations were raised mainly through advertising and postal appeals to previous donors. The BBC radio appeal for 1958, by Lord Birkett, yielded nearly £49,000. The Gift Shop raised over £19,000, and the embryonic Christmas Card operation, £1,400.

In 1959, the Oxford Committee for Famine Relief was on the threshold of a new chapter. The impetus, fittingly, was to be the refugees who had filled the 1950s with their plight.

Although refugee situations piled up throughout the 1950s, each tended to occupy a short span of public attention before fading from view until some new calamity pushed the 'forgotten people' back into the news. The intractability of many refugee situations made it difficult to inspire more than sporadic sympathy with their cause.

Hungary changed that. The mass exodus of push-cart people through the snow made a deep impression on public opinion all over the world. Hungary also proved that, with concerted international effort, an exodus of people could be gathered up and redispersed humanely and efficiently. It showed that a refugee problem could be solved.

Early in 1958, a young Conservative politician and journalist, Timothy Raison, came up with an idea: a World Refugee Year, a concerted 12-month push, to do something definitive for the world's uprooted. He was influenced by 'that strange desolation of spirit' he witnessed on a visit to Jordanian refugee camps in 1956; he was also one of the armada of sympathisers who went to the Austrian-Hungarian border. Raison enlisted three colleagues: MP Christopher Chataway, journalists Trevor Philpott of *Picture Post* and Colin Jones of *The Economist*. Philpott had covered both the Hungarian uprising and the Korean War; Chataway had visited the crowded pavements of Hong Kong.

Raison was the editor of *Crossbow*, a new Conservative Party quarterly journal. The issue of April 1958 carried their joint article: 'Wanted: A World Refugee Year'. The proposal might well have sunk without a ripple let alone a splash. But partly because it was solidly conceived and articulated, and partly because it echoed a mood of the moment, it not only floated but set sail.

Crossbow alone could never have made it happen. But there was an instant response from those organisations in Britain concerned with refugees, in particular from David Ennals, General Secretary of the UNA in London, and Janet Lacey of the British Council of Churches' refugee assistance arm, Inter-Church Aid. A key supporter, who helped to promote the idea to David Ormsby Gore, Minister of State at the Foreign

Office, was Sir Arthur Rucker; Rucker had been head of UNKRA in Korea, was the Chairman of Trustees of UNA's Refugee Fund, and an Oxfam trustee. The representative of the UNHCR in London, Nicholas Wyroubof, also took up the idea of the Year, promoting it to Auguste Lindt, the UN High Commissioner for Refugees in Geneva, and to the British press.

Mainly because of its performance in the wake of the Hungarian uprising, the UNHCR had been given an extension of its mandate, and a wider range of geographical responsibilities, by the 1957 UN General Assembly. The plan submitted in 1954, to close the European camps by the end of 1958, was nearing completion; unfortunately, the camps were not nearing closure, although donors were becoming more generous and over three years 50,000 refugees had been resettled. The need for yet another 'last push' on behalf of the increasingly abject camp population was a potent argument for the Year, and received support from all active UN sympathisers. The support of UNA was particularly important.

The Year's proponents moved swiftly. David Ennals at UNA arranged for an all-party group of MPs to sign a letter to *The Times*. In Geneva, Dame May Curwen, British Delegate to the UN Refugee Fund, raised the idea internationally. At the United Nations in New York, it was promoted by a British Delegate, Pat Hornsby Smith MP. In the autumn, she submitted a Resolution to the General Assembly, explaining: 'The basic objective of the scheme is to devote a year of intensified effort to focus public opinion, and to enlist support, both from governments and equally from peoples and charitable organisations of all kinds, to solve the problems of refugees wherever they may be throughout the world, into whatever formal category they may fall.

'If it is successful, it may help greatly, coming at this particular moment, in resolving once and for all one or two of the more manageable refugee problems with which the High Commissioner and his staff have been wrestling in recent years.' The resolution was passed overwhelmingly, by 59 votes to nine. It called upon member states to set up national organisations to pursue the objectives of the Year; the Year itself was to begin in June 1959.

The focus was placed on four specific situations. First, and most prominent in every mind, were the 162,000 European refugees mostly living in Austria and Germany but also in France, Italy, Turkey and Greece, of whom 32,000 were still lingering in camps. Then came the 915,000 Palestinians whom UNRWA resources could barely sustain, and the 750,000 Chinese refugees spilling over pavements and gutters in Hong Kong. Also singled out was a group of between 8,000 and 10,000 European Russians stranded for decades in China, now persecuted by the Communist government and unable to leave.

Of these predicaments, the key issue with which the Year became identified was the drive to 'close the camps'. Countries must be persuaded to relax immigration controls so that difficult cases could be admitted and families, long separated because of illness or handicap, reunited. The Year also aimed to raise funds; to provide the means for programmes of long-term rehabilitation and training run by voluntary agencies.

The first National Committees to be established worldwide were those in Britain, France and the US. The World Refugee Year United Kingdom Committee was a prestigious and highly effective body. Its patron was Her Majesty the Queen, and its three Vice-Patrons were the Prime Minister, Harold MacMillan, and the leaders of the two opposition political parties, Hugh Gaitskell and Jo Grimond. The Chairman was Baroness Elliot of Harwood; Christopher Chataway and Dame May Curwen were Vice-Chairmen; and the Chairman of the Executive Committee was Sir Arthur Rucker. A number of other well-known figures were included in its various committees, including Janet Lacey, David Ennals, and others from the voluntary agency world.

The Chairman of its Public Relations and Publicity Committee was H. Leslie Kirkley, Secretary of the Oxford Committee for Famine Relief. This was the first time that Kirkley, representing Oxfam, held an official position in which he rubbed shoulders with people at the heart of public and international life. Kirkley saw World Refugee Year as a launch-pad for Oxfam, a chance to elevate it from what was still essentially a provincial niche onto a much broader national stage. Equally, he saw the Oxford Committee as a major fundraiser and consciousness-raiser for refugees, both to the public and as partner with like-minded organisations. The results of the Year were to exceed his and others' wildest expectations.

During 1958, the Oxford Committee had been growing in size and confidence. In the run-up to World Refugee Year, a number of new staff members were recruited.

The most significant was Bernard Llewellyn, who was to play an important role in shaping the embryonic overseas aid programme. Llewellyn was an economist who had two areas of special expertise. He was the first person to join the staff with experience in running relief programmes overseas, most recently with Save the Children in Korea; and he was an accomplished journalistic writer with three books on Asia to his credit. He was also a thinker, not always a comfortable one to have around. Brought up a Methodist, he had become a conviction pacifist in the pre-war period. During the war he had served with the Friends'

Ambulance Unit in South West China, driving the length of the Burma Road. Two later recruits to Oxfam's aid programme, Ken Bennett and Michael Harris, served a similar apprenticeship.

Llewellyn's job title, 'Grants and Information Officer', reflected the fact that Oxfam had not yet completed its metamorphosis from the very simple and straightforward role of overseas conduit for compassion. The Committee was essentially an almoner, selecting charitable good works on behalf of donors at home, and communicating back the 'good news' about what their gifts had done. Llewellyn was expected to write advertising copy and Information Bulletins, drawing on correspondence from the recipients of grants. Searching questions about the way a programme was being run and its relevance to the overall picture of need were not yet part of the organisational vocabulary. Llewellyn, with his overseas experience and his reflective instincts, was to make them so.

Another important appointment was that of Financial Officer, Gordon Rudlin, an accountant, recruited via the Society of Friends network in 1959. And the Committee also began to build up the network of staff for local appeals Jackson-Cole had envisaged, taking on Gordon MacMillan in 1959, followed shortly afterwards by Geoffrey Petts and Peter Briggs.

These local organisers worked round the clock out of their own front rooms, driving up and down the country creating support groups and masterminding local drives. Their World Refugee Year committees, drawing on Mayoral parlours, church and voluntary groups, were an important ingredient of the Year's success in Britain. These incipient Oxfam groups were uncharacteristic of traditional blue-chip charitable committees. They were mainly ordinary folk, often professional and working people. The unwanted refugee – stateless, penniless and alone, pining away in a camp or on a pavement – was a potent symbol of wasted humanity and proved an inspiration for a new kind of workaday compassion.

World Refugee Year in Britain was launched on 1 June 1959 by the Lord Mayor of London at a ceremony at Mansion House. The Prime Minister spoke, as did the other heads of political parties; ambassadors, churchmen, and leading industrialists were present. An appeal film was made for use in cinemas by the Duke of Edinburgh, and Lord Montgomery and Lady Churchill both made radio appeals during the next six months. The degree to which the Year caught on, creating a bandwagon onto which jumped the press, public figures, civic institutions, schools, and every kind of society and organisation, was exceptional. The government gave £200,000 to the UK Committee, and Britain – like other countries – announced a special scheme to relax immigration regulations so that homes could be given to some hundreds of the TB-affected and handicapped.

Oxfam's strategy of mobilising local groups, of making the Year penetrate into homes and communities through events of every kind – coffee mornings, concerts, Youth Club drives, flag days, school competitions – paid off handsomely. Cash income for the six months to the end of February 1960 was more than double that of the same six months in the previous financial year: close to £300,000. This allowed a considerable expansion in Oxfam's grants for aid to refugees, particularly in the Middle East.

Energy was also devoted to events which conferred national visibility on Oxfam. A Gift Fair in London's West End, laid on by Joe Mitty and Leslie Durham of the Broad Street Gift Shop and opened by Anna Neagle, raised £1,500 in a week. A frugal Lenten lunch – bread and cheese for one guinea – was served to 60 peers, MPs, bishops, sports and theatre celebrities at the Westbury Hotel and lavishly covered by press and TV. Flora Robson and Christopher Chataway welcomed the guests, and Chataway launched a 'hunger lunch' movement. 'If everyone in Britain went without one meal, the money saved would raise £2 million.'

The fundraising success of World Refugee Year in Britain outstripped all expectations. After six months, the initial £2 million target was raised to £4 million, which in turn was rapidly overtaken. Of the 15 refugee-oriented charities most prominently associated with the Year, Inter-Church Aid and Refugee Service (soon to become Christian Aid) raised the most: £1,253,500; the Oxford Committee for Famine Relief came next with £755,900, gaining Oxfam recognition as a charity of national status. In no other country – 39 altogether set up National Committees – did World Refugee Year capture so much attention. The total raised in the UK was over £9 million.

Worldwide, the Year yielded $74.7 million, of which $23.2 million came from governments and $51.5 million from the fundraising efforts of National Committees. Contributions in 1960 and 1961 brought the grand total to $91 million. The voluntary agencies who produced two-thirds of this result had their own international co-ordinating committee (ICWRY) in Geneva, set up in March 1959 under the sponsorship of the Standing Committee of Voluntary Agencies Working for Refugees. At the two conferences held in January 1960 and January 1961 for the 80-odd members of the ICWRY, Kirkley was on the UK delegation and chaired one of the three Working Parties. He made many contacts in the international community which were to serve Oxfam well in coming years.

The dream of the Year – to close the remaining European camps – was not fulfilled. But it came measurably nearer. Of the hard-core cases, only 7,000 remained. And when the goal was finally achieved in the early 1960s, it was largely because of the Year's impetus. Many of the

Europeans in China were rescued; a large-scale scheme for vocational training among the Palestinian refugees was launched; extra assistance went to the Hong Kong refugees, and to the Algerian victims of civil war, a group not originally targeted. During World Refugee Year, many countries which had previously been reluctant to do so ratified the 1951 UN Convention on refugee status.

Most important of all, the continuing predicament of the refugee, the stories of lives locked up and forgotten in the rotting huts, tented camps, and pavement shanties, emerged definitively onto the international humanitarian agenda. In the subsequent decades, they have never left it.

4

A CRUSADE FOR OUR TIMES

On 18 December 1960, the *Observer* carried a brief front-page story about mass starvation in a corner of the newly independent Congo. Around 280,000 Baluba people had fetched up in a waterless and food-less plain, and there, strung out along the road, had stopped because they simply had no strength to go further. Thousands were no more than walking skeletons and many were swollen from hunger oedema. The weakest, mostly children, were dying at the rate of 200 a day.

People working for Oxfam at the time remember that story in the *Observer* with the clarity normally reserved for the deaths of presidents and the outbreak of war.

The tragedy in the Congo burnt the image of the starving African child onto the collective British conscience. Oxfam helped make that come about, and in the process itself leapt into public view as *the* British medium for prompt relief to famine victims in faraway places. When Kirkley went to the Austro-Hungarian border in 1956 he was no-one special, a helper among many. When he went to the Congo in early 1961, he was, fleetingly, a celebrity, on whom British hopes of saving lives were visibly pinned.

Chaos had steadily engulfed the Congo in the months since independence on 30 June 1960. Belgium had been extremely negligent in preparing the handover from colonial rule, holding onto all vestiges of authority till the last possible moment. There were no Congolese in senior administrative or military positions; no trained doctors or professionals – there were only 17 university graduates in the entire country. Within days of independence, Congolese troops mutinied against their Belgian officers. The country's leading federalist politician, Moise Tshombe, announced the secession of mineral-rich Katanga Province, and law and order began to break down.

The Belgians panicked. Most officials took to their heels, leaving an administrative vacuum and military turmoil. The Prime Minister, Patrice

Lumumba, turned to the United Nations for help. The UN Security Council agreed to despatch peace-keeping troops and a 'civilian operation' to restore order and maintain essential services – just while the Congolese sorted themselves out. Never had the United Nations Secretariat taken on such a complex, interventionist and controversial role; it came under tremendous strain, and the popular UN Secretary-General, Dag Hammarskjöld, was killed in late 1961 when his plane crashed in the African bush on his way to mediate the crisis.

At the beginning of 1961 when the famine hit the headlines, the UN's main peace-keeping operation was floundering. In Leopoldville, the capital, contingents of troops from Indonesia, Malaya, Tunisia, Ceylon, Ireland, Sweden, Ghana, and Egypt made occasional sorties to the bush. In New York the UN member states argued about pulling out their national forces, about extending the Cold War onto the African continent, about Dag Hammarskjöld's interference in Congo's internal affairs, and about who should pay for the UN's attempt to keep control in, without governing, a disintegrating country. Out in the vast expanse of the countryside, things fell apart.

The famine in South Kasai was months in the making, but – busy with battles for political control – no-one was looking out for the human suffering which must follow chaos and anarchy on such a scale. The source of the problem was ancient tribal friction, erupting under the pressures of mass insecurity. Over the years, some enterprising Baluba people had moved westwards into the country of the Lulua. When independence arrived, the Lulua were fearful that the Baluba would take power over the entire province, and turned upon them.

The Baluba 'refugees' set off on a 300-mile trek towards their tribal heartland without food to eat or seed to plant and quickly became destitute. Many erected miserable little huts along the road. Meanwhile their co-tribesmen, who happened to be sitting on most of the Congo's diamond wealth, followed the prevailing fashion by seceding and setting up an autonomous state under their own 'President', Albert Kalonji.

When hunger took hold in November, Dag Hammarskjöld appealed for funds within the UN family and UNICEF, the United Nations Children's Fund, came up with $150,000 for emergency feeding. But the routes and the transport for getting supplies into Bakwanga, the main local town, were complicated not only by every kind of geographical and communications difficulty but also by the political niceties attendant on 'President' Kalonji's relations with his neighbours and the central authorities. In early December, he agreed to the presence of a special UN unit and an air-lift began. A fleet of ancient trucks was despatched, and distribution centres set up. By this time the area's two hospitals and handful of dispensaries were overwhelmed by pitiful creatures starving and dying.

It took time in such adverse circumstances to build up the food distribution system and some kind of rudimentary care for those in extremity. Many children could no longer digest ordinary food. Dr. Melson, a British medical officer attached to a Ghanaian military unit, was trying to cope with 1,000 patients in a 150-bed hospital in a village called Miabi. He and a colleague from WHO began making up 'Kasai cookies' from maize flour, powdered milk, and sugar, for special feeding. Gradually the death toll began to decline. By mid-January, around 60 tons of food a day were being delivered against the 150 tons needed for full distribution.

The Oxford Committee was comparatively well-informed about the famine before it became front-page news in December 1960. Its first relief grant was made in October, and in mid-December it made an emergency grant of £5,000 to the Congolese Red Cross for child feeding. Just before Christmas, a special UN relief account was opened in a Leopoldville bank, and Oxford thereafter sent sums directly to this account: £5,000, and a further £5,000, as donations trickled in.

At that time, there was no automatic identification of Oxfam by the British press or public as a charitable saviour for remote disaster victims. The Committee sent out Congo Appeal letters to the press over the signature of Canon Milford, again the Committee's Chairman, and Sir William Hayter, Warden of New College and a trustee. On 6 January, the story of the famine hit the popular press in an unprecedented way, splashed across four pages of the *Daily Mirror*. Sir William's and the Oxford Committee's name were mentioned. Oxfam ordered 50,000 reprints of the news spread and mailed them to all its supporter groups and donors. The coverage brought a tidal wave of response.

Oxfam's press office and advertising machinery were operating in high gear. Some newspapers carried the appeal ad. free and the offices in Oxford were inundated. On one day, 9 January 1961, £20,000 arrived in the mail. Finance Officer Gordon Rudlin could scarcely manage to carry his suitcases of cheques and cash to the Bank. The Committee had to hire a church hall to house the mail-opening operation, with 30 volunteers working in shifts. In towns all over the country, regional organisers were swamped with demands for collecting tins and Congo literature.

This massive outpouring of public generosity was something completely new. It came purely from coverage in the newspapers – there were no television pictures; and even the press coverage was modest and the pictures mild by the standards of later African disasters. Other overseas aid charities such as the British Red Cross and War on Want had similar experiences. By 21 January, a total of £104,000 had flowed into Oxfam's Congo Appeal; the Red Cross had received £64,000 and War on Want, £40,000.

The following day, Leslie Kirkley flew to the Congo. The Committee had never had at its disposal such large sums to dispense so rapidly. Kirkley felt that the scale of the expenditure, the criticism of UN operations in the Congo, and the intense concern of the British public – one donor wrote: 'No child on earth should look like this' – required him to undertake a voyage of relief inspection. On Wednesday 25 January, in the company of the UN relief co-ordinator, a British Embassy official, and a party of journalists, Kirkley flew down from Leopoldville to the famine area.

Conditions were still severe with around 40 deaths a day. But things were very much better than they had been. The food distribution programme was in place and, drawing on further supplies from UNICEF, was about to step up daily capacity to 150 tons a day. Seeds and hoes had been given out by the Food and Agriculture Organisation (FAO) so that the refugees could plant in time for the heavy rains of mid-February. The worst of the crisis was over, and everyone agreed that whatever the shortcomings of the UN's peace-keeping operation, its conduct of emergency relief had been first class. Kirkley was told that Oxfam's prompt response with ready cash – vital for transport – was deeply valued. Among voluntary agencies it had led the way.

As Kirkley's heart was being wrung by the kwashiorkor babies in Miabi hospital, Edward Heath, the Lord Privy Seal, was on his feet in the House of Commons answering questions from Dennis Healey, Labour Foreign Affairs spokesman, about British government tardiness over the Congo famine. Heath rejected this charge. Indeed, he had gone shopping all around the colonies – groundnuts had been flown from Nigeria, maize seed and flour from Rhodesia, dried fish from Uganda and Nyasaland: 'FAO appealed for appropriate food and we have done our best to get hold of it.' Still, there was no question that the public response had bumped the government effort up. Heath himself paid tribute to voluntary fund-raising, singling out 'Oxford Famine Relief'.

Altogether, by the end of September 1961, £313,826 had been spent by Oxfam on Congolese relief. Some of this went towards other refugee problems stemming from the upheavals, which did not finally end until 1963. Some went on longer-term medical programmes for child health and nutrition run by the missions, in South Kasai and elsewhere. Severe as needs were during the crisis and for months to come, the key outcome of the relief effort was that no further tragedy of famine was allowed to develop from the Congolese chaos.

The starving child of the Congo in early 1961 was a temporary phenomenon and, on disaster mortality scales, not a spectacular claimant: perhaps 10,000 deaths altogether. But that starving child tapped a new well of compassion and launched a new perception of Africa, poverty, and the hungry world. For good or ill, that same perception launched the Oxfam that we know today.

The withdrawal of the Belgian authorities from the Congo in mid-1960 was only one such colonial retreat in a year known in international circles as 'the Year of Africa'. No less than 17 former African colonies achieved independence in 1960 as the 'winds of change' – a phrase immortalised by Harold Macmillan – blew over the continent in stormy gusts.

Most of the remaining British possessions on the continent – Basutoland (Lesotho), Bechuanaland (Botswana), Kenya, Nyasaland (Malawi), Northern Rhodesia (Zambia), Sierra Leone, Swaziland, Tanganyika, Uganda, Zanzibar – would raise their own flags within a few years. Meanwhile the events surrounding the various countries' independence – the wars in the Congo, the release of Jomo Kenyatta from prison, Bugandan claims for self-government, the break-up of Roy Welensky's Rhodesian and Nyasaland Federation – were daily subjects of front-page news in a Britain consumed with interest in a continent shedding the colonial past.

The rapid pace of change took most people by surprise. Africa was suddenly full of nation-states demanding an equal place at the international table, an end to the old paternalistic relationships, and the abandonment of an outworn, often racialist, mentality. For those in Britain for whom the imperial sway and the responsibilities of the civilising mission had been cornerstones of a world view and a life-time of service, the changes were greeted with misgiving. For others, they were intoxicating in their promise of renewal, of a world casting off its chains to find new paths of co-operation on terms which respected the dignity of all.

In colonial days, the typical British view of the societies which flourished in those pink-shaded areas on the map was of an endless *National Geographic* spectacular of exotics and primitives, nomads and warriors, dressed in magnificent outfits – or nothing – eating foods with curious names. These creatures were rarely seen in the newspaper, except when a Royal came by on an empire tour, at which time dances and feasts of extraordinary abundance and colour were the predominant motif. Feats of bravery were often stressed, as were the tribesmen's physical prowess, their vast numbers of wives and progeny, and their longevity. Occasionally, in a sermon or a talk at the Parish Hall, a missionary gave a more moralistic and anthropological perspective.

Whatever variations were provided in the picture of Her Majesty's brown- and black-skinned subjects, one feature was axiomatic: they were not described in the same terms – political, economic, social – as us. Comparisons using the same set of criteria were not made because the people were not comparable, they were 'not like us'. In the late 1950s, the prospect of widespread African independence, and its implication that peoples black and white, strong and weak, would now be treated on equal footing, meant that the viewpoint had to change. In a bewildered post-colonial Britain there was a sudden psychological vacuum, waiting to be filled by a new perception of those who were once the subject peoples.

With the hasty transplant overseas of Western political institutions and other trappings of the modern nation-state came the application of standard economic vocabulary. And then came the revelation: half, or was it two-thirds, of humanity lived at the very margins of existence by any comparison with our own standard of living. However deft with a spear or proficient with a talking drum, the average tribesman's material wealth was non-existent; people often had too little to eat; shelter and clothing were minimal; life expectancy was low; children died from minor causes; sickness was common and often fatal; in short they lived in poverty. Nothing about this was new – except that it was a revelation. This was because 'living standards' had not been the window on these societies through which most observers had previously been looking.

In the new age of partnership, an end to the dichotomy whereby one part of humanity lived well while the other lived in penury had to become the crusade for our times. Opinion-leaders began to call for an all-out attack on world poverty. The United Nations led the way by announcing that the 1960s would be 'The Decade of Development'. The actual declaration was made by President John F. Kennedy immediately after an inaugural address which signalled a new sense of moral purpose in international affairs: 'To those peoples in the huts and villages of half the globe struggling to break the bonds of mass misery, we pledge our best efforts to help them help themselves. ... If a free society cannot help the many who are poor, it can never serve the few who are rich.'

Kennedy's inspirational words were delivered on 20 January 1961, two days before Leslie Kirkley set off for the Congo to visit the UN relief programme for the starving children of South Kasai.

The UN Development Decade set a target for every industrialised country: one per cent of their gross national product should be devoted to official Overseas Development Assistance. This was 'aid', a word previously associated with military and strategic purpose. 'Aid' was now to become the instrument of 'development', the means whereby resources would be channelled from the better-off countries to the poorer to help build up their social and economic institutions.

To some, the notion of aid continued to carry investment and strategic overtones. Aid was something you 'gave' – actually, it was usually in the form of concessional loans – to struggling allies in Asia, Africa, and Latin America, to help build a prosperous bulwark against the Communists. But in other minds the twin ideas of aid and development were golden with promise. The rich nations should help the poor, not for reasons of strategic self-interest, but – as Kennedy said – 'because it is right'. The hopeful projected the idea of social justice and the welfare state onto an international canvas and dreamed of a world made more humane by rearrangements of wealth between the nations.

In the US, Kennedy initiated the Peace Corps, the Alliance for Progress, and 'Food for Peace'. In Britain, there was 'Voluntary Service Overseas' for young people prepared to spend a year or two helping fill a new country's educated manpower gaps. A blue-chip think-tank was set up, the Overseas Development Institute under William Clark, which pressed for a coherent government policy and more aid for the less developed members of the Commonwealth. This goal was achieved in 1964 when the new Labour Government created a Ministry of Overseas Development with a Cabinet seat and Barbara Castle as its first incumbent.

Above all there was optimism. If only aid could be given on a grand enough scale, on dimensions like those of the Marshall Plan, the growing gap between the prosperity of the rich countries and the poverty of the rest could – surely – quickly be closed. Fantastic as it now seems, many thought that the Development Decade would see the task almost completed.

The expression of acute poverty in the newly-independent countries of Africa, as people witnessed in the press reports from the Congo, was hunger. In Britain, the idea of providing help for the poorer countries reached public prominence via the 'Freedom From Hunger Campaign'. This was the springboard from which the Oxford Committee for Famine Relief became a practitioner of development assistance alongside its existing role in disaster relief.

The symbol of its involvement in both disasters and development was the starving child of Africa, an innocent whose haunting eyes and skeletal limbs made a startling impression on the British conscience.

The 'Freedom from Hunger Campaign' was initiated by the Director-General of the UN Food and Agriculture Organisation, the dynamic Dr. Binay Ranjan Sen of India. In late 1959, Sen convinced the member nations of FAO that the world's apathy towards hunger must be thoroughly shaken up by an urgent programme of action. On 2 July 1960, with applause still echoing for the success of World Refugee Year,

Sen launched his campaign in Rome, stating that this onslaught on food shortage aimed to help countries break out of the cycle of poverty and relegate hunger to the pages of history.

This was a time at which great hopes were vested in the organisational galaxy of the United Nations, invented to improve human well-being in the interests of peace and justice for everyone. As the bonds of European empire unwound, the UN found itself with an unforeseen role in world affairs. Its unbiased machinery was free from the taint of self-interest and assumed superiority which inevitably clung to the old colonial powers. The new nations sat down on equal terms with their old rulers in the UN General Assembly and on the governing boards of its member bodies. The UN might have performed disappointingly in the political arena, but with decolonisation a new day dawned: its economic and social organisations would lead the 'development' crusade.

Sen's 'Freedom from Hunger' drive was FAO's clear demonstration that it was resolved to meet this challenge with energy and determination. It also stemmed from frustration that FAO had never been given the mandate, the powers, or the budget to do more for countries with widespread hunger than offer advice or 'technical assistance'. Sen was at the same time also pushing for the setting up of an FAO 'World Food Programme', finally inaugurated in 1963, to use food surpluses to promote economic development via public works programmes, and for emergency relief.

'Freedom from Hunger' sought a worldwide partnership among like-minded groups, not for emergency relief or hand-outs but for self-generated agricultural development. Of all the rich world countries to take part, as with the World Refugee Year, Britain responded with the most enthusiasm. Ironically, this was just because of the long colonial affinities everyone was now working so hard to discard. The response was encouraged and garnered by those voluntary agencies already associated with sending help overseas. 'Freedom from Hunger' helped them to recast their own role to confront the challenge of world poverty, and to join the development crusade as partners of the big brothers in the UN system.

Oxfam was the voluntary agency – alongside War on Want and Christian Aid – to identify itself most closely with 'Freedom from Hunger'. During the Campaign's key period, 1960-65, Oxfam became the main vehicle whereby the new crusade on behalf of the poor overseas took root in British hearts and minds. This partly occurred as a result of conscious strategy; partly because at an historical turning-point a number of internal and external forces combined to propel Oxfam forward, and Leslie Kirkley was keen to run.

Three weeks after the international launch of FFH in Rome, the Oxford Committee held a week-long Annual Conference on the 'Freedom from Hunger' theme and gave the campaign its first public airing in Britain. The venue was an Oxford college, and 150 delegates attended from all over the country and from France, Holland, India, Nigeria, Sweden, Switzerland, Trinidad, and the US.

The opening lecture, grimly entitled 'The Survival of Mankind', was given by Dr. Arnold Toynbee; other speakers included Lord Boyd-Orr, the first Director-General of FAO, and Dr. Neville Goodman, the first Assistant Secretary-General of WHO. The most important contribution came from M. Veillet-Lavallee, Assistant Director-General of FAO, who spoke optimistically about the possibility of rapid increases in food production. 'Aid', he said, 'must go beyond philanthropy. It must fit in with a balanced plan for relieving the world of its food problems. Our campaign is directed not against famine, but against the causes of permanent insufficiency of food supplies.'

For many of the Oxfam audience, this kind of global view required a large perceptual leap from the good works of a Mrs. Donnithorne and child-feeding schemes in Korea, Jordan, or the slums of Calcutta. However, by such an event Oxfam took part in the growing development debate, and later annual conferences – often combined with the biennial Gilbert Murray Memorial Lecture – continued to attract major speakers: William Clark, Barbara Ward, Shirley Williams, Group Captain Leonard Cheshire, Marcel Autret of FAO, Paul Hoffman of the UN Special Fund, and Dr. A.H. Boerma, Director-General of the World Food Programme.

On 5 August 1960 at its final session, the Conference passed a slate of resolutions. Echoing the UN Development Decade goal set for the wealthy countries, the delegates stated that everybody in Britain should aim to give one per cent of their annual income to help free the world of hunger. They urged the government to establish a National Freedom from Hunger Committee and equip it to run the campaign in Britain. Finally, they declared: 'It is vital for the survival of mankind that we and all other peoples should habitually think of ourselves as members of a world community,' and described the growing gap in living standards between rich and poor countries as 'morally indefensible and inherently unstable'.

Early in 1961, the government appointed as Chairman of the National FFH Committee Earl de la Warr, a one-time Under-Secretary for Agriculture who had long been a distinguished champion of a beneficent international food policy. His deputy was Sir Arthur Rucker, Honorary Treasurer of the Oxford Committee and active on its Grants Sub-Committee. The government also provided £55,000 for the campaign's administration. But it was made clear that its activities were to be carried out by the voluntary organisations and whomever the Committee could persuade to take part. A rollcall of eminent persons did so agree, and it began work in June 1961.

Their first decision, and it was significant, was that there should be a protracted stage of inquiry into the problem of hunger in the poorer nations and careful thinking about solutions before any rush for collection boxes or appeals to public generosity. This was not World Refugee Year, with 'one last push' to end a specific problem among a specific population. Hunger was much more deep-rooted and its elimination required a longer-term and more considered approach.

This concern with education, both among those participating – the voluntary agencies and their donors – and of society as a whole, about the causes of hunger and poverty in developing countries was a striking feature of the FFH Campaign in Britain. In pinpointing its priority audience, the Education Advisory Group, chaired by Dr. Leslie Farrer Brown of the Nuffield Foundation, settled on the schools. The campaigners had a strong conviction that the generation then in the classroom should learn the facts of world hunger as an integral part of the school curriculum. One of the FFH Campaign's achievements was the first ever 'Teacher's Guide' on how to incorporate these facts into a variety of subjects. This sold 25,000 copies within a year of publication in 1962.

The other important preparatory task was to identify the projects that the Freedom from Hunger Campaign would support. Here the Committee was effectively charting new territory, trying to bridge the gap between philanthropy and the large – nowadays they would be called 'macro' – schemes funded by UN and bilateral aid. Unlike the 'micro' projects of the charitable world, these rarely involved the participation of local people. Synthesising the two perspectives was the FFH aim.

The FFH Projects Group consisted of experienced administrators and experts in tropical agriculture, and the grant selection process contained lessons for agencies such as Oxfam. The FFH team set out to consider project proposals on the basis of whether or not they would attack the root causes of low agricultural production, not on whether applicants for funds were sound humanitarians and would spend charitable money well and wisely. The possibilities included investment in some kind of seed, animal, plant, storage facility or processing gadget, or training in new cultivation methods. Thus, although the credentials and efficiency of applicants were important, FFH scrutiny was more concerned with policy issues, and with long-term impact and viability, than with capacity to relieve immediate suffering.

De la Warr and Rucker made it known at both the Colonial and the Commonwealth Offices, and at the new Department of Technical Co-operation set up in 1961, that applications from all parts of the developing world would be welcome. These might come from ambitious humanitarian entrepreneurs who normally looked for support in the private sector; or from sub-departments of government or official institutions who normally looked to the public sector and 'aid'. Submissions were evaluated against FFH criteria and proponents asked to fill in a questionnaire. This asked about the local food economy, and was progressive in its thinking, particularly in its emphasis on the need for people's participation, and for inbuilt sustainability. Many projects submitted for funding did not pass muster; by March 1962 the Group had examined 72 projects and approved only 16.

This careful development of a Projects List according to pre-set criteria, and – incidentally – before any money had been raised, was in contrast to the way Oxfam made its grants. In 1957, Oxfam had set up a Grants Sub-Committee because the load of applications had become too large for the Executive Committee to handle. The Sub-Committee met regularly to examine proposals and give its sanction to expenditures. Most members and officers were drawn from the Executive Committee, to whom they reported; but gradually more people with special expertise – many from Oxford University and some of them figures of renown – were included as the 1960s advanced.

Allocations were made within a loose financial planning framework; a growing proportion of monies granted – around 10 per cent in the early 1960s – were not 'one-off' grants to projects but envisaged continuing support in subsequent years, always assuming funds were available. Otherwise the key feature of the grant-making policy was not to have a policy – other than adherence to charitable purpose. Each scheme was judged on its merits – however 'merits' were defined at a given moment – and if the Committee agreed to fund it, the precedent became the policy. Kirkley, an arch-pragmatist, preferred to remain flexible, not to close options by statements of policy which might inhibit the organisation's freedom to act. The overseas aid programme was still largely characterised by response, grants being made in answer to the call of suffering made visible by emergency, or described by an applicant agency or mission. Thus, although the allocation of assistance was undoubtedly thorough and conscientious, it was not governed by a coherent plan, targeted objectives, or careful policy guidelines. Oxfam wanted to be all things to all varieties of needy comers.

Each voluntary agency joining in FFH had its own aid agenda and projects list. The FFH Projects Group resolved the problem of fusing private philanthropy with a planned developmental approach in a constructive manner. It sought financial contributions for FFH Projects from the agencies: in Oxfam's case, the original commitment was for £500,000, later rising to £1,800,000 including £300,000 to the World Food Programme. The Group also studied the food-related projects on Oxfam's projects list which could be described as developmental – improved sheep in Greece; Musa Alami's heifers; Winifred Coate's farming plots; fishing boats in Vietnam; poultry breeding in Morocco. While most did not match FFH criteria, many were put on an 'FFH seal of approval' list. This meant that Oxfam could talk about certain of its own projects as part of the Campaign and raise funds for them on that basis.

The main FFH fundraising drive was launched in June 1962, a year after the education work began. A grand ceremony was held in the Royal Festival Hall, addressed by the Duke of Edinburgh, the Campaign's patron. Present were civic leaders from all over Britain. As with World Refugee Year, the three heads of the political parties all served as Campaign Vice-Presidents, as did the Archbishop of Canterbury and every top churchman.

Over 1,000 FFH Committees were eventually set up in towns and villages all over the country, many with help from Oxfam's growing network of local organisers. Typically, they raised between £1,000 and £4,000, but some did spectacularly well: Birmingham raised £63,000, Somerset, £76,840, Swansea, £23,400, Nottingham, £43,500, Glasgow and the Clyde Valley, £114,360. Every group adopted one of the growing list of approved FFH Projects. These ranged from £170,000 for the construction of three farm institutes in Tanzania, adopted by Somerset, Devon and Exeter, and East Central Scotland; to £1,247 for two bulls and a rotovator for Tristan da Cunha, adopted by the national WI; to £30,000 for laboratories to control disease in groundnuts in Nigeria, adopted by Oldham. By 1965, the Campaign had raised a superb £7 million, for over 400 projects.

The Freedom from Hunger Campaign profoundly influenced the philosophy and approach of Oxfam and other overseas aid agencies towards the longer-term development objectives of the projects it supported. In fact, such was the new passion for 'development' as opposed to 'relief' that Bernard Llewellyn began to question whether hand-outs to the hungry were unfairly being given a bad name. Time would show that investment in development schemes was much more problematic than many enthusiasts with their rosy prognoses of egg-laying, fish-farming, and bumper crops for years to come were yet able to envisage.

Optimism was, for the moment however, the order of the day. Among the huge oceans of need in the world, the sense was that grants for relief must simply vanish into bottomless depths. Giving out a dole was intellectually and psychologically unappealing to those people, especially young people, wanting to build the new Jerusalem. Proponents of the new school of thought quoted what became a much over-worked Chinese proverb: 'Give a man a fish and you feed him for a day. Teach him to fish and you feed him for life.' This was the new faith to which the Freedom from Hunger Campaign began to give currency. It had a ring, it chimed with the go-out-and-do-it age of Kennedy, the Beatles, 'Ban the Bomb', and 'Beyond the Fringe' – the swinging sixties.

In Autumn 1962, Oxfam announced to its supporters that among many grants allocated to Freedom from Hunger projects it had committed funds to a 'Big Four'. The largest was a feed-compounding plant for a dairy project among poor farmers in India, the Anand District Milk Producers' Co-operative; the £108,000 needed was raised by the Glasgow and Clyde Valley FFH Committee, an achievement which helped to launch Oxfam in Scotland. The other three were: £25,714 to develop an improved variety of maize in Pakistan; £60,000 for a range of agricultural activities at Thesprotia in Greece, including olive-canning and cheese factories; and £90,000 for a programme in the three British High Commission Territories in Southern Africa, Basutoland, Bechuanaland, and Swaziland.

This last, the first set of projects ever to be carried out with the government as Oxfam's main partner, and much the largest undertaking in Africa unconnected to disaster relief, represented Oxfam's plunge into the age of development.

The Oxford Committee's involvement in Africa pre-dated the Congo crisis, but similarly stemmed from emergency situations. From 1954 onwards, grants had been made for relief among Kenya's Kikuyu people around whom had swirled the horrors and dislocations of Mau Mau. In 1956 came the first grant to church groups in South Africa. This grew into a programme of school feeding and recreation centres to compensate black African children in the townships for cutbacks – in school hours, school meals, school activities – imposed under a new Bantu Education Act.

The people of the three British High Commission territories – Basutoland, Bechuanaland, and Swaziland – had escaped apartheid domination but their social and economic condition was on a par with black African neighbours in the Republic. The British were sensitive to their responsibilities in these Protectorates, and wanted to make them 'a shop window for the Commonwealth'. Leslie Kirkley wanted to take up the Protectorates as a destination of project funds. He began by looking for a partner in Basutoland to copy the South African churches' effort to combat child malnutrition via school meals. In time the Save the Children Fund took on this role, providing a meal of milk, soup, and biscuits to nearly half the Protectorate's primary schoolchildren, with Oxfam's assistance.

In early 1961, Kirkley began to explore whether an Oxfam Freedom from Hunger programme might be developed in the Protectorates. Through contacts in left-wing circles then caught up with African liberation, Kirkley came across Tristram – always known as Jimmy – Betts, an ex-colonial servant who had spent 24 years as a forestry officer in Nigeria. Since Nigerian independence he had been doing research for the Fabian Colonial Bureau. Kirkley sent Betts off to Southern Africa to look around and see what he could come up with.

In October Betts returned with a persuasive recommendation for a 'crash programme' of several dozen projects designed to improve agriculture in the three territories. Up to this time the Committee had mainly depended on Kirkley, Llewellyn, and – more recently – Colonel Widdowson, a retiree from the Salvation Army with long experience in the Far East, to visit projects on tour from Oxford. It had, in fact, been a Committee boast that working through local voluntary agencies avoided the unnecessary expense of posting its own officers in the field – Frankie Hamilton in Greece being an honourable exception; but she was regarded as a project in herself.

With the list of grants to Africa rapidly growing, and with the Charity Commissioners beginning to take an interest in Oxfam's selection and monitoring of disbursements, Kirkley decided that the time had come for what seemed like a drastic change. He invited Betts to return to Africa and set himself up in one of the territories to ensure that the programme moved ahead on track. Betts accepted. He was thus appointed in late 1961 as Oxfam's first Field Director, a move which had far-reaching implications.

For his base Betts picked Basutoland, later to become the independent kingdom of Lesotho, the tiny mountainous and eroded enclave of 900,000 farming people entirely surrounded by South Africa. He worked closely with the Department of Agriculture, and most of the schemes he promoted – credit for smallholders through the Co-operative Bank, farmers' training centres, fish farming, experimental work in hydroponics and reafforestation – were Oxfam-funded increments to government services. Betts assumed the colonial officer role with which he was familiar, except that, in his personal style, he was a thoroughly unconventional type of operator and enjoyed cocking a snook at boffins and bureaucrats.

Jimmy Betts became something of a legend in Oxfam, regarded with a mixture of horrified admiration and affection. A brother of Barbara Castle, his left-wing sympathies put him solidly behind the anti-apartheid struggle: he eventually tangled with the South African authorities too successfully to reside in a country whose access routes they controlled. He was a larger-than-life personality, given to extravagant behaviour which could estrange as well as endear. But whatever his idiosyncrasies, he brought tremendous energy to his Field Director role, travelling relentlessly and building up a vast portfolio of projects. He broke new ground for Oxfam, moving the centre of gravity of the overseas programme to the field.

The Basuto project which Oxfam worked hardest to promote was 'The Progressive Farmers' scheme, originally started by the Department of Agriculture in 1958. Through demonstration and example, farmers working unproductive soil on small plots were introduced to good seed, fertilisers and pesticides. A loan of £25 was advanced to cover the cost of these inputs over six acres. In an average year, the extra yield of maize and sorghum would – theoretically – permit the farmer to pay off his loan, with £20 still in pocket to invest in next year's crop. 'Progressive farmers' were given advice about contouring the hillsides, binding the soil, preserving grass for winter fodder, and other aids to higher productivity.

Another approach was short courses for farmers in two specially-built training centres – the first institutions of their kind built with Oxfam money. The contribution was held down to £81,310 after many brisk exchanges about architects, specifications, sloppy planning, and suitability – exchanges which Oxford was only too relieved to leave to the man on the spot. The first centre at Leribe was opened in May 1964 by Paramount Chief Moshoeshoe II, and thereafter ran short courses on everything from bee-keeping to book-keeping, pisciculture to child nutrition. Up to 40 farmers at a time could stay in residence, each paying a token fee for board and lodging.

Betts and his colleagues in the government service were ahead of their time in recognising that many African farmers were women. This was particularly conspicuous in Basutoland, where low agricultural incomes meant that 46 per cent of the menfolk went off to seek work in the South African mines, leaving their wives behind to cultivate the family plot and tend the family cow. Some women attended not only home economics but the farming courses and – as seemed worthy of comment in a 'Freedom from Hunger' film – turned out to be as capable of using the information as the men.

Bechuanaland – later to become Botswana – presented a very different set of agricultural problems. Here, instead of a high and eroded sierra, the arid landscape of the Kalahari Desert stretched away endlessly into the horizon like the sea. Ragged scrub and wispy grassland supported migratory herds of cattle on which the farming economy depended. In the early 1960s, a succession of drought years afflicted this most marginal of grazing land. Many of the 600,000 people – 90 per cent relied upon farming – lost livestock: a third of the country's 1,200,000 beasts died in four years. The conditions concentrated cattle around the remaining water holes and destroyed the pasture. Changes were needed if the traditional ranching economy was to survive.

In Bechuanaland, too, Betts took on government departments as Oxfam's main partners. One of the earliest grants he recommended was for £5,070, to pay for building repairs to 21 small catchment dams. These were positioned so that water courses which seasonally ran dry would leave behind a reservoir large enough to last until the next rains. The cost was low because dam construction was done by employing human labour on public relief works, which also enabled some drought victims to receive an income during difficult times.

Stabilising herds in smaller numbers around particular watering places and pastures also made their owners captive for another service: advice from agricultural extension teams. These moved from community to community to talk up the virtues of deticking, dehorning, castration, all-day grazing, bonemeal diets, and other attentions to bovine health. The creation of this Animal Husbandry Extension Service was another Freedom from Hunger project, to which Oxfam gave £60,000 in 1964, and continued support for many years. Training centres for short residential courses were also built; as in Basutoland, graduates were dubbed 'Progressive' and eligible for small loans; they could even go on to become 'Master Farmers' with a smart diploma to hang on the wall.

Persuading farmers to fence pasture was the most tricky of all improvements to introduce because fencing tribal land was diametrically against landholding tradition. The idea of fattening cattle before slaughter was peculiar: old, feeble, animals no longer up to life on the hoof were the ones normally sent to the abattoir. To hype the advantages of the fat and profitable carcase, Oxfam paid for the Department of Agriculture to set up seven livestock holding grounds in tribal areas. Each was endowed with a small demonstration herd to cross-breed with local stock and show what a plump cow looked like. At Mahalapye, the local agricultural officer was surprised that, in the first year, nearly 200 local Tswana beasts joined his health farm. When they went to the abattoir six months later their owners found they were worth an extra £15 a head. Within three years, 450 farmers had taken advantage of the holding ground pastures at Mahalapye.

During the 1960s, Oxfam invested around £500,000 in Botswanan dam construction and agriculture, getting on for £1 for every member of the population. In every dimension – size, scope, coherence – this was a comprehensive development programme in a different league from the past, and Oxfam was proud of its contribution to rural Botswanan livelihoods. By the end of the decade Jimmy Betts had gone off to Nairobi and left Oxfam. But the seeds he had planted had born fruit. Out in the thatched hut settlements of the Kalahari, so it was said by officials in town, 'a farmer tilling his field knows about Oxfam'.

However favourable the climate for Oxfam's great leap forward in the early 1960s, it could not have happened without the creativity and hard work of certain individuals. Among these was Richard Exley, the most dynamic of Kirkley's bright young men. Exley originally joined Oxfam in 1957 as a substitute for national service, from which he was exempted on conscientious grounds. In 1959, after a year away, he wrote to Kirkley outlining a new fundraising scheme. Kirkley, who was always open to ideas, simply said: Come and do it.

The idea for 'Pledged Gifts' came to Exley when he was wandering round Manchester contemplating its rows of back-to-back houses and trying to work out how to interest their occupants in an Oxfam appeal. They might be unsusceptible to newspaper advertisements for covenants and cheques, but a monthly doorstep request for a small but regular amount to save lives in Leribe or Bhagalpur would surely not be refused. Exley started by advertising for door-to-door collectors. When people responded, he went to see them personally, travelling all over the country to visit and cajole.

'Pledged Gift' collectors gave out cards and stamps to a circle of donors – neighbours or workmates – who gave a shilling a month in return for a tiny Newsletter. In its first year the scheme scarcely covered its costs, but Kirkley had confidence in Exley's determination. Within another year it had taken off and in three more, nurtured by its own officer, Joan Chapman, yearly proceeds had risen to £200,000 from over 300,000 subscribers and 26,000 collectors. 'Pledged Gifts' was seen as the most promising source of increasing regular income, particularly from those not in the usual social band of charitable givers. It was promoted as a way of meeting people while doing good. In 1963 Stella Humphries, a collector in Stockport, 'won' an air fare donated to Oxfam and an adventure trip to a mission hospital in the Sierra Leonian bush. A film was made – 'Mrs. Humphries goes to Africa' – to encourage other housewives to join.

Exley – still only in his mid-twenties – injected a burning urgency into whatever he did. He helped foster the sense of an organisation ready to take on the problem of world poverty as if every little counted, now, today. Oxfam was part of a new consciousness about the world. Just as the image of the starving child of the Congo was new, so too was the image of the 'progressive farmer' leaving hunger behind on the basis of a sum well within the reach of anyone's comprehension.

Press advertising became more hard-hitting. This was the heyday of the hungry child. Between them, Harold Sumption and Richard Exley began to fix Oxfam's identity with that child, blasting something uncomfortable and unforgettable into the British conscience. The strong hint of accusation in the message might put some people off and probably added to Oxfam's aura of controversy; but any negative impact was more than outweighed in financial terms. In the 1950s, Sumption reckoned to raise £5 for every £1 spent on a press advertisement. In the early 1960s, the ratio peaked at £31 to £1. Exley capitalised by bumping up the advertising budget at key psychological moments, particularly at disaster times.

As the Oxford Committee's income rapidly rose – from £500,000 in 1958-59 to £1,400,000 in 1960-61 – success built upon success. The index of supporters had grown to well over 200,000 by 1960. On 9 July 1961, Richard Dimbleby made the fifth BBC Radio appeal for the Oxford Committee on the Week's Good Cause and, with the push given by supplementary advertising, raised a record £105,941. In many ways this particular year, the Congo year and the year Jimmy Betts went to Basutoland, was one of the most significant in Oxfam's history.

The rise in income enabled – indeed, forced – Oxfam to take on more staff. In 1960, Kirkley appointed a second in command, Henry Fletcher. In the early sixties expansion was rapid: from around 30 paid staff, the total grew to 200 by the end of 1963, of whom 40 were regional organisers fostering 250 voluntary groups. There was a geographical spreading of wings: offices opened in Scotland, Northern Ireland and Wales. There was also a greater degree of specialisation in the allocation of responsibilities among the staff.

Early in 1962, Bruce Ronaldson joined as Secretary; Ronaldson had been a colonial administrator in Tanganyika, now reaching independence. As the paid establishment grew, the relationship with the trustee and advisory bodies changed, as did their role in decision-taking. As advisors and policy-makers, their role remained important; but they became less involved in day-to-day affairs. Ronaldson eased these transitions, bringing a quality of kindly patience and administrative tidiness to an organisation rapidly growing and gaining a national reputation, but still loyally surrounded by many of its original sponsors.

Another recruit from the shrinking requirements of the colonial service in Africa was Humphrey Hilton, who acted as the intermediary between Betts in the field and the African submissions to the Grants

Sub-Committee. This pattern became set for other geographical areas as the programme expanded and other Field Directors were appointed. By 1960, grants had been made to 56 countries; by 1963 the figure had risen to 73 – not the most useful gauge of expansion considering the size of some of the grants but nonetheless one in which Kirkley and Jackson-Cole took considerable pride.

Although there were some highly professional people on the staff and serving in a voluntary capacity, Oxfam was still a family of individuals whose links were forged by motivation and idealism. Credentials for employment owed more to commitment to the cause and an enthusiasm to use abilities in its service than to any notion of building a career in the charity world or in the still nascent science of 'development'. No-one joined the staff for financial reward: salaries were low and many who could afford to gave up most or all of their entitlement. Joining Oxfam was rather like joining a church, although it was a distinctly secular organisation and its shared creed open to many interpretations.

Unlike many other charities, its senior ranks were never dominated by public servants, civil or military, pensioned and in early retirement; although there were some. Nor did any particular social background prevail: those from the gentry and the odd progressive aristocrat assumed a kind of spiritual and social camouflage among more typical ordinary folk. In the regional offices the range was particularly wide, with former steelworkers and Methodist lay preachers rubbing shoulders with retired Majors and leftist sympathisers with double-barrelled names. Much has been made of the Quaker influence, but although this was a part of the genesis, the Committee was always a broad church in which no one denomination prevailed. Many of the influential Friends in Oxfam were so by conversion, inclined by personal philosophy to take that particular spiritual path rather than another, sometimes before they joined the organisation, often afterwards.

Whatever the elusive quality of Oxfam fellowship and however ill-defined its articles of faith, for many of those who joined its crusade then or since, membership – even temporary membership – of this 'church' has been the most important influence in their lives. It has not only helped to fashion their world view but its values have affected their personal lifestyle and aspirations. An underlying element of fervour helped power Oxfam's physical and perceptual expansion; it has also been a yeast fomenting away inside the organisation, always creatively but sometimes divisively as well. Controlling and channelling this fervour has given more than one Director headaches; it did not however faze Kirkley very often – in fact, he rather enjoyed it.

In late 1962, in a psychologically important way, organisational size brought unity and a sense of permanence. The staff moved from five scattered locations in central Oxford to a new purpose-built Oxfam House in Summertown, a northern Oxford suburb. The move entrenched Oxfam in its *alma mater*: a move to London was contemplated but rejected.

The site on the Banbury Road was negotiated with the help of Jackson-Cole and Leslie Swain, and funds raised specifically for the purpose. An existing house was demolished to make way for the £75,000 office block, whose ground-floor shops were leased out to help recover costs. There was, inevitably, criticism from those who imagine that professionally-managed charities can somehow run cost-free. The investment in a proper headquarters quickly repaid itself, helping promote a Summertown boom in retailing which multiplied the site's value many times over.

In the 19th century, Matthew Arnold described Oxford as 'the home of lost causes and forsaken beliefs'. Fair and square in its new office block along the Banbury Road, Oxfam had convincingly broken with any such tradition.

The last three months of 1963 witnessed the most frenzied and exciting campaign of Oxfam's history. This was the 21st anniversary year, and plans were long in the making. It was Oxfam's good fortune to come of age with the groundswell of public opinion running its way. At no other time has it more completely caught the crest of a popular wave in its favour; but not only by luck, by good management too.

The campaign was launched on 6 October at a Bread-and-Water lunch in Trafalgar Square. This 21st birthday party event was organised by Philip Barron, Oxfam's Press Officer, and it set the ball rolling magnificently. Around 2,000 supporters turned up. Messages of congratulation came from HRH Prince Philip, Duke of Edinburgh; Trevor Huddleston, Bishop of Masasi in Tanganyika; and Felix Schnyder, UN High Commissioner for Refugees. Peter Finch, Susannah York, Sylvia Sims, and Mike Sarne the pop-singer were there, collecting one-pound notes on African spears. But the real star of the show was three-year-old Moses, a refugee child from the Congo, held aloft on the shoulders of Ted Willis and grinning bemused into the lenses of half the press cameras in London.

Oxfam announced that it would try to raise £1 million by the end of the year in aid of urgently needed projects. This 'Hunger £Million' campaign managed to inspire an extraordinary surge of activity. The £1 million target and whether it could be reached by the New Year became, as December wore on, truly matters of national preoccupation.

The campaign's chief architect was Richard Exley, and he drew upon a number of other similarly energetic Oxfam people, including his press officer, Pat Davidson. The *Daily Mail* acted as the Hunger £Million sponsor, and press advertising and the regional network of Oxfam organisers were used to orchestrate a gradual climax of local and national attention. But the name publicly associated with the campaign's most strenuous effort is that of Jeffrey Archer.

Archer was then a student in Oxford. One day in December he breezed into Oxfam House, and convinced Exley that he could distribute 10,000 collecting tins among Oxford and other university students. Pat Davidson had managed to persuade Brian Epstein to allow the Beatles to lend their name to the campaign. With the help of Nicholas Lloyd, editor of the University Newspaper, *Cherwell*, and a stringer for the *Daily Mail*, this guaranteed the *Mail*'s sponsorship. Archer went up to Liverpool to secure the necessary photograph. This picture, in which Ringo, Paul, George and John grinned from behind an Oxfam poster and held up 'Hungry £Million' cans, was endlessly hyped in the *Daily Mail* and made a big difference to momentum. It helped bring in a number of other figures from the entertainment industry, including Adam Faith, Harry Secombe, and Stratford Johns. The *Daily Mail* built up the story, incidentally giving Archer a generous share of accolade.

The high moment of the campaign was a 'carol service with the stars' on Sunday 22 December, again in Trafalgar Square, complete with showbiz float and Christmas tree. Leading the singers were Acker Bilk, Dennis King, Bert Weedon, Pearl Carr, Vince Hill, Frankie Vaughan, Matt Monro, Bruce Forsyth, Alan Freeman, Lionel Blair, and Kathy Kirby. Blaring 'OXFAB!' across its front page, the *Mail* reported a crowd of 60,000, with Jeffrey Archer and 300 Oxford students jangling collecting tins.

A snowball effect had been created and the campaign had taken on a life of its own. The *Sunday Telegraph* put the ultimate Oxfam dream into words: 'Something is starting which transcends politics and religion. For the first time the people of the affluent countries have been aroused to a sense of responsibility for their less fortunate brothers. There is every indication that a new Crusade is in the making, a Crusade animated by duty and humanity.' On 31 December, Oxfam announced that the targeted million had been raised.

These were heady times for those involved with Oxfam. No door seemed barred, no appeal met with indifference, no great name in any field of endeavour turned them down. Just a few weeks back, days before his assassination in Dallas, John F. Kennedy had spoken to the UN General Assembly in support of a 'world food policy' that would ensure for every child in every country a healthy and plentiful diet. The British Labour Party, soon to win a general election, supported the same policy as a part of its political programme. Truly, it seemed, the day had dawned when the world had committed itself to 'Freedom from Hunger' in our time.

Not for another decade would there again be a sense of such unanimity about the appalling injustice which allows children to starve in a world of plenty. But by then, the banners were no longer new and some painful lessons had needed to be learned.

5

THE SHOALS OF CONTROVERSY

The Hunger £Million campaign gained Oxfam widespread national recognition. But public visibility also brought controversy and less welcome attentions. In late 1963, while the campaign was at its height, the Charity Commissioners delivered a bombshell. They called in question Oxfam's right to provide 'development' aid – grants given to long-term prevention of hunger overseas rather than to its direct relief – suggesting that such grants, now absorbing 40 per cent of its assistance, might not be charitable.

There were a number of ways in which Oxfam's activities had recently been bothering the Commissioners, and these had become the subject of ongoing dialogue between the Chief Commissioner, C.P. Hill, and Leslie Kirkley. Kirkley was at his best in handling the protracted awkwardness these enquiries engendered, consistently helpful in manner while non-confrontationally standing his ground. He calmly pursued the view that long-term projects to prevent hunger had to be charitable. As the storm widened, bringing in other overseas aid charities, his Quaker spirit persisted in believing that if the parties were not driven to take stands from which they could not retreat, the fuss would die down and consensus emerge around the only sensible viewpoint. His low-key handling of the affair meant that operations were hardly affected and many staff and supporters were scarcely aware that, for over a year, Oxfam's mission balanced on a knife-edge.

One of the Commissioners' concerns mirrored the Oxford Committee's own sense that larger expenditure overseas – now over £2.25 million a year – needed closer scrutiny. Jimmy Betts' appointment as Field Director for Africa showed the Commissioners that Oxfam was doing something on this score. His overseas appointment was followed by others. Bernard Llewellyn went out to Hong Kong as Field Director for Asia in 1964, promoting a new pattern of on-the-spot inspection.

But the Charity Commissioners found a lot else to question. They complained that Oxfam's appeals were 'vaguely worded'. Unlike charities such as the Red Cross or Save the Children, who themselves ran their projects or did so through sister organisations, Oxfam entrusted a wide variety of others to do so on its behalf. But this was by no means obvious in its press appeals for funds. Who were these unnamed organisations which carried out the work in far-flung corners of the world beyond the reach of British jurisdiction? If Oxfam did not itself feed 'the starving child', if the individual child pictured was an idiom for hunger generally, then some advertisements were arguably misleading.

Also queried were calls for more international concern to be given to the problem of world hunger. Taking its cue from the Freedom from Hunger Campaign, Oxfam frequently took pains to point out that world poverty was too large a problem for private philanthropy alone and should be a concern of governments. 'Propaganda and advocacy for legislation, whether in this country or overseas, have been described by the courts as political, and not charitable; so, too, has the promotion of international friendship', stated the Report of the Charity Commissioners for England and Wales for 1962. This report announced that the activities of overseas aid agencies would come under active investigation during 1964. They were not named, but Oxfam and the UK Freedom from Hunger Campaign were the twin targets.

The Commissioners' multiplying questions were, in fact, symptoms of a more general malaise about what it was right and proper to do in the name of charity in the contemporary world. The Charities Act of 1960 – which had for the first time legally defined the Charity Commissioners' functions and brought all charities within their purview – had done much to tidy up the law and its administration. But the Act had chosen not to lay down a definition of 'charitable', preferring to leave the courts to make decisions as and when cases arose. Such decisions could only be based on previous judicial pronouncements; the key ones dated from the 19th century, and they were based on a statute dating back to 1601.

During the recent past, attitudes towards helping the victims of social distress had undergone important changes. The 20th century had done away with the old language of indigence and pauperism; modern society reached beyond the condition of destitution to understand its causes and how they might be removed. The second World War brought to a head the growing feeling that dealing with social distress must be a state responsibility. The war had been fought to ensure freedom; Sir William Beveridge, main architect of the Welfare State, defined five freedoms: freedom from want, from disease, from ignorance, from squalor, and from idleness. What else was 'Freedom from Hunger' but the same notion of mankind's entitlements writ large into the international context?

Oxfam drew attention to itself because it did not behave in the circumspect way of conventional charity. With the discovery of the

'Third World' – a phrase coined around this time – it had come to regard its cause as larger than itself and had set about building momentum behind ideas belonging to the realm of public policy. In its fundraising and publicity it persistently broke new ground, motivated by conscience and by Cecil Jackson-Cole's drive for the application of business techniques to voluntary action. At the same time, the objects of its charity were very far away, and increasingly the subjects of countries outside British control. Oxfam's word had to be taken largely on trust both concerning their needs, and on the means to relieve those needs deployed by partners similarly outside British jurisdiction.

Patient explanation of the system whereby grants were screened by trustee committees, and some modification of advertising copy, did something to assuage the Charity Commissioners' protests. But on the issue vital to the evolving character of Oxfam's overseas programme there was a serious problem. The press caught wind of it. 'We interpret our general charter as being for the relief of distress and suffering,' Kirkley told the *Oxford Mail*. 'Not only feeding hungry people today but helping them to be fed tomorrow. We haven't rigidly separated this in the past.' Nor would he wish to do so in the future. However, if the Commissioners took the opposite view, then the options were to accept it, or to contest it in the courts. Neither was attractive.

At the Chief Commissioner's instigation, the Inland Revenue requested a list of grants made for projects of the 'public works' variety. Oxfam was instructed that, until a decision was reached about whether such projects constituted a proper use of charitable funds, no further grants should be made for purposes other than relief and welfare. Oxfam had recently increased its commitment to Freedom from Hunger from £500,000 to £1.8 million, and had just completed a triumphant campaign in which £300,000 extra income, much of it destined for FFH projects, had been raised. Under the moratorium, how was this to be spent? Worse, if the Inland Revenue found previous development grants 'non-charitable', the trustees would be liable to pay the taxes due on the amount spent on these non-charitable purposes.

The interpretation of the law applied by the Charity Commissioners had been laid down by Lord Macnaghten in a judgement of 1891. To be charitable, something had to relieve poverty, provide education, advance religion, or be otherwise beneficial to the community. Many of the development projects supported by Oxfam fell into the first two categories; training courses for farmers, for example, promoted education. Here the Commissioners' complaint was that Oxfam's formal name – 'Famine Relief' being the key phrase – and its 'objects' clause implied that donations would be spent on direct relief, not on education or other measures to obviate its need.

The law bound a charity and its trustees to stay within the remit of its stated purposes. The expression of these and their evaluation by the Charity Commissioners decided whether or not an organisation could be registered as a charity, and thereby gain the tax-exempt status to which charities were entitled. There were, therefore, two separate but interrelated issues: Could aid for development be charitable? And could Oxfam rewrite its 'objects' clause to cover the full range of its grants in wording that the Charity Commissioners would accept? In early 1964, legal work to draw up a new clause for approval by the trustees was set in motion.

Meanwhile, the charitable outlook for development aid did not look good. In February, Mr. Hill addressed a meeting of the Standing Conference of British Organisations for Aid to Refugees, chaired by Lord Astor, whose members included Christian Aid, War on Want, Oxfam, and the FFH Committee. Counsel's advice was still pending, but Hill was not reassuring. Shortly afterwards, the Inland Revenue required Oxfam's trustees to sign an indemnity for £20,000 covering tax refunds from covenanted income, which might have to be recalled. This the Executive Committee agreed to do, but many members strongly resented the imputation that they were lacking in responsibility towards Oxfam's donors, or had acted illegally.

What type of projects were those for 'public works' and 'general economic improvement' to which the Charity Commissioners took exception? Hill's view was that money given to people to dig irrigation canals, terrace hillsides, or build roads in neglected rural areas was unconnected to charitable purpose.

One Oxfam/FFH grant to fall under scrutiny was a 24-mile stretch of road in Western Kenya close to the shores of Lake Victoria. Here, the local community development officer, a British colonial servant, had encouraged some farmers on marginal land to plant sugar cane as an experiment. In 1962, the first marketable crop was harvested from 180 acres of previously eroded soil. Unfortunately, the farmers found themselves unable to take their crop to the sugar mills: the earthen track could not withstand heavy vehicles. To wait their turn on a government road-building list would have doomed their cane and the venture.

Although major road works were outside a voluntary agency brief, this small stretch of 'feeder' road to reinforce a very local effort at self-improvement was rather different. This was just the kind of scheme in which a modest input from Oxfam – the sum requested was £6,000 – could fill a gap, setting up for the future not only the initial group but perhaps a whole community. This grant was made in August 1963, and the community development officer reported enthusiastically on progress. Could it really be that the Inland Revenue would not accept that the road was *bona fide* charitable?

Similar projects already approved by both the FFH Project Committee and Oxfam's own Overseas Aid Committees were held in abeyance. One of these was a £1,000 proposal for building a small bridge across the River Khubelu in the Basutoland mountains. Villagers high in the sierra were isolated and unable to get crops to market or people to hospital. But they could not have their bridge: it was a 'public work'. The next winter was phenomenally cold and emergency supplies had to be flown in. Jimmy Betts made an emergency grant – following due procedures. The grant was for £1,500, some for relief works; with part of it, the villagers built a bridge across the River Khubelu. Betts duly reported back on the use to which the money had been put; he elicited no comment.

On 6 May 1964, the question of whether humanitarian aid for development was charitable was raised in the House of Lords during a debate on 'Refugees, disasters, and international aid'. Lord Astor was to lead the debate, but was summoned away at the last moment. Baroness Elliot of Harwood, Chairman of the World Refugee Year in Britain, took his place. She pointed out that it would be ironic indeed for the government, after encouraging the voluntary societies to join the WRY and Freedom from Hunger Campaigns, now to describe the long-term projects they advocated as uncharitable. Lord Dundee, speaking for the government, agreed. He said that the lawyers had now told the Charity Commissioners that 'the great majority' of projects brought to their notice did meet charitable criteria. The agencies breathed a sigh of relief.

The Commissioners themselves reported in detail to Lord Astor. Measures 'reasonably closely connected with the relief of poor people' were now seen as charitable anywhere in the world. But the charities must be satisfied 'that the poverty to be relieved actually exists in observable cases and is not merely inferred from statistics'. Most of Oxfam's activities were now covered by the charitable umbrella, with the understanding that there must be better 'observing' of needs and checking on expenditure on the ground. But public works and projects for economic improvement were still beyond the pale.

The Commissioner's opinions were only semi-judicial, unlike findings laid down by the courts. As far as Leslie Kirkley was concerned, this meant that they could and should continually be re-argued with the Commissioner until his position – already dented – gave still further. While quietly exerting pressure, every effort should be made in other areas – publicity as well as grant-making – not to antagonise.

In early June 1964, Kirkley and his new Overseas Aid Officer, Ken

Bennett (replacing Llewellyn who had left for Hong Kong) paid a visit to the Charity Commissioners to reiterate the case for development aid. Some room for manoeuvre began to appear. For public works, the Chief Commissioner informed his visitors, Macnaghten's final charitable heading – 'purposes beneficial to the community' – was the only applicable principle. This applied in the UK, by extension in its dependent territories, and perhaps throughout the Commonwealth as well. Thus, bridges and roads in Kenya and Basutoland might, after all, clear the hurdle.

But there was no way in which 'the community' could be interpreted to include people who were not British subjects and who never had been British subjects. Such a usage of charitable funds would have the effect of relieving taxpayers in foreign countries. That there might not be too many of those in the poorest corners of the developing world was a point the Charity Commissioners did not consider. Questions of scale were similarly overlooked. The Aswan High Dam – quoted as a palpably uncharitable public work – was in no way analogous to a small stretch of road costing £6,000, built by poor farmers to earn a bare living from a crop of sugar cane.

Threatened by the indictment on aid to non-Commonwealth countries was Oxfam's growing portfolio of FFH and other projects in Latin America. An example was a £100,000 scheme to research and introduce better strains of tuber and grain crops among Indian farmers on the Andean plateau in Bolivia. This project, however, scraped past the Commissioners' indictment because both they and the Inland Revenue agreed that commitments made before the argument arose should be honoured. But Oxfam and the other overseas aid-giving charities were determined not just to find ways of protecting existing programmes, but to gain acceptance of the charitable principle.

On 16 July 1964, shortly before the Charity Commissioners were due to publish their Report for 1963 and the results of their investigation, the 15 members of the Standing Conference of British Organisations for Aid to Refugees met to discuss its anticipated conclusions. Lord Astor had received a letter from the Commissioners. Their position on economic improvement, public works, and the idea that the charities should restrict their activities to British Commonwealth countries, incensed the international thinking of many present.

Some of their views appeared a few days later in the *Sunday Times* 'Insight' column. Donald Tweddle, Director of UK Freedom from Hunger, was particularly exasperated. 'What the government is saying', he pointed out, 'is that it is OK to indulge in short-term palliatives, but illegal to do anything more fundamental. This conflicts with the whole trend in British charity work overseas. It is only by public works that we can tackle the problem of poverty at its roots.' Lord Astor adopted a fighting tone: 'The government must make legal the present emphasis on long-term operations. If they can not amend the law, they should change it altogether.' Others muttered about testing the Commissioners' opinion in the courts, and the sooner the better.

A few days later the Chief Charity Commissioner wrote to Kirkley. Having examined grants made during 1962-63, the Inland Revenue, Hill was glad to say, had found that 'the greatest part of Oxfam's income in the period covered was expended on projects that are charitable in law', and that tax rebates on covenants would therefore now be upheld. However, there was a clear discrepancy between the purposes of some expenditures, notably those on health and education, and the purposes – 'relief of distress' – expressed in the Memorandum of Association. The relevant clause should be changed, with the Commissioners' guidance; it could then cover all types of grants made by Oxfam with the exception of public works and economic improvement outside the Commonwealth.

By early the following year, even this stricture had been relaxed. But not because Kirkley continued to argue the case. A new 'objects' clause had been drafted. This, with amendments now suggested by the Commissioners, now by the trustees, now by the Inland Revenue, finished its rounds in March 1965. It stated that Oxfam's main object was: 'to relieve poverty, distress and suffering in any part of the world (including starvation, sickness or any physical disability or affliction) and primarily when arising from any public calamity (including famine, earthquake, pestilence, war or civil disturbance), or the immediate or continuing result of want of natural or artificial resources, or the means to develop them, and whether acting alone or in association with others'. This was broad enough to encompass anything Oxfam was likely to want to support, inside or outside the Commonwealth.

The Executive Committee congratulated Kirkley on his handling of the negotiations, and rightly so: he had achieved what he wanted without the Charity Commissioners having to climb down explicitly from the line they had taken. The storm had blown over.

The new clause was adopted at an Extraordinary General Meeting of the trustees, held on 6 May 1965. At the same time, the old official title – the cumbersome and by now inaccurate 'Oxford Committee for Famine Relief' – was legally dropped in favour of the simpler 'Oxfam' by which, anyway, the organisation was now widely known. That the word was technically meaningless was a legal advantage.

The changes were widely reported in the press as a natural updating of Oxfam's affairs to match its contemporary role. No-one mentioned the crisis about the charitable nature of development aid which had prompted the necessity. Hill retired at the end of 1965. And no-one ever mentioned it again.

While Kirkley was busy dowsing this bout of organisational heat, he was trying simultaneously to keep a rather different pot from boiling over. Should Oxfam, or should it not, provide support to family planning?

In the early 1960s, the issue of population control took on the dimensions of an international *cause célèbre*. Alarm about the failure of the world to increase its food production fast enough to keep pace with population growth became widespread. During the 1950s, public health improvements brought about dramatic declines in the death rates in developing countries without any corresponding declines in their birth rates. The lack of data from such countries meant that the scientists and statisticians took some time to notice what was going on. When they did, their slide-rules told them that the kind of population increase that took Europe three centuries would take only 50 or 75 years in parts of today's world – invariably the hungriest parts. Malthusian prophecies of doom were suddenly on their way to fulfilment.

Dr.B.R.Sen, FAO's Director-General, was keenly aware of the implications for world agriculture. The demographers' rising tide of numbers required food production to grow by much more than the current 2 per cent a year even to combat existing levels of poor nutrition: hence the FFH Campaign. Now the image of too many mouths to feed was given new drama by the scaring notion of a population 'crisis'.

Oxfam already saw itself as making an important contribution by its involvement with Freedom from Hunger and the philosophy of hunger prevention for which – as we have seen – it was prepared to defend a new piece of charitable turf. But by early 1964, support to one side of the equation only – the food side – began to seem to some wholly inadequate. Bernard Llewellyn, whose vast Asian Field Director patch included the most populous and poorest corners of the world, found himself confronting the population crisis at what the Charity Commissioners called an 'observable' level, as a genuine human problem, not an 'extrapolation of statistics'.

In the shanties of Hong Kong, Macao, and a growing number of Asian cities, crowdedness added greatly to squalor and suffering. Llewellyn described a visit he made to a settlement in the seasonal mud-flats of the Han River on the edge of Seoul, filled with Korean families with six or more children. 'The social worker accompanying me enquired about their needs. For long Korea had been corrupted by relief hand-outs and I expected to be asked for all the usual things. But no. The women wanted money for abortions which cost more than they could hope to earn. They wanted help to avoid future pregnancy. And one mother, her two-weeks-old baby lying on the mud floor at her feet, asked me to take it away. She couldn't feed it.' His eloquent voice continued to demand that family planning should become an object of Oxfam grants.

Since time immemorial, human society had found ways of dealing with unwanted births. Much of the pioneering effort devoted to birth control had been undertaken not only to free women from the bondage of endless childbearing, but to replace abortion, infanticide, and child abandonment with better ways of dealing with unwanted pregnancy. In the early 1960s, new contraceptives – the pill and the inter-uterine device (IUD) or loop, easier to use and more reliable than older techniques – were just entering millions of people's lives. They appeared to offer the means of helping the world cope with a crisis of human surfeit, as experienced in the family and in society. When Llewellyn put the case for support to family planning to Oxfam, he did so for strictly human-itarian reasons.

Unfortunately, the case was impossible to make in such straight-forward terms. Roman Catholic theologians objected to artificial tampering with the sacred process of creating new life in the womb. Moralists believed that widespread availability of the pill and the loop would mean a relaxation in the codes controlling sexual behaviour. Many developing countries still associated large families with national virility and questioned why they should enforce a policy of fertility restraint when no Western government did so. Left-wing ideologues perceived the whole idea as a means of diverting attention from the main problem, which was one of too much poverty rather than too many people. From every direction, persuasion and conviction, the issue inspired passion and emotion.

Because of the financial support lent from Christians of all persuasions, including Catholics, the overseas aid charities had all ducked the family planning issue. Oxfam's line was that this was a matter for those specialist organisations set up to deal with birth control. But Kirkley, in spite of the fact that the Pope had just made him a Knight Commander of the Order of St. Sylvester, decided that it was time to grasp the nettle. The second Vatican Council (1962-63) was blowing fresh air into doctrinal debate, and it was widely assumed that Rome would soon modify its position on contraception. But the first attempt to change Oxfam's stance – in 1963 – was defeated in the Oxfam Council of Management: those not bound by conviction believed that Oxfam stood to lose too much support by a pro-family planning stand. Kirkley persisted with a campaign of quiet persuasion. Among his allies were Sir Arthur Rucker, whose Korean experience predisposed him to Llewellyn's reports, and a Lancashire businessman, Frank Kershaw.

In March 1964, Kershaw introduced a new resolution at the Council. It stated that Oxfam would not in principle refuse a grant application submitted by the International Planned Parenthood Federation (IPPF). Family planning – despite what some might have wanted – would not be among Oxfam's main purposes, and supporters with conscientious scruples might restrict their donations to other schemes; but they should not be allowed to impose their views on others who felt that some measure of family planning was essential to the overall aim of relieving suffering. After a day of heated debate, the resolution was passed by 11 votes to seven.

The passage of this resolution – an agreement to disagree – was an illustration of Kirkley's gift for compromise. He would have preferred to avoid a vote; his Quaker instinct was always for consensus. But with people of strong conviction on the Council, a vote was unavoidable. In putting the new policy into effect, however, there was a convenient breathing space. The decision came at the height of the tussle with the Charity Commissioners over whether development aid was charitable. In order to avoid muddying the waters still further, action on the policy decision had to await the redrafting of the 'objects' clause. It was nearly a year before the policy was publicly announced, and by then passions had cooled and public opinion was known to be on Oxfam's side.

The groundwork for the announcement was carefully laid. The Indian High Commissioner, Dr. J.N. Mehta, was enlisted to make the case in its favour. India was deeply aware of the way in which what Mehta called 'a vast bottom bulge' of youngsters in the population was threatening to derail economic progress, and was leading a campaign at the UN to persuade member agencies to aid family planning: as yet, not even the World Health Organisation did so. But Oxfam, in the bulletin announcing its policy, gave equal space to the alternative view. Father Arthur McCormack, a leading Catholic authority, wrote persuasively that family planning was no panacea, and that converts to the doctrine of mass contraception must not be allowed to distract the world from the main tasks in the war on poverty: boosting agriculture and economic life.

Before the announcement was made, Kirkley went to see Archbishop Heenan at Westminster, through the good offices of Father Thomas Corbishley, a Jesuit member of the Oxfam Council of Management. Corbishley, a liberal among the Catholic clergy, had abstained in the Oxfam Council vote. He took the line that, since family planning would absorb a very small proportion of Oxfam's future grants – at most five per cent – there was a great deal that Catholics could still support and should be encouraged to do so. The Catholic hierarchy endorsed this view, as long as Oxfam fulfilled its promise to respect the wishes of any donor who specified that their contribution was not to be spent on birth control. By this procedure, Kirkley hoped that the damage to Oxfam's support – and everyone anticipated damage – would be minimised.

The uproar that greeted the announcement on 14 February 1965 took Oxfam by surprise. 'OXFAM BOMBSHELL' was the front-page lead in the *Sunday Mirror*, and the story was prominently carried everywhere. The mollifying tone of the Catholic establishment, in comments from Father Corbishley and Archbishop Heenan's spokesman, Mgr. Bruce Kent, was helpful. At this time, 'Humanae Vitae', the Papal Encyclical on contraception, was due out and it was widely expected that it would liberalise the Church's position. It was finally issued after long delay in 1968; if it had already been out in 1965, Catholic leaders would certainly have felt more constrained.

When the furore had died down, the tenor of the reaction, even in Catholic newspapers, was gauged as almost universally favourable. The population 'crisis' was a major contemporary issue and Oxfam's courage in taking it up ahead of UN and other British aid organisations was applauded. On 24 February, *The Times* reported that only four Catholic groups, three schools and a youth club in Birmingham, had so far found it necessary to withdraw their support from Oxfam. The Oxfam spokesman commented: 'We are saddened to lose them but fully understand their feelings.'

Immediately, grants for family planning projects were sanctioned by the Asia Committee. The Family Planning Association of Hong Kong received £625 to run a three-month radio propaganda campaign; this was designed to increase attendance at birth-control clinics. The Planned Parenthood Federation in Seoul was given £6,680 to establish two model clinics and train 200 doctors and other medical workers in IUD insertion and follow-up. This project, in which family planning was added to an existing maternal and child health service, was a pattern later followed in grants to the Christian hospitals in India and other medical programmes. Oxfam aid to family planning soon rose to between £30,000 and £40,000 a year.

The passionate urgency many felt about the need to dispense contraceptives among the multiplying millions of the Third World turned out in a sense to be misplaced. Entrenched cultural mores, particularly where intimate physical relations were concerned, meant that couples whose hopes of wealth and personal security were founded on the need to produce a large number of healthy children, did not seize joyfully upon pills and loops as their answer to a prayer. And it took time for many developing countries to recognise the effect of rapid population growth on their economic prospects. The crisis of over-population was not susceptible to a contraceptive fix; modern technology, it transpired, had a role to play but was not the determinant many had assumed.

Like the disappointments connected to so many remedies devised by industrial mankind, for solutions to problems perceived by industrial mankind – and to a large extent created by industrial mankind – the false expectations attached to family planning took a while to uncover.

An issue raised during the saga with the Charity Commissioners was the complaints they had received about 'high pressure fundraising'. Oxfam was the prime culprit. When a Committee was set up by the Commissioners to examine the substance of these complaints, Leslie Kirkley and Harold Sumption – both members – learned that nearly half the complaints came from other charities. With its application of modern marketing techniques, its hard-hitting press ads, its sophisticated set-up for postal appeals, and its audacity, Oxfam was cutting a new style in charity fundraising. Where some organisations carped, others imitated.

In the mid-1960s almost anything Oxfam did attracted attention. The word 'Oxfam' appeared in films and plays, and was tossed about by newspaper columnists to indicate their affinity with a world view that took in the immorality of widespread human suffering alongside 'the affluent society'. The organisation was treated as a phenomenon; its activities prompted commentary on the nature of modern charity, even philosophical ruminations on the new philanthropy as the inheritor of instincts that organised religion used to attract.

Offers of assistance poured in from every side: everyone wanted to be identified as a supporter. Plane fares, services and facilities, goods of all kinds, were given free of charge or at knock-down rates without demur. Officialdom and governments were unhesitatingly supportive, as was the press. In 1964, *The Economist* published a graph showing the dramatic upward curve of Oxfam's income since 1949 without adding even a caption of explanation. Some Oxfam staff kept scrap-books of press cuttings, mesmerised to find that almost everything undertaken by their humanitarian employer took place in a fish-bowl of publicity.

Oxfam's go-getters had touched that special spring in the British conscience that attaches to different causes at different times. Kirkley's young enthusiasts were always looking for another hill to climb, another barricade to lean on. They did so with the confidence gained from the conquest of the last. But they had to keep out in front, be there before other charities caught up and presented givers and providers with competing demands. Charities such as Shelter, another creature of the 1960s, were following hard on Oxfam's heels.

In establishing Oxfam's name before a much wider public, the *Daily*

Mail's sponsorship of the 1963 Hunger £Million campaign was very important. The relationship had worked out well for both organisations, and it continued. In February 1964 Richard Herd, a *Mail* reporter, was despatched on a tour of Africa, and wrote a series of splashy articles under a masthead of 'your OXFAM money in ACTION!' With headings like 'These twins would have been THROWN OUT TO DIE' and 'It isn't often you meet a man you REVERE', Herd's articles introduced readers to the small miracles their pounds and pennies made possible. Jeffrey Archer continued to help, inviting the Beatles to tea in Brasenose College and pulling off the kind of stunts which gave the *Mail* good, exclusive, copy.

Came the autumn of 1964, and the *Mail* again agreed to sponsor Oxfam's Christmas push. This time, readers were invited to send in gifts. This cross between Antiques Roadshow and the bric-a-brac stall at the Parish Fair built on another part of Oxfam's fundraising machine: the Oxfam Gift Shop. By 1964, three more Gift Shops had been opened around the country, the first in Guildford in 1960, then in Leeds and Cheltenham, both in 1963. These shops were all run by a small staff under Joe Mitty, the first Manager of the Broad Street Shop in Oxford, and modelled on the original.

Although willing to turn around almost anything – dentures, old spectacle frames, and broken fountain pens were on Mitty's list of desirable items – he was a stickler for quality. He was able to find a buyer for a houseboat, a donkey, or a stuffed porcupine if that was what turned up. But he preferred jewellery and silver teapots – things of finery and value. These, naturally, came in more slowly than books or records, china or cutlery. What he was not prepared to run for Oxfam was a junk shop or a second-hand clothing stall. One line he added was Oxfam Christmas cards. The first of these were designed in 1957 by Leslie Durham, who later became Mitty's assistant. Sold both through the shops and by mail order, the cards quickly became a flourishing business, bringing in £18,500 profit by 1963.

In 1959, Oxfam hired a Gift Appeals Organiser based in Leeds, and in 1963 another was taken on to look after the south. The main problem was to keep the shops stocked with an adequate supply of good merchandise. Shop income grew steadily. In the financial year 1962/63 they brought in £79,000, almost doubling their proceeds in only two years.

One of the attractions to Oxfam of the 1964 *Daily Mail* gift appeal was that of providing the shops with a tremendous boost in stock. The *Mail* ran a series of classic human stories about giving: the unmarried elderly lady of 80 who gave 'my dearest earthly treasure', her mother's engagement ring; the Brownies who held a toy party; the Crufts' *habituée* who gave her pedigree poodle puppy; the poultry firm who gave a champion turkey weighing in at 61lb. The *Mail* enjoyed itself: 'When I met Joe Mitty at the Oxfam headquarters reception depot, he was rubbing shoulders with a full-sized stuffed brown bear, a set of glass domes, a Victorian snow scene more than 8ft. long, several sets of wooden-shafted golf clubs, an 18th century fowling-piece, enough battered violins to equip the Philharmonia and, on a plinth, an alabaster lady called Giuditta.'

The biggest lift came from the celebrity presents. Harold Wilson gave a Gannex mac. Sir Alec Douglas-Home, a cricket bat. Jackie Kennedy, Harold Macmillan, and umpteen others gave signed copies of books by them or about them. Mary Rand gave her winning Olympic running-shoes, Cilla Black her teddy bear, the Rolling Stones an electric guitar, Sir Laurence Olivier a copper bracelet he wore in 'Othello'. Jeffrey Archer was in his element. Courtesy of PanAm, he dashed to Washington and managed to get President Johnson to autograph an album of Sir Winston Churchill's records. These, along with the cream of the gift crop, were sold at a grand auction at Mansion House hosted by the Lord Mayor.

The *Mail* gift drive raised about £225,000. Even the Queen gave a cash donation, and her Christmas Day message that year included some stirring words about 'the fight against poverty, malnutrition and ignorance'. Meanwhile Oxfam's regional organisers put their energies into distributing door-to-door five million collapsible cardboard 'Family boxes' with an appeal to put in £1 by Christmas. £150,000 was raised but the returns – as with the *Daily Mail* gift drive – did not rise to the heights of Hunger £Million the year before.

Not only Oxfam's prominence but its conspicuous willingness to risk money to raise money inevitably excited controversy. Small charities without the resources to do the same resented the way Oxfam seemed to be cornering the market in British generosity by up-front investment in publicity. Wary of criticism about overhead costs, Oxfam publicised its expenditure ratio *ad nauseam*. Canon Milford, frequently quoted, was always slipping in that only 'a penny-ha'penny in the shilling' was spent on fundraising, 'and another ha'penny on administration'. But the visibility gave another impression. A Gallup Poll of 1963 found that 43 per cent of middle and upper income respondees thought the expenses ratio was higher. For whatever reasons – higher competition, a publicity backlash – the momentum of rising income slackened and dropped around the mid-1960s. A report prepared at the end of 1964 on 'publicity and the changing patterns of response' commented that the organisation had been over-optimistic in its forecasts. Graphs drawn heading dizzily upwards had in fact flattened out. 'It was easy to mistake the successes of the time', wrote the author, 'for the bottom rungs of a ladder, when in fact they were the crest of a wave.'

In 1965, a fall in income of £300,000 on the previous year's £2.7

million rang alarm bells. The shortfall represented a much bigger drop on projected income, and an S.O.S. – by no means the last in Oxfam's history – went out to the field that grants would have to be held back. In the meantime, the entire range of fundraising and publicity activities was examined. The trend was downward on press ad. returns – the 'starving child' had lost some of its shock impact; and the return on Pledged Gift expenditure had begun to fall after reaching a peak in 1963. It seemed that the days of the cut-price donation were over.

The most promising outlook was in the local offices around which the network of support groups was steadily growing. By 1964, Oxfam had a presence in 20 towns and cities including Edinburgh and Belfast. The 'Family box' campaign, with its dependence on local publicity and volunteer action, was designed to bring the regional fundraisers behind a unified national effort. Some grassroots stalwarts were inclined to run their own, individualist, shows and resisted attempts to orchestrate them from Oxford. In spring 1965, an Assistant Director – Philip Jackson – was taken on. From this point onwards, a major attempt was made to weld the disparate machinery of local appeals into a more coherent and productive team effort. With a marketing and sales background, Jackson was expected to wave an organisational wand over the 'home front' – including all fundraising and publicity – and make it march in unison.

Quite a number of Oxfam supporter groups had begun to engage in a new kind of activity: running temporary shops in premises lent for a few days or weeks. The first were in Reigate and Redhill in 1962. To begin with, these volunteer-managed shops were quite different from Joe Mitty's fiercely professional enterprise. Unlike Mitty, they usually took in clothes, selling those unsuited for sending overseas, and were less like a down-market version of an antique shop than an up-market version of a jumble sale. Gradually, the two types of Oxfam Shop fused; it took some time to persuade Mitty that the sale of second-hand clothes would not detract from the Gift Shop image and performance.

At the end of 1964 a trading company was set up to market Christmas cards and other products through the shops. Oxfam's involvement in trading came about – like so many of its activities – more by piecemeal involvement than grand design. In 1959, Pastor Ludwig Stumpf of the Lutheran World Service in Hong Kong was invited by Oxfam to speak at their World Refugee Year Conference. He brought with him a suitcaseful of pincushions and embroidered boxes made by Chinese refugees. Initially, Oxfam itself showed little interest, but another conferee seized upon them with enthusiasm. Elizabeth Wilson of the Huddersfield Famine Relief Committee – the only other such Relief Committee to survive since 1942 – took Pastor Stumpf's handicrafts back to the north and thereafter imported and sold them with considerable success.

Within a year or two, Oxfam picked up the idea. Lynn ten Kate, an energetic Gifts organiser, not only began to import from Pastor Stumpf, but bought African handicrafts from British suppliers for sale in the shops at Christmas time. She then persuaded Jimmy Betts to bring beads, bowls, and ornaments from Bechuanaland and anywhere else he was travelling. This turned out to be the start of another major charitable enterprise by Oxfam: the import and sale of Third World crafts as a means of benefiting their producers.

The formation of the trading company, Oxfam Activities Ltd., later to become Oxfam Trading, formalised the framework for selling both manufactured goods and those imported from overseas. With legal advice and after consultation with the Charity Commissioners, articles were drawn up for what was then a novel kind of business. The company functioned as did any commercial concern, but covenanted back to Oxfam all of its profits, allowing its operations to escape taxation. Imported craft goods entered the country without levy, initially at the discretion of HM Customs; later the principle was established at law.

The birth of the trading company encouraged supporter groups running temporary shops to take up merchandising. They were able to put up attractive window displays of cards and handicrafts to front their trade in second-hand goods. Shops caught on with volunteers and with customers; by mid-1966 around 50 were functioning at any one time, paving the way for the charity shop bonanza of the 1970s.

In the spring of 1963, an enterprise long nurtured by Leslie Kirkley and Cecil Jackson-Cole bore fruit. The international extension of the Oxfam family of organisations took its first step with the establishment of a Canadian Committee in Toronto. The next year saw the inauguration of Oxfam-Belgique. The latter was the creation of a wealthy Belgian aristocrat, Antoine Allard, an idealist of pacifist and internationalist persuasion. Allard heard of the British Oxfam, presented himself and his ideas for inspection, and – with Kirkley's support – set up a modest imitation with the patronage of his Queen. But the Canadian move was different, very much promoted and inspired from Oxford as a planned *démarche* to spread worldwide the Oxfam crusade against world hunger.

Kirkley and Jackson-Cole had begun to think in terms of internationalisation back in the 1950s. Jackson-Cole's was an evangelistic perspective. He cherished some words once spoken to him by Gilbert Murray: 'There is a responsible spirit behind the universe who is seeking to remedy the suffering.' Jackson-Cole believed that if this spirit could work through the British, it could surely also be summoned from the peoples of other countries.

Kirkley had a less ethereal vision. Ever since 1959 he had been a member of the formal non-governmental network, attending meetings in Geneva as a guest of UN agencies and, from 1962, playing an active part in the International Council of Voluntary Agencies (ICVA). He yearned to set up like-minded bodies in Oxfam's non-sectarian image, one day to become an international federation such as the Save the Children network or the World Council of Churches. Kirkley's dream occupied much of his own and no little organisational energy during the 1960s and beyond. Although an international Oxfam network of sorts emerged, it fell far short of Kirkley's ambitions.

His initial hopes lay in the US. After a preliminary visit by Colonel Widdowson, Kirkley set off for North America in 1962. He did the rounds of friendly organisations, having breakfast with Mrs. Eleanor Roosevelt, being interviewed by the *New York Times*, and travelling to a number of cities. After all, Kirkley decided, the place to start was Canada. He took on a retired Salvation Army Officer, Colonel Albert Dalziel, to set up an embryonic organisation in Toronto. This Dalziel accomplished, gaining the patronage of key people and negotiating the all-important tax deductible status. To obtain this, the new organisation had to undertake charitable activity in Canada. Accordingly, a grant of C$10,000 was made for Salvation Army work with Canadian native peoples. Costs were met by Oxfam UK on the understanding that donations overseas would, initially at least, be channelled through Oxford.

Unfortunately, the assumption that the Oxfam UK momentum would buoy up an Oxfam of Canada was a misjudgement. Dalziel withdrew in 1963 and the small National Committee became moribund. So Kirkley sent across Lynn ten Kate, a forceful and energetic lieutenant. She set up a number of local fundraising groups, but after she left in mid-1964, they became directionless. Kirkley's deputy, Henry Fletcher, then began a series of visits to try to get things moving. Hot from success in Britain, he found it incomprehensible that the same spirit and energy could not be tapped. In spring 1966, he accepted an invitation to go out and run Oxfam of Canada himself, and from this point onwards things began to look up.

This was only one aspect, if the most significant, of Kirkley's efforts to develop co-operative ties, at home and internationally. He formed a relationship with the Austrian Freedom from Hunger Campaign Committee; he fostered links with an Italian group, Manitese. But the truth was that, however impressed potential allies were with the Oxfam story, this was a peculiarly British animal and it did not thrive easily in other environments. Organisations which transplanted well were those which had a very definite constituency – children, the elderly – around which support could coalesce. Oxfam was an idea, and it was not a tightly defined idea. Neither the idea nor the marketing methods used in Britain instantly moved the spirit which Kirkley and Jackson-Cole had counted upon.

It took the radicalisation of North American youth in the late 1960s, largely wrought by Vietnam and a sense of disgust with Western imperialism, to create a more conducive climate. And then the Oxfams that flourished in such a hothouse were different, radically and controversially different, from the careful balance of British pragmatism and passion.

In its desire to open up hearts and minds as well as purses to the problem of poverty in countries overseas, the Oxford Committee took seriously the task of public information and education. Kirkley was a strong believer in 'the educated pound'. But efforts went further with a programme specifically directed at the nation's youth.

In 1959, World Refugee Year, Stella Dyer was appointed as Oxfam's first Schools Organiser to co-ordinate what had been up to then a haphazard series of classroom appeals and competitions. She set about forging systematic links with schools, universities, colleges of further education, teacher training institutions, and the whole educational establishment. Then came the Freedom from Hunger Campaign with its strong focus on putting across the facts of world hunger in the classroom. Oxfam's education team grew, one of its key recruits being Bill Jackson who joined in 1962. By 1964, Oxfam was in touch with 12,000 schools and the department was raising around £150,000 a year.

As they hopped from school assemblies to staff rooms to lunchtime talks at training colleges, Oxfam's education staff were constantly asked for materials for classroom use. Other than FFH materials, there was virtually nothing ready-made for teaching young people about world poverty. In 1963, Oxfam was contracted by UNESCO to produce a series of teaching resources for primary school teachers, and this set off yet another area of pioneering activity. To begin with, the Oxford Committee had seen schools mainly as a source of money. But by the mid-1960s, the importance of the educational role in schools had outstripped the fundraising one. Oxfam materials were produced in close co-operation with Freedom from Hunger.

Stella Dyer and Bill Jackson took the line that no direct appeals should be made to students. The emphasis should be on laying the facts about hunger, disease, and deprivation before young people, and letting them respond in the way they wanted. That this would often redound to Oxfam's advantage was axiomatic. But a very important part of the educational message was that the problems were too large for charities like Oxfam to handle; that only governments and international organisations commanded resources on the necessary scale. That there could be tension between education for development and fundraising for the overseas programme soon became apparent. When Jackson proposed to Kirkley that Oxfam should set up a separate educational trust, he was told: 'Nothing doing'. The idea was premature. It was to re-emerge in the future.

In 1965, the year marking the formal end of the five-year Freedom from Hunger Campaign, a co-operative mechanism between the overseas voluntary agencies was set up: the Voluntary Committee on Overseas Aid and Development (VCOAD). This Committee, which included ODI, UNA, and FFHC, as well as the relevant charities, was expected to become the mouthpiece of the voluntary aid sector, succeeding the Standing Conference of British Organisations for Aid to Refugees. Its inspiration came from Barbara Castle at the Labour Government's new Ministry of Development, who hoped that it would serve as a joint platform with the government on aid issues, as well as prevent duplication among the burgeoning charity programmes.

In spite of a number of meetings by a working group, the areas in which the agencies were prepared to work in a truly co-operative spirit appeared to be few. Oxfam was one of the members which saw the creation of VCOAD as a chance to stimulate educational and fundraising action throughout the entire private sector. But, like others, it was very unwilling to move towards any merger of its overseas aid programme. In the upshot, this attempt to build co-operation – as in the international arena – did not fulfill what appeared to be its potential. But VCOAD did undertake seminal work, particularly in relation to the formal education system. It provided a useful forum for the agencies, and a clearing-house for the growing range of materials each was generating.

Oxfam's education programme derived great strength from the decision to create a separate information department both to service organisational needs and to field public enquiries. In early 1963, Elizabeth Stamp, previously with the Economist Intelligence Unit, joined Oxfam as Information Officer. Her great-uncle, Dudley Stamp, was a well-known geographer, and one of the earliest academic writers to popularise the notion of 'a developing world' in books foreshadowing those by Ritchie Calder, Gunnar Myrdal, Paul Streeten, Hans Singer, and others establishing 'development' as a new field of scholarship.

Elizabeth Stamp played a very important part in positioning Oxfam intellectually, between the simplest response to world hunger – 'I am 79, I can't spare much but here is 6s. I saved on fuel' – and what was fast becoming a subject of significance and complexity, spawning new disciplines and professions. It was not easy to straddle, almost single-handedly, an exhortation to ladies knitting blankets, and a background briefing on the implications of GATT negotiations for developing economies which would pass muster with statesmen.

The information service was an earnest of Oxfam's intention to play a role in bringing the many issues connected to world hunger to a wider audience. The information literature developed – for use with supporter groups, in schools, by speakers, for organisational sponsors – presented a view of the world which chimed with the standard geographic 'land and people' text, but which differed in one important respect: its point of view emanated from the need to eradicate poverty and hunger, and incorporated projects Oxfam was supporting towards that end.

Gradually, image by image, Oxfam was helping develop a new way of looking at the world, an ideologically charged view of other countries and cultures, a more considered version of the predicament symbolised by the starving child.

It is difficult to appreciate just how novel this was only a generation ago. It is a great tribute to Oxfam that, in today's Britain, almost no-one's idea of the world beyond Europe and North America is untouched by the perception of humanity in need. However, the redefinition of 'lands and peoples' in the light of poverty and underdevelopment, and the attempt to market a new notion of international friendship – help for the poor – had an effect both on organisational consciousness, and on Oxfam's public image.

At that time, for any audience other than the academic, the main source of information about world poverty was the overseas aid charities, among which Oxfam was the pacesetter. Thus, not only did its information output help fill the information vacuum left by the end of empire, but it also had a tendency to convey a grander importance of Oxfam projects in the scheme of things, and a greater belief in Oxfam's ability to solve the problems of world poverty, than was realistic.

However carefully Oxfam proclaimed 'this problem is too large to be solved by philanthropists like us', the implication was that villagers in Africa, Asia or Latin America turned the corner out of poverty thanks to an Oxfam grant. Problem and solution were married, intentionally or otherwise; the organisation which brought people's attention to world hunger was identified as the mechanism for solving it. The scale of the problem and the proportionality of the Oxfam response became blurred. Thus the importance of Oxfam as a weapon in meeting mankind's greatest contemporary challenge was unconsciously overstated. This tendency was reinforced by the need to maximise fundraising, and by the passion Oxfamers brought to their cause.

One reason why Oxfam images took such a powerful hold was that, except for a handful of ex-colonial servants, intrepid travellers and foreign correspondents, few people had any alternative images with which they had to conform. Television had not yet penetrated the mysteries of the Third World; few people went abroad for their holidays, nor if they did were they likely to travel somewhere so exotic nor witness the workings of an Oxfam-type project at first hand. This was still an age of innocence as far as the average British view of distant foreign parts was concerned.

In 1966, Bill Jackson conceived the idea that 800 schoolchildren should be given a development education tour: they should visit the Oxfam version of 'abroad'. This was a brave idea. On a concessionary basis, Oxfam chartered the *Devonia*, a ship fitted out for educational cruises; and for £49 a head, offered places on 'Operation Oasis'. Teenagers prepared for the trip by learning about Algeria's geography and economic problems in the aftermath of civil war; stepping ashore at Algiers, they would visit Oxfam-funded projects in action. The venture was non-profit-making; but it taxed Oxfam's information and education staff to the limit.

Oxfam had provided aid to Algerian refugees for many years, and since 1962 – the year of peace and independence – to Algeria itself. Feeding and medical schemes, particularly 'Gouttes de Lait' mobile milk stations, had been set up for the children of returnees. In the Saharan south, Oxfam had given £3,000 to the White Fathers to equip vocational training centres for boys. These in their oasis settings provided the final destinations of parties of British schoolchildren, camping under the stars like their nomadic Arab hosts.

'Operation Oasis' was a successful adventure, as well as an introduction to the problems of poverty. The authorities in Algiers started by treating the arrival of a ship-load of schoolchildren as an early swallow of the tourist season, and conducted the party around the smartest city 'developments' newly independent Algeria had to offer. When they set off in bone-rattling buses for villages on the edge of the Sahara, the poverty they had come to witness was masked by an Arabian Nights fantasy.

The children were greeted everywhere by cavalcades of Arab riflemen on camels firing volleys into the air. Surrounded by hordes of friendly faces and waving hands, they enjoyed traditional desert hospitality – mountainous feasts of *couscous* and roasted sheep. Bill Jackson and his Oxfam colleagues tried to compensate for the contradictory impressions of desert pride and poverty, while White Fathers shepherded youngsters round their modest training workshops, and Save the Children workers gave them cups of milk to hand out to crowds of friendly children.

'Operation Oasis' was an educational experience for everyone concerned. It was not an experience Oxfam attempted to repeat. The effort was out of proportion to the benefit to Oxfam and the cause of development. The complexities of poverty were not easy to unscramble while you were simultaneously warding off marauding bottom-pinchers from crocodiles of schoolgirls and trying to keep 800 youngsters dysentery-free. On the way home, the children wrote essays, and the journalists on board wrote copy. The *Sunday Mirror* reporter, John Knight, quoted Peter Smith, 17, of Hackney Down School, London: 'I felt choked when two little Arab girls without two halfpennies to rub together gave me a souvenir. It was a wonderful gesture, but I wish they were taught more how to look after themselves.'

The complexities of development aid caused less soul-searching in Oxfam in the early 1960s than parallel questions of scale.

Year by year, Oxfam recorded the expansion of its overseas programme: 'last year Oxfam funds were spent in 89 countries' declared the annual report for 1965. But to say: 'We now work in 89 countries', however true it might be, and couple the statement with global or national statistics, was misleading. The few thousand pounds spent in many countries, on a clinic extension here, a consignment of high-protein food there, the salary of an agriculturalist in some mission outpost, was negligible against mass poverty.

On any physical scale above that of a particular individual, family or small community, it had to be clear to the thoughtful mind that a typical Oxfam grant could exert no conceivable influence on the problem of poverty. For those it helped, it might represent – as Bernard Llewellyn pointed out – 'the most important thing that ever happened in their lives', and on that basis alone was absolutely justifiable. But increasingly there grew up a school of thought for whom helping a handful in an ocean of need provided an inadequate sense of reward, whose unhappiness with the modesty of the Oxfam aid achievement led them in new directions.

As early as November 1962, Peter Burns, a young writer working with Richard Exley, put up to Kirkley a set of radical proposals. Burns quoted Aldous Huxley on the threat posed by world hunger: '"We will go through poverty to social unrest, through chaos to dictatorship",' continuing apocalyptically: 'In 40 years our civilisation could be usurped. I believe that these prophecies are *felt*, but not generally understood. Their significance has not penetrated deeply enough for people to take the steps that must be taken now – whilst there is still time.'

Burns' idea was that Oxfam should step up its role as a pressure group and a moulder of public opinion. He even suggested that the current publicity and fundraising style might be having a damaging effect: 'It is not enough to ask people to adopt a herd of buffaloes. It is possible, in fact, that this last tactic may lull people into a false sense of security by making them feel that the adoption of a project will, in itself, solve the problem of world hunger.' Burns wanted extraordinary pressure to be put on the British government. He envisaged a petition with a million signatures, and a delegation of 'respected minds' calling on the Prime Minister. 'I further suggest that Oxfam should present its case for world action directly to the United Nations.'

As Burns well knew, this kind of action would propel Oxfam further into the jaws of controversy than it had previously ventured. It would antagonise certain political and religious leaders and excite accusation of engagement in politics. 'I feel', he said, 'that Oxfam must be prepared to enter into such a controversy. The war against world hunger is, after all, a political war. It must be fought on that level.'

Burns' ideas were discussed at a special Executive Meeting on the future of Oxfam held over the course of two days in January 1963. The meeting, after long discussion, 'accepted in principle that propagandist activity is a function of Oxfam'. But this consensus was reached at a time when the Charity Commissioners were hovering menacingly over Oxfam's charitable status and any such public action as Burns suggested was put under wraps until times improved. As a start in building 'political' support, Kirkley despatched Burns to work in London as Oxfam's first lobbyist. He developed useful contacts in both Houses of Parliament, as well as in the Trades Unions and the Co-operative Movements.

As the 1960s progressed, Oxfam put increasing stress on the role of educating people about world poverty, but without de-emphasising its aid programme. The idea that Oxfam was one of the standard bearers of a new movement – inheritors of a fading CND, a philosophical catchment area for 1960s' energy and idealism – continued to appeal. Overseas aid was popular, and – more important – 'with-it'. In 1964, a youth department was set up as an extension of education work. The idea was to capture young people's enthusiasm outside the confines of school and the classroom project.

David Moore, who built up 'Young Oxfam', had an infectious sense of fun, and he prompted Young Oxfam groups to go in for all sorts of stunts and record-breaks – non-stop knitting, distance hikes, dance-ins – for which they obtained sponsorship from parents and friends. By 1966 there were over 100 'Young Oxfam' groups, a 15,000 circulation 'Young Oxfam Bulletin' – *YOB* – a name calculated to rile conservatives, and a series on Radio Luxembourg. And there was an epidemic of marathon walks.

CND had established the long-distance march as a form of popular political statement. Oxfam's version was an altogether softer vehicle, primarily an enjoyable outing with a social purpose. From Oxfam's point of view sponsored walks had many attractions, not least their high rate of return. David Moore and the regional organisers expended energy on logistics – police, wardens, refreshments, first aid posts – but the young people themselves obtained their sponsors and raised the money. In 1966, sponsored walks brought in £50,000; in 1967 a Food Trek in relays around the country raised nearly £100,000.

But here too controversy struck. A girl lost her life in Newcastle United Football Stadium when a crowd of 12,000 marchers surged against the gate. After this, mass starts and appearances by pop stars were banned. Worries about safety turned walks into less free-wheeling affairs. In April 1967, 500 Young Oxfamers pushing prams from Tolworth to Brighton were stopped by the police because of the nuisance they were causing to traffic. Nick Cauldwell, 18, the organiser told the press: 'This has completely dampened our efforts.' Dampened or otherwise, the surge of youthful enthusiasm for Oxfam's cause continued on throughout the decade.

In July 1966, 200 Young Oxfamers, kitted out in badges which read 'Make Love, not War', met up in an Oxfordshire School for their second annual discussion week. The mood was distinctly militant. Trevor Huddleston, then Bishop of Masasi in Tanzania, was the principal guest speaker. He delivered a slashing attack on the West's patronising attitude towards the developing countries and received an ovation for demanding justice for the world's have-nots.

Like some of their elders in the Oxfam ranks, the mismatch between the scale of Oxfam's aid programme and the problem of world poverty was bothering the Young Oxfam activists. They passed a resolution condemning the government's threat to cut back by 10 per cent on overseas aid: any such cutback would nullify at a stroke the programmes – gauged in financial terms – of all the agencies together. There were calls for Oxfam to become a political pressure group, a rallying-point for radical opinion on international justice and peace.

The debate about the weight Oxfam should give to public information and education as opposed to overseas aid was to rumble on for many years. Indeed, it has never died down, merely evolved. And the key question – how much pressure can a voluntary agency exert within the political arena without jeopardising its charitable status – will always remain open to revised adjudication. It, too, is subject to the evolution of attitudes in society at large.

In 1966, these issues had not yet reached boiling point. That happened a few years later, when the conundrum of education v. aid reached its most dramatic expression at the hands of the then Deputy Director, the Reverend Nicolas Stacey.

6

ACTS OF GOD AND ACTS OF MAN

Earthquake, wind, flood, fire, war, pestilence, drought, famine: whatever else the starving child of the 1960s might symbolise, to most people it meant catastrophe, disaster. Oxfam was seen as a fire brigade for dousing distress overseas, 'always ready,' in the words of Richard Dimbleby's 1961 radio appeal, 'day and night, to send immediate help to any danger point'. Emergency relief, Oxfam's genesis, has always been the activity for which it is best known.

Kirkley – at the Hungarian border, in the Congo – had built up a reputation for responding fast to crisis whether of the natural calamity or man-made variety. The emergency relief role was integral to the organisation's psyche and programme as well as its image in the public mind. As Oxfam grew and necessarily became more bureaucratic, financial management and grant-screening procedures had special circuits built in to safeguard the treasured flexibility, which permitted speedy reaction to disasters. Planning for the unplannable was a part of the Oxfam repertoire.

Every month, a number of small grants were made to help house, feed, or tend victims of floods, crop losses, blights, epidemics, and other localised disasters in faraway places. The aid-giving machinery, originally supply-driven by the concern at home to send help overseas, gradually became more demand-driven from the field as the Field Directorate became established. Oxfam became increasingly better known as an instant source of help to mission outposts suddenly confronted with drought, monsoon floods, or an influx of refugees in their parish. The grants list, issued annually, enumerated these inconspicuous emergency actions: 'Congo: medical programme for people who left their villages following rebel activities, £2,000'; 'Brazil: stoves, mattresses and roofing materials for flood victims in Recife, £5,165'; 'Laos: to purchase corned beef after crops destroyed, £1,000'; 'Uganda: food and blankets after earthquake, £62.'

In the case of major disasters, special initiatives were taken: for the Algerian refugees; the victims of the 1960 earthquake in Agadir,

Morocco; earthquakes in Iran, Turkey (1966), and Sicily (1968); refugees fleeing Vietnam and Tibet; war in the Middle East (1967); drought in many parts of Africa. Besides any other consideration, responding to major disasters was a matter of organisational credibility, whatever the new emphasis on development. Disasters were also a time for emotive fundraising appeals. Money thus raised could be used among the victims not only for immediate relief but for longer-term purposes – schemes which built a better future.

Britain's response to major calamities in remote places was transformed by the media revolution. In the 1960s, the television camera became part of the dynamics of disaster relief. For the first time, people in the West were confronted with images in their homes of other peoples, many in unfamiliar settings, undergoing traumatic crisis right before their eyes. The effect on the viewing public was an outpouring of compassion in the form of cash donations for disaster relief, and demands that the government rush to give aid. In the capacity of angels of mercy, the charities were part of the news event, both as purveyors of help and as anguished critics of the sluggish nature of officialdom's response.

A less fortunate aspect of the media's growing influence was the tendency of charitable emissaries to rush to a scene of devastation and compete for publicity – and the funds it produced – while doing things of dubious usefulness on the ground. Although the horror stories about diversion, chaos, and wasted aid – 'relief goods piled on docksides' – were often exaggerated, there was amateurishness and inefficiency. The government and Charity Commissioners had an uphill battle trying to persuade Britain's overseas aid agencies to co-operate with one another, but their efforts did bear some fruit. In 1963, in the wake of the Skopje earthquake in Yugoslavia, a Disasters Emergency Committee (DEC) was formed consisting of the five main agencies: the British Red Cross Society, Christian Aid, Oxfam, Save the Children Fund, and War on Want.

In the past, the charities had run their own appeals at disaster times; the argument in favour of competition was that the total amount of money raised by several appeals must be larger than the amount from one single joint one. But television's new importance changed things. Although commercial advertising for charitable causes was not allowed, the TV authorities were prepared, for a major disaster, to run a peaktime appeal for the victims. What they would not do was to run several different appeals or give one charity preferential treatment. It was therefore agreed that, in future, the five agencies would mount joint DEC disaster appeals and split the proceeds. They were pleased to co-operate thus far; hopes that collaboration would extend to joint field operations mostly proved stillborn. They tried to avoid overlap, but all wanted to stay within their own mandate, help their own constituency, use their own partner network on the ground.

In the mid-1960s, two influences were pushing Oxfam towards a more operational role in disaster situations. One was a supply-led impulse, in the form of the large sums of money produced by DEC appeals: the first, in the wake of a 1966 earthquake in Turkey, raised £495,662. Even split five ways, this was a considerable sum by the standards of the time. The other was Oxfam's desire to develop a more active disaster response than shipping goods into the maelstrom of relief or making cash grants to the local Red Cross or Crescent Society. A case, it was felt, could be made for an exception to Oxfam's usual rule not to become operational.

After the earthquake at Skopje in 1963, Oxfam came to an arrangement with a team of Bristol Civil Defence volunteers. They were set up as a disaster-ready, stand-by team, able to set off for the scene at a moment's notice. Oxfam provided three Landrovers and other emergency equipment, while Civil Defence paid for uniforms and training costs. Oxfam would pay the team's travel and living expenses to and at the disaster site. The 22-member team went on training week-ends in the Welsh mountains, practised first aid, emergency feeding, and sharpened up their rescue skills.

The team was eventually called into use in 1966, in the aftermath of a Turkish earthquake. Within 48 hours of its departure from Bristol, the team had set up a feeding station and was giving out 2,000 meals a day. Some of the Bristol volunteers performed a similar exercise after the 1968 Sicilian earthquake. But shortly after this, Oxfam withdrew its backing. The Landrovers were costly items to keep sitting around, and since air freight would be inordinately expensive, they could not be sent to a disaster further afield than Europe. Oxfam had also learned that a Civil Defence team from Britain could not perform more usefully or cheaply than volunteers recruited on the spot. This was not the first nor the last Oxfam emergency relief experiment to merit an entry in the 'lessons learnt' disasters ledger.

In 1965, India suffered a failure of the monsoon rains. The drought, one of the worst of the century, covered a large belt of central and southern India. Crop damage was extensive and, by early 1966, there was acute food shortage in a number of states including Rajasthan, Maharashtra, and Mysore.

At this time, before the 'green revolution' had transformed the output of its grain harvest, India was struggling to overtake its annual increase in population with a corresponding increase in food production. The year 1964-65 had set a record in foodstuff production of 88 million tons; but even so, India had imported six million tons of grain from the US on the concessionary terms laid down by US Public Law 480. In late 1965, President Johnson announced a stepping-up of exports over the next few months, and efforts were set in motion to increase Indian port capacity to handle the forthcoming armada of grain shipments.

In 1966, the monsoon failed again. This time the drought was less widespread but particularly intense in the two north-eastern states of Bihar and Uttar Pradesh. Bihar, one of the poorest, most densely populated, and worst administered states in India, was the most vulnerable. Nine-tenths of the 53 million inhabitants lived entirely from the land, and more than a quarter were landless and without reserves of any kind. Every year in Bihar was a food shortage year. Less than 7 per cent of the land was irrigated and therefore shielded from the impact of a bad monsoon. From June onwards when the rains should have come, the sun beat down relentlessly. The autumn crop produced next to nothing. By now the ground in the south was too hard to be turned by the farmers' wooden ploughshares and in extensive areas the spring crop was not sown. By October, famine began to threaten.

In November 1966, Mrs. Gandhi toured Bihar and Uttar Pradesh in response to an outcry in the Indian press about the failure of the Bihar authorities to respond to the crisis. The first reports of death from starvation – 13 were admitted – coincided with Mrs. Gandhi's visit. According to *The Hindu*, 48 million people in Bihar were affected by shortages of food, fodder, and water. There were stories of villagers eating grass, giving away their children, and committing suicide. Oxfam's Field Director, Jim Howard, wrote from Bihar in the same month: 'It is quite clear to me that the wolf is through the door and we are faced with a massive disaster. The failure of the rice crop is 85-95 per cent. Prices are up 300 per cent. In some of the villages, groups of people are already prostrate with starvation.' He argued that Oxfam's usual rule about not becoming operational on the ground was inappropriate and should be ignored. Kirkley agreed.

Jim Howard, the third Field Director to be appointed by Oxfam, had set off for India in January 1965. A water engineer by training and a Quaker by conviction, he had already spent from 1956 to 1960 in India working in rural development with the Friends' Service Council. For Jim Howard, the opportunity to go back to India for Oxfam came simply as a calling. This rough-hewn figure, big-hearted and gifted with a passionate eloquence, epitomised the Oxfam spirit at its best. Howard threw his energy into the unfolding tragedy in Bihar, and set up an operation based in Patna, the state capital. This quickly developed into by far the largest relief programme Oxfam had ever contemplated.

In India, the word 'famine' has special connotations. According to the 100-year-old Famine Code, a state declaring famine took upon itself responsibility for feeding the victims, remitted all land taxes, suspended credit repayments, and gave extra power to magistrates and district commissioners to carry out relief. The declaration also entitled a state to be given extra food grains from the national stocks. 'Famine' is thus a sensitive issue in India, and whether true famine exists or not can become a matter of contention between central and state governments. Although a famine was not declared in Bihar in late 1966, government relief efforts were dramatically stepped up after Mrs. Gandhi's tour.

A Bihar Relief Committee was set up under J.P. Narayan, a celebrated Gandhian and Indian elder statesmen. The authorities creaked into action, setting up 150,000 'fair-price' food ration shops, one for every four villages, in the worst-hit areas. Public works were established; to help solve the drinking water problem, a crash programme of borehole drilling and well-digging was instituted. With their wages, victims of the drought were – at least theoretically – able to buy a ration of 8oz of food grains a day.

With his engineering background, Howard had already fixed upon village water supplies as a main plank of Oxfam's general programme of aid to India. From the small network of water projects already helped by Oxfam, Howard sought to redeploy water-well specialists from elsewhere. John Macleod, a Scottish missionary in Jalna, Maharashtra, brought in his driller and the rig – a Halco Tiger – already provided by Oxfam. Halco Tigers became quite a feature of Bihar famine relief; Oxfam ordered two others, one on behalf of the Vatican; UNICEF air-lifted in another nine. But these were high-speed percussion machines for hard rock; much of Bihar's geological terrain was soft, and shallow wells were as important. Over the crisis period, half a million shallow wells were dug and 10,000 old wells deepened.

Howard's November visit to the South Bihari hinterland made him deeply concerned about the state of the children. Children's bodies are a barometer of scarcity, showing nutritional stress long before those of adults, and becoming extra susceptible to infection. At that time, the instinctive reaction to the predicament of the hungry child was high-protein foods, especially milk. So Howard cabled Oxford for milk, and Oxfam determined to send him as much milk as possible.

The British government was asked for help, not with purchase but with shipment. In December 1966, the Royal Navy loaded 300 tons of dried milk on board the *Hebe*, displacing military equipment to do so. The *Hebe* docked in the southern Indian port of Cochin on 31 December, and a special milk-train left for Patna. A young British VSO called Simpson, temporarily commandeered by Howard, was put on board to fend off pilferers for the 15 days of its journey and delivered all 12,000 bags of powdered milk miraculously intact. Howard wrote: 'If you could see the truckloads of milk arriving from the station you and all of Oxfam would feel as grateful and as pleased as we are. Now comes the task of feeding it into the right mouths.'

By this time, an assistant Field Director, Bert Stringer, and four Oxfam volunteers had arrived from Britain. The Bihar Relief Committee was planning a feeding programme through the state's 25,000 elementary schools, based on grain provided by the US organisation, CARE. Oxfam offered its milk as a supplement. Another 300 tons of British milk was soon in the pipeline. Difficulties in finding further supplies ended when Community Aid Abroad, Oxfam's sister organisation in Australia, tracked down 1,100 tons and shipped it to Calcutta. Within weeks, the Oxfam-organised part of the programme was feeding 90,000 children in Gaya, one of the worst-hit districts. The volunteers supervised stocks and distribution.

Meanwhile, the wife of a British businessman in India, Tigger Stack, had been searching the country for supplies of locally-manufactured high-protein foods. Stack had spent most of her life in India, moving in the privileged circles of post-Raj society. She believed that it was possible to harness the social conscience of Indian businessmen and professional people through a channel such as Oxfam, and had offered her assistance at any time it might be useful. As crisis loomed in Bihar, Jim Howard decided to take up her offer.

Nutritional thinking of the time – later modified by the recognition that calories mattered more – was then heavily focused on protein deficiency as the root cause of child malnutrition. In India, as in other countries where dairy produce was a luxury commodity, Food Technology Institutes had been experimenting with mixes of local pulses and legumes for manufacture as a 'tonic' children's food. Existing contacts with the Central Food Technological Research Institute in Mysore led Howard to pin his trust in 'Multi-purpose food', a bran-like substance with a 46 per cent protein content, made of peanut and chick-pea flour with added vitamins and minerals.

MPF had been manufactured in India for some years but only in a small quantity. For the emergency, production needed to be dramatically increased. Tigger Stack visited factories in Mysore, West Bengal, and Sitapur, both closer to Bihar. A gracious and persistent operator, Stack used her contacts in government and business circles to unblock logjams and confer an aura of VIP status to speed things along. She obtained scarce peanut flour for the food factories so that they could raise their output; she borrowed vehicles and sent the MPF up to Bihar at minimal cost. The first loads arrived in December 1966, and by mid-January, deals were made for 50 tons a month and trucks were arriving regularly.

The scale of need remained severe. In January 1967, Howard reported: 'I cannot find the words to describe the misery and starvation I have seen. It staggers me that so many people in Patna are so unaware, so misinformed, accept so casually the authorities' inertia.' Everyone was preoccupied by the general election, due in February. In Patna itself, markets were bursting with fruit and vegetables. But 20 miles to the south, the bright green of irrigated paddy field gave way to a brown, concrete-hard wasteland. In the villages, hunger was becoming daily more visible.

The spring wheat crop, as expected, failed throughout most of the state. On 18 April 1967, the government of Bihar finally declared that a state of famine existed in seven districts, including Gaya. This was the first time since Independence in 1947 that any state had invoked the Famine Code. Against opposition from central government – from whom 400,000 tons of food a month were sought – the authorities had assumed responsibility for feeding 13 million people, one quarter of the state population. No-one believed that the administrative or distribution system could manage such a load.

As the heat of the pre-monsoon season in India built up and many remaining streams and wells went dry, observers believed that a calamity of Biblical proportions was in the offing. But somehow, the threatened calamity passed by. Deaths from starvation, and far more deaths from epidemics of smallpox and all the infections to which the weak and starving are prone, did occur; the full mortality toll probably reached a few thousand, an unexceptional hot season figure in one of India's poorest states.

Where did the Bihar famine go? Disaster was kept at bay mainly by the massive scale of food imports from North America and Australia. The US sent nine million tons of wheat, one quarter of the annual US crop, with ships docking at the rate of three a day. And that wheat, against all the odds, travelled the full length of the relief pipeline. For all its slow-moving start, the Government of Bihar managed to make the relief machinery – public works and ration shops – function adequately. The supporting agencies played a valuable part; but in the end it was the Biharis themselves who saved their people from mass starvation.

At the peak of the relief effort, five million children were being fed daily, 450,000 with a meal that included Oxfam milk and nutrition supplements. A correspondent for the *Birmingham Post* wrote: 'Famine in Bihar has brought into being a relief operation of unparalleled magnitude and complexity. Oxfam crops up all over the place – I saw its ration-cards in a village of half a dozen huts.' An ITV documentary, 'Famine', which showed the scheme at work, produced £32,000 in donations and 10,000 letters to Oxfam. Between December 1966 and November 1967, Oxfam spent £345,500 on drinking water supplies and child feeding. Howard and his team were justifiably proud of their effort.

The distressing feature of the relief programme was that there was more milk to drink in Bihar in 1967, more healthy children, and more people vaccinated against disease, than there had ever been in the past. In a report prepared at Mrs. Gandhi's request, her adviser, George Verghese, wrote with only slight exaggeration: 'In a normal year, these people hover on the breadline. They are beyond the pale, nobody's concern, they starve. In a famine year, they eat. Their health is better and the children are gaining weight. For them this is a year of great blessing. This was the deep irony, the grim tragedy of the situation.'

In July 1967, after a slow start, the monsoon broke and a new round of planting – the first for a year in parts of Bihar – began. The rains were good. Within three months, crops were being harvested and feeding centres closed. The next year, 1968, produced a bumper crop. The new hybrid seeds of the 'green revolution' were gradually transforming India's food deficit problem and helping to fill the national granary, even though poverty and malnutrition remained.

India has not since faced drought without sufficient grain in hand to avoid mass imports from elsewhere. Bihar 1966-67 was a historic landmark. Verghese wrote: 'The famine has been a revelation, a trial, a shame; but also an opportunity and an awakening.' It had aroused the conscience of many better-off Indians and government officials and given a new impetus to efforts to conquer child malnutrition.

For Oxfam, the deep involvement in Bihar famine relief was also a turning-point. It opened a new chapter in the evolution of its aid, both to the sub-continent and elsewhere.

In April 1967, just as the Bihar famine was reaching its climax, Oxfam launched one of its largest campaigns to date. Posters on 9,000 hoardings ambiguously declared: 'Help Oxfam STOP feeding hungry children' and 'Oxfam HATES hungry children'. This was Oxfam's most brazen effort to use mass advertising to put across the message that – with hunger as with disease – prevention is better than cure. The campaign was entitled 'Food for Tomorrow' and attracted much attention.

1967 was Oxfam's 25th year. The highlight of Anniversary celebrations was a National Hunger Lunch in the Banqueting Hall in Whitehall, with Reg Prentice, the new Minister of Overseas Development, as chief guest. Prentice was committed to raising Britain's level of overseas aid, which – with economic problems at home – had lost popularity with the Wilson government since the 1964 election.

Prentice told his audience that he wanted to be pressured by demands that Britain give more overseas aid. 'The kind of effort we can put into helping development throughout the world is going to depend on public opinion, and this government and governments of the future ought to be nagged and bullied by those who care strongly about these things.' This was music to the Oxfam ear. 'I want to live in a world where Ministers of Overseas Development are considered more important than Ministers of Defence.' Amidst cheers, the Minister of Defence, Dennis Healey, nodded agreement. The heyday of overseas aid as a political issue might be waning, but it still packed some moral and political punch.

Meanwhile in Bihar, Oxfam was entertaining David Frost. Frost, approached to front the pre-Christmas 25th Anniversary appeal, and to do it from the field, accepted enthusiastically. He doled out milk into small brass cans held by lines of Indian children. He was photographed in the rain to show joy that the drought had broken. He wrote: 'I shall never forget some of the scenes – the mother appealing for more food as her child lay dying on her breast, the old men waiting all day for a children's emergency feeding to end, in the hope that there might be something left over for them.' On 26 November, Frost launched the campaign in London. The appeal was a success. For the first time, in 1967-68, Oxfam raised over £3 million.

As the 25th year of Oxfam's existence gave way to the 26th, another emergency was building. This was no natural calamity of drought and crops withering in the earth, but a bloody and man-made affair: the Nigerian Civil War.

The end of British rule in large chunks of Africa left a political legacy with many in-built flaws. To suit their imperial ambitions and adminis-trative convenience, the colonisers had knitted together in unitary states peoples of widely different cultures who, left to their own devices, found the national flag and national anthem less compelling than their many ancient rivalries.

One of the national patchworks with poorly-sewn seams was the Federal Republic of Nigeria. By the historical accident of British rule, and because Lord Lugard had favoured the common destiny of the desert kingdoms of the Moslem North with those of the Christianised farmers and traders of the South, Nigeria came to independence in 1960 as one gigantic country. Britain, the creator, and nationalist Nigerians, the inheritors, were proud of their achievement. But the varnish of unity quickly began to crack.

A military coup in 1966 brought to power a group dominated by Easterners, the Ibos. A backlash of violent reprisal led to another coup, and a young Northerner, General Yakubu Gowon, took over. Continuing massacres of Ibos living in the North profoundly scarred the collective Ibo consciousness. While Gowon tried to exert control and redesign the federal structure, Ibo from all parts of Nigeria began to converge on their homeland, swelling the population by one-third, to around 12 million. In May 1967, Colonel Odumegwu Ojukwu, Military Governor of the Eastern Region, announced the secession of the independent Republic of Biafra. Biafra happened to contain Nigeria's oilfields. In July, the Federal forces of General Gowon attacked.

When the fighting began, the problem was seen by the outside world as a tribal rebellion of concern only to Nigeria. But as the months went by and Colonel Ojukwu's Biafran troops continued to hold out, world opinion and the ex-colonial powers began to line up on either side of a bitter civil war. At stake was the ability of the largest independent African country to resist the forces of disintegration – forces which, as the Congo had demonstrated, were explosive elsewhere. Early in 1968, however, Tanzania and Zambia accepted the claim to Biafran self-determination. Their recognition of the breakaway state was in breach of continent-wide agreement to uphold pre-independence borders, and it transformed the Biafran adventure into an issue of international significance. This was enhanced by international involvement in the oilfields.

Britain, as the ex-coloniser, the head of the Commonwealth, and a key Nigerian trading partner, was bound to support the Federal side. But domestic opinion – and these were the turbulent 60s, with the Vietnam war at its height and student campuses in turmoil – took the underdog's side. There was much sympathy for the Ibo and the massacres they had endured: an industrious, go-ahead Christian people had been put to a savage Moslem sword. The Wilson government, supplying arms to the Federal side, was painted as the partisan supporter of formalised brutality. In vain did Michael Stewart, the Foreign Secretary, point to international backing in the Organisation of African Unity (OAU), and suggest that to cancel arms agreements with a Commonwealth ally in their hour of need would amount to active support for the rebel group and the abandonment of British commitment to African nationalism.

General Gowon, a self-effacing Christian, young and Sandhurst-trained, was far from the ogre his critics implied. To him, the principle of Federal unity was as important as it had been to Abraham Lincoln. Ojukwu was as uncompromising. Sovereignty for a separate Ibo-dominated state was, he claimed, vital for the very survival of his traumatised people. Gowon claimed that pacification and integration, not Ibo extermination, were his aims. Ojukwu told the Biafrans that the Federal Army was out to kill every one of them. They, and much of the world, believed him.

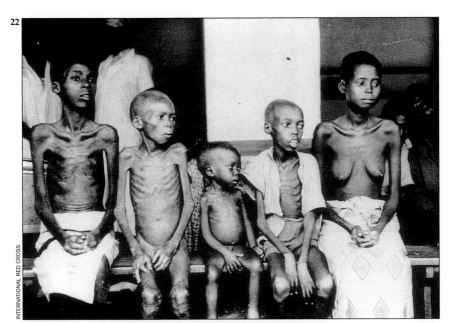

INTERNATIONAL RED CROSS

22 *The photo that launched the earliest outpouring of British generosity towards people in newly-independent Africa: Congo 1960, the first famine horror.*

OXFAM ARCHIVE

23 *Early grants (1956) to South Africa were for a cup of classroom milk for black children suffering from the effects of a new Bantu Education Act.*

COI/BECHUANALAND INFORMATION SERVICES

24 *Botswana 1963: Oxfam's first major involvement with comprehensive agricultural development. 'Progressive farmers' took to the tractor.*

SYDNEY ROSE

25 *Oxfam's 'Hunger £Million' campaign of 1963: on the crest of a wave of popular support for its cause, scores of celebrities gave their support. Acker Bilk and Frankie Vaughan.*

JOHN HOPKINS

26 *The launch of the Hunger £Million campaign in Trafalgar Square: Susannah York collects pound notes on the tip of an umbrella.*

27 *The picture of the Beatles, used to good effect by the* Daily Mail, *Hunger £Million sponsor, made great impact.*

28 *Susan Hampshire, Rupert Davies, Jon Pertwee, with heart and voice: a 'carol service with the stars'.*

29 *Sunday night in Trafalgar Square: the 'carol service with the stars' on 22 December 1963, was front-page* Daily Mail *lead story.*

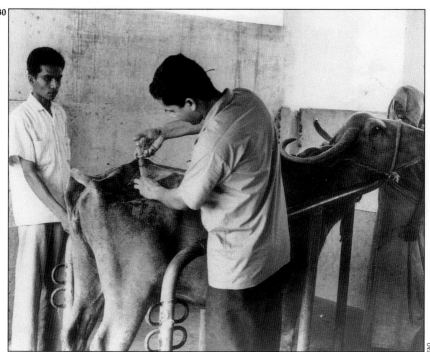

30 *Anand Dairy Co-operative, Gujerat, India: one of the 'Big Four' Freedom from Hunger projects supported by Oxfam.*

31 *The Family Box - to be put on the table at meals - was the mainstay of the Oxfam campaign for 1964.*

32 *By 1964, Oxfam had 20 local offices and an active grassroots support network. Delivering the Family Box on horseback.*

33 *Gifts on display by Oxfam helpers at a Christmas Gift Fair in Yorkshire, 1964.*

34 *Rev. Austen Williams blesses gifts donated to Oxfam's 1964 appeal on the steps of St. Martin-in-the-Fields.*

35 *Joe Mitty, Manager of Oxfam Giftshops from 1949 until 1971 and an architect of the charity giftshop idea, had a keen eye for items of value.*

36 *The heyday of Young Oxfam and the sponsored walk. In 1967, a 'food trek' all over Britain brought in £100,000.*

37 *Oxfam was one of the charities to pioneer support for family planning overseas. By 1970, the Christian Medical Association of India had received £58,000 for IUD insertions.*

38 *The Halco Tiger drilling rig on emergency duty by night in villages in Bihar, during the drought of 1966-67.*

OXFAM

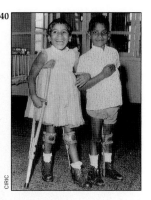

CIRIC

40 *Polio victims at the St. Antony's Home, Bombay. Oxfam Field Directors insisted on the value of social welfare in spite of the new fashion for 'development'.*

39 *Bihar drought: 300 tons of Oxfam milk, arrive at Cochin in December 1966. Jim Howard second from left and colleagues on the dock.*

AB PHOTOGRAPHY

41 *David Frost visits the slums in Delhi to bring his own eye-witness account to the appeal for Oxfam's 25th anniversary, 1967.*

42 *A 25th anniversary event at the Whitehall Banqueting Hall in London. The theme: 'Food for Tomorrow'. Key speaker was Reg Prentice, Minister for Overseas Aid.*

43 *The Park Lane Giftshop: by the late 1960s, more than 50 Oxfam Shops were operating in temporary premises, paving the way for the charity shop bonanza of the 1970s.*

This polarity of views affected not only the conduct of the war and every effort made to negotiate a peace; it also ensnared every effort to bring relief to its victims.

In early 1967, when Ibo people from the North had been fleeing homewards to find sanctuary, Oxfam had given help to them through the Irish Holy Ghost Fathers in the Eastern Region. After the war began in earnest, several trucks were provided to the Nigerian Red Cross for medical relief. Tim Brierly, Field Director for the vast area of West and Equatorial Africa, had set up an office in Lagos in early 1966. Before this, through its Catholic relief contacts, Oxfam had had a relationship with the missions in eastern Nigeria, one of the most Christianised parts of Africa. Some Biafran emergency grants went directly to the Irish Fathers inside the embattled territory, where increasing numbers of people were retreating as the fronts hemmed them in.

However, Brierly was careful to ensure that a near equal amount of Oxfam aid was channelled to areas re-taken by the Federal Army, especially through the National Relief Committee, a co-ordinating body he helped to set up. As an ex-Colonial Officer, and having served in the Congo during the famine crisis, Brierly was sensitive to the political ebb and flow. He made every effort to emphasise 'help to victims on both sides of the conflict', in keeping with the Oxfam mandate to give aid according to need, without political or religious consideration. By February 1968, £59,300 had been spent.

At this stage Oxfam's aid to Nigerian civil war victims reflected the careful attempt at political neutrality of the efforts made at the international level. Under the terms of the UN charter, no UN agency can meddle in the affairs of a member state by providing relief to those in rebellion against it (although, over time, the humanitarian agencies – UNHCR, UNICEF, and the World Food Programme – have established a *de facto* right to do so). Under the circumstances, the International Committee of the Red Cross (ICRC) was accepted as a neutral umbrella for all UN, government, and Red Cross aid to 'Nigerians on both sides of the war'. With Federal agreement, ICRC teams were sent to Biafra, and a relief airlift was organised from the (Spanish) offshore island of Fernando Po.

As the Federal forces tightened their noose around the enclave in March and April 1968, the disruption to farming and market life, the swollen numbers of people in a compressed area, and the blockade by land and sea, began to put pressure on the food supply. People were short of the protein foods – stockfish, meat, and legume sauces – which normally accompanied their starchy yam and cassava diet.

The Irish Fathers, distressed by the increasingly malnourished state of their parishioners, took a radical step: they began to airlift relief goods into Biafra along with the rebels' arms supplies. Through Caritas International, the Vatican relief organisation, an agreement was made with Ojukwu's gun-runner, Captain 'Hank' Wharton, to carry mercy cargoes on his missions from Lisbon and the Portuguese island of Sao Tome. The ICRC had promised General Gowon to keep their air route separate from that used for Biafra's arms supplies. The churches felt under no such obligation. Nor were they internationally criticised for their action. On the contrary. The key organiser, Irish Father Tony Byrne, was known as 'the Green Pimpernel'. In March 1968, Oxfam made a first £10,000 grant for goods to go in on the Wharton/Caritas run.

On 21 May 1968, Port Harcourt fell to the Federal forces. This meant that Biafra had lost the oilfields; also its link with the sea, and the airport used for bringing in arms and relief supplies. Surrender looked a matter of weeks away. Peace negotiations under OAU auspices began in Kampala, while the Federal forces waited, poised for a final assault. The hope was that Ojukwu would agree to withdraw the claim for sovereignty so as to avoid the bloodshed and the bitter legacy a conquest would entail. To put pressure on Ojukwu to come to terms, Gowon peremptorily withdrew permission for the ICRC airlift. The blockade was tightened.

But Ojukwu had no intention of coming to terms. His emissary to Kampala, Biafran Chief Justice Sir Louis Mbanefo, had no brief to compromise the sovereignty issue. As the talks dragged on into early June with neither side willing to shift, not only did the prospects of a cease-fire dwindle. The ICRC-led relief operation also became deadlocked. Gowon would not accept an airlift through Federal airspace from islands outside his jurisdiction. Ojukwu would not hear of a land corridor from Federal territory – the only sensible route for the necessary 200 tons a day – under ICRC supervision. With the relief pipeline all but cut off, conditions in the rebel-held area drastically deteriorated.

Two months back in *Oxfam News*, Dame Margery Perham, a famous authority on the area and a member of Oxfam's Africa Committee, had written about 'Nigeria's Agony'. 'A terrible and bloody war is going on. Why do we hear little or nothing about it in the Press or on the radio?' She pleaded for aid for the victims. 'But the need must be known. The strange silence in Britain about this war must be broken.'

In June 1968, the silence was indeed broken. It was broken with the force of a thunderclap. First in the *Sun*, then elsewhere, came the horror exposures of starving Biafran children. On 12 June, the ITN *News at Ten* carried a film to tug a thousand heartstrings, unleash a thousand angry voices, launch a thousand mercy ships. The statistic of 3,000 child deaths a day was widely quoted. The words 'genocide' and 'extermination' were used to describe the prospect of death by slaughter, or death by starvation, imminently facing the Ibo people. Passions in Britain began to run high. The clamour to save the Biafrans became deafening.

What was not immediately obvious was that Ojukwu was playing the 'starvation card' in a desperate gamble to stave off defeat. The version of the Biafran situation which burst so spectacularly upon the world in mid-1968 was put out by a European public relations firm hired by Ojukwu to present the Biafran case in its most heartrending light. While there certainly was great suffering and dying in the enclave, the more sensational – and unverifiable – claims about death rates and atrocities were being made by the entirely partisan, and by journalists and missionaries passionately persuaded in their cause. Ojukwu, who understood the power of the press, wanted to exert pressure via public opinion on the British and other governments to stop the supply of arms to the Federal side. He still hoped to change the international – and thus the military – tide in his favour.

The relief agencies were unscrupulously, and unwittingly, to be used as Biafra's allies and spokesmen. In their humanitarian zeal and naivety, many took on trust the Biafran claims of 'genocide' and the 'thousands dying daily'; they accepted British complicity in an act of mass criminality; they fell for it, hook, line and sinker.

On 6 May 1968, a new Deputy Director joined Oxfam: the Reverend Nicolas Stacey. The position had been vacant since Henry Fletcher set off to revitalise Oxfam of Canada.

Stacey was a bird of brightly coloured plumage, out of the run of Oxfam's more stolid senior statesmen. He had made a national name for himself, first as a runner in the Roger Bannister class; then as Rector of Woolwich. He had tried to shake decades of solidified dust off the Church of England by a mix of showmanship and radicalism designed to regenerate its role and replenish its congregation. After a self-publicised declaration of failure, he applied for the Oxfam job, and won it from a large field of candidates.

Stacey was the new look for the 1960s generation, an energetic dazzler, a young people's leader for the aid lobby. He was well-known as a television and newspaper journalist, and soon began to use his publicity talents on behalf of Oxfam's cause of the moment: the starving children of Biafra.

Earlier, in March 1968, Tim Brierly had been home on leave from West Africa. He had attended a meeting of the Africa Committee to take part in a discussion of the war in Nigeria and how best to provide relief to the victims. Brierly had explained the Federal authorities' extreme sensitivities about aid to Biafrans, with its implicit connotations of support for Ojukwu's cause. He pointed out that there was suffering not only within the enclave, but also in parts of the 'Biafran' countryside recently taken over by Federal troops – which he had just visited.

It was agreed that Oxfam would continue to give aid on both sides, but that no publicity should be given to direct aid to Biafra. In time the rebellion would almost certainly be defeated, and Brierly believed that nothing should be done to prevent Oxfam taking part in the major post-war relief and rehabilitation effort which would be desperately needed.

In the weeks following, Oxfam and the other members of the Disasters Emergency Committee – the British Red Cross, Christian Aid, Save the Children, and War on Want – discussed whether to ask the BBC and ITV for a national television appeal for Nigeria. A decision was taken that the agencies should jointly hold back, waiting for the ICRC relief pipeline to be fully secured, and then commit the results of a joint appeal to the Red Cross-led programme.

In mid-June, when the popular press in Britain set up its clamour about starving Biafra, Oxfam threw its agreed policy line, its understandings with the other agencies, and its caution to the winds. With the pressure of '3,000 dying daily', carefully-worded statements of neutrality seemed to many Oxfam crusaders like so much foot-dragging. There was a humanitarian tiger to ride and, since its partners in the business of compassion were holding back, Oxfam would ride it alone. On 13 June, it announced that 1,000 tons of milk was being purchased for immediate shipment to Biafra, and launched an appeal for £100,000 to cover the costs. To the other DEC agencies, Oxfam's sudden assumption of the 'Saviour of Biafra' role was a breach of previous understandings.

Popular opinion – fired up by the Biafran propaganda campaign – blamed the starvation in the enclave on the Federal army and its British backing. It was hard to believe that the Biafran leader himself could be obstructing the mass import of relief foods: as the *Guardian* pointed out, it was his people who were starving. Accordingly Kirkley, in a blaze of publicity, went to Lisbon to fly into Biafra on a Wharton arms run to persuade Ojukwu to let in relief. Somehow Oxfam believed that a voluntary agency, representing nothing but a compassionate section of British opinion, might succeed where the massed ranks of governments, the OAU, the UN, the Pope, and the Red Cross establishment had so far failed.

Kirkley did manage to see Ojukwu. He took part in a meeting set up by Red Cross negotiators. No dice. No land corridor: anything coming from Federal territory, whoever brought it in, would be poisoned in

Ojukwu's view, literally or metaphorically. No mass mercy airlift. Only a vague promise about permitting the use of Biafra's last airstrip for daylight relief flights if this did not interfere with the landing of the most important cargoes: arms. The promise about daylight flights was never fulfilled.

The problem with Kirkley's mission was not only that it did not succeed; by going direct to Biafra without passing first through Lagos in the correct diplomatic fashion, he had imperilled Oxfam's relations with the Federal government by clearly identifying Oxfam with the Biafran cause. This might be good for fundraising at home, and highly popular with the anti-arms-to-Nigeria lobby. But for a voluntary agency claiming to be non-partisan it was, at best, unwise.

The pro-Biafra impression was reinforced by press activity at home. Nicolas Stacey took to the airwaves and newspaper columns in typically ebullient style and – new to the delicacies of parleying relief in situations of great sensitivity – told the world that Oxfam would fulfill its mission to save the Biafran people from starvation in ringing 'come hell or high water' tones. In early July, the Wilson administration, putting together a humanitarian mission to Nigeria under Lord Hunt to try and unblock the obstacles to aid on both sides, included representatives from the Red Cross and Save the Children, but pointedly left Oxfam out.

In Lagos, Tim Brierly found himself in a very uncomfortable situation. Oxfam's statements were making angry Nigerian headlines – 'Oxfam a hostile agency says Gowon', and 'Do-gooders we don't want'. Not only the Federal authorities but a furious British High Commission wanted to know why Oxfam was taking unilateral action in support of the rebels instead of working through the same channels – ICRC and Nigerian Red Cross – as everyone else. Brierly was extremely annoyed by Oxfam's behaviour – in breach of all agreed policy and adopted without reference to himself – and he did his best to explain to Oxford that more of this kind of public statement would jeopardise Oxfam's entire response to the civil war, not to mention his own credibility in Lagos. In vain. Ken Bennett, Director of Overseas Aid and the voice of caution within Oxfam, was unable to generate calm.

Oxfam was trying to establish its own airlift into Biafra, and was negotiating the use of a Canadian Hercules carrier. This initiative collapsed when the Federal authorities announced that planes on unauthorised missions over their airspace risked being shot down. On 5 July 1968, Oxfam publicly demanded that Harold Wilson put pressure on Gowon to have this announcement rescinded, and embarked on a new flurry of 'Britain must stop this apocalypse' publicity. From the Nigerian perspective, Oxfam was acting as if the Federal desire to defend the nation's integrity was irrelevant and the colonial sun had never set. But this was not intentional on Oxfam's part. To a protest from the Nigerian High Commissioner in London, Kirkley replied on 5 July: 'We never take political sides, and our one and only concern is to help those in greatest need.' He insisted: 'An appeal on purely humanitarian grounds ... does not involve us in political judgements on the rights and wrongs of this tragic situation.'

By this time, Kirkley had seen that a more careful tone was required. Brierly in Lagos had found his position untenable and asked to be relieved. Kirkley flatly denied to the press that 'our man in Lagos' had resigned, but Brierly's protest had registered. Kirkley did the rounds of Whitehall and Westminster, and sent Bennett to Lagos on 11 July to fence-mend. The feedback from senior British officials was salutary. From this point on, Oxfam became more circumspect in its statements and worked more consistently within the ICRC-led operation. Brierly returned to England a few weeks later, but not before receiving a carpeting from Gowon. 'Oxfam apologises', screamed the Nigerian press.

Throughout July 1968 and into August, the relief situation remained deadlocked and the hue and cry carried on while protein-deficiency disease – kwashiorkor – reached what was seen as epidemic proportions. The Biafran child, with a grotesquely swollen stomach, was becoming a metaphor for 20th century African misery. Neither Lord Hunt, nor Henry Labouisse, Executive Director of UNICEF, nor Dr. Auguste Lindt, the Swiss ex-UN High Commissioner for Refugees heading the ICRC effort, managed to put forward a plan for relief that both Gowon and Ojukwu would agree to. Meanwhile, shiploads of grain and protein foods from all over the world were arriving in the Gulf of Guinea. By August, 10,000 tons – including Oxfam's 1,000 tons of milk – was sitting, some of it perishing, on island docksides while thousands of people were starving just a few hundred miles away. To the humanitarian conscience, the situation was appalling and incomprehensible.

Abandoning the land corridor idea, Auguste Lindt began to focus once more on the airlift. While the ICRC waited in vain to gain clearance from both sides for a schedule of flights from Fernando Po, the churches, led by a Scandinavian consortium, began to build up their illegal airlift from Sao Tome. They recruited as their squadron-leader Count Carl-Gustaf von Rosen, a Swedish pilot who performed heroic feats of hazardous flying at treetop height to break the Nigerian blockade. Cargoes were landed at night on the last remaining Biafran airstrip at Uli, half-lit by flares, taking turns with arms shipments. At times the operation became a chaotic combination of zeal and daredevilry, attracting humanitarian adventurers of every kind.

The Oxfam cargo in the ship *Mitropa* was off-loaded at Fernando Po in late July for onward passage via the ICRC route. Kirkley sent his unflappable Company Secretary, Bruce Ronaldson, to see the milk safely landed and to do anything he could to speed it into Biafra. Ronaldson found a frustrated Auguste Lindt shuttling in and out of Biafra and Lagos. Except for the odd sortie, planes sat on the runway while the Federals refused to agree not to shoot them out of the air. The Biafrans continued to balk about anything coming in by day, which would expose their operations more fully and make them more vulnerable to Federal attack. Finally in early September Lindt announced that he would start the airlift, threats notwithstanding, and would personally go in the first plane.

On 4 August, Ronaldson and a relief worker, Duncan Kirkpatrick, managed to fly into Uli with the first seven-ton cargo of Oxfam milk. They travelled to Queen Elizabeth Hospital in Umuahia to meet Biafran Red Cross and UNICEF people who were setting up feeding programmes in which the Oxfam milk could play a part. Along the roadside, markets were functioning and people looked well-fed. But in the refugee camps things were very different. The condition of many children was terrible; their distended stomachs, spindly legs and red hair indicated advanced kwashiorkor. The Red Cross was mobilising teachers and professional people as helpers to run feeding schemes and child rehabilitation programmes.

By September, the two airlifts were functioning effectively and no planes had been attacked. Both the ICRC and the churches gradually increased their carrying capacity, and over the month 3,500 tons of supplies were flown in. This was little more than half the lowest estimate of need, but the death rate began to decline and the children's condition to stabilise. In October, the church airlift became regularised when the Scandinavians set up a special ecumenical umbrella organisation – Joint Church Aid – to run it. Support groups sprang up in a number of countries. Canairelief was one of these, through which Oxfam of Canada provided two Super Constellation aircraft. (Tragically, one of these crashed on the Uli runway, killing its entire crew.) Running up to 12 planes between them, the airlifts landed 200 tons of goods a night.

By this time, the prospect of an early end to the war had receded. After the failure of more peace talks, first in Addis Ababa, then in Niamey, a Federal 'final push' began. Advances were made, but Gowon's troops failed to clinch the conquest. Ojukwu's strategy for cultivating influential allies was finally paying off. In September, France took Biafra's side and started airlifting arms into Uli via Gabon and Ivory Coast. No matter how small his shrinking domain – less than 100 miles in any direction – Ojukwu was clinging on. The secession was by no means over.

While worldwide attention had been focused on the Ibo heartland, other victims of the war were – genuinely – equally in need. Already by mid-1968, much larger parts of 'Biafra' were in Federal than in Biafran hands. Although there were some incidents of atrocity, the much talked-of massacres by Federal troops had not occurred. Once reassured that they would not be butchered, villagers had re-emerged from the bush and returned to their normal rounds of yam barns and market days. But there were many in a sorry condition.

To the south and east towards Calabar, the 'Biafrans' were mostly other peoples over whom the Ibo had assumed domination. Many were pleased to be liberated – they were not 'Biafran' by choice; but the process left great disruption in its wake. The area was remote, the terrain riverine, and the destruction of bridges during the Biafran retreat had made the movement of goods and people along roads and waterways even more tortuous than usual. Representatives from aid organisations found mission hospitals full of children in a pitiful state. Close to the front, people were fleeing, hiding out and camping in the bush for days without food or water.

By August 1968, not only Sao Tome and Fernando Po but Lagos too were awash with food aid, sent by donors scrupulously sticking to 'aid to both sides'. In an effort to improve the situation in the stricken south-east, many agencies now offered to provide relief teams under the ICRC umbrella. Brierly was inhibited from visiting the area because of Oxfam's still suspect status; but through the Red Cross he gave support to a Salvation Army team, in July 1968. This was one of the earliest relief teams to reach the area.

Oxfam then recruited its own group of seven medical and relief workers. This was only the second time – the first was in Bihar – that Oxfam became operational, and the first on which the team included doctors and nurses. Led by Patrick Kemmis, an ex-colonial officer with 15 years of Nigerian experience, the team arrived in Lagos in October. It took time for them to gain permission to move out into the field.

In November, Kemmis and company set themselves up in a small town called Itu on the Cross River, three miles back from the Federal frontline. They distributed by truck ICRC and UNICEF food rations – milk, stockfish, *gari* (cassava meal), rice, beans, CSM (corn-soy-milk, the US equivalent of India's high-protein food) – to camps of refugees. Altogether, around 50,000 people were under their care. Kemmis split his medical people into two teams and supplemented them with local

Nigerian volunteers. By a system he described as 'appalling medicine – it would send shivers round all the professional bodies', they managed to treat 1,000 patients a day. 'With the numbers involved – 10,000 need urgent treatment – perfectionism isn't on. Kwashiorkor is such a rapid killer – untouched, it has 70 per cent mortality, but if caught, you have 80 per cent chance of recovery in a few days.'

The most tragic part of their work was the discovery of children hiding out along the roadside, in disused buildings or pockets near the fighting, many orphaned, some in too bad a shape to have any hope of survival. They dug many graves in their first few weeks, but thousands of children began to recover. What they initially expected – a Federal military advance which would bring crowds of starving Ibos through the lines and into their care – did not materialise. By mid-December, Kemmis reported that the worst of the emergency was over. Of the 5,000-8,000 lives at risk when they had come, he reckoned that 750 had died, 250 were still at risk, and the rest were out of danger.

Following Bruce Ronaldson's visit to Biafra in August, Oxfam also provided staff support to the Queen Elizabeth Hospital in Umuahia. Dr. Bruno Gans, a leading paediatric consultant, helped Dr. Aaron Ufekunigwe, chief of Biafran paediatric services, develop an extensive child recovery programme in schools andclinics. They also ran a measles inoculation campaign starting in December 1968 with joint support from UNICEF and Oxfam, which managed to reach 350,000 children by March 1969. The density of population in what remained of Biafra at least had one advantage: once stocks of medicines and protein foods were available, the logistics of feeding and child health monitoring were relatively straightforward.

In March 1969, a new uproar developed in the British press about Biafra, this time against Federal bombing attacks on civilians in the embattled territory. In another debate in the House of Commons, the government was once more attacked over its policy of military support to the Federal side. This policy was still almost universally condemned in the press, and treated – thanks to the Biafra propaganda machine – as if it was the major determinant of the outcome of the war.

In the run-up to the debate, the Oxfam propaganda machine, led by Stacey, was itself highly active. Speaking on behalf of the humanitarian conscience, Charles Coulson, Chairman of Oxfam, issued a public statement which effectively added Oxfam's voice to the chorus of opposition. 'What Britain – both the government of Britain and the people of Britain – must now face is that the price for a united Nigeria is likely to be millions of lives.' Still the muddled assumption persisted that the suffering in the enclave was the fault of only one of the hostile parties, and that this starvation conferred a moral superiority on the Biafran cause. Nonetheless, the government won a substantial majority. Later in the month, Harold Wilson visited Nigeria nominally in the role of peacemaker. He was welcomed by Gowon; predictably, therefore, Ojukwu snubbed him.

In spite of the doom-laden prophecies, the basic supply of harvested yam and cassava and the airlifted tonnages of protein foods held starvation in Biafra – just – at bay. The US government stepped in to help finance the stupendous costs of the airlifts, and by April 1969, 8,000 tons a month was being landed at Uli. But the situation was fragile: around the fighting lines, one million people were dependent on food relief, and within the enclave, another 1.5 million of the seven million remaining. Any break in the supply-line, and famine on the scale of mid-1968 would once again threaten.

Crisis descended on the whole operation in June. It was prompted by a new round of derring-do by the Swedish Count von Rosen, the churches' blockade-busting flier. Von Rosen put together a 'Biafran Air Force' of tiny single-engined planes and began hedge-hopping attacks on Federal aircraft on the ground. This was proof to the Federals that the humanitarians were absolutely partisan; their military commanders also became jumpier about who and what was flying around. On 5 June 1969, an ICRC plane crossing the coast just before dusk was shot down by a Nigerian fighter.

Lindt protested vigorously in Lagos and ICRC flights were suspended. Tensions had been mounting for some time between the ICRC and the Federal authorities. The latter were increasingly frustrated by their inability to bring the war to an end and they blamed the agents of humanitarianism for inhibiting their efforts to do so. A few days later Lindt was unceremoniously declared *persona non grata*. Agency representatives in Lagos were informed that, from now on, all assistance for victims of the war must be channelled through Nigerian relief organisations.

Great heat was generated in Geneva, London, New York, and elsewhere by this Federal decision. A new spate of negotiations began for land corridors, sea corridors, and daylight flights. Ojukwu, now hard-pressed, initially seemed accommodating; but however much his people were suffering, he would not accept a neutral land corridor nor flights by daylight into Uli. In September, with 8,000 tons of relief supplies still stockpiled in Fernando Po and starvation in the enclave imminent, the endless attempts at negotiation collapsed. The role of the ICRC – or anyone else – as a neutral co-ordinator of international succour acceptable to both sides was over.

This failure was devastating to the humanitarians. In spite of all their efforts, a population of several million civilians was to be starved to death in a futile sacrifice to the political intransigence of Federal and Biafran leaders. But the plain fact was that, from a military point of view, a blockade or a siege cannot with precision make a distinction between combatants and civilians; and the gaping hole in the blockade created by the relief operation was actively aiding the secessionists and helping to prolong hostilities.

The idea that the humanitarian principle of saving the innocent can transcend the rules of war is a modern, and a Western, concept; it was not surprising that both belligerent parties in Nigeria found it incomprehensible and ultimately rejected the right of the outside, ex-imperial, world to impose it upon them. It is more surprising that, for such a long period, Gowon allowed the relief effort to go ahead. At the time, a few observers in the West recalled the Allies' use of blockade in the first World War to defeat the Germans. No-one recalled its use in the second, an even more intransigent use, and one which, incidentally, was the genesis of Oxfam's existence. Shock might be expressed at Federal behaviour; no-one recalled that Churchill's war cabinet had taken the same line.

The collapse of the relief effort for the people in the enclave opened the final chapter in the war. During the late summer and autumn of 1969, the Joint Church Aid airlift continued to operate, but under great strain. Those agencies – Oxfam included – which had previously assisted the ICRC airlift quietly transferred their support to the unofficial Sao Tome operation. Gradually the tonnages taken into Uli by night began to creep back up to their previous levels. But after more than two years of warfare and siege, the people in the Ibo stronghold were exhausted in mind, body and morale.

More important still, the potency of the genocide threat as a Biafran propaganda weapon had waned. Since late 1968, international observers invited by the Federal side to view military operations and judge for themselves the genocide claims had declared them specious. Half of the total Ibo population of 14 million were living in reasonable security in Federal Nigeria, and the property of those who had fled to Biafra was being protected. As this became more widely known, Ojukwu's refusal to compromise on sovereignty lost credibility. Those who had backed the moral case of the Ibo to their own state not for pragmatic reasons but out of sentiment, as an expression of sympathy with their suffering, began to wonder whether their goodwill had been exploited.

In mid-December 1969, the Federal advance began again. By Christmas, the enclave had been cut in two. On 10 January 1970, Ojukwu fled abroad and the Biafran secession finally ended. The bloodbath, so often predicted, did not occur. Nor did Biafran fighters retreat into the bush for a guerrilla struggle. The universal reaction to the end of the war was relief. Gowon expelled from the ex-rebel territory all foreign journalists, relief workers from overseas, and Catholic missionaries. The only external assistance organisation allowed to remain was UNICEF. Gradually, administrative authority was established, and through the Nigerian Red Cross and with help from abroad, a programme of post-war relief and rehabilitation began.

Oxfam had withdrawn its original team from the south-eastern war zone area late in 1969 when emergency conditions no longer prevailed. Now the new Field Director in Lagos, Derek Robinson, offered Oxfam support to the Nigerian Red Cross, and another emergency input of relief was set in motion. As well as despatching vehicles, food, and drugs, to support the Red Cross programmes, eight doctors and two nurses were sent out from England to work in various hospitals in the area where staff were short due to the withdrawal of medical missionary personnel. Most stayed for around two months until the post-emergency phase was over.

During the period of the Nigerian civil war, Oxfam spent around £500,000 on relief for victims on both sides of the conflict; another £100,000 was given to Oxfam to spend by the British government in the final stage of the war when, because the ICRC programme was no longer operational, governments had no official route for helping Biafrans other than through Federal channels. Altogether, the relief effort cost the international and voluntary community an estimated $200 million. It also cost many organisations, including Oxfam, their innocence regarding the politics of relief in independent Africa.

When the reckonings came to be made, no-one really knew or will ever know how many Biafrans lost their lives, from starvation or war-related causes. Some estimated two million in 1968 alone; another authority placed the figure much lower, at 600,000 for the entire period of secession. Like everything to do with the Nigerian civil war, estimating the size of the tragedy in human lives was an exercise inextricable from the competing propaganda claims.

The story of Biafran relief leaves an outstanding question. Did the mobilisation of the world's concern for the starving children of Biafra in mid-1968 – a mobilisation in which Oxfam played an important part – have the effect of prolonging the war and thereby increasing the suffering? The criticism that their concern was achieving the very opposite of their intention plagued the churches and relief agencies in the last stages and the aftermath of the conflict.

The most that can be said is that the maintenance of the food airlifts was one factor among many that helped to keep the war going. In the balance of military forces, the relief of hunger in the enclave – where starvation was being used as a weapon – cannot rate higher than the arms delivered by the French; the inexperience of the Federal forces; or the bravery – spurred by the conviction that they were fighting for their very survival – of the Ibo.

In the end, the principle that the lives of innocent civilians count for more than the political aims of belligerents must be the mast to which the agents of humanitarianism nail their colours. Whether or not actions based on that principle may subsequently be manipulated by players of the political game is immaterial as far as humanity's wider interests are concerned. In the bewildering maelstrom of the Nigerian civil war, prey to one of the most extraordinary public relations campaigns in the history of warfare, Oxfam hovered at the brink of abandoning that principle. It was not the only relief organisation to do so.

The problems of bringing relief to the victims of the first major civil conflagration in independent Africa was a fiery baptism for other conflicts, in this and other continents, yet to come.

7

IN GANDHI'S FOOTSTEPS

When Gandhi was killed in 1948 he left behind many disciples, who embraced his ideas as a political and personal philosophy. Their vision of a regenerated India required a process of non-violent change in which the poor, the landless, and the outcast discovered their dignity as human beings. The locus of these efforts must be 'the village', those thousands of social units dispersed throughout the plains, highlands, jungles, and deserts of the subcontinent, whose eternal rhythms under-pinned the appalling poverty endured by so many of their inhabitants.

As a social and political campaigner, Gandhi centred on the village in his championship of the poor. In this, as in his credo of non-violence, he was a spiritual forbear of much voluntary agency thinking, including that of Oxfam.

Among many well-known Gandhian followers, the mantle of leader-ship fell upon two men in particular. The political inheritance was assumed by Jaya Prakash Narayan, for many years a prominent socialist politician, whose services Mrs. Gandhi called upon in 1966 when famine threatened his native Bihar. The spiritual succession fell to the saintly Vinoba Bhave. Bhave personified the Indian ideal of the sage purified by a life of simplicity in service to the poor.

In 1951, at the scene of village disturbances in Andhra Pradesh, Bhave witnessed a landowner make a *bhoodan* – a gift of land – to local untouchables in an attempt to extinguish the touchpaper of communist agitation. This gesture of reconciliation inspired his *bhoodan* or 'land-gift' movement. For the rest of his active life, Bhave adopted the Gandhian expedient of the march, walking the byways of India with his entourage, in a crusade of land redistribution on behalf of the poor. If a number of villagers pooled their holdings (this was usually among the poor or untouchables whose holdings were uneconomic), this was *gramdan* – 'village gift'. Bhave's crusade was celebrated in India and overseas as an attempt to reform and democratise rural Indian society. He even appeared on the cover of *Time* magazine, over the caption: 'I have come to loot you with love.'

The pivotal centre of the *gramdan* movement was Bhave's ashram at Khadigram in Bihar, set up in 1952. From here, he attracted groups of Gandhi's disciples into a federated body, the Sarva Seva Sangh – The Society for the Service of Truth. *Gramdan* became an established formula, mainly suited to *harijan* or untouchable villages: for caste Hindus it had little appeal. Three-quarters of the landowners in the community must commit their land, and over half the village land come under the sway of the *gram sabha*, a representative council, which redistributed a portion of the land to the landless. By 1968, 50,000 villages in India had officially joined.

During the Bihar famine of 1966-67, J.P. Narayan's Bihar Relief Committee set in motion a two-year programme of minor irrigation works – hand-dug wells, catchment tanks, dams, and borehole drilling – both as a means of employing the drought-afflicted and to reduce Bihar's future vulnerability to a bad monsoon. Oxfam's participation in Bihar famine relief created a close contact with J.P., and Jim Howard needed no persuading that small-scale water development was the key – alongside improved agricultural practice – to helping India's villagers transform their fortunes.

For some years, Oxfam's Asia Committee had been pushing the Field Directorate to seek out a higher number of 'indigenous agencies' as channels for assistance. Apart from the neo-colonial overtones of working almost exclusively through expatriate bodies, most of them were church-related. Christians represented a tiny proportion of India's population; yet almost all Oxfam grants were made to Christian missions, whose future in India was precarious. In its effort to identify itself as a partner in Indian development as well as a source of charitable funds, Oxfam was keen to find organisations working within India's social and economic fabric which represented an essentially Indian impulse for social improvement.

This sounded wonderful at a distance, but in the field it was far from easy. At the end of 1964, when India was still part of his Asian beat, Bernard Llewellyn complained strongly when Oxford – without reference to himself – gave £35,000 worth of milk and vitamins to the Indian Red Cross in response to world news headlines about Indian food shortages. 'The reputation of the Indian Red Cross is not very good and among foreign-based agencies there is much suspicion of the integrity of its distribution agents. For Oxfam to be using such a channel on such a scale at a time when the Indian papers are full of corruption stories scarcely enhances our reputation.' There was no control over such a grant, no way of being sure that all the milk would get into the right mouths, however admirable and sincere the Major-General Llewellyn called upon at Indian Red Cross headquarters. Llewellyn disliked his presence in Asia being used as an alibi to British donors to support the claim that 'we know every penny gets there'.

If one needed to be certain of organisations to which emergency grants and foodstuffs were consigned, it was even harder to be sure of a local group's credentials and competence where the much more nebulous process of development was concerned. Jim Howard wrote to Oxford soon after he arrived in India: 'I am at one with the Committee in its desire to seek out and support reliable indigenous groups. Over these past months I have looked very hard and found very few. There are many people appealing for funds who are obviously dishonest. In my recent visit to Nagpur, the talking point of the town was the deliberate misuse of substantial funds given by a foreign agency to local groups.'

Both Howard and Llewellyn were forceful spokesmen on behalf of the traditional recipients of charitable aid. 'The size and quality of the work by the Christian missions is unparalleled in the sub-continent,' wrote Howard. Was Oxfam to allow the fashion for development aid to eclipse the needs of those who would otherwise be forgotten? 'Often it is only the Christian missionary who will tackle some of the desperate needs we see around us in leprosy work, medical work, and among the destitute.'

In those days a Field Director had to cover a vast geographical area and check up on scores of projects. The most he could do was to visit each one for a matter of hours or a day at most, and make a judgement about everything from technical suitability to likely social impact before moving on. At that time, exercises in planning, surveying, technological review, or field-testing, were rudimentary. However dedicated they were – and most Oxfam Field Directors were exceptional individuals – they had to depend on instinct, their field of expertise, and the record of a project manager's performance; their own checking-up process was not scientific, nor more than cursory. Regular reports were mandatory; but they had their limitations. 'When a visit is at most a twice-a-year phenomenon, this is neither supervision nor control, which must be left to the operating agency,' advised Llewellyn.

The relationship which developed with J.P. Narayan and the Gandhian ashrams in Bihar during the 1966-67 drought provided Howard with the indigenous agency opening for which he had been searching. The Gandhians, with their concern for the very poorest members of Indian society, the untouchables or *harijans*; their ascetic lifestyle in close proximity to the villages they worked amongst; and their advancement of *gramdan* provided impeccable credentials.

Discussions between Jim Howard, the ashrams, and the Sarva Seva Sangh led to a joint rural development programme, the Oxfam Gramdan Action Programme, or OGAP. Activities were to be based on four ashrams within 132 miles distance, and the villages involved were *gramdan* villages. Promoting social change was the Gandhians' affair; Oxfam was more concerned about economic improvement in the communities which – it was assumed – were already pre-selected by the Gandhians for their poverty and need. Each project area was to contain irrigation schemes and agricultural extension – the twin technological pillars of the Green Revolution. Oxfam would provide funds for seed and equipment, and pay the costs of several United Nations Association (UNA) volunteer technicians to work with the Gandhians. These were seen as the vital lever for precipitating the Bihari village economy into the 20th century.

This programme was an important new departure for Oxfam. Not only did OGAP represent the first in-depth collaboration with an agency authentically and inspirationally Indian. It was also Oxfam's first attempt to be operational in the development context, to put people to work in a programme which was actually situated in 'the village', thus becoming much more pervasively involved than usual. OGAP was launched in excellent faith and a pioneering spirit; it was, as many commentators remarked, a natural. But new ventures often fail to flourish in quite the way expected. OGAP was to prove a laboratory in which Oxfam came face to face with some of the flawed assumptions on which its development aid was based.

As in other geographical regions, Oxfam's 'programme' on the Indian sub-continent was not a programme in any formal sense. Built up in response to *ad hoc* requests, it bore no resemblance to the plans negotiated for this sector or that by government administrators and international bodies. Rather, it consisted of a miscellany of projects of every variety. Oxfam's policy of maximum flexibility meant that almost any scheme, so long as it helped the needy, could be included – agriculture, water supply, education, welfare, medical.

A project location might be a clinic, a home, a hospital ward, a settlement scheme, or a training centre; it might take the form of equipment, instruments, vehicles, buildings, stipends for training; aid could supply a poultry house, a vegetable garden, a fish pond, a set of tools, a drilling-rig, a camel cart, or a spinning-wheel. The beneficiaries were as heterogeneous; they might be children, women, landless farmers, leprosy patients, *adivasis* (tribal people), the handicapped, the unemployed, the low caste. And a Field Director had to be a jack-of-all-trades. A typical tour would find him inspecting rice paddy and irrigation works in the morning, orphanages in the afternoon, refugee camps, family-planning clinics, and skills training for destitute women on the day after and the day after that.

In spite of the demands such incredible multiplicity put upon him – 117 grants were made to India in the financial year 1967-68 – a Field Director was naturally inclined to influence the programme in certain directions. Although its grants were so tiny as to make no difference on a large scale, Oxfam could not fail to be aware of the major problems of poverty in a country such as India. So it tried to help combat such problems at the localised village or family level where its funds could make a difference. Very often, a Field Director's own background – professional, personal and ideological – affected the general course he steered.

In the India of the 1960s, the constant nag of food shortage led Jim Howard, with his water engineering background, to focus on technical inputs to farming and small-scale irrigation. There were two achievements about which he was particularly enthusiastic. One was known as the 'fertiliser scheme'; the other was concerned with technical inputs to agriculture.

During the 1965 countrywide food shortages which preceded the Bihar famine, Oxfam provided the foreign exchange for the purchase and import of 5,300 tons of fertiliser for a crash food production programme in Mysore State. The scheme was run by the University of Agricultural Sciences in Bangalore, which repaid the £105,000 cost to Oxfam in rupees, which were then used for other grants.

All sorts of calculations were made about the fourfold increases in crop yields, and the 600,000 mouths for six months that this dramatic rise in output would feed. These sums proved wildly optimistic; but the crop yield was doubled and the fertiliser introduced local farmers to the benefits of high-yielding maize. Howard was bowled over. 'I went out to our project area and saw acres and acres of beautiful maize at all stages of growth. The crops are as good as or better than I have ever seen them. The market is good, the prices attractive, and the demand is leaping up.' The scheme was 'Food for Tomorrow' incarnate; Oxfam felt that it was helping to make the Green Revolution happen.

Howard also enthused over the creation of a joint organisation for giving technical guidance to food production projects run by voluntary agencies. This was AFPRO: Action for Food Production, and Oxfam was a founder member. 'At last,' wrote Howard, 'there is an organisation where concerned people, Catholic and Protestant, Hindu and Moslem, can plan together with Government and share the skills available.' He went on: 'Alone we have little to give India, whereas in consultation and joint efforts we are slowly coming to grips with the massive problems that confront her 500 million people.' He looked forward to a time when each agency might opt for complementary specialisations, 'rather than the hotch-potch that everybody tries to cope with now'. AFPRO went through many ups and downs. But it remained a worthy attempt to make the total impact of voluntary efforts for food production add up to more than their constituent parts.

The other side of the food equation – every year, 12 million more mouths were added to the population – was also a major concern. Oxfam's main contribution to family planning was to support the Christian Medical Association of India (CMAI) in promoting the IUD through mission hospital family-planning clinics. By the end of 1966, more than 100 mission hospitals had joined the CMAI scheme, and of these 33 had received Oxfam funds for loop insertions. The CMAI could not on its own work the miracle of fertility control in India. 'What it is doing is to reduce the population pressure at specific points, making it easier for a family to feed its children and the wage earner to cope.' By 1970, Oxfam had given the CMAI £58,000, and support continued throughout the 1970s.

Oxfam's assistance to the Christian missions was not confined to hospitals and health programmes. In his sturdy defence of the Christian missionary, Howard had pointed out that many undertook welfare work that others would not touch. Mother Teresa of Calcutta, with her homes for the dying and destitute, was one compelling example. Major Gardiner of the Salvation Army, who delivered thousands of daily meals from a mobile canteen in the heat and stench of the Calcutta slums, was another remarkable servant of the poor. Oxfam regularly supported the ministries of both these exceptional individuals. But there were others out in the countryside whose activities were less well-known, and whose commitment was the more extraordinary for the isolation in which it was fulfilled.

Like the Gandhians, certain priests and missionaries lived and worked in village India, as close to the people as they could get. Although they became *de facto* development workers, they did so as a specific response to local problems of which they had personal knowledge. These were often set before them by farmers and villagers whom they knew, and who regularly lamented the vagaries of the monsoon, the rapaciousness of the moneylenders, or the inadequacy of their landholdings. To such people, 'helping the poor' by means of economic inputs was not initially perceived as categorically different from 'helping the indigent' by means of social welfare.

Here was no master plan to solve India's problems of food production or population growth, developed in Delhi or Bangalore with the aid of experts and statistics, to be put into action on a mass scale. The scheme worked out by a priest sitting under the shade of a peepul tree might be a rough and ready affair, but what it lacked in scientific application, it gained in local knowledge of what the real – not the assumed – obstacles were to the improvement of villagers' lives. Some missionaries were technical wizards in their way; others were efficient managers and entrepreneurs; a few had a profound understanding of the cultural environment.

Because some outstanding individuals brought special strengths of local acceptance and close community relations, their initiatives were often more successful than those dreamt up by the professional planners and imposed from outside. Thus some of Oxfam's partners became pioneers on the development frontier, even though their perspective was limited, the scale of their activity extremely localised, and their impetus purely humanitarian.

A humble priest trying to break the mould of poverty in village India had few other options than 'small-scale technology', 'low costs', and 'maximum self-sufficiency' – ideas later embraced by all the development pundits. A classic example was a project started in 1968 by a Breton priest, Father Godest, attached to the Catholic diocese of Mysore. The construction of a major dam had forced thousands of Tamil people to move to a remote valley and set up new communities, one of which was the village of Otterthotti. During the droughts of the mid-1960s, the water table dropped and Otterthotti's 254 village families no longer had enough well-water for irrigation, with disastrous consequences for their crops.

Father Godest came from a farming family in the hard, rocky conditions of Brittany, and had made himself something of an expert in groundwater management. A number of streams flowed into the valley, and at the height of the rains their swollen waters poured away and were lost. He devised a system of small check dams to capture their flow in order to raise the water table and recharge local wells. Villagers manoeuvred boulders large enough to withstand the torrent across the river beds, and piled smaller stones in the gaps. When the rains came, the flood filled the interstices with sand and clay, making the dams impermeable. Elsewhere, by blasting and digging, existing wells were deepened.

The Otterthotti farmers were also gradually persuaded to try high-yielding varieties of seed, fertilisers, and new crops – maize, sorghum and *bajra*. But nothing was given free. Farmers took out loans for well-deepening, to purchase bullocks for ploughing, to buy seeds and fertilisers, and repaid them out of harvest profits. The progress of repayment was painfully slow, but the principle was nonetheless maintained. Godest also ensured that *harijans* were eligible for loans, and insisted upon some sharing of water sources with the less fortunate by those whom the project had helped.

By 1970, 1,300 acres of Otterthotti land were under constant irrigation, producing three crops a year and quadrupling many incomes. With £6,000, the humble Breton had wrought a miracle which successive Oxfam field staff applauded without reserve. One visitor wrote: 'Father Godest is so obviously a model for others in development that one must ask: What is the secret of his success?' Part of his winning formula was to ensure that all the changes in Otterthotti were within the villagers' own technological and organisational grasp. 'He is a man of foresight but essentially practical, never trying to make people do more than is realistic,' the visitor continued. 'And, perhaps as a consequence, he has a relationship with the community of quite unusual mutual affection and trust.'

At the end of 1967, Jim Howard moved to Delhi and a second Field Director, John Staley, took over responsibility for Oxfam in the southern part of India. An economist who had taken the unusual step of obtaining his doctorate from the University of Lahore, Staley was the first Oxfam Field Director with a primarily academic background. Unlike Howard, the man of action, Staley was quiet-spoken and naturally inclined towards reflection. In a different way, he was as remarkable a person and his influence on programme thinking – and on many Oxfamers – was to be profound.

His first reaction to the 150-odd projects he visited on his southern beat was that those selected for support were remarkably successful, judged in relation to their own criteria and intentions. But he pointed out that there was very little data, and it was difficult to have any objective sense of their value. As time went on, his doubts increased. In August 1969, he told Oxford that, with hindsight, he could not justify some of the grants he had earlier recommended. There simply was not enough evidence that good intentions and worthy ideas had produced the desired results, nor that the benefits had accrued to those whose neediness was the justification for the project in the first place.

Staley found the lack of information which characterised the planning of projects and the making of grants 'astonishing and crippling'. He believed that Oxfam was inclined to put a misplaced emphasis on the 'project holder', as if the project holder and the project's capacity to improve poor people's lives were the same thing. Oxfam's aims and the project holder's aims were not necessarily identical; the latter's priority might be to build up his own institution. Without proper information before a project started and regular evaluation as it went along, there was no guarantee that an Oxfam grant was making any truly meaningful contribution towards transforming the lives of the poor, even though it might well be helping some badly-off people.

Oxfam must give more attention to these matters, Staley believed, and more funds. 'What, for example, do we know of the impact of the University of Agricultural Sciences' extension programme upon poor farmers? It is not enough to know only the acreages under high-yielding varieties. What do we know about the increased farming output from the Oxfam-financed well-sinking projects? It is not enough to be told the numbers of boreholes drilled. Is Oxfam's contribution to leprosy work helping to control or reduce the incidence of leprosy? It is not enough to know the number of ulcers treated.' Not having answers to the questions did not necessarily nullify the benefit of Oxfam's aid; but answers, and the means to get those answers, must be found. Too much was being taken for granted as far as the beneficiary was concerned.

The notion of accountability for Oxfam's overseas expenditure was changing. Field Directors were beginning to ask questions about the impact of projects which took accountability far beyond 'the money has arrived and the farmers are thrilled'. In fact, many of the questions Staley was asking were ones that many donors and fundraisers would not have dreamt of, and which some might find confusing, even off-putting. To ask such questions was an earnest of Oxfam's sense of responsibility about its contribution to 'development'. To fundraisers, however, organisational self-doubt is not easily marketable as a reason for charitable giving, whereas boreholes drilled and maize harvested show simple and solid achievements.

Thus, accountability to satisfy the needs of ordinary donors and fundraisers, and accountability to satisfy overseas aid programme criteria were beginning to part company. Ultimately, Staley was saying, Oxfam must be accountable to the poor themselves, not to the image of the poor which happened to be marketable in Britain.

In an echo of Bernard Llewellyn's frequent admonitions, Staley underlined that development was difficult and risky, that it required preparation, research, evaluation and professionalism. 'It is not enough for Oxfam simply to announce a shift in emphasis from welfare to development: if the intention really is to contribute to development the implications must be accepted – otherwise opportunities will be limited, the effort partly wasted, and the results doubtful.'

In Bihar, at the four OGAP locations, the tensions between technical inputs and social benefits, between the goals of project holders and the goals of Oxfam, between wishful thinking and proven results, were beginning to show.

When Sarva Seva Sangh and Oxfam sat down in late 1967 to plan the OGAP programme, a sense of great urgency had driven them on. The famine had sent shock waves through the rural system and the Gandhians had been energised by their work in famine relief. They believed that speed was of the essence, that the drought had stung the villagers out of their usual apathy and inertia, ready to embrace change with alacrity.

The project document read like a classic blueprint for rural development. It talked of 'setting in motion a process of integrated development', of supporting agro-industrial inputs with 'a strong educational movement of value and attitude change', of drawing up area plans with 'the participation of the people'; of credit and technical guidance, of self-help construction of schools, roads, dams, and community centres, of mobilising local resources for production, of marketing and consumer co-operatives. The problem with this vision of village nirvana was that it was elaborated by outsiders, British and Indian, without proper data about local situations or local needs. Here was a case of wishful thinking substituting for realistic project planning and preparation.

The British volunteers seconded to OGAP were given the opportunity to live and work truly at village level. This had its rewards, but life in the ashrams was primitive and tough, and the heat and dust of Bihar took their toll on health and morale. In spite of culture shock, lack of language training, and the difficulties of working in uncharted waters, the group did well. Most were agriculturalists or mechanics; an irrigation expert was later added. Four were based at Khadigram, Vinoba Bhave's original headquarters. Others were based at three other ashrams.

The OGAP management structure was far from tidy. Sarva Seva Sangh was nominally in charge; in practice, the ashram leaders – all individualists with their own versions of Gandhian service – were the men who counted. Few sprang to attention with the vigour anticipated by OGAP's devisors; they had their own priorities. Many felt their main task was to achieve converts to *gramdan*, help the landless gain their rights, and whittle away at the landowning and debt-bonding systems enslaving the poor. They did not want to go around extolling the benefits of modern farming methods.

The volunteers – supposed merely to be technical advisers – found themselves obliged to take the lead. Oxfam placed an Assistant Field Director, Alan Leather, in overall charge of the four OGAP areas; but it was not really clear who, if anyone, reported to him. A great deal depended on personal relationships, which could easily be strained by the volunteers' urge for activity, clashes in perspective, and the lack of workable project plans.

Many volunteers established great rapport with Gandhians and villagers; but there were also frustrations. Unable to accept the irrationalities and convolutions of the world in which they had been plunged, some complained that the ashrams were the wrong medium for the urgent delivery of an agro-industrial revolution. In this they were almost certainly right; but it took time for anyone to admit that an imported agro-industrial revolution might have been the wrong prescription in the first place.

John Hunt, a farmer from Dorset, set up a training programme in improved agricultural techniques for young village farmers. He put together special manuals for imparting basic techniques and adjusted his teaching programme to suit local conditions. His aim was to promote cultivation with the Green Revolution 'package' of new seeds, special varieties, extra crops, fertiliser, irrigation, and the associated technological and management frills. Results on the Khadigram demonstration farm were good. But non-trainee farmers were most unwilling to follow suit. They had their own reasons – which no-one had attempted to discover in advance – for not wanting to grow bigger plants or different crops; for not using more water for irrigation, or harvesting three times a year. Some simply could not afford to go further into debt to do so.

This was not 'peasant apathy and inertia'. After the devastating experience of the drought, farmers had fewer means and less enthusiasm for taking risks; what they wanted was to feel more secure within the system they knew. So the British agriculturalists found that customers for their 'package' were painfully slow to come forward. And then the maize yields were disappointing, partly because the new seed was still experimental in local conditions and its cultivation needed great care. In 1970, only on half the plots planted to maize did the farmers' profits cover their extra inputs.

Nevertheless, some farmers persevered and some fortunes flourished. But rarely the very poorest. John Hunt cited the case of a traditional farmer from a low-ranking caste with a small landholding. 'His family has owned the land for generations. He has two buffaloes, six cows giving plenty of milk, and two bullocks for ploughing which also provide manure. He has farm implements, all his family work regularly in the fields, the yields are good and they live a good life.' Twenty low-caste families in the same village had recently acquired plots of land under *bhoodan* – plots as large as the traditional farmer's. 'But they used to be landless labourers. Few have bullocks, none have cows, there is no milk and no manure; none have farm implements, and their women and children rarely go to the fields. Their farm gives poor results and they are poverty-stricken.'

What Hunt and his co-workers were discovering – that within the ranks of low-caste Indian villagers there were great differentiations of means, capacity and aptitude – was only to be expected. But in those days it was a revelation, at least to those addressing problems from the narrow perspective of 'technological backwardness'. The evaluations of OGAP carried out by Alan Leather in the late 1960s and early 70s were pioneering documents of their time; to begin with, they were greeted by the practical idealists as too academic and nit-picking by half. But these analyses and others taught Oxfam a very great deal.

Designing OGAP so as to target the poorest farmers had not been attempted; indeed without data about patterns of income, landholding, employment, and indebtedness, such questions did not surface until the programme was underway. The assumption had been that the glittering new farming technology – with some local investment to get it established – would aid all; in fact, such technology, its costs, and the sophistication with which it had to be applied belonged to another planet as far as most poor Bihari farmers were concerned. The co-operative banks and marketing enterprises which would underpin the new farming economy also turned out to be pie in the sky. A declaration of *gramdan* did not suddenly implant durable co-operative institutions in one of the most stratified rural cultures in the world.

OGAP obtained supplies of relief wheatflour to use as wages on public works. The flour was difficult to preserve, so dam construction, land levelling and well-digging works were swiftly mounted. Too swiftly and amateurishly in some cases; without geological data, hard rock strata confounded some of the well-digging plans. Worse, the distribution of the flour was influenced by the Gandhians' desire to spread their influence. Food went to families who were by no means in need. Some volunteers were upset, and outraged by Oxfam's unwillingness to take on the role of food policeman.

In fact, the employment of villagers on these public works provided the necessary security for many to take the risks OGAP volunteers were pressing upon them. This was positive; maize did become an established crop. In one area, regular 'wages' had a much more profound consequence. Alan Leather found that the security of a regular income had helped *bhoodani* farmers break away from their crushing subjugation to the landlords. He wrote: 'I believe the psychological change in the attitude of the ex-landless labourer towards the landlord is one of the most important achievements of OGAP. They are aware of their rights and prepared to fight for them. This provides a good base for future development.'

OGAP was Oxfam's first full immersion in the complexities of rural development, in India or elsewhere. It led to the discovery that the main barriers to the transformation of opportunity for the rural poor had more to do with entrenched social attitudes and structures than with the ability to use a pumpset, plant in rows, or dismantle the insides of a truck. The course of true development did not run smooth; in fact, unless it ran bumpy, it was unlikely that any lasting developmental change which would help the poor was underway.

For £150,000 invested in OGAP, Oxfam could feel that some successes were achieved, if on a more modest scale than envisaged. Above all, when it was prepared to face them, there were lessons to be learned. By the early 1970s, in their own different ways, many Oxfam Field Directors had begun to absorb these lessons, and to tread more carefully where once the technical angels had rushed in. In southern India, an important new corner was turned when John Staley took on an Indian Assistant Field Director, Srikanth, to help reorient Oxfam away from its old alliances towards a more satisfying partnership with Indian organisations. In Bihar, another Indian – Subramanian, a Gandhian associated with OGAP – was appointed as Field Director in 1972.

With all the shortcomings and mistakes, Oxfam was one of the earliest overseas voluntary agencies to take on the difficult challenge of development in 'the village', and have the conviction to press on towards the new Jerusalem.

If Gandhi was the first Indian thinker to describe the village as the linchpin of social regeneration, the first to do so in Africa was President Julius Nyerere of Tanzania.

On 6 February 1967, *Mwalimu* – Nyerere's title meant 'Teacher' in Swahili – spoke for two and a half hours to an audience of 50,000 in Dar es Salaam on 'African Socialism and Self-reliance'. The policy he outlined – known as the Arusha Declaration – represented a turning-point in Tanzania's affairs and was applauded by development enthusiasts the world over. Here was an authentically African vision of the national way forward, a rejection of the route designed, and still largely controlled, by the ex-colonial masters.

The cornerstone of Nyerere's drive to create a just, equitable social structure aimed at the advancement of human well-being was his philosophy of *ujamaa*. The word meant 'the oneness of brothers and sisters together', and evoked the tradition of co-operation and sharing within the extended African family. The same notion, Nyerere argued, must now guide Tanzanians towards national unity and progress. Tanzania's only political party, TANU, was to be the instrument for ensuring that the spirit of *ujamaa* governed the management of community resources in such a way as to promote equitable growth, and did not allow the already rich and powerful to decide matters on everyone else's behalf.

At the national level, the means of production were placed in public ownership. This was to ensure that Tanzania, not the manipulators of foreign capital, controlled the Tanzanian economy. At the community level, every citizen would be able to participate in the creation and distribution of wealth, by membership in TANU. Over 90 per cent of Tanzania's population were subsistence farmers living in the countryside. Not only did their voices play little part in decision making, but their agricultural productivity was low. Nyerere hoped that by redesigning the power structure so that they could have a genuine say in their own and in national affairs, and by redirecting social investment to meet the needs of the majority, he would create both a more egalitarian society and a more productive one. It was a brave vision, and extraordinarily influential in development thinking in Africa and internationally.

The philosophy of *ujamaa* was music to the ears of voluntary agencies like Oxfam, particularly those busy repudiating the colonial inheritance. It was centred on the need to uplift the poor; although nominally socialist, it was democratic; and it was heavily influenced by Nyerere's Christian faith and his belief – like Gandhi – in the power of the injunction to 'love thy neighbour'. Here was a Third World leader who articulated as national policy the precepts guiding the Oxfam world view and, increasingly, its programme of development aid. Because of this, the relationship with Tanzania was to be very different from that with any other developing country. In Tanzania, the indigenous agency Oxfam could embrace as funding partner was the government itself. In some countries, such as Botswana, grants had been made to specific government agencies for specific projects. Tanzania was different. The whole country was perceived as an Oxfam-type project magnified to national scale.

The relationship did not begin as a direct partnership, although personal contact with Nyerere was established by Jimmy Betts in 1961 when newly-independent Tanganyika was afflicted by drought. A grant of £35,000 was spent on supplies for famine victims, and this was followed up by help to refugees from Rwanda resettling in western Tanzania.

Gradually, Oxfam had built up a typical portfolio of grants to Tanzania, most of them concerned with health and nutrition through mission hospitals and government clinics. Agriculture and community development were supported through the Anglicans at Masasi in Mtwara Region, where Trevor Huddleston was Bishop during the 1960s; and through the Ruvuma Development Association in the remote south-west. Here, a group of educated young idealists tried to transform the nascent idea of *ujamaa* into practical living and working arrangements. This experiment, the test-tube for much of Nyerere's thinking, was much praised for the way in which it involved and enthused local farmers in dynamic co-operative enterprise. Oxfam contributed £22,500 up to 1969. But Ruvuma then ran foul of local TANU party politicos, and regretfully, Nyerere banned it.

For many years, Oxfam's single most important partner in Tanzania was an organisation called the Community Development Trust Fund (CDTF). This 'indigenous agency' was originally set up by Marion Lady Chesham, one of the relatively few British farming settlers in Tanganyika, a great sympathiser with the independence struggle and a friend of Nyerere's. Originally she put aside £300 to help local villagers with water problems – pump repairs and well-deepening. Under the umbrella of the Prime Minister's Office, CDTF began to receive funds from voluntary agencies all over the world and channel them into rural development. Within some years, Lady Chesham handed over the directorship to a Tanzanian, Martha Bulengo, under whom CDTF flourished.

The administering agents of CDTF-supported schemes in the villages – the choosers of sites, the deliverers of materials, the inspectors of works – were the district development officers and other local functionaries. CDTF was a facilitator, sometimes an extra source of advice; but its essential role was to enable overseas charities to support Tanzanian development via the government, and yet keep tabs on the actual projects to which their funds were committed. From the late 1960s, after the Arusha Declaration triggered the liberal love affair with Nyerere's ideas, CDTF enjoyed a boom. From the Tanzanian perspective, CDTF funds gave a useful boost to the official development budget down at village level where budgets and benefits tended to run out.

The CDTF's Field Officer and Martha Bulengo's right-hand man was the colourful figure of Daudi (David) Ricardo. During the War, Ricardo was invalided out of the Hussars after the back of his head was shot off. To recover the use of his faculties he began walking about the African continent. He eventually decided to settle in Tanganyika and became a highly unconventional farmer, ranching cattle, befriending his pastoralist rivals, the Masai, and personally herding his cattle to market on foot over the length and breadth of the country. After independence, he gave up farming, converted to Islam, and – at Marion Chesham's request – joined CDTF. Ricardo spoke many local languages as well as Swahili, and the wise and wiry figure of Daudi was known and respected in many unlikely corners of his chosen country of citizenship.

Among Tanzania's development goals were the provision of basic services to the entire population: one medical dispensary for each 10,000 inhabitants; universal primary education; and safe, permanent water supplies for every village. But except in the country's few intensely fertile areas, Tanzania's population was widely scattered, making service provision virtually impossible. This led to Nyerere's carrot-and-stick policy of 'villagisation', encouraging and, in the early 1970s, compelling people to relocate into villages where they would have access to schools, roads, clinics, wells, and other facilities. If villagers worked together on communal farms and enterprises, they were seen as moving towards *ujamaa* and received favoured treatment from party and government.

CDTF appealed to Oxfam to help provide villages with water. One part of their case was that unsafe water was a public health hazard, spreading bilharzia, malaria, dysentery, and typhoid. But CDTF put even greater emphasis on the burden of water-carrying for village women: 'In thousands of villages and settlements the woman of the house must walk in the hot sun to the nearest water hole, sometimes as much as five miles away, and carry on her head a heavy pot or 'debbie'. She cannot carry in one trip enough water to last her household 24 hours so she spends a disproportionate time trudging back and forth. This is slavery, and leaves her no time to learn the best way to bring up her children, keep her house clean, or go to adult literacy, cookery or hygiene classes. She is held back in every way and this in turn holds back improvement in her family and development in her village.' This focus on the importance of women in the development process was in advance of its time.

The first, modest, Oxfam grant to CDTF for well-digging was made in 1967. In 1968, after the arrival of a new Field Director in East Africa, Malcolm Harper, Oxfam made a major commitment of £31,000 for 233 wells and 'supervision costs' – Ricardo's salary, vehicle, and inspection safaris. The villages selected by the Tanzanian Water Development Division for new wells were all committed to *ujamaa*, and were expected to provide labour for digging, burnt bricks or stones for well-lining; concrete rings for lining were only used where nothing else was practicable, and made on-site. All this helped to keep costs low and was meant to give villagers a feeling of responsibility for 'their' well.

The programme was very popular. By 1971, it had expanded to the point where 430 wells were constructed in a year, costing between £120 and £175 depending on depth. When each well was approved by Ricardo and the Water Department, it was covered to prevent contamination and to stop people falling in, and a simple handpump installed. The District Medical Officer from Nachingwea wrote: 'The wells have been very helpful in improving hygiene and reducing diseases like conjunctivitis and scabies.' Another, from Sumbawanga, commented that dispensaries in local villages with wells were seeing fewer cases of bilharzia, dysentery and gastro-enteritis.

Oxfam had so much confidence in CDTF and Ricardo that £145,000 was committed over a period of ten years to help water-supply construction. But as time went by and the number of schemes mounted, it became clear that too little attention had been given to maintenance.

Enthusiasm was all for new wells; when pumps on old ones broke down or the well silted up, neither government nor villagers did much about it. In 1975 as a condition of a new grant, Oxfam insisted that someone from each village be sent for maintenance training before the well was sunk and the pump installed. This helped, although it did not entirely solve, the problem.

In 1973, Oxfam – still in partnership with CDTF – moved a step closer to a direct relationship with the government. A 'Development Secretary', Adrian Moyes, had recently been appointed in Oxford to explore ways of enhancing the impact of project assistance on the poor. Ricardo helped Moyes identify a suitable district in Tanzania for a more concentrated Oxfam programme, and a more direct exposure to, and partnership with, the intricate mechanisms of local government and the *ujamaa* village. The district was Chunya, one of Tanzania's poorest, in the southern Mbeya region.

Oxfam committed £20,000 to the district development authorities in Chunya, to be used for small-scale co-operative village enterprises as an addition to the family food production and cash crop schemes already in hand. One such enterprise was a carpentry workshop for making furniture out of local *mninga* wood; there were others for goats, pit-saws, bee-hives, and poultry. Ploughing oxen were provided to be managed communally by villagers who did not own draught animals.

This modest handful of enterprises inspired great theoretical excitement: they would help newly-settled villagers still unfamiliar with joint activities to learn how to organise their affairs. They were the beginning of a step-by-step process which would flower into self-sustaining equitable growth. But for all the visits and discussions and the strivings with the district staff over the complexities of *ujamaa* in action, the modest handful of projects, some successful, some less so, remained no more than that.

Working hand in hand with government, even Tanzanian government, was not necessarily a dynamic or scientific process, as people like Ricardo were sagely aware. On their side, the Tanzanians did not understand why, having made such a modest contribution to their grand Chunya district plan, Oxfam agonised so long and hard about a few goats and beehives and asked so many detailed questions. They were used to the larger sums and more detached behaviour of the international donors; the World Bank was also active in Chunya. The *modus vivendi* for a useful partnership between voluntary agency and local government, even where both were aligned with the poor, needed a lot more time and effort to work out.

Nyerere expressed his confidence in Oxfam when he visited its head-quarters in Oxford in late 1975. He also knew that some of *ujamaa*'s keenest supporters in the West were frustrated by the slow pace at which his ideas took root back home. 'If we state that some new Jerusalem is where we are going, our friends should not be disappointed when they come and find that we are still in the desert. Sometimes they want to find we are already there!' In their enthusiasm for *ujamaa*, many Westerners had a tendency to see the African village as a blank piece of paper on which development could be written. 'We come from a long history of tribalism, of superstition, of malnutrition, of slavery, of colonialism,' Nyerere said. 'We are describing a society that is the opposite of what we have inherited. It will take us a very long time to get there.'

In the early 1970s, as Oxfam Field Directors in different parts of the world were evolving a more thoughtful perspective on the application of charitable aid to 'development', those in the Indian sub-continent were suddenly distracted by a series of calamities natural and man-made. For well over a year, staff and resources were consumed by emergencies; OGAP's structure never fully recovered.

The first catastrophe was in the Bay of Bengal. On the night of 12 November 1970, a cyclone of unprecedented intensity struck the coast and the off-shore islands in the low-lying Ganges delta. Half a million people were drowned, crops on a million acres were destroyed, and homes, boats, and livestock swept away by a tidal wave. More than four and a half million people were affected.

In the chaotic aftermath of the worst natural disaster of the century, international sympathy fuelled a massive relief operation. In Britain, an appeal by Richard Attenborough for the Disasters Emergency Committee raised the unprecedented sum of £1.4 million. Oxfam, which did not at the time have a Field Director in Dacca, joined British partner agencies in airlifting out tents, and water purification and medical equipment. Further supplies were sent up from Singapore, consigned to CARE and to the East Pakistan Red Cross. Altogether, £375,000 was spent on flood relief.

In the aftermath of the cyclone, existing political tension erupted into turmoil, and within a few months civil conflict engulfed the Bengali half of Pakistan. A terrorist campaign for secession began and the Pakistani army retaliated, clamping down mercilessly throughout the countryside. From March 1971 onwards, hundreds of thousands of people began fleeing across the border in search of sanctuary in India. Providing them all with shelter, food, and care presented the Indian authorities with problems of almost inconceivable magnitude.

Late in April 1971, Oxfam's Alan Leather set off for Calcutta from Bihar armed with $10,000 from Oxfam of Canada. The enormity of the influx and the problems it posed only came home to him after he had travelled out of the city. On 3 May he reported: 'The first place we stopped was a small town between Krishnanagar and the border. All the talk about numbers and the state of some camps had not prepared me for suddenly finding 6,000 people clustered along verandas, under trees, around handpumps, queuing for food, ration cards, registration, spilling out of makeshift offices.' And every hour, every day, more were arriving. 'The camp started seven days ago. The Block Development Officer was organising it as best he could, but was extremely worried about news of another 10,000 people on the roads. 500 had arrived that morning.'

The picture everywhere was similar. The refugees arrived on foot with little more than a few bundles. Many were in a state of shock. The only shelter was in a nearby school or under tarpaulins stretched over bamboo poles. At another stop 'we found that 13,000 had gathered at a site for a new camp. Here again there was no shelter, just a great mass of people waiting to be fed ... ' This was to be the story, endlessly repeated, in the areas around the East Pakistan border for the next seven months. After the rains began, and the monsoon was unusually heavy that year, canvas and bamboo offered little protection. The camps were quickly reduced to a muddy squalor sprouting umbrellas and harbouring every agent of infection.

Alan Leather's three years of experience in India were of immense value in guiding the course he took on Oxfam's behalf. This was a determined step away from the old, neo-colonial way of doing things. All the priority needs – shelter materials, medical supplies, clothing, transport, and trained administrative and professional personnel – were available in India. He therefore cabled immediately to Oxfam for money with which to purchase goods and hire helpers. Tarpaulins, clothing, baby foods, medical supplies, ambulances, petrol, and daily allowances for volunteers, were distributed to Indian agencies, Gandhian and others, already working in the camps alongside government personnel. He told Oxford: 'No expensive and inappropriate expatriate inputs, either goods or people,' though he did bring up from Bihar the remaining OGAP volunteers.

In this early stage of the crisis when the world had not yet grasped what was happening, Leather found that Oxfam's speed and flexibility were invaluable. Until large-scale aid was mobilised, there were important gaps to be filled. In early June, an outbreak of cholera in a district near Calcutta rang alarm bells around the world, unleashed a deluge of international attention, and prompted action on a massive scale. Appeals were mounted, and in Britain the DEC again raised over £1 million. The pressure on Oxfam to fly out relief goods – dried milk, plastic sheeting for shelter, medical equipment, and large butyl septic tanks for sanitation – became for a while overwhelming. Meanwhile, Leather recruited 250 young doctors and medical students to carry out mass vaccinations in camps and villages. In a month, 100,000 people were inoculated, helping to contain the outbreak and prevent it entering Calcutta.

Although the attention of Oxfam supporters in Britain was absorbed by the drama of RAF mercy missions and DEC charter flights, the real merit of Oxfam's Bengal programme was its Indian-ness, characteristics that do not fit with the rescue mission mentality which fuels British generosity to disaster relief. The advantage of the upsurge in donations was that Oxfam could begin to consolidate its programme and plan ahead.

As the monsoon rains started to beat down, the condition of the weakest, especially the children, began to deteriorate. In July, Oxfam decided to concentrate on five areas with a refugee population of around 500,000, supplementing the basic food rations from the Indian government with medical care, sanitation, clean water, child feeding, clothing, and shelter. The programme teams were all made up of Indian volunteers and refugees, including doctors, nurses, and social workers who came from as far away as Bombay and Gujarat. Between July and October 1971, £350,000 was spent by Oxfam on maintaining these teams in the field and keeping the programme supplied. This sum represented almost as much as was spent in those months on the entire Oxfam programme in the rest of the world. But no-one doubted its value. Senator Edward Kennedy was so impressed when he visited the camps that he invited Alan Leather to make a presentation later in the year to the US Senate Sub-Committee on Refugees.

During the summer, Oxfam in Britain worked hard to publicise the plight of the Bengal refugees and to raise money. But as autumn approached and press interest died, a cash and attention-span crisis developed. By the end of August 1971, Oxfam was beginning to wonder how it could possibly go on finding an extra £120,000 a month to maintain its work in the refugee camps. But the spectacle of international generosity faltering was even more alarming. The cost to India of refugee relief was running at over £1 million a day. The Oxfam headquarters team, led by Communications Director Philip Jackson, therefore felt that an attempt must be made to rearouse the conscience of the world. A campaign was mounted – the first of its kind: a public information campaign aimed at governments and the UN.

Remembering Nigeria, and worried that Oxfam would be accused of overstepping the political line, Kirkley was initially hesitant. But the humanitarian predicament of eight million uprooted people called for something special. Kirkley undertook a round of meetings with the Editors of major newspapers and media news programmes. A bus-load of Oxfam staff and volunteers called personally on the Ambassadors of all UN member countries, to ask that they raise their aid contributions and do more at the UN itself.

Advertisements were placed in the press, inviting people to sign a coupon and send it to their MP: 'I add my plea that the United Nations use the power invested in it to press for an urgent political solution to the Pakistan problem, and immediately organise the relief programme desperately needed to avert further suffering.' In late September, Michael Rowntree, Chairman of the Oxfam Council, and Ken Bennett, Director of Overseas Aid, went to New York to lobby at the General Assembly. Other NGO partners around the world, especially the church organisations and the other Oxfams, were invited to join this international lobby, and did so.

The campaign's centrepiece was a publication, *The Testimony of Sixty*, to which 60 aid workers, politicians, and journalists contributed eye-witness accounts of the misery in the camps. Its contributors included Senator Edward Kennedy, Mother Teresa of Calcutta, Nicholas Tomalin, Martin Woollacott, James Cameron, John Pilger, Bishop Trevor Huddleston, Gerald Scarfe, Donald McCullin, Michael Brunson, Clare Hollingworth, and many foreign journalists. This plain but eloquent document was published on 21 October 1971, and distributed worldwide. J. Banerji, an Indian social welfare worker, wrote: 'Imagine the whole population of Scotland trekking south, leaving hearth and home with a basket on their heads. Leading their old parents and ailing children by the hand in continuous streams day after day, and finally taking shelter under improvised sheds, only God looking after them. Imagine heavy rains, cholera, and death on the roadside. This is the picture. How will the world accept it?' The concern of many writers was the unendingness of the problem. What was the refugees' future? How could they go on being cared for? Yet who would persuade them to go home?

By late November, the exodus from East Pakistan had swollen to over nine million people. On 3 December, India took matters into her hands and despatched her army across the border into East Pakistan on the side of the secessionists. On 16 December 1971, Pakistan surrendered, and the exultant Bengali freedom fighters declared independence. The new state of Bangladesh was born.

The bleak underside of their triumph was that the world's newest country was also its poorest. The land once celebrated as Golden Bengal in the poetry of the great Tagore had not only been devastated first by cyclone, then by warfare, but had become overburdened with people and poverty. As the millions of refugees swarmed back across the border to home and freedom, a new development challenge awaited.

8

BARGAINING FOR A BETTER WORLD

By the late 1960s the cause of the hungry world was faltering. At the beginning of the decade, the 'rich world' had shouldered a new version of the white man's burden and set out enthusiastically to fulfill its obligations towards what was now no longer the 'colonial world' but the 'poor world'. In Britain, the image of the starving child with which Oxfam popularised the new mission had caught people's imagination and inspired a heartfelt response. By 1970, things had changed. While Oxfam's own torch continued to burn strongly, out in the wider world among politicians, commentators, and the public, the lustre of 'overseas aid' had faded.

One reason was the violent and chaotic events in Third World countries such as Congo, Nigeria, and in a different way, Vietnam and the Middle East. In the midst of such turmoil and political intractability, it was hard to believe that aid and charitable giving were able to provide any lasting solution to distress. Another problem was that, as an instrument of 'development', the record of 'aid' was disappointing. In their different ways, economists, social scientists, administrators, and plain humanitarians were discovering that 'development' – however you defined it – was much more complex than they had realised. Some of the old colonial hands might have given them a hint or two; but views from those quarters were distinctly out of fashion.

The euphoria of the early 1960s, the excitement of 'Freedom from Hunger' and the 'Development Decade', had raised unrealistic expectations about what overseas aid could do. Analogies had been made with the Marshall Plan; but this had been a massive short-term investment programme to rebuild what had been destroyed by war. Aid for the Third World was supposed to do something much more fundamental: to help launch a process of economic and social transformation which, in the European context, was already part of history. In many poorer parts of the world, such history had yet to be made.

At the beginning of the Development Decade, people had looked for a twentieth century miracle, a crusade using space age technology to banish poverty from the face of the earth. When the fantasy began to recede, the prospect of a long and grinding haul did not have the same appeal. Governments, including the British, became more half-hearted about overseas aid as domestic issues beset them. Bad aid stories affected public attitudes, which became distrustful about largesse towards the poorer world. 'Charity begins at home', with the implication that it also ended there, was a sentiment Oxfam found itself increasingly contesting. Oxfam had difficulty adjusting to the new climate, in which it was harder to find allies, launch appeals, and make headlines than it had been a few years back.

To rekindle international enthusiasm, the World Bank under its new President, Robert McNamara, launched a 'grand assize' into why the development cause had run out of steam. Lester Pearson, recently Prime Minister of Canada, was invited to head an international commission which published its findings in late 1969. Their report *Partners in Development* disputed the notion that the Development Decade had been a failure and that overseas aid did not work. Some aid had been thoroughly inappropriate, either because it was ill-conceived or because it had been given for short-term political or trading gain; but there was no call to be so down-hearted when many Third World countries were getting richer at a rate far exceeding that of industrialised countries at a similar stage of their own development.

Pearson called for revisions in the why, what, and how of aid, and for its rapid increase. He suggested that all donor countries should raise their allocation as soon as possible to one per cent of their GNP. The Commission also called for an end to the restrictive import policies which kept many developing countries' key products out of first world markets, reflecting a growing emphasis on trading relationships as well as aid as a vital part of the 'rich world, poor world' equation. The Pearson Report was influential in setting the agenda for the next UN Development Decade, declared by the General Assembly in 1970, particularly the one per cent GNP aid target; it was also seized upon by those who had picked up the development banner in the 1960s in a spirit of conviction and were determined not to abandon it. Quotes from Pearson sprinkled Oxfam's and others' literature for many years.

Almost simultaneously with the late 1969 publication of the Pearson Report, the British overseas aid charities launched a joint campaign entitled 'Action for World Development' arguing for many of Pearson's precepts. Its keynote was struck by a *Manifesto on Aid and Development*. The agencies had decided to take a radical step. Since the British government and others were going off the boil about aid, they would have to be put under pressure. Political pressure. This meant straying into pastures where the law said that charities were not supposed to go.

This decision had been many years in the making, and it derived from an accumulation of forces.

The rumblings in Oxfam about the need to take on a stronger educational and propaganda role dated back to the early 1960s. The 1963-64 brush with the Charity Commissioners had quelled them, but only temporarily. Harold Wilson's government, which had put overseas aid high on its agenda after coming to power in 1964, cut the aid budget after its second election victory in 1966, by £20 million. This, as Oxfam's activists pointed out, was a larger sum than the amount the organisation had spent on aid in its entire history.

The proverbial drops in the ocean provided by Oxfam's £3 million annual expenditure seemed a puny response to the massive problem of world poverty. The scale of the poor world's predicament was too vast, its iniquities too entrenched. Evidently, only those operating on a massive scale – governments and international monetary and trading institutions – could make a major difference. A report prepared for Oxfam in 1967 by Dr. Cyril James, ex-Vice Chancellor of McGill University, then Secretary of Oxfam's Council, stated: 'It is clear that the relief and development of peoples in all parts of the world cannot be accomplished by voluntary agencies alone. Massive effort by all governments is essential, and to encourage such effort, Oxfam must sometimes play the role of Socrates and be a gadfly to sting the State to action.' The James Report, as this document was known, reflected important trends in Oxfam thinking.

In the late 1960s, not only was Pearson conducting his grand assize, but figures such as Barbara Ward were talking of the population time-bomb ticking away, and other prophets of environmental catastrophe were starting to make their voices heard. The sense of crisis, of time running out, was palpable and it affected thinking in all the aid agencies. True, to lobby for a change in public policy was to undertake political action, and this might lead to a clash with the Charity Commissioners. But so overwhelming did the case for action on behalf of humankind appear that many believed the Commissioners could not be so unenlightened as to interpret the law about political action against them. Where a charity was convinced that public policy in its area of expertise needed correction for humanity's sake, surely it would be lacking in responsibility not to seek the necessary changes?

Although mass popular interest in eradicating hunger had dwindled, informed minority interest was growing. This owed a great deal to the long-term education and youth programmes of Oxfam and other agencies. Some of their key people – Og Thomas who headed up Oxfam's education work from 1966-71, for example – were also influential in helping set up ginger groups on aid and development issues outside the formal charity network. The most important of these – because it had the backing of many influential names – was the Haslemere Group. In mid-1968, the Group issued a 'Declaration', price 1/-. It sold out immediately, to the membership of a growing network of World Development and Poverty Action groups. This call to arms took a radical line on the causes of underdevelopment, essentially adopting the Marxist critique of the evils of colonialism developed by writers such as Renée Dumont and Frantz Fanon, then becoming highly fashionable in left-wing circles.

In this view, the rich world was not merely obligated to help the poor world because it happened to be better off; it was itself responsible for the poor world's parlous condition, and must redress the imbalance as a matter of justice. Although the Haslemere Group included many Oxfam sympathisers, their analysis suggested that aid of the kind Oxfam gave was almost irrelevant, a sop to the conscience of the donor which might even be shoring up the oppressive structures crushing the poor. Socialist analysis and a vision of the Third World in justifiable revolt against exploitative Western capitalism were beginning to characterise an ideology of development whose primary context was neither economic nor humanitarian, but political.

The activity propelling the agencies towards a propaganda role was diffuse and emerged in a spontaneous fashion. At Oxfam, the arrival of Nicolas Stacey as Oxfam's Deputy Director in 1968 helped to stoke up the debate. Kirkley was a very steady type of person. He liked the feeling of organisational energy generated by his young hotheads, but he was inclined to let the thunder roll around him and wait for it to subside without feeling the need to bring matters to a head or reach any definitive conclusion. Stacey, a far more dynamic figure, had quite opposite instincts. He wanted to fire up the debate and encourage the forces he saw as Oxfam's main source of vitality; he wanted a driving sense of excitement and action.

Kirkley never paraded his views and rarely expressed them except in the most general terms. In a middle-of-the-road kind of way, he believed that – although the wider educational role was important – nothing should be done which risked damage to the *raison d'être* of Oxfam, its overseas aid programme. The Haslemere-ists, at one extreme, saw the programme as good so far as it went, which was almost nowhere at all; education and public policy change were far more important. The view at the other extreme, whose champion was Ken Bennett, Overseas Aid Director, was that all the hot air generated over socialism, self-reliance, and sisal quotas achieved very little that was concretely detectable for the poor – unlike Oxfam's aid, which did things of great importance to those individuals whose lives it touched. Meanwhile the trustees had endorsed the James Report's recommendation that Oxfam engage in public opinion-forming, to 'sting the state to action'. Nic Stacey threw himself into the fray with gusto.

Stacey had been asked by Kirkley to take overall charge of the Oxfam 'home front' – fundraising, regional staff, volunteer groups, education, youth, shops, advertising, press, PR. Within all this, the high energy ex-Vicar was willing to do his duty and exploit his publicist talents by opening charity bazaars, kissing celebrities, and giddying up gift shop helpers; but something of real significance such as championing development as a political cause was much more up his alley. Stacey was an enthusiast for big ideas and good at making things happen. He was very bright, had a handy network of contacts and ready-made fame as a TV and newspaper commentator. If anyone could push aid and development back up the political agenda, from second in command at Oxfam, surely he could.

Stacey (who had just turned forty) identified with the younger, activist elements within Oxfam and on its fringes. Early in 1969, a group of Oxford students arrived at his house one evening. Peter Adamson and his wife, Lesley, and Philip (son of Robert) Maxwell wanted Oxfam's backing for a campaign. Their idea echoed the theme of '1 per cent of GNP' being sought internationally for development. They believed they could persuade Oxford undergraduates to sign banker's orders worth at least one per cent of their student grants to overseas aid charities. If the campaign worked, it would be financially worthwhile for Oxfam and the other agencies, and would secure a platform for further educational activity. After a bottle of wine round Stacey's kitchen table, he agreed that if they could collect one thousand signed promises in three weeks, Oxfam would take them on. They did so.

This led to the creation of 'Third World First' with its own accommodation, office and staff, established on the strength of a grant from Oxfam. By the end of the first year, 3W1 had managed to start a support group in every university in the country, and 16,000 students had signed a banker's order to Oxfam, Christian Aid, War on Want, or some other charity. The financial results paid off; within three years, 3W1 brought Oxfam over £50,000 annually. Adamson, never at a loss for ambitious ideas, began to produce a good-looking, thrice-yearly magazine for members: the *Internationalist*. In 1973, he persuaded Oxfam and Christian Aid to back the *New Internationalist*, the first monthly magazine on development issues available to the public. Establishing the magazine was to cost the agencies more than they had bargained for; but, somewhat to their surprise, it became in time a successful independent concern.

During 1968-69, Stacey's first year as Deputy Director, Oxfam made plans to launch its own political campaign. Position papers were prepared on a variety of topics – aid, trade, agriculture, population. Oxfam also drafted a 'manifesto'. But Kirkley was not entirely happy with the way things were headed. Gradually, he steered Oxfam away from a go-it-alone campaign towards joint action with other members of the Voluntary Committee on Overseas Aid and Development (VCOAD).

This co-ordinating group had been set up in 1965 largely at the instigation of Barbara Castle, then Minister of Overseas Development, as a new mechanism for agency collaboration. As well as the usual allies, it included the Overseas Development Institute, UNA, and the UK Freedom From Hunger Committee, and it offered a joint platform for representations to government. VCOAD's purpose was to dovetail the agencies' educational and opinion-forming work, and Kirkley – always seeking to build a common front in a co-ordinated voluntary sector – vigorously supported it. In the context of active political work, VCOAD offered a ready-made umbrella under which the agencies could shelter from Charity Commissioner storms; and if legal opinion happened to blow their way, joint action would add a puff in the right direction.

Thus the stage was set for the 1969 'Action for World Development' initiative in the wake of the Pearson Report. Its *Manifesto on Aid and Development* was a redraft of the manifesto originally prepared by Oxfam. Oxfam and Christian Aid were the prime movers, seconding members of staff and paying the lion's share of the budget. The position papers originally prepared by Elizabeth Stamp, Oxfam's Information Officer, were now issued as AWD materials, under the rubric 'Stamp on Poverty'. The Churches also launched a 'National Sign-In on World Poverty', inviting congregations to sign a declaration to be presented to MPs throughout the country. This supported the allocation by 1972 of 1 per cent of GNP to overseas aid, and the negotiation of more favourable trading arrangements with the poorer countries.

In Oxfam, once the commitment had been made not just to the idea, but to the implementation of the 'wider educational role', a great deal of energy was consumed in reaching lift-off position. The experience was sobering. People began to discover that it was relatively easy to agree on the moral imperative to try to save the world from hunger, disease and illiteracy, and to sit up all night penning ardent declarations to this effect; it was much more difficult to develop an effective strategy for actually doing something about it. It required producing authoritative position papers on complex subjects to which several agencies could subscribe; arguing a convincing case for real policy alternatives; avoiding the politics vs. charity minefield; reconciling voices within each agency, and those of several agencies with different agendas. All of this was merely a preparation for the main task of conjuring into existence a popular mass movement clamouring at the gates of Westminster.

The launch of the Manifesto was something of an anticlimax. There was no echoing roar as there had been for Hunger £Million, for Biafra, and for other emergencies. A hundred or so committed development action groups – Haslemere emulators – beavered away, trying to disentangle growth rates from commodity agreements, unearth the mysteries of ODAs and GATTs, unhook multilaterals from intergovernmentals, and work out where the poor fitted in. They helped to collect over a million signatures for the churches' National Sign-In, and presented these to some 500 MPs. But for all the achievements of the emerging development lobby, no-one could pretend that '1 per cent of GNP' and 'fair trade' evoked in the public mind the passionate concern that a Biafran child could conjure.

In a January 1970 report to the Oxfam Executive Committee, Kirkley spoke of 'teething troubles and a slow start'; but he was convinced that backing AWD was the right course of action. Others were disappointed. After all the efforts and the internal discussions, the plans and the policy documents, the mountain had laboured and brought forth a mouse.

The casualty was Nic Stacey. His vision of Oxfam at the head of a national movement on behalf of the hungry millions, himself holding aloft the leading banner, was slipping away.

In October 1969, Stacey set out his views on the future of Oxfam in a confidential memo to Kirkley. His analysis of the social trends influencing Oxfam's fortunes was wide-ranging. He saw the tide on which Oxfam had swept to success as turning, with threatening implications for future income and ability to keep expenses below 20 per cent. 'Oxfam policies must again catch the prevailing tide, which is so different from that of ten years ago. To do this demands a radical reappraisal of Oxfam's priorities and policies at a much more fundamental level than has been envisaged up to now.'

Stacey's prescription was a major restructuring of the entire home front. The prevailing tide he wanted to ride was the demand among 'the articulate liberal minority' for lobbying and propaganda work, a task he described as essential for any organisation which took its commitment to the Third World seriously. (Stacey was among those who believed that Oxfam's aid programme was too tiny to be useful on any scale that mattered.) He regarded AWD as an under-funded, mealy-mouthed response to the demand for educational activity; the action groups could make no real headway without more funds and backing. Stacey argued that only Oxfam was big enough and powerful enough to carry the political torch effectively. He also undoubtedly thought that the movement needed him, not some anonymous committee of well-meaning agency deputees.

He suggested to Kirkley that Oxfam should commit around £500,000 for educational work annually. He saw that a public appeal for this amount of money for educational work would be certain to fail. His suggestion, therefore, was that the income from Oxfam's trading company and from the growing network of shops should be put into an Oxfam Educational Trust. He believed that the middle-aged women volunteers who ran the shops did so because they liked running shops, and that they were not fussy about how the money they raised was spent as long as it went to a good cause. He saw the shops as a way Oxfam had found of raising money 'which involves neither commitment nor sacrifice', and that this liberated Oxfam from the obligation of spending the proceeds directly on relief and development overseas.

Independently of the main questions – whether such a high proportion of income should be allocated to educational work and what the Charity Commissioners would have to say about it – there were a number of flaws in this proposal. As Stacey himself pointed out, all fundraising efforts were currently under stress, with the exception of the shops. The loss to the overseas programme of Oxfam's most promising source of income would have to be compensated in some way. This Stacey recognised; but the solution he proposed – a kind of sponsorship scheme with town-twinning and intensive campaigns by 'mobile flying squads using Kennedy-type election techniques' – was fanciful. Too many of his ideas were not sufficiently grounded in the mundane realities of Oxfam's existing organisation and public profile. His urge to think big and visionary was his undoing. And many regional organisers were deeply opposed to their own eclipse as the backbone of Oxfam's motivational presence in Britain's towns and cities. In Stacey's scenario, they would be confined to the management of shop networks selling second-hand goods and Oxfam products.

Stacey was too loyal to Oxfam to mount an internal lobby on behalf of his proposals. To do so would have been to set himself up in opposition to Kirkley in a leadership contest, a contest he neither sought nor could be expected to win. He counted on the force of his ideas and the internal momentum behind campaigning to win the day. But whatever tide he had identified, he had misjudged the strength of the one running in his favour. Kirkley wanted campaigning to be altogether more circumspect and was very disinclined to court the Charity Commissioners' wrath, or alienate the other agencies recently enlisted in AWD by taking a separate, unilateral initiative.

Stacey's proposals never explicitly reached the trustees although their tenor was well-known. Instead, Kirkley put up his own case for discussion. In February 1970, the Council of Management reconfirmed that Oxfam's primary purpose was to raise money for overseas aid and development, endorsing Kirkley's suggestions and thereby consigning Stacey's – at that time and in that form – to the organisational out-tray.

The tensions in Oxfam reached the *Sunday Times*. Stacey's own visibility had helped sustain Oxfam's visibility; now his dissension with a key decision on organisational priorities could not remain invisible. Stacey was a public figure, a far better-known one than Kirkley, whom he had been expected to succeed. That could no longer happen. Although Stacey stayed on for a few more months, and even went on a trip to Tanzania to try and interest President Nyerere in town-twinning, the writing was on the wall. Without being able to commandeer a sizeable chunk of resources to set about what he saw as the vital challenge of the day, Stacey lost heart. Cutting ribbons, opening fetes, chairing meetings, and worrying about expense ratios did not ultimately satisfy. His departure came a respectable few months later.

Meanwhile, after a pause for thought, the Charity Commissioners decided to take issue with the AWD *Manifesto*. Although couched in the most cautious terms, its suggestions about government aid targets and trade deals had used the phraseology: 'We call upon'. Direct calls upon government for policy change were uncharitable, according to the Commissioners. Their June 1970 Annual Report warned charities that if they strayed into the field of political activity, 'their action will be in breach of trust', and that 'those responsible could be called on at law to recoup to the charity any of its funds which have been spent outside its purposes.' If the agencies had hoped that the moment had come for a more liberal interpretation of charity law, they were now disabused.

In late 1970, the action groups and the parties to AWD decided that it was in all of their interests to set up an independent non-charitable body, the World Development Movement. This would allow the groups to develop a separate identity: they were finding the agencies' concerns restrictive. Freed from the constraints of charity law, WDM could develop its own positions and campaigning strategies, calling on the agencies for support where appropriate. Oxfam, Christian Aid, and some others helped to fund WDM, letting go their co-ordinating role and conceding – for the moment – that campaigning in the political arena could not legally be undertaken in their name by their own volunteer constituencies.

WDM developed as an organisation, but its numbers did not significantly grow. By the 1970s it was becoming clear – if not easily admitted – that the momentum within the aid and development constituency was not gaining the kind of strength required for a mass movement. Radical sentiment among the young focused on the overtly political, not the social and economic: Vietnam and Southern Africa, not kwashiorkor and textile quotas. Most development issues were too complex and too remote from the day-to-day preoccupations of most people, even among the liberal intelligentsia. The prevailing current in favour of political action at home on behalf of the poor overseas had been less a flood tide than an eddy.

The Nicolas Stacey episode was an important passage in Oxfam's story. The question of how much money and energy should be given to educational activity on the domestic front was a big contemporary issue among Third World sympathisers, and has continued to be so in one form or another ever since. Stacey was not the only person to leave Oxfam because of its refusal to adopt a more radical stance or risk alienating middle-class, middle-aged, middle-of-the-road supporters. Given his independent status as a public figure, Stacey could have split the organisation and caused lasting damage. That he did not do so is in part a tribute to Kirkley and the respect and affection in which he was held; but credit must also go to Stacey himself, who conducted himself in such a way as to minimise the impact of the parting of the ways.

Stacey or no Stacey, the campaigning issue continued to be hotly debated. In November 1974, a new proposal cleared the upper reaches of the policy-making apparatus. The Council of Management decided that in future, public information and education should be regarded not as an organisational cost, like fundraising expenditure; but as an organisational purpose, like overseas aid. From this time onward, Oxfam allocated five per cent (later raised to six per cent) of its donated income to educational activity, a sum roughly akin to what had previously been spent as a cost. The principle argued by Stacey five years before had now been established; but the effort came nowhere near the scale he had envisaged.

Nor did regular educational work take on a political character. In certain specific instances, such as the 1971 campaign on behalf of aid for the Bengal refugees in India, Oxfam invited supporters to 'write to your MP' and sent senior representatives to see government and UN officials. But ongoing campaigning work on aid and trade was firmly left to WDM, 3W1, and the *New Internationalist*, all of which Oxfam continued to support financially through the 1970s. It was to be another ten years before Oxfam again tried to advance the barriers constraining its own role as a critic of public policy in the international arena that it believed to be against the interests of the poorer members of the human race.

Although Nic Stacey did not achieve the fundamental shake-up he looked for at Oxfam, he did help to bring about some much-needed reorganisation. Kirkley always preferred the back of an envelope and a hand-shake to structures and lines of bureaucratic command; and he was content to allow staff extraordinary freedom both of expression and action. But Oxfam had grown rapidly over the past decade and sorely needed not only the coherent statement of priorities which Stacey had forced upon Kirkley and the trustees, but a more streamlined organisational structure.

The next few years saw various consultants trying to make sense of this erratic organisational animal. This was far from easy; where idealism was the essential ingredient of job motivation, and its expression an important component of job satisfaction (salary levels were way below market rates), whatever structures were erected were constantly in danger of being undermined in the name of the latest moral imperative. The larger Oxfam became, the more unwieldy and potentially anarchic. The problem was exacerbated by the vast scope of Oxfam's philanthropic remit – poverty and distress arising out of any cause anywhere in the world – which meant that there was no new issue – population, environment, trade – that it could bear to leave alone. This made of its own body of energy a diffuse and volatile mass, constantly surging off in new directions.

The modest 1970 programme of reorganisation established a directorate to head up the key organisational activities. There was no more home front supremo in the form of a Deputy Director. A system of divisions was developed which, with reshuffling and consolidations, has remained the essential Oxfam structure. The regional network of local organisers had been already given some shape and a pecking order; they now came under a Regions Director, Richard Matanle. All the opinion-forming work – press, education, information – came under Philip Jackson as Communications Director. Administration was under Bruce Ronaldson; Finance under Gordon Rudlin; Overseas Aid under Ken Bennett. The sixth division was under Oxfam's newest senior recruit, Commercial Director Guy Stringer.

Within a year or two, Guy Stringer was to become Stacey's successor as Deputy Director. A bluff, quintessentially good-hearted person who described himself as 'a commercial man with a conscience', Stringer came to Oxfam in 1969 to beef up Oxfam Activities Ltd. and generally put Oxfam on the map in the commercial world. His background was in business, as managing director of a Pilkingtons ceramics firm, and before that, in the army. It was his wife Mary who converted him to Oxfam; she ran an early Oxfam shop in Dorset. Stringer, who ended his career with Oxfam with a spell as Director, always remained a little startled that he had been persuaded to abandon a successful business career to work for such a problematic and wilful creature as Oxfam. But the simple conviction that led him to do so never dimmed, and its eloquent expression on public platforms down the years won many hearts and minds to the Oxfam cause. Like Kirkley, he inspired great affection.

By the early 1970s Oxfam was increasingly finding fundraising tougher. An unfortunate episode took place in 1969, when Oxfam dumped 50 sacks of shoes left over from jumble sales and judged unsellable on a rubbish tip in the Oxford area. A few good pairs of plimsolls donated by a manufacturer were mistakenly included, and their discovery led to a national scandal in which Oxfam was accused of everything from wastefulness and ingratitude to lack of charitable instinct towards people at home. The impact of this negative publicity was out of all proportion to the misdemeanour, and its bad effect clung to Oxfam's reputation for some time. Oxfam-bashing – 'they spend everything on administration' and other myths – became familiar on the public grapevine.

There were also by now a number of new charities, notably Shelter under Des Wilson, using the aggressive marketing techniques that Oxfam had pioneered. The whole business of modern philanthropy was changing and becoming more competitive. Oxfam's advertising revenue continued to decline. With the new emphasis on solidarity with the Third World, there was now resistance within the organisation to starving child images except during real emergencies. In their over-simplification of the world poverty problem, such images perpetuated an inaccurate and offensive picture of day-to-day life in the Third World, and a wrong idea of Oxfam's overseas programme. However, advertisements with more educational messages did not yield as well, sometimes barely covering their costs.

By 1970, half Oxfam's income was being raised in the regions, where the long-term build-up of staff and support groups was paying dividends. The most promising area of financial growth was the Oxfam Shops, of which there were now 250. The decision to promote the Oxfam Shop had been taken in 1968, when the existing Giftshops were handed over to local organisers. In future, organisers encouraged volunteer groups to replace gift drives and coffee mornings with retailing.

The average Oxfam shop's weekly income – £42 in 1970 – might sound small; but on a year-round basis it was far higher than the returns from a group which organised an annual tin rattle and sale of work. Shopkeeping was a more focused and regular activity. It was also less up-market. Shops needed a different kind of person from those used to genteel meetings with a speaker, slides and a few well-chosen remarks from the Chair. Shopkeeping required scrubbing floors, fitting shelves, sorting garments, and minding the till. Organisers had to be able to find enough helpers to take on these responsibilities; some shop rotas ran to 70 members. And whatever some headquarters staff airily thought about middle-aged ladies' desire to run shops, helpers needed motivating. They had to open and close on time, they had to be disciplined about cash and stock control, and since they gave their time free they must enjoy the experience or they would drop out.

By 1973, the number of shops had risen close to 500, and their total profits to over £1 million. With their increasing numbers and the day-to-day nature of their dealings with the purchasing public, shop volunteers also became the most frequent standard-bearers for Oxfam's cause. This had an impact on Oxfam's overall presentation of its message. However well-motivated, few shop helpers matched the image of the articulate radical that some Oxfamers were keen to mobilise. In fact, some shop managers – with the protection of some regional organisers – were reluctant to devote more than minimal space either in the window or on the counter to Oxfam's information material: their twin priorities were to raise money and service their bargain-hunting clientele.

The degree to which Oxfam Shops should be utilised as education and information centres continued to excite debate for many years. Bill McGuire, Director for Scotland, reflected on the issue in a 1971 edition of *Oxfam News*: 'Could our army of shop helpers become so intent on keeping their heads down over their work that they have no time to gain a real understanding of what Oxfam is about? Is Oxfam in danger of losing its heart?'

In opting for shops as the fundraising way forward, Oxfam subconsciously made a choice about what kind of organisation it would be in terms of the character of its support and the broad public perception of its activities. Shops assumed in the 1970s and 1980s the role that advertising hoardings had played for Oxfam in the 1960s. In fundraising terms, the Shops were by far the largest contributor to Oxfam income, their proceeds peaking in 1988-89 at £19.5 million from over 800 sites. They were the vehicle through which most of Oxfam's 27,000 volunteers made their contribution of time and effort, the means whereby its name was placed constantly before the public, and a model for fundraising and community service copied by hundreds of charities in Britain.

The decision to boost the Oxfam Shops also paved the way for the expansion of Oxfam Trading. Under Guy Stringer's directorship, sales of Christmas cards and a range of other special Oxfam products – tea towels, toys – began to climb. Between 1970 and 1975, the company's annual sales rose from just under £300,000 to nearly £750,000. The most important growth area was the sale of handicrafts from the developing world, whose share of the total rose from 9 per cent to 46 per cent. What had begun with a few orders for bags or cushions made by refugees and the destitute had grown into an import scheme called 'Helping by Selling'. This enterprise was developed and run by Roy Scott, who combined enthusiasm for the handicrafts with a very particular commitment to equitable trading.

At this time, a new theme associated with the nuts and bolts of poverty in the developing world was emerging: unemployment. The overabundance of manpower for the available jobs in most developing economies was seen as an outcome of the population explosion, and of the export of inappropriate capital-intensive Western technology. In 1971, Oxfam published a report called: 'Unemployment: the Unnatural Disaster' written by Peter Adamson. Quoting Hans Singer of the Institute of Development Studies at Sussex University, the report pointed out that 30 per cent of the potential workforce in developing countries were either out of work or desperately short of it. Some were seasonally unemployed in agriculture, others earned far less than the minimum wage, and many barely survived on the margins of the economy, shining shoes, washing clothes, and selling a few of this and that from a stall, a tray, or a roadside pitch.

This picture of the competitive, and often exploitative, conditions in which so many men, women and children tried to scrape a livelihood, was Roy Scott's inspiration. Small-scale handicrafts enterprises were often set up by missionaries trying to provide occupational activity for their social welfare caseload: widowed and abandoned women, people with disabilities. 'Helping by Selling' originally offered an overseas market for these products, many of which came from workshops and training centres which Oxfam grants had helped set up. Scott wanted to go further: he wanted, through Oxfam, to help such enterprises establish themselves as viable businesses, enhancing their capacity to provide employment to people from very low socio-economic groups in a way that increased their opportunities and improved their lives.

A typical example of a Helping by Selling producer was a women's training centre or *kendra* in the slums of Ahmedabad set up by Sr. Lucia Carabias, a Dominican nun, in 1970. Oxfam originally gave a grant to cover the costs of staff to teach tailoring for two years. When Sr. Lucia saw that the women were already skilled in Gujerati embroidery and mirrorwork, she diversified. The first retail order came from Oxfam: 5,500 embroidered wall-hangings. This provided regular wages for 75 workers, and helped to get their products established. Oxfam continued to place orders, and the *kendra* branched out into cushion covers, shopping bags, table linen, and bedspreads, using hand-woven cotton cloth and the designs that Gujerati women traditionally embroider onto the clothes and linen of their dowry.

From 1972 onwards, Scott began to develop an idea for a business partnership with handicraft producers such as these. In his view, simply picking up pretty items off the ethnic shelf on which Oxfam could turn a useful profit did not guarantee help to producers of any but the most transitory kind. For example, if Oxfam Trading made a large order for a mirrorwork shoulder-bag for the Christmas Mail Order catalogue, this could put a producer under pressure to expand the workforce to fill it; once completed, there might be no new order for years until existing stock was sold. If the fashion for shoulder-bags died, that was that. How could Oxfam justifiably claim to be helping poor producers if it boosted their prospects and then dropped them flat? Something must be done to offset their vulnerability.

Scott was also concerned about the nature of the enterprises from which Oxfam purchased. The poor and illiterate, particularly if they were women, were easy victims to exploitative labour practices. In many Third World countries they were not in a position to assert their rights to decent wages or a share of profits, even where laws existed for their protection. Child labour and indentured labour were not unusual. For Helping by Selling, Scott had always preferred to buy products from enterprises with a co-operative structure, and avoided middlemen at all costs. This allowed Oxfam to develop a direct relationship with the producers, an essential ingredient of the venture he now proposed.

Scott called his concept 'Bridge' because it exemplified the philosophy of a new kind of trading relationship in which the underlying theme was partnership. 'Bridge' was truly radical and visionary, and it took time to persuade Oxfam's policy-makers to accept it. The key principle was that Bridge's reason for existence was to serve the producers, not to serve Oxfam. In the first place, prices must be fair and up to 40 per cent of an order's value must be pre-paid. But much more important, profits from the sale of handicrafts would not simply fetch up in the general pot for Oxfam's aid programme. Instead, they would be ploughed back into the producer enterprises themselves. A small proportion would also be spent on educational work about 'fair trade' in Britain.

Bridge was, therefore, to be an independent operation; this was the feature that many of the Oxfam policy-makers and trustees found hard to swallow. Up to this point, the overseas aid programme under the scrutiny of the Field Directorate had been the sacrosanct destination of profits earned by Oxfam, on handicrafts or any other item. The claim about 'helping' by selling had been taken at face value; the idea that Oxfam might be failing the makers of those attractive hanging baskets and leather sandals by participating in their exploitation – rock-bottom wages, no security – was not easy to convey. Some sceptics thought that Scott was a dreamer trying to tinker by remote control with societal or market relationships which were none of Oxfam's business.

Eventually, with backing from Guy Stringer, the Bridge proposal won approval in mid-1975. In the future, suppliers of handicrafts to Oxfam would occupy the same slot as projects did in the aid programme: small craft enterprises would be seen as a context in which 'development' could be fostered and their employees' quality of life improved. Unlike most trading companies, Bridge would single out the weakest, the least secure, the least confident suppliers, and try to elevate their manufacturing and business skills to the point where they could become successfully self-sufficient. At the same time, Bridge would try to keep its own balance sheet healthy and its customers satisfied.

Bridge's policy was to build up producers' capacity by ploughing its profits back into their activities in the form of capital investment, expertise, and dividends. One quarter of the profits went directly to the producers. The rule was that this dividend should be spent by them as a group, not split up between employees individually; and they must tell Oxfam what they had spent their dividend on. This was a revolutionary idea; in very few handicraft workshops, including those run by missionaries, would anybody consider giving a say in affairs to the humble basket-makers or embroiderers themselves. This was a means of making them take at least one decision about their enterprise in a democratic manner. The first dividend in the Ahmedabad *kendra* caused quite a stir among the women workers. Reaching a decision about what to buy took an entire day; Oxfam's Guy Stringer happened to be present. 'When they finally agreed to buy a large, lidded cooking pot with a ladle to prevent the children putting their hands in, a huge frisson went through the hall.'

Most of the rest of the profits went into the Bridge Development Fund. From this, grants were made to producers for equipment, the construction of a warehouse or stockroom, or social improvements in the workplace. Others needed technical advice: what kind of kiln to buy, how to weave wool instead of cotton, how to fix dyes, how to size shoes to fit British feet or label skirts to go in German washing machines. On the marketing side, Bridge might help a group prepare their own catalogue or open a local shop. But the most important advice was on product design. A consultant might spend two weeks with a group of caneworkers developing a range of furniture. A weaver from one project might be sent at Oxfam's expense to develop new textiles on the loom of another. In a way that other charitable importers of handicrafts did not, Bridge spent time and effort working with producers to make their business viable, their products saleable, and the future of their workers secure, independently of whether Oxfam ever bought another pincushion or batik tie from them.

In the early 1980s, Bridge sales rose to over £1 million annually. It took on its own field officers in India and Bangladesh, countries which together provided 50 per cent of orders; these were later followed by others in Thailand and Mexico. Their main task was to select the groups Bridge bought from and invested in, and thereby to develop closer links and a better understanding of who producers were, and their real, as opposed to assumed, needs as workers and as people.

Like all idealistic ventures, delivering on Bridge's promise was fraught with pitfalls, given that commercial viability rather than charity was the underlying requirement. However immaculate their embroidery or carving, those artisans weakest in education and means were, by definition, also weakest in business and marketing skills. Bridge tried to deploy most of its resources in helping the weaker groups; but as in the aid programme, investing in the poorest is difficult and risky. Whereas in the aid programme an ill-judged grant could be written off, in the case of Bridge, if investments went wrong the company and its dependents – suppliers and customers – suffered. Thus there was an unavoidable tension between the concentration of Bridge's resources in accord with its philosophy, and the need to remain profitable.

Although there were still many practical and philosophical bumps to be flattened, Oxfam's experiment in 'alternative trading' grew from strength to strength during the 1980s. By 1990, Oxfam Trading's 25th anniversary year, Bridge was importing items from 295 groups of producers in 43 countries, and its annual turnover was £8 million. It was now just one member of an international network of 'alternative traders' with links to the consumer – and green consumer – movements. Roy Scott's dream of commercial activity between North and South which did not exploit the poorest and weakest had proved infectious among the socially concerned, and successful enough to boost the contemporary taste for ethnic wares.

Not only in Britain, but in North America, Lester Pearson's grand assize into the Development Decade coincided with a profound awakening to the problems faced by the world's poorest people. In the late 1960s, when US involvement in Vietnam was opening the eyes of the young to the nature of international relationships between the powerful and the weak, Oxfam of Canada suddenly found its fortunes blossoming. In 1967, Canada's centennial year, its Ottawa Group introduced the sponsored walk to North America. 'Miles for Millions' raised money for well-drilling in Bihar, attracting 4,000 walkers. At their head was the then Prime Minister: Lester Pearson.

Sponsored walks took off in Canada like brush fire. In 1968, Oxfam more than quadrupled its income, to $680,000, as a result of walks and the publicity they generated. The following year, 250,000 walkers turned out simultaneously, in cities and towns across the country from Vancouver to St. John's, Newfoundland. In Britain, Oxfam's big national event of the year was also a sponsored walk, 'Walk '69', in which thousands of walkers converged on Wembley Stadium; but the total never even came close to the 45,000 who walked in Toronto alone. In 1969, Oxfam of Canada's income not only topped $1 million for the first time; over $1 million was raised just from walks.

Oxford, which had nursed Oxfam of Canada into existence, spending £60,000 and lending Henry Fletcher to tide it through its awkward early years, now saw its investment amply repaid. By the end of 1970, Canada had spent £1,200,000 on overseas aid, of which £600,000 had been channelled directly through Oxford. No-one was more pleased than Kirkley, who still strove after the vision he had shared with Jackson-Cole of an international network of Oxfams representing a non-sectarian and non-partisan constituency as the new character of worldwide voluntary endeavour.

Canada was the jewel in the crown of the extra-Oxford network, but the 1960s had seen a consolidation of links elsewhere. Oxfam Belgique had developed its own identity, and by 1970 contributed a useful annual £30,000 to the Oxfam programme. In 1965, instead of attempting to start an Oxfam Australia, Kirkley had been persuaded by David Scott, Chairman of Community Aid Abroad, to forge a mutually beneficial partnership and regard CAA as the Oxfam of down-under. CAA similarly promoted the development goal of 'helping people to help themselves'; like Oxfam UK, it also had a trading arm which imported and sold handicrafts in Australia; and its 160 voluntary groups carried out an energetic educational programme about the lives of neighbouring peoples in Asia. In 1971, without changing its name, CAA became a formal member of the Oxfam international fold. Oxfam America was also newly launched, and there were Oxfam fundraising groups in Italy, Denmark, Bahamas, Gibraltar, and Hong Kong.

Kirkley also made every effort to develop Oxfam's credibility in the international world, particularly among UN member agencies. Contacts were often made during emergencies – Congo, Nigeria, and East Pakistan/West Bengal – when an Oxfam-style voluntary agency had a freedom of movement denied many international bodies because of their intergovernmental character. In 1971, Kirkley was elected President of the International Council of Voluntary Agencies (ICVA), and he used the opportunity to try and gain the whole voluntary sector a higher degree of recognition. His aim was always to promote humanitarian fellowship based on the principles that Oxfam stood for; and to demonstrate that this spirit was capable of generating a methodology of aid which made a special contribution. Kirkley always claimed for voluntary assistance something far more elevated than marginal do-gooding which merely saved a few extra lives.

In a 1971 paper for the trustees Kirkley described Oxfam's high international reputation as deriving from: 'the quantity and quality of our aid programme, and the internationalism inherent in the humanitarian approach of Gilbert Murray and his co-founders'. The quantity of the aid programme rested on the organisation's ability to raise funds, and to underpin fundraising with longer-term education; its quality depended on the careful grant-making and project-checking procedures developed over the years, and the linchpin role in that process played by the Oxfam Field Directorate. So high a value was placed by Kirkley, and by Oxford generally, on the quality this system guaranteed that it did not really occur to him that other Oxfams might see things differently.

Where Oxfam support groups overseas raised money for Oxford to spend, there could be no divergence of view on eligible projects and beneficiaries: they chose a project on the Oxfam list and, goodness knows, the choice was wide. Problems could only arise where there was a separate, autonomous Oxfam. These had been encouraged: in their domestic programmes, other Oxfams needed an identity suited to their own fundraising, cultural, and political climate. It was also assumed that they would make some grants directly to projects of their own choosing: central control was not intended. A network of autonomous bodies in an international federation – like Save the Children or UNICEF – had been Kirkley's dream.

For a while, all went smoothly. Oxfam Belgique was content to pass its funds for overseas aid through the regular Oxfam machinery. CAA maintained a separate identity; so while it might participate in projects or share field services, what it chose to spend its money on was its own affair and need not affect Oxfam because it was not done in Oxfam's name. But the rapid growth of Oxfam of Canada in the increasingly radical North American climate began to disturb the Oxfam peace.

In the late 1960s, Canada began to assert its own independence of view about project funding. During the Nigerian Civil War, for example, some funds were channelled through Oxford, but a far larger amount was spent quite separately. Canadian support for the Scandinavian churches' airlift into beleaguered Biafra was extraordinary. In the mood of the moment, Henry Fletcher and the head of the Presbyterian Church in Canada bought a plane, set up an organisation called Canairelief to run it, and then bought three more. These four planes, manned by Canadian crews, carried 11,000 tons of relief goods into the Biafran enclave between January 1969 and the end of the war a year later.

This extraordinary $3-plus million effort, run by a volunteer board of Directors who neglected their own jobs and businesses to do so, was a profoundly formative experience. It was maintained entirely by public generosity. The loss of a Canairelief plane, which crashed on the approach to Uli airstrip killing its crew, was a moment of national tragedy.

By the turn of the decade, Oxfam of Canada was showing the same internal tensions about its political and educational role as Oxford was experiencing. The Canadian radicals, influenced not only by Pearson, by Vietnam, by Biafra, but by their dislike of Oxford's paternalistic attitude towards its colonial offspring, made a much stronger showing than their counterparts in Oxford. The crucial policy document, agreed by the Board in mid-1969, read: 'Oxfam must strive continuously to awaken the conscience of the public so as to develop a deep concern for the underprivileged peoples of the world. ... The organisation must be prepared to undertake activities which are sometimes of a political nature; the basis of development aid is one which calls for political decisions.' However, as in the UK, this agreement on the principles governing the Canadian Oxfam's way forward left open many questions about how to give them practical application. Far from dying down, the debate went on gathering steam.

Their new self-confidence encouraged Canada to flex their muscles in the public policy arena. In 1971, a submission was made to Canada's Parliamentary Committee on External Affairs, attacking a government White Paper on Foreign Policy produced in response to the Pearson Report. This had failed to recommend the adoption of any of Pearson's goals or recognise a need for change in Canada's trading or public investment relationships with the developing world. From this point onwards, Oxfam Canada began to become much more vocal in its criticism of federal policies, forcefully adopting the type of activity Cyril James had called 'the role of gadfly to sting the State to action'. But it also became a recipient of government resources for project aid: the Canadian International Development Agency (CIDA) was the first official donor body to channel funds through voluntary agencies.

Now under entirely Canadian management – Jack Shea took over from Henry Fletcher in 1971 – Oxfam Canada continued the process of redefining its own aims and policies. The process was ideologically driven and was a deliberate effort to distance Oxfam Canada from Oxfam UK. A signal that this might lead to trouble came when a grant was made to an institute run by FRELIMO in what was still the Portuguese colony of Mozambique. Oxford wanted discretion; it was anxious about the potential damage to its name and programme if it was known that 'Oxfam' support was associated with the armed southern

African liberation struggle. To Oxfam Canada, however, most of the point of making the grant was to express publicly its solidarity with the victims of Portuguese colonialism.

A full-scale showdown between the Oxfams finally erupted in early 1973. The immediate cause was a 'White Paper on Political Affairs' produced by a leading Oxfam Canada radical, Professor Meyer Brownstone. (Brownstone subsequently became the Oxfam Canada Chairman.) When this document arrived in Oxford it provoked instant alarm. Its analysis derided what it saw as Oxfam UK's devotion to charitable rather than 'developmental' aid, allocated through paternalistic structures – Committees in Oxford – mostly to projects run by missionaries and other expatriates. These were overseen by a Field Directorate more concerned with technical questions than the political and social inequities which ought – in Brownstone's view – to be their starting point. 'Developmental', in Canada's interpretation, could only mean the pursuit of social justice by the undermining of existing power structures. Oxford would have not narrowed the definition so far, although much current thinking was similar. The difference between the two Oxfams lay in the prescription; and in the fact that Oxford had what by voluntary agency standards was quite a large programme to protect, and Canada did not.

Oxfam Canada was already committed to a domestic education and political action programme which drew attention to the inequities governing relationships between the rich and poor worlds. Now it wanted its overseas aid programme to reflect the same preoccupations; the inequities governing the relationships between the elites in Third World countries (and their Western capitalist allies), and the poverty-stricken majority. This meant concentrating its aid both in type and in place, and spending it through those indigenous groups – decidedly not expatriates or missionaries – working to 'eliminate the material and political poverty of the oppressed'.

Decisions about project funding would be made by special committees set up in the countries in question 'composed of nationals with the relevant skills and a strong commitment to social justice'. Oxfam Canada realised that this course of action might not endear it to the authorities in many countries. But it welcomed the idea of becoming known as a critic of right-wing governments. It singularly failed to recognise the full implications of what it was proposing for those whose cause it was intending to champion.

As far as Oxfam UK was concerned, public campaigns about projects which were trying to change the balance of social forces stacked against the poor were out of the question. Delicately, it was trying in many countries to shift its aid in this direction, often under the umbrella of the liberal, missionary church. Shouting about projects which were already in dubious political odour was hardly likely to ease their already difficult passage. One result might be that 'Oxfam' – and who would recognise the difference between the Canadian Oxfam and any other? – would be thrown out of a country. Worse: in certain countries, Oxfam-funded projects and the people running them might find themselves in serious danger.

In early 1973, Oxfam Canada announced its intention of 'withdrawing' from Brazil, then under military rule, as a prelude to mounting a public attack on Canadian investment in Brazil and the policies of the regime itself. Oxford was appalled; this action would jeopardise the safety of just the kind of projects and indigenous personnel Oxfam Canada said it wanted to support. To Oxford, the value of the programme and the modest help Oxfam offered came above all other considerations; Canada, which did not have the same long-standing and intimate contact with a programme on the ground, saw mainly a bossy, centralist and neo-colonial Oxfam UK presuming to tell them what to do.

Eventually, the action campaign on Brazil was modified. The breach between the two agencies was patched up, but not resolved. The sense of divisiveness within the Oxfam family increased when the Quebequois arm of Oxfam Canada broke away to form a separate Oxfam Quebec. Oxfam Canada decentralised into regional groups within a federal structure, and suffered further deep divisions. Oxfam America, still in its infancy, was also beset by problems of every kind. In the absence of a common framework of policy governing activities overseas carried out in Oxfam's name, the viability of an international Oxfam network was in doubt.

Early in 1974, a working party was appointed by trustees in Oxford to consider the future of 'Oxfam International'. This attempt to put the growth of an international movement back on track was an effort to salvage Kirkley's dream. Although a joint Disasters Unit was set up as a result of its recommendations, little harmony greeted the rest of the working party's proposals. The best that could be achieved was agreement on the need for proper consultation and information-sharing; the opening up of the Field Directorate to candidates from other Oxfams; and common assent that alliance with like-minded agencies, such as Community Aid Abroad, was in future to be preferred to any extension of the Oxfam name.

The original Kirkley vision of a worldwide Oxfam with a shared overseas programme and field staff had to be put aside. The idea of non-confessional assistance to community projects in the vast reaches of the developing world was too loose a concept to be centrally controlled, especially by that reconstructed colonialist, the British philanthropist. This does not mean that new Oxfams in other countries have not subsequently emerged, nor that special relationships within the Oxfam fold cannot survive; but in a world increasingly full of competing views of the rich world/poor world divide, and of how to tackle it, the Kirkley dream of Oxfam International with a unified structure and policy was doomed.

Kirkley himself, at this moment of disappointment, was on the verge of retirement. After 22 years at the head of Oxfam, and at the age of 63, he felt that the moment to hand over had come. The succession had been in the back of his mind since the appointment of Nic Stacey; now an external candidate was appointed: Brian Walker, 43, Manager of an engineering company in Northern Ireland. His selection exemplified the need felt for the modern management man with professional organisational skills who could weld the disparate energies of Oxfam into a more disciplined unit.

Leslie Kirkley's legacy to Oxfam was – Oxfam. In the early days, when he had sat every morning at the table in the office above 17 Broad Street, opening the mail with the volunteers and feeling bucked if the day's take was high, Jackson-Cole had provided the vision and much of the driving force. But Kirkley had absorbed that vision and given it enduring organisational expression.

In 1951, Oxfam had been a successful local charitable committee. Under Kirkley's stewardship, it had become one of the largest, most creative, most widely respected voluntary aid agencies in the world. It had helped to transform the business of philanthropy in Britain. Overseas, its Field Directorate, both as a means of accountability to donors and of shaping an effective programme, was the envy of many other organisations with a similar mandate.

HLK never claimed, as some have tried to do on his behalf and others would certainly have done in his place, the credit for Oxfam's extraordinary success. The climate of the early 1960s in which Oxfam surged to prominence was not a climate anyone in Kirkley's position could independently have created. There was a degree of luck in being there at the right time. Kirkley recognised this. But his canniness, and his particular style of management, in which he led not from in front but from the middle, enabling the energy of brighter stars to radiate, allowed Oxfam to catch the mood and harness its power to its own advance. And when the tide receded in the late 1960s, leaving a residue of Haslemere activists and Stacey acolytes who wanted to challenge the first principles of Oxfam's existence, it was Kirkley's performance which kept the organisation steady: the tortoise caught up with, and overtook, the hares.

In his cardigan, saying 'Well, I don't know really' in answer to some impassioned exposition, windbagging the trustees around to consensus, eating his lunch unceremoniously in the Oxfam canteen, HLK did not always indicate his mettle. He certainly did not set out to impress, and as a public speaker did not impress; he did not 'director' his way about. But all those who had the chance to find out what he was made of had enormous respect for him, and for what he achieved. No-one has ever done, or could ever do, as much for the organisation he nurtured, or for the voluntary aid sector in which he earned it a leading role. In 1977, his continuing contribution to the British overseas aid and charitable world was recognised with a knighthood.

Sir Leslie died in 1989. There are people all over the world who remember him plodding his Oxfam path with feelings of gratitude and deep affection.

9

TO HAVE MORE AND TO BE MORE

The early 1970s were a time of great intellectual and spiritual energy concerning the theory and practice of development. Thinkers of heroic stature strode about the world stage unleashing a maelstrom of ideas, inclined to challenge every prevailing orthodoxy about underdevelopment and poverty in 'the South'. Their inspirations were many but they shared a common ingredient: rejection of the Western economic model as the one and only instrument of human advancement. In all directions of the compass, and under a number of different disciplinary and ideological banners, the search for alternatives was on.

One of the earliest icons to tumble was rapid growth of GNP, previously the patron saint of instant social transformation. Up to this time, few had questioned the application of Western standards to the process of 'development' decision making. Economic expansion, brought about by the march of Western science, technology, and industrial know-how into developing societies, had been expected to sweep more and more people into its embrace as it spawned jobs and services, upgrading the quality of life for all.

No such thing had occurred. What had tended to happen instead – with different emphases in different places – was that a small section of the population had become educated, modern, and outward-looking, their fortunes and life-styles integrated with the Western economic system. Meanwhile, the traditional economy, which still supported the overwhelming majority of people, had become downgraded, even as the numbers of those depending upon it swelled. This had not been the typical end-result of the industrial revolution in the West whichever ideological model you looked at. Something – and it was not just the unprecedented rate of population growth – was going drastically wrong.

In 1972, Robert McNamara made a landmark statement to the Board of Governors of the World Bank. He suggested that the governments of the developing countries should reorient their policies to attack directly the poverty of the poorest 40 per cent of their citizens, and that the world's financial and investment machinery should reorient itself to help them do so. Traditionally, economists and planners looked down on social expenditures – food, welfare, health, education – as 'consumption'; their business was with productive enterprise, with the build-up of technological and managerial capacity. This, according to McNamara, must change. Since the fruits of growth were not 'trickling down' to them, ways must be found of targeting the poor with investment policies that paid dividends in their lives. In other words, McNamara suggested, what was happening to the poor mattered; it was a sickness in the international body politic and needed a cure.

McNamara was only one of many contemporary figures to champion an attack on world poverty as the challenge for the 1970s. Academics such as Hans Singer, Gunnar Myrdal, Raoul Prebisch, Michael Lipton, and Richard Jolly characterised the new line of economic thought with slogans such as 'redistribution with growth' and 'meeting people's basic needs'. The international community countered with a series of global UN conferences, on the environment (Stockholm, 1972), population (Bucharest 1974), food (Rome 1974), women (Mexico 1975), human settlements (Vancouver 1976), water (Mar del Plata 1976), desertification (Nairobi, 1977). At all these fora the voluntary agencies made their presence felt, playing their 'gadfly, to sting the state to action' role.

The countries of the Third World were beginning to make their own voices heard more strongly. In the wake of the 1973 oil crisis, the possibility of using their control over certain commodities – of joint action to raise the price at which they sold raw materials, to match the price at which they were obliged to buy Western products – seemed for a while to open new bargaining horizons. The 'Group of 77' – the developing countries – demanded a 'New International Economic Order', a call endorsed at the UN in 1974. There was much sympathy in the development lobby towards the Third World's desire to escape the chains of economic dependency which decolonisation had failed to unshackle. Aid, in whatever form, was a poor substitute for a fair deal; and it could never do more than top up the national development budget.

By now, the major league players – government and international – had accepted that most of the aid-for-development plans and blueprints had so far made a negligible impact on the condition of the poor. This had important implications for the minor league, the voluntary agencies. Reaching poor families and engineering some small but lasting improvement in their lives was all that the philanthropists had ever aspired to do; they could not have afforded to invest in hydroelectric dams and groundnuts schemes even if they had wanted to. The scale of their activities might be modest, but they had developed special skills and expertise. Casting around for alternative models in which the benefits of a scheme managed to reach people at the bottom of the social ladder instead of bunching higher up, the economists – with some prompting – began to notice that some of the projects funded by the charities met this criterion rather well.

The most progressive of the voluntary agencies, of which Oxfam was but one, had developed a methodology of aid which made its own special contribution. The programmes they supported did not simply succour the destitute; neither were they mini carbon copies of 'aid' as defined by government, but were qualitatively different. They were certainly smaller, even lilliputian by government and international standards. The miniature size of their operations both in population coverage and geographical spread was, however, the source of their most striking advantage.

The philanthropists tended to be better at reaching the poor. This was not because of their brilliant grasp of economics and sociology, but because the poor were their deliberate target. In keeping faith with their donors to ensure that 'the money really gets there', they distributed their resources as close to the poor as they could reach. The projects they supported focused on the specific needs of a specific group of people, not on the overall needs of a large administrative area. This meant that they were by definition designed – if sometimes amateurishly – to fit a particular micro-environment. The sensitivity of most voluntary agency projects to the human condition – what people thought, how they behaved, whether they were motivated, what they themselves could contribute – was beyond that of large impersonal government programmes. The latter's planning and management procedures rarely reached closer to their poorer clientele than a provincial urban centre; their agents in the form of government functionaries were often regarded with mistrust by local people, whom they in turn treated with disdain.

It took many years for the special characteristics of voluntary agency programmes to be fully appreciated by the 'experts'; indeed, the mutual admiration of official and voluntary aid protagonists has always remained ambivalent. But the role of informal structures and 'barefoot' technicians began to gain widespread recognition, as did the 'micro projects' of the voluntary agencies now identified as a special breed. In Britain, a dialogue began between the agencies and the Overseas Development Administration about whether the government should follow the Canadian and Scandinavian example in channelling some official aid through the charities.

Oxfam first submitted a proposal to the Select Committee on Overseas Development for a suitable framework for co-operation in mid-1973. In 1975, Judith Hart, Minister of Overseas Development, introduced a scheme whereby £500,000 a year from the ODA was offered for the co-funding of approved voluntary agency projects. Oxfam, now under the leadership of Brian Walker, played an important role in helping to bring this partnership to fruition. Walker also took a lead among non-governmental aid organisations in Europe in promoting similar arrangements with the EEC's assistance programme.

While the official development establishment pursued 'basic needs' and other alternative strategies, the agencies' own quest was propelled forward from other directions.

One thinker whose ideas were of seminal importance was E.F. Schumacher. In the mid-1960s, Schumacher set up the Intermediate Technology Development Group, the first organisation from North or South to seek out and build upon existing technological capacity within traditional societies instead of behaving as if they were pieces of pre-Iron Age paper on which modernisation and mechanisation must be written. His treatise *Small is Beautiful: A study of economics as if people mattered* was published in 1973. Its criticism of the assumption of power by large impersonal institutions in extensive areas of people's lives so resonated with audiences around the world that Schumacher rapidly developed a worldwide following.

In the development context, the concept of 'appropriate technology' – ('intermediate' had connotations of second-class unwelcome in the Third World) – contained a self-evident truth of blinding simplicity: the tools of development, whether artefacts or social arrangements for deploying them, must be reconciled with the needs and the capacities of the people they were meant to serve. This required that those trying to introduce them should acquaint themselves properly not only with the real parameters of a given problem, but also with the locals' usual methods of dealing with it. Control over technology was a factor in the distribution of power, and people's interests were likely to be best served when their own hands were on the levers.

Although Schumacher attacked the spiritual emptiness of the modern behemoth of progress, his ideas were essentially secular. The voluntary agencies, rooted in Christian and humanist persuasion, were as strongly influenced by currents of thinking emanating from the churches. One of the most pervasive moral influences in Oxfam had been the ideals of pacifism and consensual fellowship espoused by the Quakers. In the 1970s, its thinking – in common with many other agencies – began to be affected by the radical energies in the Catholic Church unleashed by Vatican II. Like the Gandhians who articulated an alternative Indian vision, and Nyerere's philosophy of *ujamaa*, the voice of those demanding the 'preferential option for the poor' came authentically from the Third World, this time from Latin America.

This was an urgent voice and a revolutionary voice, a voice which described the Christian duty to 'love one another' as inseparable from active rejection of the socio-economic injustice deeply ingrained in Latin American society. Bestowing crumbs of charity upon the poor was not enough, especially now that the existing pattern of development could be seen to be entrenching, not diminishing, the gulf of wealth discrepancy. No longer was it possible to pretend that under-development was merely retarded growth and that everyone would catch up in due course. Underdevelopment and poverty were structural phenomena; the poverty of many was a natural corollary of the social, economic, and political system controlled by a few.

In Latin America, those forces, internal and external, which designed and upheld these structures were strengthening their grip. The rise of socialist movements throughout Latin America following the 1959 Cuban revolution had led to rapid polarisation within societies. Liberal and leftist tendencies received a setback when the Brazilian government was militarised in 1964; thereafter many countries followed suit, stamping out democratic expression. The darkest day for the South American reformist movement dawned when, in Chile in September 1973, Salvador Allende's government was violently overthrown by General Augusto Pinochet. The flight of hundreds of thousands of refugees, not only from Chile but from other Latin American dictatorships, was to have an important effect on awareness in North America and Europe about the agonies suffered in many countries during the 1970s and 1980s.

The repressive actions accompanying military rule made a profound impact on the Latin American church, and on the attitude of many originally conservative bishops towards the reformist movement. An important expression of their position came with the rejection of rich world 'developmentalism' at an international meeting of Roman Catholic bishops held in Medellin, Colombia, in 1968. From this point onwards a new school of doctrinal debate developed a 'theology of liberation', and many priests strove to realise its radical precepts in partnership with their poorer congregations. The gospel was henceforward to be propounded as an instrument of self-realisation; those marginalised by the forces of modernisation would discover their worth as human beings, and become the subjects of their own version of development instead of the victims of someone else's. In the new definition of pastoral function and duty, the foot soldiers of the Latin American church found a convergence of view with partners in Europe and North America. The Oxfams and many other funding agencies became their keen supporters.

Despite its Marxist rhetoric, liberation theology did not envisage a direct and violent challenge to the *status quo* so much as an erosion of the mechanisms whereby the *status quo* was protected and perpetuated. The most important of these was the colonisation of the human spirit by which the poor were bound into acceptance of a miserable existence and abject dependency. The word 'education' could not be used to describe the enlightenment they needed, because the existing educational system was part of the philosophical and institutional framework enforcing their oppression. For this reason Ivan Illich, an influential 'alternatives' prophet based in Mexico, went so far as to advocate – in *Deschooling Society* (1970) – the removal of schools altogether. 'The mere existence of school,' he wrote, 'discourages and disables the poor from taking control of their own learning.'

Illich was prolific in his condemnation of institutionalised social progress. Like Schumacher, he developed a following among the disciples of development; on visits to Britain, many Oxfamers were to be found in his audiences, although he consistently excoriated the humanitarians for being wide-eyed and gullible extensions of the system causing all the damage. For this he received their adulatory applause. His combination of arch-conservatism and subversive radicalism embodied the schizophrenic attitude towards philanthropic aid that tangled many debates in Oxfam at that time, acting as both stimulus and depressant. To help was to interfere, sometimes with unforeseen and negative consequences. But if even the humanitarian establishment contained more potential for social damage than for repair, what hope on earth was there?

On the positive side, Illich helped put the emphasis back on people as the rightful subjects, not the objects, of their fate. All the new prophets agreed that development could not, and should not, be done to people or for them; the *campesino* (peasant farmer) and the slum dweller must carve their own path out of their predicament. But for this to happen, they would first have to abandon their passive and fatalistic outlook. A new type of learning was needed which would spark an awakening within the abject mind. This was why so much importance was attached to the concept of 'conscientisation'.

Although many efforts were made – not least in Oxfam – to translate the Portuguese *concientizacao* more comfortably into English, no other word really worked. Invented in the early 1960s by Paulo Freire, a Brazilian educator, and adopted into liberation theology, the concept embraced intellectual and spiritual nourishment as in learning, awakening, becoming motivated; and practical action such as organisation for some kind of project. Freire described the poor as submerged in a 'culture of silence'. Learning to read and write – Freire mounted literacy campaigns in his native north-east Brazil before being

JENNIFER A BOOTH/OXFAM

44 *Father Godest, a Breton priest, whose simple but effective groundwater management technology transformed the lives of the villagers of Otterthotti, in Mysore, India.*

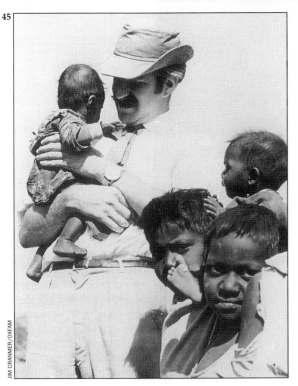

JIM CRANMER/OXFAM

45 *Living and working truly at village level: Adrian Marshall, an agricultural 'volunteer' in Oxfam's first operational development enterprise, the Gramdam Action Programme in Bihar.*

46 *President Julius Nyerere of Tanzania at Oxfam House, 1975, with Brian Walker (Director) left, and Michael Rowntree (Chairman). 'If we state that some new Jerusalem is where we are going, our friends should not be disappointed if they find we are still in the desert.'*

47 *In 1973, Oxfam embarked on an unusual partnership with Tanzanian local authorities to boost development in the* ujamaa *village: a carpentry workshop in Chunya for making furniture out of* mninga *wood.*

48

48 *1971: refugees in India from what was then East Pakistan, soon to become Bangladesh. Oxfam's largest-ever relief programme, costing £150,000 a month.*

49

49 *Lester Pearson,* left, *Prime Minister of Canada, steps out with Henry Fletcher in Oxfam of Canada's first national event: 'Miles for Millions' in 1967.*

50

50 *Nicolas Stacey kisses Rita Tushingham: an Oxfam 'Fun Run' in 1970. The extrovert Deputy Director had great publicist talents, but his real ambition was frustrated.*

OXFAM

51 *The Oxfam Shop, high-class jumble sale variety. In the 1960s, many volunteer groups ran temporary shops in end-of-lease premises, raising a few hundred pounds a year.*

CAMILLA GARRETT-JONES/OXFAM

52 *In the 1970s, Oxfam modernised its shops operation, investing in premises, marketing, and volunteer training. Shop income topped £1 million in 1973 and never looked back.*

53 *'Helping by Selling' 1970: in Ahmedabad, 75 women who would otherwise have been destitute and unemployed made mirror-work wall-hangings, and sold them to Oxfam.*

54 *Combining fundraising with fun. Youngsters taking part in a 1972 event to 'Find the Monuments', map read with Maggie Black.*

55 *The launch of 'Bridge' in 1976 brought Third World handicrafts into the shops via a fair-trading policy that invested profits back into producers instead of donating them to Oxfam.*

56 *1977: with Archbishop Helder Camara in Brazil.* Left to right, *Brian Walker (Director), Michael Harris (Overseas Director), Lesley Roberts (Field Director, Caribbean)*

57 *Irma (Sister) Dulce, Brazil's Mother Teresa, who ministered tirelessly to the sick and destitute of the city of Salvador. Oxfam began helping her in 1969.*

58 *Agricultural trainees in Guatemala. Oxfam set up an office in Guatemala in 1975; it was closely involved with an early 'integrated development' programme based in Chimaltenango.*

59 *Illiterate Indian villagers in the remote highlands of Ecuador tune into 'classes' on animal husbandry, hygiene, and child care.*

60 *On 4 February 1976, a devastating earthquake struck Guatemala. Reggie Norton, Oxfam Field Director, in the ruins of San Martin Jilotepeque, discussing relief plans.*

61

SHEENA GROSSETT/OXFAM

61 *BRAC in Bangladesh, set up after the liberation of 1971 and supported by Oxfam. Cheap materials, low-cost technology, and a focus on women gave BRAC staying power.*

62

OXFAM

63

NICK FOGDEN/OXFAM

1973: Oxfam tried to draw attention in Britain to drought in India and raise funds for an imaginative, development-ally conscious, programme. **62** *Above, a vigil on the steps of St. Martin-in-the-Fields;* **63** *left, Judith Hart MP doles out relief rations – bowls of porridge.*

jailed and subsequently exiled in 1964 – must not only equip people to wield a pen; more significantly, it must equip them with the energy and creativity to be able to reflect upon their own environment as a step to changing it.

Freire's *Pedagogy of the Oppressed* was published in Britain in 1972. Like Ivan Illich's outrageous propositions, Freire's ideas were very difficult to follow, but this did not make them any less popular. Their impact on the more radical minds in Oxfam was profound, particularly since this quest for alternatives invited not only the poor, but everyone, to challenge the values inherent in their own *status quo*. Among many senior Oxfam staff and trustees, this latest form of preoccupation with intellectual, left-wing precepts within the ranks was greeted with misgiving. This new debate had all the hallmarks of subversion; it was not only about an alternative vision of the Third World, but of society as a whole and the role and relationships of every human being within it.

During the late 1960s and early 1970s, as this whirlwind of ideas gathered force, Oxfam had begun to build up its programme in the Americas.

The Oxfam programme in the Western Hemisphere began in the mid-1950s in the traditional way: help for victims of a hurricane (St. Lucia), and a famine (Haiti). These emergency grants were given via the Methodists and the Salvation Army, and once these contacts had been made there was a gradual increase in requests for assistance. It took time, however, for a programme to develop. Compared to Asia and Africa there were few British ties with a part of the world whose conquest by sword and cross had been accomplished by Spaniards and Portuguese. The Americas were also more developed than most ex-British colonies, and wealthier.

The Freedom from Hunger Campaign opened up a range of new projects to Oxfam funds. One of the largest of these was the Bolivian venture for improving traditional Indian crops, that caused so much vexation to the Charity Commissioners. In 1964, great Oxfam excitement was generated by a big-spending Jimmy Betts tour of British Guiana in which his intention was to set up a programme similar to that in Lesotho; it languished for want of a locally-based Field Director. In 1965, Oxfam began to support village credit co-operatives in north-east Brazil for small farmers normally fleeced by local merchants. A range of health, nutrition, and other projects followed in other countries of the region, many funded through Catholic Relief Services (CRS) and missionary bodies.

By 1966, Oxfam had become enthused by radio schools in Ecuador and Peru. These 'schools' enabled illiterate Indian villagers living in inaccessible mountain areas to tune in to classes in agriculture, animal husbandry, hygiene, and child care. One request read as follows: 'The Prelature of Yauyos plans to open 87 new radiophonic schools. They asked us to transmit to Oxfam their ardent wish and petition to continue to help them with their generosity. It means progress for their simple and good population.' The Vicar General of Yauyos resolutely visited these far-flung communities on muleback, recording his long rides in the mountains in a diary he sent to Oxfam House. This was still the old world of calm, sometimes stoic, beneficence; not yet the confusing one of deschooling and conscientisation.

Like Asia and Africa, Latin America had its saints. One of these was Irma (Sister) Dulce, a nun who dedicated her life to the poor in the city of Salvador, Bahia, on Brazil's east coast. Her first ministry was to a group of derelicts sheltering under a bridge. When their space was condemned as an eyesore she found a small, empty, dilapidated house, invited an astonished passer-by to break in, and took it over. This was the start of her 'Albergue', or refuge. Within a few years she was also running a shelter for destitute migrants from the countryside, an orphanage and a hospital, somehow managing to persuade local benefactors to stump up £30,000 a year.

Irma Dulce came to Oxfam's notice in 1967, and a grant of £10,000 was made for a new hospital building. In 1969, Oxfam's first Field Director in the Americas, Peter Oakley, visited Bahia and was deeply impressed by Sister Dulce's work. 'She overcrowds her wards with the sick and begs everyone who will listen to help her do more for the only free hospital in the State. There are 14 doctors and surgeons working for her voluntarily, including Professors from the State University. The new hospital is now built and ready for use ... all Irma Dulce needs is equipment.' £4,000 was duly sent, and the building opened that year. Her work continued to be admired and supported by Oxfam through the early 1980s.

By 1970 the Americas were absorbing £276,000 a year, 13 per cent of Oxfam's total aid overseas. The comparative scale of programmes in different regions was largely a product of history. By far the largest amounts were spent in the Indian sub-continent (one-fifth) and in Africa (nearly half) where Field Directors had been first on the scene. But by now, the rate of programme growth in South America was among the fastest. As Field Offices opened up – Brazil 1969, Peru 1970, Mexico 1971 – the pattern was set for change. By 1974, the proportion of Oxfam aid going to Central and South America and the Caribbean was 22 per cent.

North-east Brazil, the poorest and most climatically vulnerable swathe in the hemisphere, was selected as the location for the first Field

Director. In 1969, Peter Oakley – young, confident, energetic – took on the role of Oxfam itinerant in a vast parish which included problems as varied as threatened Indian tribes in the Amazonian rain forests, drought in marginal rural lands, peasant land dispossession, the proliferation of slums and shanties in the cities, child abandonment, prostitution, as well as poverty's basics: low income, low skills, illiteracy, hunger, and ill-health. It was no coincidence that this was the crucible of radical thinking on the continent. The Archbishop of Recife was Dom Helder Camara, a leading voice for the progressive church, later to become known worldwide for his championship of liberation theology; Recife was also Paulo Freire's home town and thus conscientisation capital.

Like Field Directors in other parts of the world before him, Oakley at first had great difficulty in identifying indigenous agencies with whom to work. This was mainly because, in the prevailing climate of repression, the church was the only institution able to defend the interests of the down-trodden. Oakley's difficulties were not made any easier by the fact that Oxfam was almost entirely unknown in Brazil. Some of those who did get to hear that there was a new source of funds in town had a tendency to arrive on his doorstep talking in vague and ethereal terms; concrete projects rarely materialised. Oakley therefore depended heavily on priests and missionaries to build up the programme, despite a wish to do otherwise. Both because of their courage in the face of threats to their activities, and because of their commitment, he deeply admired their work: 'In many areas the missionaries constitute the only hope that many people have.'

One promising development was the creation of an entirely Brazilian voluntary agency, the Federation of Organisations for Social and Educational Assistance, or FASE. The brainchild of a priest working for CRS, this was an attempt to set up a Brazilian equivalent to run its own projects and raise its own funds from church and non-governmental sources. In 1970, FASE separated from CRS, and became a secular organisation. Two of its offices were in the north-east, in Recife and Belém.

FASE had its fair share of early difficulties and relations with Oxfam were sometimes strained. But as Oakley constantly underlined to the Latin American Committee back in Oxford, FASE was one of the only private Brazilian organisations working in community development: 'In FASE, Brazilians are helping Brazilians.' Therefore this was a special kind of partner, and if its behaviour did not always conform to Anglo-Saxon attitudes about project formulation or accountability, Oxfam must be understanding. How to encourage the evolution of local agencies by supporting their projects without being directive or culturally judgemental, and yet adhere to procedures devised in Oxford, posed constant dilemmas to the Field Directorate.

FASE's *modus operandi* was to appoint teams of *'tecnicos'*: agricultural-ists, social workers, hygienists, teachers, to act as advisers and community organisers in the *barrios* – slums – and in rural parishes. By 1972, FASE's full complement of Brazilian staff was 133. Oxfam supported health activities, housing improvements, work with leprosy patients, village co-operatives, and small-scale irrigation schemes for marginal lands; it also paid salaries and costs of one group of *tecnicos*, and helped pay for a national research and development team. Thus, Oxfam not only aided FASE projects, but helped support its core establishment.

During the early 1970s, Church and the military-dominated State in Brazil seemed set on a collision course. Radical priests were being arrested and detained. 'Base communities' set up by the liberationist clergy represented the only popular democratic structures of any kind and this progressive Christian movement was constantly under pressure. Oakley, while hopeful of its potential for the poor, alerted Oxfam to the implications. 'The essence of the clash is the word *"concientizar"*. A lot of priests preach the need to wake the people up from their dormant acceptance of their miserable lives, to point out to them the injustices of Brazilian society and in many cases to urge them to 'right the wrong'. All of this is a slap in the face for the stern, disciplinarian right-wing government which is openly suspicious of grassroots community movements.'

FASE, and other recipients of Oxfam grants such as MOC (the Movement for Community Organisation) in Feira de Santana, Bahia, were right in the thick of things. In 1972, several FASE-Rio personnel were arrested. Oakley wrote: 'This is an indication of the authorities' determination to control any organisation melodramatically called "subversive".' Already, some projects supported by Oxfam had aroused the authorities' suspicions. This was a new ingredient in the careful balance of forces governing Oxfam aid: however obviously humanitarian a grant to basic literacy or slum improvement might be in the eyes of British donors or charitable law, their intent might be quite differently interpreted by those in power in countries at the receiving end. In some parts of the world, development was becoming a very sticky business. And, since in such places much project work was labelled 'subversive', it became extremely difficult to publicise it in Britain or elsewhere for fear of placing in jeopardy both the work and the safety of those involved.

In mid-1972, another Portuguese-speaking young British dynamo, Bill Yates, took over the north-east Brazilian beat. Yates had spent his early childhood in Brazil, worked in marketing, and been an energetic

Pledged Gift collector for Oxfam. This was his first appointment in an organisation to which he was to make a very important contribution, not only in Brazil.

He joined at an exciting time. Freire fever was invading Oxfam House, and he was the man posted to the place whence the infection was blowing. It fell to Yates to shift Oxfam's Brazil programme into a wholehearted commitment to conscientisation and alignment with – he called it *'caminhar junto'*, 'walking with' – those organisations trying to put the concept into practice. He also had the task of persuading the Oxfam powers and the Oxfam constituency back home that this pursuit of the unpronounceable and incomprehensible was not just an addiction to intellectual hot air but the adoption of a sound and effective strategy on behalf of the poor.

Yates' own 'conscientisation' took place against the backcloth of continuing repression and courageous Christian activity. Every few months news came that a priest or worker involved in an Oxfam-supported project had been detained. Oxfam itself was suspect and the need for discretion complicated a process of communication with Oxford already befogged by the growing lexicon of -isms. One of Yates' most testing moments came when, early in 1973, Oxfam of Canada announced its intention to campaign against Brazilian development policy and its backing by Canadian business interests. Yates went to Quebec to explain that, if an organisation called Oxfam campaigned publicly in this fashion, the safety of some of Oxfam's partners and those they were helping would be threatened. His eloquence was persuasive.

Yates' condemnation of 'assistencialism' – a misplaced notion of doing good while actually shoring up the forces oppressing the poor – echoed certain other Oxfam voices around the world. Alan Leather described the violent tactics of Bihari landholders against a powerless labouring class in much the same terms. The importance of this analytical starting point was that it gave an entirely new purpose and meaning to the concept of community development.

In the past, a community development project – such as Father Godest's catchment dams in Otterthotti or Daudi Ricardo's wells in Tanzania – had envisaged the community coming together to construct or grow something which would augment their collective and individual fortunes. The management of this activity and the technical know-how were provided by the project-holder, as were money and materials. At the end of the activity, there would be a product: a dam, a well, a bund, a field of waving corn. After the next harvest, the value of this could be counted, in bushels of extra crop, in cash value, in improved health and nutritional standards. Material advance was the natural measurement of success.

'Small is beautiful' dethroned the miracle of glittering Western technology from its previously hallowed role: technology must be affordable and manageable by the community. Conscientisation – as interpreted by Oxfam – did the same for project design, organisation and management. To be effective and long-lasting, development must emanate not from outside the community, but from the beneficiaries' own articulation of their needs, by activities they themselves had planned and were committed to carrying out. The role of outsiders in this scenario was to try and help the community develop the capacity to do this, and lend support appropriately, preferably from an increasing distance as the community's capacity to handle its own development expanded.

The ultimate goal here was to precipitate a process; whether an extra crop of waving corn was harvested this year or next was seen as a by-product – an essential by-product but a by-product nonetheless and not the key measure of 'success'. Measuring the process was less a matter of counting physical outcomes than monitoring the strength of community groups and how well they were led and organised. As Yates was fond of repeating, it mattered not what people did – they might build a chapel, a jail, even a football pitch if this was what they wanted. (He actually submitted a request on behalf of a mountain-top village that wanted to blast away part of its perch to build a football pitch, rendering his counterpart in Oxfam House temporarily speechless.) What mattered was the self-confidence, and the sense of fellowship, and the know-how a group garnered in the process of doing.

This would not occur if the group saw themselves as employees on a venture dreamed up by someone else. If someone else drilled the borehole, built the latrine, constructed the community centre, there was no sense of community ownership or responsibility; if it leaked or broke down, no-one bothered. So if they wanted to build a cinema, let them build it. Once they had made a start, their sense of achievement would lead them on -perhaps to start a loan fund, a community clinic, a co-op, or something else more solidly within the usual Oxfam frame of reference. Of course this would all take time; but gradually a new, mutually supportive society would emerge to build a better and a fairer world. This was the dream, and it was a potent and an optimistic dream.

Yates argued the case for the dream from a profound and passionate conviction which deepened as his experience of north-eastern Brazil lengthened. Visiting the MOC (Movement for Community Organisation) programme in Feira, in 1973, he described how the community associations were developing their muscle and taking initiatives. But witnessing the process could be painful. 'The meetings take an hour to get started; someone with important information does not turn up; the subject under discussion gets lost; the meeting goes on for hours. But decisions are taken, people are appointed to do things, and a little progress is made each time.' He concluded: 'Personally I have no doubt that this kind of activity – by FASE, MOC, and others – is the most important development work we are supporting.' Some members of the Latin American Committee, not to mention Oxfam's own senior establishment, found such statements hard to swallow.

Not all Oxfam's partners in Latin America maintained the same implicit faith that this process would lead to concrete results. One Bolivian organisation set up in 1971 by Jesuit priests, the Centre for the Study and Promotion of the Campesino (CIPRA), began with conscientisation, training peasant leaders to become 'active agents of social and economic transformation': the project proposal read like a text from the gospel according to Paulo Freire. Within a few years came the discovery: 'Conscientisation is not enough.' Soon, CIPRA was also offering technical assistance, and encouraging the *campesinos* to form co-operatives to produce and market their most important crop, potatoes. Awareness-building had been a first step along the road, but was not able to propel the *campesino* and his family the entire distance.

Within Oxfam, an important advocate for the incorporation of conscientisation into a wider economic strategy was the newly appointed Development Secretary, Adrian Moyes. Moyes joined the Overseas Aid Division in 1972 to try and develop a handful of special projects in which Oxfam aid would be concentrated geographically. This was an attempt to overcome the random effects of supporting whatever projects happened to be submitted from a country or area provided they met Oxfam criteria. This had led to a scattergun programme with few internal links or connections, often very widely dispersed. The notion of 'concentrated aid' quickly evolved. The new fashion in development thinking was 'integrated development': projects whose economic benefits would dovetail with social improvements in an area of geographical concentration.

The theory behind 'integration' was that investments in different activities – carpentry workshops, tinsmithing, poultry-raising, bee-keeping – would reinforce each other; the overall economic benefits would enable communities to enhance social services such as schooling, health care, or water supplies. This would multiply the impact of aid so that small amounts of money made larger differences. Moyes, who had a worldwide remit and was a great absorber and disseminator of ideas, was quick to take on board conscientisation (he insisted on calling it 'alertment', for which he won few converts). Conscientisation, in his view, was another force for multiplication; but via an analysis stressing attitudinal transformation and the growth of organisational capacity rather than one stressing technological or economic change.

One of the places Moyes selected for an 'integrated project' was north-east Brazil, under the auspices of FASE. Yates and Moyes and the FASE office in Belém took some time to develop a project that the Latin America Committee would support. The area they picked was a flat, riverine peninsula called Curucambaba at the junction of the Rio Tocantins with the mighty Amazon. FASE's preparatory team drew up a plan for a pepper cultivation scheme whose proceeds would fund what the local people really wanted: health care. The Committee agreed with the idea in principle but tore several large holes in the plan's economics, particularly in its dependence on pepper. Support for a team of *tecnicos* was agreed, but on a temporary basis on condition that more information be collected.

The development musketeers Yates and Moyes went back to FASE, back to the team in Curucambaba, back to their dug-out canoes on the lower Tocantins, back to the drawing board and the budgetary plan. In January 1976, Yates made a concerted effort to persuade his mentors back in Oxford not just to back the team for another 12 months but to make a forward commitment for at least two years. In the period since the scheme had first been under discussion, FASE's, his own, and Moyes' ideas about how to go about the business of aid had undergone considerable change. But the Committee's absorption of the new thinking was not yet complete.

Yates submitted that grants to FASE and similar teams should not be made as if to finite projects with time-bound objectives, but as allocations to a budget period of an ongoing process. The idea of an 'integrated programme' had evolved. It was no longer a pre-planned programme with interlocking parts, but a framework within which linked projects could emerge as the local people wanted and planned them.

In response to the Committee's queries on the economics of black pepper production, Yates dutifully produced an essay on the local costs and prices of pepper trees and peppercorns, but added: 'The Committee appears to interpret the programme very much in economic and materialist terms – produce more crops for stable markets.' This sounded depressingly like the strategy for Brazil's 'economic miracle', everyone's least favourite model of how to help the poor. He went on: 'FASE's analysis does not allow the problem to be reduced simply to a need for economic growth. The objectives are social and structural.' The team's main focus was on *educacao de base*, 'popular education', which would gradually extend the programme's outreach and reinforce its social and economic impact. He concluded: 'Leaving crystal balls aside, FASE's presence in the region can only be seen as indefinite.'

Yates' words proved prophetic; and the Committee's misgivings equally justified. 'Integrated development' and the lower Tocantins never seemed to gel; the idealised image of harmonious group dynamics around carefully dovetailed activities remained elusive. It turned out that, with or without *educacao de base*, such activities were not what the farmers wanted. However, they were quite keen on pepper trees. By 1978, 23,000 pepper trees had been planted by the farmers of one community, their loans had all been repaid and they were doing nicely. By the old numbers yardstick, something was going well. But as a model of 'integrated development' inspired by a conscientisation process, the project was a flop. Conscientisation could not substitute for proper planning, nor could economic factors outside the project's control – such as the fluctuating market price of pepper – be ignored.

In the late 1970s, the emphasis of FASE's Tocantins team changed. In the past few years, powerful commercial interests had been enclosing land in the north-east for cattle ranching. Effects on the *campesinos* were disastrous. They were thrown off land they owned but to which they held no written title and treated as if their existence was merely an impediment to the march of progress. To defend their rights, the Rural Syndicates or unions – originally a tool of landowner control – were transformed and revitalised into representative bodies. Membership grew rapidly as land seizures and disputes increased. A lawyer joined the Tocantins team to hold courses on tenure and help sharecroppers obtain documented title to land rightfully theirs but often taken from them by practices of dubious legality.

Elsewhere in the north-east, FASE teams similarly began to focus less on *educacao de base* as a stimulus to economic improvement, promoting it instead in the Rural Syndicates as a means of helping farmers defend their rights and livelihoods. By 1980, support to FASE's teams in Tocantins, Maranhao, Garanhuns, and Recife, and helping FASE itself become more financially self-sufficient, was one of Oxfam's largest commitments in the hemisphere, amounting to $200,000 a year.

By the early 1980s, many of the social education programmes supported by Oxfam in Brazil had similarly begun to concentrate on human rights and legal aid. In Salvador, Bahia, Oxfam supported the Centre of Study and Social Action (CEAS) set up by Jesuits 'to develop and adapt Christian social doctrine to respond to the reality of north-east Brazil'. CEAS worked with factory workers and plantation labourers on collective bargaining and labour legislation; it also mounted a strong campaign through the church to highlight the violent expulsions of *campesinos* from their land. In Aratuba, Ceara, Oxfam had long supported the highly respected programme of *educacao de base* run by Father Moacir Leite, which up to 1979 concentrated on loans and technical assistance. Here too, the emphasis abruptly changed when the seizure of their lands became the *campesinos'* chief concern. Without land, there was nothing to improve. So all effort was redirected into strengthening Rural Syndicates and registering land titles.

During the 1970s, Oxfam's programme in Brazil had gone through a major evolution, exemplifying trends and currents of thought some of which were specific to the Brazilian environment, many of which were mirrored elsewhere. This evolution from support to missionary projects of the traditional kind, into support for a multifaceted development process based on educational enlightenment, was a product of the passionate convictions of the times; and of the special contribution made to Oxfam by having people in the field who were highly responsive to local problems and opportunities.

In Oxford meanwhile, Freire fever had given rise to another process of critical awareness. The questions it raised back home not only concerned the need for an alternative model for development assistance; certain voices in the organisation were asking whether Oxfam needed an alternative model for itself.

On 1 August 1972, Michael Harris took over from Ken Bennett as Director of Oxfam's Overseas Aid.

Harris was a Quaker who detested conflict and injustice, a person of deep convictions which he carefully hid behind an idiosyncratic style modelled somewhere between George Bernard Shaw and Bertie Wooster. During the second World War Harris had been with the Friends' Ambulance Unit in China and the Far East, an experience he shared with Bernard Llewellyn and Ken Bennett, and which gave a unique grounding in the complexities of relief and welfare work in distant and unfamiliar environments. He then joined the Colonial Service. After some 16 years in Africa he came to Oxfam in 1964, and in 1967 went out to Lesotho as Field Director for Southern Africa. In 1969, he returned to become Bennett's deputy.

His long experience with Oxfam and his instinctive flexibility were useful attributes at the head of the Overseas Division at a time of ferment. Harris always listened to his Field Directors, took great pride in them and defended their judgement through thick and thin. He therefore encouraged a climate in which innovative ideas and action flourished; and where civil conflict or human rights violations caused terrible pain on the ground – as in Central America and South Africa – Harris was never one to protect Oxfam at the expense of its mandate to relieve human suffering. Although at the start of his tenure, the Field Directorate was uniquely male and almost entirely British (the first woman Field Director, Gaby Taylor in Zaire, was not appointed until

1977), this gradually changed during the 12 years of Harris' overlordship of the Oxfam aid programme.

As always in Oxfam, activity in the Indian sub-continent – the new interest in Latin America notwithstanding – was at the frontier of policy evolution. The fiery creation of Bangladesh in January 1972 was greeted by Oxfam with the largest aid package in its history: £1 million for water transport, re-housing, and agricultural rehabilitation, to which the other members of the Oxfam family – Canada, USA, Belgium, Australia – gave a generous share. In the heady aftermath of independence, with the charismatic figure of Sheikh Mujibur Rahman struggling to repair a birthright of upheaval and devastation, there was enormous pressure to spend too much too quickly. Oxfam made mistakes. But it backed one venture which was to write a chapter in community development as important in its own context as anything elsewhere in the world.

BRAC began life as the Bangladesh 'Rehabilitation Assistance' Committee, later changing its name to 'Rural Advancement'. F.H. Abed, its founder, had worked as an accountant in Dacca, becoming involved in relief following the 1970 cyclone. He and 11 colleagues picked Sulla, a remote area of their native Sylhet, for a rehabilitation programme. One-fifth of Sylhet's four and a half million people had fled to India; many returned to find their villages in ruins and no boats, fishing nets, or housing materials with which to restart their lives. The BRAC team ran a reconstruction programme which avoided the trap of dependency with cheap materials, simple technology, and affordable loans. Unlike some other ventures BRAC had staying power; its approach to reconstruction provided a base for a solid development programme, and Oxfam's initial grant of £161,000, including £69,000 from Oxfam Canada, was a more than worthwhile investment.

Like FASE, all of BRAC's staff were nationals. The team in Sulla promoted fishing and agricultural co-ops so as to generate income for health care, family planning, women's groups, and literacy: in other words, 'integrated development'. The second phase of the project, which began in 1973, had as its objectives: 'to create and develop the human and institutional infrastructure in the project area to make development activity self-generating and self-sustaining. It is hoped that ... a long-term change in attitudes will be achieved.' Here were ideas echoing those from halfway round the world.

And in Sylhet, too, a programme could run foul of the authorities for threatening 'subversion'. BRAC and Oxfam were forced to withdraw from a new project area, Rowmari, in 1974. A local landowner found their activities undesirable because they bypassed the power structure he dominated and emphasised women and children over men. So he harassed the field workers and laid false charges against them until they went away. But BRAC survived and prospered, becoming a well-known and much copied force for village-level progress throughout the country. Its success helped to establish local voluntary agencies as an important vehicle for Bangladeshi development, attracting funds from UNICEF, CIDA, and other bilateral agencies.

Another type of crisis, the Indian problem of drought, pushed Field Director John Staley several leagues along his own path of conscientisation. Late in 1972 he toured Maharashtra in western India, where the monsoon had failed for three consecutive years. He described the scene as 'May in December': the dry river-beds, dust and glare, were typical of the period just before the rains. But there were six months to go, six months in which wells would dry up and hunger take hold.

The drought relief programme mounted for Maharashtra in 1973, backed by a fundraising and publicity campaign in Britain, was a testing experience for Oxfam. Staley moved his establishment to Poona, took on extra Indian staff, and made an intensive effort to supplement local government and agency relief for 100 villages in the worst-hit districts.

Apart from well-drilling, Oxfam's efforts went into a daily feeding programme for children under five, nursing and pregnant mothers. The scheme was operated by a group of organisations running medical projects, some previously well-known to Oxfam, some new. The formula was developed by Drs. Raj and Mabelle Arole at the Comprehensive Rural Health Project at Jamkhed. Its basis was local wheat and pulses in varied menus; villages had to contribute with labour, premises, cooking pots, and firewood; the food – a helping of porridge providing 500 calories – had to be cooked and consumed on the spot. At its height, a daily meal was given to 23,000 mothers and children through 25 different organisations.

Staley, the overall co-ordinator, was strongly influenced by this daily contact with Indian organisations and workers, and the unaccustomed proximity to those on the receiving end. He was specially impressed with the vision of people like the Aroles who were developing a methodology for working with people at the grassroots, and who stuck to their principles of local effort and self-sufficiency even in the face of crisis. The intensive experience of several months convinced him that 'development' in India must be defined, initiated and managed by Indians. He found himself rejecting the usual hierarchies of donor-recipient relationships, and felt out of tune with the old paternalism of disaster relief – helpless victims, mercy missions, Western know-how and largesse – which fuelled the Oxfam fundraising machine.

The Maharashtra programme – and Staley's whole approach – were keenly admired inside and outside Oxfam. But his scruples presented the fundraisers and the publicists with a serious headache. There was a drought and there was a human damage-limitation programme of great importance: Oxfam was spending £400,000 it badly needed to recoup. But this was not Bihar 1967 and there was no famine. The Maharashtra authorities were paying wages for stone-breaking on public works, and however back-breaking and unpleasant it was, no-one was starving. Staley was determined not to allow any publicity which gave the impression that, in the face of widespread hunger, inert and incompetent India stood by while the Oxfam fire brigade rushed in to help.

Oxfam had sculpted the image of Third World suffering in the public mind; now, when it did not follow the visual and verbal code used to denote disaster, neither press nor public responded. By mobilising its regional teams Oxfam managed to raise an extra £100,000 for Maharashtra relief. But there was almost no media coverage; and some of what there was caused offence in India. With a modulated message about long-term prevention and building on local capacities, Oxfam could not put an emergency on the media map. Judith Hart, then Shadow Minister of Overseas Development, dutifully doled out cracked wheat porridge in Trafalgar Square; Rita Tushingham paid her 'tap tax', and no-one took the slightest notice.

A tension had arisen between the obligation to the compassion of the donor, and the obligation to the dignity of the receiver. Staley's view was that singlemindedly serving the former ruled out any hope of an equitable relationship between them. Whom ultimately did Oxfam exist to serve? Bill Yates posed the same question. 'Is Oxfam primarily a service to the Victorian charity ethic in Britain, or is it a service to the marginalised populations of the world?' When asked by the fundraisers how they could put across the idea that Oxfam was paying for the poor to discuss their problems because it did not itself know what to do about them, Yates responded: 'Have you tried?' No they had not, and most did not wish to do so.

During 1974, this tension, articulated in the new language of the alternative order, convulsed Oxfam House in the way that the aid vs. public education debate had done in the Stacey era. That the concept of conscientisation was of vital importance in working with the poor had by this time gained some acceptance with the Oxfam establishment, in spite of its radical and Marxist undertones. This was largely due to Michael Harris, on whom Adrian Moyes' encapsulation of its purpose, 'to have more and to be more', made a deep impression. Harris himself helped to communicate this idea to the organisation's supporters. Even the new Director, Brian Walker, on his first field visit to India in early 1974, returned talking of 'motivation', his choice of pseudonym for the new enlightenment.

Rather less welcome was the idea that if conscientisation was so important that Oxfam must encourage the process in others, then surely it should engage in the process itself. If the poor old poor were supposed to 'reflect upon their reality as a first step to changing it', then many Oxfamers felt that they too should reflect on their reality and their roles and relationships in society. This also meant reflecting on the – to them – very important part of society represented by the organisation they worked for. How equitable and participatory was Oxfam's structure? Was it truly championing the wretched of the earth, or simply reinterpreting the white man's burden to coincide with British charitable impulses?

Oxfam was in the middle of a major change: the handover to a new Director, the first such change since its inception. A recent working party on fundraising had talked of doubling Oxfam's income to £8 million within five years. To Walker, the incoming Director, the target made eminent sense. But a number of staff, including Harris, were by no means sure that rapid growth was inherently desirable, nor that large amounts of extra money could be well and wisely spent. There was a worry that the quality of the programme and its still embryonic new philosophy might be sacrificed to the assumption that the only thing that mattered was growth. In development circles, growth was distinctly out of fashion.

In May 1974, a number of middle-level staff formed a study group on Oxfam policy, and set about their own consciousness-raising exercise. The group's informal leader was Reggie Norton, Field Secretary for Latin America, a radical in thought and theology but a figure respected at all levels in the organisation. He saw the group's task as: 'To explore our own ideas on what Oxfam should be for the Third World, and see whether there can be an 'Oxfam vision of the world' to which we could all subscribe with enthusiasm and genuine commitment.' He saw the range of views within Oxfam as divisive and unhealthy. 'To have a vision of the world means to have one vision for the whole world. At present, we are inclined to preach one gospel overseas and another at home. Many of us feel that we must try not just to eliminate such contradictions, but to have a clear and coherent policy reflecting an authentic and prophetic view of the world.'

The policy group drew in opinion from all parts of the organisation, including Staley, Yates, and others overseas, as well as education and fundraising staff at home. By the time Walker took over the reins of directorship from Kirkley in September 1974, a dialogue had begun with trustees and senior management. A commitment had been made to reach organisational consensus around a new definitive statement of Oxfam's *raison d'être*.

A draft was discussed by the trustees in January 1975, and agreement to a final version of 'Oxfam: An Interpretation' reached in March. Many minds, including Brian Walker's, bent themselves earnestly to its articulation. The setting down of this 'Oxfam vision of the world' was – in the spirit of *concientizar* – important as a process as well as for its product. It represented the moment at which the maelstrom of alternative ideas reaching Oxfam was tamed and incorporated into its institutional character.

'Oxfam: An Interpretation' begins: 'Oxfam believes in the essential dignity of people and in their capacity to overcome the problems and pressures which can crush or exploit them. ... Oxfam is a partnership of people who share this belief – people who, regardless of race, sex, religion or politics work together for the basic human rights of food, shelter and reasonable conditions of life.' The statement did away with 'we' and 'they', with all implicit notions of superiority and double sets of values. There was to be no more muddling of 'poverty' with supine helplessness; no more confusion between accountability to the givers and accountability to the receivers.

This statement was an important marker in Oxfam's evolution, recording a turning-point in its own perception of the world and of its mission. The sense of solidarity with the poor, supplanting the old idea of beneficence towards them, was to lead Oxfam in new directions and has remained ever since at the heart of its philosophy.

Soon after the acceptance of 'Oxfam: An Interpretation', Reggie Norton left Oxford to become Field Director for the Caribbean and Central America. Late in 1975, he moved Oxfam's field office from Barbados to Guatemala. His purpose was to position the office closer to the regional epicentre of human need. Half of Guatemala's population of six million were native Indians, whose subjection to Spanish conquest and settlement over 400 years had deprived them of most of their land, banished them to the highlands, and exploited them as dirt-cheap labour in coastal sugar fields and fruit plantations. Their vulnerability was acute; but this was not the whole of it.

On 4 February 1976, a devastating earthquake struck the small and mountainous country. In the steepest parts of Guatemala City, the flimsy dwellings of the poorer inhabitants plunged wholesale into gaping ravines. Landslides cut off all forms of communication with much of the surrounding highlands. Repeated tremors in the following days provoked terror and pandemonium. When all the dust and debris had settled, 25,000 people were dead, 80,000 injured, and one million homeless.

When the earthquake struck, Norton rushed back from Haiti where he was on a field visit. Managing to beg a helicopter ride, he reconnoitred the mountain areas close to Guatemala City; thousands of little fires out on the cold hillsides indicated the extent of homelessness and fear among the villagers. Emergency aid arrived from Oxford: water storage tanks, a sanitation unit, marquees and medical supplies. His presence on the spot encouraged other British agencies and Oxfams to use Norton and the team gathering around him as a channel for assistance. Large sums became available from a DEC television appeal and energetic fundraising. But no-one in Oxford was prepared for the scale of the rehabilitation programme the normally sanguine and dependable Norton suddenly sprung upon them.

The area he focused upon consisted of four municipalities in the department of Chimaltenango, a poor and perilous part of the Western Highlands where Oxfam was already working with the US agency, World Neighbors. Over the past eight years one of the municipalities, San Martin Jilotepeque, had become well-known to Oxfam as the site of another 'integrated development' scheme. Since 1972, Oxfam had spent £45,000 on an agricultural and community health programme run by World Neighbors. The programme was regarded by Oxfam as one of the brightest stars in its firmament. It had all the right ingredients: appropriate technology, capacity-building among membership groups, co-operative structures; and it had generated enthusiasm for new techniques among farmers who could have been expected to be fiercely conservative and highly suspicious of outside ideas.

San Martin's success had much to do with the methodology developed by World Neighbors. Dr. Carroll Behrhorst, the programme's founder, and Roland Bunch, its agricultural director, were pioneers of the 'barefoot' approach later adopted internationally as the model for extending all kinds of services into the community. They trained volunteer farmers from the villages to become promoters of soil conservation measures critical to highland farming. Targets were set for contour ditch construction, soil analysis, fertiliser use, and for their end-product: doubled yields of maize, healthy fruit trees, improved incomes and diet. The strategy worked. Not only did the ideas spread, but some promoters – notably the leading instructor, Anacleto Sajbochol – joined the project staff, which gradually became completely indigenous.

In the early 1970s, the use of villagers as extensionists in farming or public health was seen as revolutionary, particularly since it originally emanated from Maoist China. The approach contained the shocking suggestion that local people, even the barely literate, were better agents of development than highly-qualified outside 'experts'. Bunch thoroughly agreed with this perception, and argued the case persuasively on behalf of Anacleto and his team: 'The Indian promoters are able to teach their classes at times when they don't interfere with work in the fields, and they all know the people they are working with.' They understood local attitudes, were more plausible among their fellows, and also much less expensive. At Jamkhed in Maharashtra, the Drs. Arole were pursuing an identical strategy for the same reasons, as was Abed at BRAC.

When the 'quake struck in February 1976, San Martin was devastated. Hillsides collapsed, the roads were blocked, and the town of San Martin Jilotepeque was flattened. Nearly 3,000 people lost their lives in its rubble and every single house was wrecked or damaged. The same story was repeated in many surrounding villages. The area of San Martin and three other equally devastated municipalities therefore became the focus of Reggie Norton's attention. Not only did both Oxfam and World Neighbors have a natural desire to help those with whom they were already so closely involved, but the network of promoters and co-operatives built up over the years could form the basis for post-earthquake reconstruction.

Any rebuilding programme for temporary or permanent shelter would require materials, the most important of which was roofing. Norton and Bunch on their visits to the San Martin area were told repeatedly by the extensionists that people's most critical need was corrugated iron sheeting, or *lamina*. After the 'quake, Oxfam's office in Guatemala had become a mecca for helpers from the aid agency network. One of these was Bob Gersony, a young US entrepreneur-philanthropist working in Central America, extremely bright and business-minded. At Norton's request, Gersony worked his contacts and came up with a large and cut-price supply of *lamina* in El Salvador. This material was in great demand. So without a moment's hesitation Norton bought the entire supply for Oxfam. As a Field Director, his discretionary spending limit was $5,000; the *lamina* cost $845,000.

Although there was no possibility that the DEC appeal and other earthquake donations could cover this amount, Michael Harris and the Oxfam trustees took a large gulp and swallowed Norton's proposals. Never in Oxfam's history had such a large amount of money been spent on one item, nor at such speed and by so unconventional a procedure. Here was 'flexibility' stretched to its limits. As a result Oxfam had cornered the market in a sorely needed item at a critical moment; the risk of being landed with unusable rehousing materials was almost nil. The plan was to recover part of the cost by selling the 157,000 sheets at half price to the 10,000 homeless families of San Martin and surrounding areas. Here, Oxfam and World Neighbors became responsible for housing reconstruction at the request of the government.

From the start, the *lamina* was in hot demand. Its distribution along with other materials – timber, nails, wire, creosote – was organised through the San Martin promoters, farmers' groups, and co-operatives. Those who had no money to purchase their entitlement of ten sheets earned it on '*lamina*-for-work' road works, while the elderly and those unfit for manual labour obtained their roofing free.

In the run-up to the wet season people used the sheeting for temporary repairs. But the long-term plan was to help people build better houses with cross-braced supports, safe against the kind of tragedy they had just endured. So an educational programme was started to teach people how to rebuild their houses from scratch according to a design easily mastered by local masons and carpenters. In July 1976, a school for training builders was set up, and over the next two years 191 students were launched into a new profession.

The post-earthquake programme around San Martin was not confined to housing; the key to its entire organisation was that all action was based upon close consultation with the community, and depended not on giveaways but on reinforcing the earthquake victims' own efforts and resources. It drew upon years of lessons in local organisation and managerial experience. As with the Aroles in Maharashtra and BRAC in Bangladesh, the programme upheld the vital principle that a condition of dependency must not be created in a misguided effort to speed up disaster relief.

Amidst all the post-earthquake problems, commitment to agricultural improvement did not flag. Contour ditches, the planting of retaining grass, soil analysis and composting were not forgotten. An Oxfam visitor in November 1976 found it hard to believe that farmers showing off their six-fold maize increases and neat terraces topped with fruit trees had suffered such ruin only months ago. One villager explained: 'You can't destroy what is now in the minds of men and women and what we have learned to do for ourselves.'

Although an earthquake could not wipe out the work at San Martin, darker forces could cause damage of a still more terrible kind. World Neighbors had tried to keep their scheme for community agricultural improvement at a distance from the political struggle between the reformists and the reactionaries in Guatemala. The attempt turned out to be futile.

During the late 1970s, the political climate in Central America began to change. In Nicaragua, a radical opposition movement gained widespread support and after a violent civil war, the hated dictatorship of General Anastasio Somoza was sent packing in July 1979. Other regimes in the area, equally elitist and authoritarian, saw in the demise of their neighbouring strongman a possible portent of their own future. In El Salvador and Guatemala, extreme repression began.

Their governments held that the world was riven by two opposing and warring forces: evil atheistic communism and Western Christian civilisation. The need to defend the latter was used to justify the most grotesque violations of human rights and freedoms. People who worked for any kind of social improvement – even literacy or family planning – were branded as subversives. Those who defended the rights of peasants to their land, who sought to alter the traditional balance of power, who called for the rule of law and the growth of democracy, were systematically hunted down. Many priests and religious who had 'opted for the poor' were singled out. The outrage which most shocked the world was the assassination of Archbishop Oscar Romero, gunned down while administering mass on 24 March 1980.

No regime in the region was more cruel or repressive than that of Guatemala. In 1979 began a long night of brutality which over five years was to see 50,000 Guatemalans (mainly Indians) slaughtered, hundreds of villages destroyed, and one million people on the run, 200,000 of them across the borders. The leader of any group, even agricultural promoters like those in San Martin, risked being 'disappeared' and shot. Anacleto Sajbochol and many others fled to Mexico. Their families left with them or vanished into the anonymity of Guatemala City. In spring 1982, at the height of the terror, the army surrounded the municipality of San Martin for several months, and in the course of its occupation massacred over 5,000 people. Their victims included many who had been active in the earthquake reconstruction programme.

By this time Oxfam had been forced to close its office in Guatemala and move to Mexico. Its staff, now led by a Guatemalan, Rolando Lopez, were at risk and the programme in ruins. The 'partnership of people committed to a process of development by peaceful means' envisaged in 'Oxfam, An Interpretation' was extremely difficult to realise in an environment where social and political injustice were so inextricable that even a contour ditch and a lemon tree could inspire state murder in the name of security and civilisation. Instead, Lopez and his team offered humanitarian and emergency support for refugees and those displaced inside their own countries; and tried to find ways of upholding human rights against the deluge of misery being poured upon those whose only crime had been to be poor and oppressed and to want to be less so. In their efforts to work in such a politically charged environment, their target was to create 'humanitarian space': to respond to human need in a way that took account of political reality, but was firmly based on humanitarian intent, independently of unavoidable association with individuals or organisations belonging in certain ideological or political camps.

The 1970s, the era of alternatives, had begun in a spirit of excitement and optimism. There had been a sense that the old moulds of power and privilege were crumbling and that a new order was emerging. Some people had glimpsed a vision in which the poor nations and the poor within the nations could 'have more and be more', could become participants instead of spectators of this thing called 'development' pursued in their name. There had been heroes, there had been martyrs, there had been great hope and deep disillusion. Oscar Romero had championed the rights of the poor on the grounds that human dignity was all-important, more important than any struggle between communism and capitalism, atheism and Christianity. For this belief he had given his life, joining thousands of others for whom the hope of 'having more and being more' had ended in persecution, torture, imprisonment, and death.

However bleak the future in many countries, events at the end of the decade had their positive side. The Nicaraguan revolution had succeeded. In one country at least, the Christian leftist and liberal movement had achieved a victory. The 'liberation theologians' flocked to take part in the Sandanista experiment; land and labour reform was introduced; basic health care and education for all were incorporated into national policy. Not surprisingly, many of those voluntary agencies committed to solidarity with the poor became stalwart allies of the Sandanista regime, some of the more idealistic among them heralding a socialistic utopia. As in Tanzania, Oxfam found itself able not only to support small-scale local projects, but to add its modest contribution to the general thrust of social action nationwide.

But the threat of destablisation by forces opposed to the Sandanistas and the mounting oppression in countries nearby confronted the humanitarians with continuing problems and dangers. One reaction in Oxfam was to speed up the indigenisation of the local staff, who with their deeper understanding of the political environment, could carve out 'humanitarian space' more successfully than less personally vulnerable expatriates. Another was to re-think the range of policy options that charity law, safety, and practicality would permit in the face of conflict, oppression, and violent infringements of human rights.

By the end of the 1970s, not only in Central America, but in South Africa and to a lesser extent elsewhere, the ways in which Oxfam could work in deeply polarised societies had become a major preoccupation.

10

TO THE KILLING FIELDS

When Brian Walker was appointed Director of Oxfam, he was given to understand by senior trustees that what was needed was modern management and the smack of firm leadership.

Walker, a Quaker, had an impressive record as a man of conscience: he had worked for reconciliation in Northern Ireland as founder chairman of the New Ulster Movement, an alliance of moderate Catholics and Protestants, sometimes at great personal danger. But his management credentials (in an engineering company, Bridgeport Brass Ltd.) were also decisive in his selection. In Kirkley's last years when he concentrated on the international arena, there had been some loss of direction on the domestic front.

Although Walker had been the Northern Ireland representative on the UK Committee of the United Nations Association, the field of overseas aid and development was relatively new to him. He was not, therefore, encumbered by doubts about Western economic models, nor did he perceive any dichotomy between Oxfam at home as a vehicle of British compassion and Oxfam overseas as an effective partner of the poor. Dichotomies and ambiguities were not his cup of tea. He liked clear lines of argument and decisive action. Over the next ten years, his singlemindedness, which could be a powerful force, made of Oxfam a more focused, businesslike, and less volatile organisation. As a personality he could be austere and defensive; privately he was capable of great kindness and no-one ever doubted the depth or sincerity of his commitment to the Oxfam cause.

Walker fully took over the reins in September 1974. He was impressed by the calibre of the staff, their liveliness and degree of motivation; by the part played by volunteers; and by the projects he visited on overseas familiarisation tours. But he did not approve of what he saw as the blight of make-do-and-mend which permeated Oxfam's operational and institutional character. The shoestring mentality was natural to many working in the charity world, and it was laudable in its way, but lacked efficiency.

One of its worst symptoms was the lack of a personnel and training policy, either for staff or for volunteers; and the payment of salaries which, in some cases, were unbelievably low. This led to heavy dependence on staff who were young and left almost as soon as they became productive. Kirkley had accepted this because he saw them taking their Oxfam vision out into the world and expanding the community of like-minded. Walker, with a personnel background, saw things differently. He introduced a salary structure and other measures designed to develop Oxfam's own human resources; he wanted Oxfam to lead the charity world in creating a proper career path for the modern humanitarian.

Walker also identified a lack of long-term investment and solid financial planning as inhibiting to Oxfam's future prospects of healthy growth. Oxfam had always spent virtually its entire income as it was received, never holding back sums for capital investment or financial security. And in the effort to keep fund-raising and home-based costs below 20 per cent, there was a tendency to scrimp not only on salaries but on facilities in shops, offices, and the trading company. Some of the thrifty housekeeping practices amounted to false economy. Walker determined not only to make the operational picture healthier, but to set Oxfam on a growth curve. By late 1974, whatever qualms had been earlier expressed about growth-for-growth's-sake had been swept away by the oil crisis and high inflation. At his first trustees' meeting as Director, he announced changes in organisational structure designed to promote the drive for new funds. The three key fund-raising areas – Shops, Trading, and Appeals – were to be overhauled and upgraded. Walker's diagnosis – and it was correct – was that, with an investment of energy and resources, these existing routes for funds could be improved substantially.

The key was to professionalise by calling upon expertise available in the commercial world. This strategy was most pronounced in the Oxfam Shops, which were built up as a retail chain under the guidance of a National Shops Committee. In May 1975, a Shops Development Fund was set up so that shop properties could be improved and, in some cases, purchased. This marked the beginning of Oxfam's deliberate streamlining of its merchandising activity. The same drive to maximise on modern marketing methods was applied to the appeals machinery for covenants, legacies, cash donations, and goods such as blankets and clothing.

The new fund-raising broom had the effect of concentrating minds and energies. The only problem – and it was not a new problem – was that it placed great stress on the regional staff. The teams of volunteers and shop helpers they depended on for all their fund-raising activities were a very special kind of workforce which could not be treated as pawns in the corporate game. The idiosyncrasies of their performance were integral to the free provision of their time; it took cajoling, not line management, to get them to fill in the right forms, notice which handicrafts sold well, put this month's posters in the window, and run the shop 'correctly'. Many regional organisers found themselves fighting to protect their volunteers from 'management by objective' and became somewhat bruised in the process.

However, the strategy paid great dividends to Oxfam. By 1978, shop income had tripled since 1973, to over £3 million. Improved professionalism was one reason for success. Jumble and bric-a-brac in temporary, rent-free premises had been abandoned in favour of permanent sites in good retailing situations, with proper facias and attractive displays. The Shops Unit in HQ introduced a common 'look', and offered advice on pricing, staffing, publicity, and other management functions. Special training schemes were introduced for shop helpers. Over the course of ten years, Oxfam shops became an institution in their own right, providing a service to the community as well as an important source of funds.

Although Walker's main thrust was financial growth, he by no means downgraded Oxfam's educational role. But he wanted the informational and educational role more strictly defined. He wanted to end what a report on communications policy described as 'the confused face of Oxfam' and to focus publicity resources on things which had a clearly definable impact on Oxfam's image or income. Philip Jackson, Communications Director, had been building up an Oxfam public information role with press and other media concerning development issues. Disaster relief remained the only context in which Oxfam itself could expect media limelight. Rapport with prominent journalists during an emergency – Alan Hart in the 1971 Bengal cyclone, Jonathan Dimbleby in the 1973 Ethiopian famine, Gerald Priestland in the 1974 Maharashtra drought – helped promote their interest in deeper Third World coverage. But Oxfam's role in development was too modest to command extensive coverage in its own right, a reality Walker did not find easy to accept.

This had been the reason for Oxfam's joint financial backing with Christian Aid for the monthly *New Internationalist* magazine, whose masthead declared it to be about 'the people, the ideas, and the action in the fight for world development'. The *New Internationalist* went in for interviews with Nyerere and Dom Helder Camara, clarion calls for the New International Economic Order, and *exposés* of the marketing practices of babyfood companies in the Third World; it was not meant to be a house organ for the overseas programmes of Oxfam and Christian

Aid. But with Oxfam paying a large chunk of the bill, Walker sometimes found the editorial independence of these radical journalists disconcerting. In late 1975, the magazine was in financial difficulty having exhausted in two years the £80,000 provided for three. Eventually a new schedule of support was agreed by the Oxfam trustees. Walker accepted the decision with a good grace, but he was never really comfortable at the presence of this kind of loose cannon in the Oxfam fold.

Walker's dislike of broad brushstroke education and communications projects with other agency partners was not to do with fear of controversy or ideological perspective. It reflected his urge for corporate control, the discipline of the balance sheet, and a desire to push Oxfam's name. One important step he took was to set up a Public Affairs Unit in London. The PAU, which reported directly to him, set out to develop links with MPs, Trades Unions, and professional bodies over topics of mutual interest. This was a courageous step given that it meant that Oxfam would assume for itself a public information role located close to the grey area known as 'political activity'.

In the international arena, Walker showed similar instincts. Since 1974, when Oxfam Canada and Oxfam Quebec had decided to go their own way as far as overseas funding was concerned, the relationship with Oxford had soured. Their increasing independence of outlook had distressed Kirkley since it rang the death knell on his dream of a common international Oxfam programme. With Walker, it rang loud alarm bells. He disliked an alliance with organisations of the same name whose policies were radical and different, whose actions were beyond control, and which might do something prejudicial to Oxford's reputation. The relationships between the Oxfams remained fraught during Walker's directorship, particularly after he offered Canada financial compensation if they would drop the Oxfam name. In 1976, the six organisations (Oxfams in UK, USA, Canada, Quebec, Belgium, and Community Aid Abroad in Australia) reached an agreement designed to protect the name while accepting each other's autonomy. In time, this became the basis for looser, and warmer, co-operation.

Walker directed most of his international networking energies towards Europe and the EEC. This attempt to build up relationships with German, French, and Dutch agencies helped to fill the gap left by the loss of funds from other Oxfams, and also placed Oxfam UK in the forefront of European overseas aid non-governmental organisations (NGOs). In 1977, the EEC set up a mechanism for funding voluntary agency projects; Walker was a key member of the UK delegation to the EEC NGO Liaison Committee, and played a formative role in the emerging relationship between aid NGOs and the Community. He was also on the League of Red Cross/Voluntary Agencies Committee in

Geneva from 1974-83. These connections were to be of vital importance in late 1979 during the Cambodia crisis.

Walker also took on board a new and somewhat risky domestic venture developed by Guy Stringer, his Deputy Director. This was 'Wastesaver', a commercial project designed to capitalise on growing public disillusion with the throwaway society. Originally it had been Leslie Kirkley who, pondering the connections between environmental conservation and the progress of the poor, had asked Stringer to work out how items surplus to household requirements in the form of waste could be alchemised into development aid. The initial survey, into the re-usability of everything from LP records to little metal bottle tops, was carried out by Adrian Moyes.

The Oxfam Wastesaver Centre, launched in 1975, was the first comprehensive waste-recycling scheme ever set up in Britain. Kirklees Council gave it a home. Its premises were a derelict textile mill in the centre of Huddersfield. This was converted into a plant where 60 staff and 60 young people on Job Creation schemes sorted, processed, and packaged glass, tin, paper, aluminium, plastics, textiles, clothing, and furniture. Some of this junk mountain was cleaned up and sold in the 'biggest Oxfam shop in the world'. Most of the rest – tin chips, rag, paper, empty bottles – was resold to industry after being granulated, pressed, or shredded.

The basic unit for collection was the 'dumpy', a tubular stand with plastic bags in four different colours for different types of rubbish. Oxfam vans collected the sacks from co-operating households. The dumpy caught on, and 6,000 found homes with people willing to go to some trouble to sort and clean their waste. But within 18 months, inflation had wrought havoc with dumpy economics. The cost of collection had risen by 40 per cent and the cost of the dumpy itself by 60 per cent, while the prices received for waste end-products were static. Other means of acquiring waste were tried, including special containers in supermarket car parks. Oxfam Shops also sent aluminum scrap and unsaleable clothing to Huddersfield.

Oxfam's investment in capital equipment was £92,000 for the first two years. In the first year, sales reached £48,000 against costs of £98,000, a slightly better result than expected. The resourceful manager of the Wastesaver Centre, Jon Vogler, was optimistic that the Centre would soon show a profit. But it failed to do so because the market in waste continued so depressed. In July 1977 part of the building collapsed, along with morale and the price of paper. In early 1978 it was decided to drop household collection and set up a new centre specifically geared to the more modest recycling effort which Oxfam now knew was viable.

Wastesaver had turned out to be a useful adjunct to the 575 Oxfam

Shops, themselves now spruced up and becoming more profitable. It absorbed all the garments shops were unable to sell, processing them for resale in special 'surplus' shops, or selling them off for rag. This released more selling space in the shops as well as helping to reduce the volume of low quality stock they were carrying. In 1979, Wastesaver moved to smaller premises specially designed for sorting and handling textiles. They also sorted aluminium for processing – foil, ring pulls, bottle tops, cans – collected through Oxfam shops. Within a short space of time this venture repaid its capital costs and was making a profit.

Brian Walker's first full financial year as Director was promising. In spite of inflation, in spite of salary rises, total income for 1975-76 burst through the £6 million barrier, helped by a hugely successful appeal in the wake of the Guatemala earthquake. During the next few years, the investment in shops and general appeals began to pay dividends. In 1978-79, income reached £9.7 million. This had not been achieved painlessly; but there was satisfaction that the end-decade target of £10 million was well within reach.

Five years earlier, Michael Harris had doubted whether the overseas programme could absorb a large injection of extra money and maintain its quality. It had done so because, spurred on by the search for alternatives, its direction had undergone major change.

By the mid-1970s, 'targeting the poor' had become the new orthodoxy in development philosophy. At every level, from the international to the micro-project, minds and budgets were exercised by the search for ways to reach the poor.

'Targeting the poor' was very difficult. Their condition of poverty was directly related to their lack of access to existing services and institutional structures. Logically therefore, such structures would either have to be by-passed; or they would have to be reformed. New structures would have to be created or existing ones adapted; but how and who by? And how could anyone be sure that, operating in the same environment, they would not soon manifest the same in-built inequities? In Oxfam, this period was one of 'anti-institutionalism' in its overseas programme, expressed both practically and philosophically.

One of the reasons why official aid donors were becoming keen on NGOs was that they were the only available route for bypassing existing structures. Official aid went to government services and, in a poor country, the reach of government services was often limited to those with economic and political muscle. The official donors therefore had no route into the places where the poor were to be found. But the NGOs, or some of them, were already there, if not actually in the village or slum at least close by, with staff and an organisation. Thus while governments could be encouraged to reform their services so as to reach the mass of the people – a process bound to take some time – at least some good people were getting on and doing something.

But from Oxfam's perspective, from a position closer to the poor, the problem looked almost exactly the same. The good people, be they local or foreign, who had set up their ashram, their centre, or their clinic, in a particular locality, had done so for all sorts of reasons. Some – such as Mother Teresa's home in Calcutta and Irma Dulce's hospital in Salvador – were set up specifically to serve those singled out by indigence; others to serve leprosy cases, the disabled, refugees, or particular kinds of social distress. But many organisations were by no means positioned or geared to serve the really poor even if the people they served were poor by Western standards.

They might primarily serve a religious congregation; or, if they were agriculturally-minded, farmers; or, if medical, the sick; or, if vocationally-minded, the young; and so on. Most of those who enlisted in the course or went to the clinic already had some means, could afford the fee or the medicines and the bus-fare to get there. Such organisations were also very thin on the ground. Yet the location of their projects and the income-levels of those they served set limits to any donor agency's programme. These were major limiting factors even before one took account of programme quality.

There were thousands of villages in virtually every developing country which were not reached by any agent of social improvement, government or philanthropic. Inevitably, they included the poorest and most neglected. And within the poor communities covered by some of the best projects Oxfam supported, the poorest people were often excluded. A 1978 evaluation of the World Neighbors agricultural programme in San Martin, Guatemala, pointed out that contour ditches and fruit trees yielded benefits for the small owner-farmer; but that 50 per cent of the local population were landless. The programme concentrated on the most dynamic farmers assuming that they would bring along 'slow adopters' – another version of 'trickle down'. But landless farmers were 'slow adopters' for good reason: the benefit of any improvements on land they tilled went to their landlords.

Here was one of the eternal conundrums of trying to help the poorest. Handouts created dependency and destroyed initiative. But how did you invest in people who had nothing? You could give a farmer a loan to deepen his well and irrigate his fields. But what about the farmer who had no well? And if you left out the poorest, the gap between them and the slightly better-off would widen; the people you had helped might join the group exploiting the poorest, whose situation would then deteriorate. The San Martin evaluator found that the World Neighbors programme had indeed encouraged such a process. The landless in the area were asserting legal claims to land they had worked for years. But farmers in the World Neighbors programme had become well enough off to buy this land illegally from the landowners, thus helping to cheat the landless of their rights.

One response to the problem of how to reach the poorest was to try and encourage the growth of local indigenous agencies. This was the rationale behind support for FASE in Brazil, the Community Development Trust Fund in Tanzania, BRAC in Bangladesh, and many others. Meanwhile in India, John Staley began to pursue the problem from another direction: the almost total absence of awareness among educated and idealistic young Indians of 'development' as it was understood by Oxfam. Only a tiny handful of very special characters, usually Gandhian, such as the remarkable Vikhasbhai in Varanasi, took up this kind of development work as a personal mission or career.

Without such a workforce, how were local organisations to emerge which would pursue a vision distinct from the usual Indo-Victorian welfarism with all its built-in hierarchies? And how were project staff, and for that matter Oxfam's own, to be Indianised? Expatriates, unless they were saints on the Mother Teresa pattern, could not reach the poor whatever their commitment or aptitude. By 1977, five out of 11 Oxfam staff in India were Indian. They had not been easy to recruit, in a country of 600 million people.

In 1976 Staley left Oxfam to work with Indian colleagues in setting up an organisation called 'Search'. Search recruited apprentices, or trainees, from a number of different social backgrounds, and set out to engage their intellects and personal motivation partly by discussion, and partly by assigning them to work on projects. Staley saw their conversion to development – their conscientisation – as a developmental force in its own right. Oxfam had great faith in Staley and underwrote Search to the tune of around £20,000 a year, even though Staley's almost spiritual commitment to participatory principles tended to exasperate the management-minded. Gradually Search evolved into a training centre for development workers. Search also played a part in trying to communicate through Indian channels what 'development' meant when it had nothing to do with industrialisation or targets for the Five-Year Plan, but was to do with people and the human condition.

If reaching the really poor was difficult because there were no routes into the village and few educated Indians ready for the pilgrimage, there were more problems once you finally arrived. The poorest had almost no capacity to absorb funds. They had no land to improve, no bullock to yoke, no cow to fatten, no barn to make rat-proof; they were illiterate and ignorant of the modern world. Their plea to any outsider was for help and they were clearly in need; yet how was their plea to be transformed into a viable project meeting minimum standards of competence? As one agonised paper from Bangladesh put it: 'Most of the proposals which come to us from village groups are so poorly thought out, so lacking in detail as to how the activities will be organised, who will participate, who will benefit, that there is no hope of us accepting them as they stand. A great deal of work in fleshing them out is required.' And there were leadership problems. 'Because of their organisational ineptitude the poor are likely to end up as employees in a business controlled by better-off members of the village. And this simply replicates the age-old pattern of authority and opportunity – not at all what we want to do.'

In 1977, ten years after the first operational programme in India was launched in the wake of the Bihar famine, Oxfam embarked on another major operational experiment, this time in neighbouring Orissa. This was a new evolution: not quite an 'integrated programme', not exactly 'barefoot technician', nor yet 'conscientisation', but with elements of all three. Orissa was one of India's poorest states, drought- and cyclone-prone, and the scene therefore of many Oxfam emergency relief efforts. In consultation with the Orissa government, Oxfam put together an ambitious scheme to surmount the barriers on the path to the poor. Theoretically, the programme would create a network of new participatory and popular structures which would generate micro-projects for Oxfam funding. The key philosophical architect of this was Andrew Clark, an Oxfam Field Director who had earlier worked in South Vietnam, and whose concern for the minutiae of social development was encyclopaedic. His key ally on the practical side was A.V. Swamy, the programme's Co-ordinator and a star of the embryonic Indian cadre in Oxfam's field service.

OXWORP, the Oxfam West Orissa Programme, chose for its home a neglected corner of the state where the railhead ended on the way to a dusty little town called Khariar. Apart from a mission hospital there were no local voluntary agencies; the partners were government officers at Block level (a Block is an administrative area of roughly 100 villages). In the years since OGAP began, Oxfam had reached a better understanding of the complexities of trying to transform the far from arcadian face of village India. Swamy was always begging patience of those who expected OXWORP to solve instantly the puzzle of how to reach the poorest. OXWORP did not fulfill all the expectations it raised; but it did many valuable things and, like OGAP in its day, was an important learning experience.

To reach the village, Oxfam invented a new kind of pilgrim: the

'Community Contact Person'. (Much of the programme terminology was new: Swamy was the 'Action Consultant'.) The CCPs were recent men and women graduates, rigorously selected, trained, and then posted to one of the Blocks within the programme area. Their job was to go into the villages and meet people, and gradually encourage interest groups – women, artisans, farmers – to coalesce. This might lead to an application to Oxfam for a loan fund for seed, basketwork, or irrigation channel construction. Having handled this successfully, the group might be put in touch with a government programme which they had not previously known about or felt able to approach. They were also introduced to banks and credit facilities whose tentacles did not usually extend beyond the towns.

As time went by, groups in several villages could combine in a Block-level association, which itself developed an organisational capacity to handle funds and projects. This was the vision: the growth of democratically run structures whose strength would endure when Oxfam removed itself after the predetermined span. In fact, an Oxfam review conducted in 1987, four years after they had withdrawn, found many village groups still operational. The number of mini-projects to have made an improvement in village lives ran into hundreds, and applications still flow into Oxfam today. Many of the OXWORP graduates went on in a development career, running their own projects, working for Oxfam or other agencies.

OXWORP, however, did not solve the problem of how to reach the poorest inexpensively. It was a classic illustration of one of the ironies of development aid: the costs of programme delivery tend to mount in proportion to the depth of poverty of those you are trying to reach. Over seven years, OXWORP cost Oxfam £700,000, including £200,000 for emergency drought relief in 1979-80. As a model for instigating social and economic change among the poorest, OXWORP – Oxfam felt – was too cumbersome to be cost-effective.

Other Field Directors in India pursued the same quest via a different route. In 1979, Tony Vaux in Ahmedabad took on a young Gujerati with a trades union background, M.D. Mistry. Gujerat had a large population of extremely poor tribal people living in areas where there were no agencies and few project possibilities. The political atmosphere was relaxed and there were special programmes budgeted by the state for the benefit of tribal people. Vaux and Mistry picked two districts, and Mistry set off by motorbike to make contact with the villages. His results were striking. In the early 1980s Mistry, as the personification of a new type of programming which did reach the poorest, became something of an Oxfam celebrity.

By visits and by letter, Mistry identified villages where there was an existing nucleus of people wrestling with a common problem: an avaricious trader, who underpaid for farming produce and overcharged for inputs; a group of farmers who had thought about better irrigation but not known where to start. Often those he corresponded with were young and keen to try something. He helped them to register themselves as formal societies to become eligible for government finance. This was not easy, as Mistry explained: 'It requires a constitution, members, membership fees and approval either by the charity commissioner, in the case of *yuvak mandals* (youth groups) or *mahila mandals* (women's groups), or by the registrar, in the case of societies. Such groups have to audit their accounts each year and submit them to the authorities.'

Not surprisingly, semi-literate people in remote villages stumbled on some of these hurdles. In one case, they collected the money and the papers and entrusted them to a man who conveniently lost the documents. In another, they could not afford the bus-fare to go 200km to Ahmedabad to take the papers for registration. Here, Mistry took on the role of facilitator, to help people overcome such hurdles and then go on to use their new group structures to dissolve or bypass the forces which held their lives in pawn. A small Oxfam loan might get them started. One village, for example, purchased a pair of weighing scales to replace those used by the local merchant and dramatically lowered his takings. Another set up a bank to enable dispossessed farmers to buy back their land from the exorbitant clutches of the moneylender.

The effect of this approach, which was soon to dominate the evolution of Oxfam's India programme, was to spend proportionately more, but still a relatively modest amount, on the intermediary activities needed to reach the poorest: staff time, most of it spent helping villagers formulate ideas and proposals. Actual grants were small. An example was a lift irrigation scheme for a village called Tembda. After long preparation, the villagers put in a request for a Rs. 2.5 lakhs (around £14,000) subsidy from the Tribal Sub-Plan, a government programme. Oxfam's contribution was a fee for a professional engineer to draw up the plan, and money to cover their transport costs to meetings with the officials. Few grants were for sums above Rs. 10,000 (£600).

The trap the field staff did their best to avoid was to create groups, or modify existing ones, which then became dependent on Oxfam. Mistry ensured by the way he worked with the groups that their own capacity to run their affairs was augmented, not diminished. He also insisted on all loans being repaid and all moneys accounted for. Dr. Anil Bhatt, a well-known Indian social scientist, evaluated Mistry's work in 1985. 'I have never seen any effort, voluntary or governmental,' he said, 'which has made such impact on very poor people with such meagre financial input, in such a short time and with such limited manpower.'

In one adaptation or another, the Mistry experience became a major influence on Oxfam's development approach, not only in India, but worldwide.

Of all the colonial disentanglements in the generation after the second World War, the most protracted and painful was in Indo-China. In 1975, Saigon fell to the North Vietnamese and the turmoil at last seemed over. Four years later in 1979, increasing signs of human distress began to filter through the bamboo curtain.

To begin with, the Vietnamese refugees, especially those setting out to sea, attracted the spotlight of public attention. But for the humanitarian agencies, the ultimate challenge came later in 1979 with the crisis that consumed Cambodia – then called Kampuchea. In its scale, this was not the most serious emergency in their experience; the birth of Bangladesh and the long years of African drought affected many more people. But in its intensity, Kampuchea was unique. Its attendant horrors were more awful and its political intricacies more complex than any in the post-war world.

In April 1975, the people of Cambodia had been 'liberated' by the Khmer Rouge, who had then closed the country off from the world and subjected it to a ruthless revolutionary experiment. In early 1979, 'Democratic Kampuchea' was again 'liberated', this time by the forces of their traditional enemy, the Vietnamese. By the autumn, when the enormities of four years of Kampuchean suffering began to be known, it seemed to the world that the entire nation was poised on the verge of extinction. A tiny handful of Western relief agents were holed up in Phnom Penh desperately trying to organise aid in the face of every conceivable obstacle. Oxfam was one of that handful. Because of this, Oxfam played a role in the Kampuchean crisis which catapulted it onto the international stage, hugely enhancing its reputation and resources. But in the process, its own efforts and those of others attempting to aid the Kampuchean people became swept up in the complex maze of Indo-Chinese affairs. From the crisis in Kampuchea, few of the players emerged unscathed.

Oxfam had been a very minor humanitarian player in the endless turmoil of Vietnam since back in the 1950s; its involvement had ended in 1975. With the build-up of US forces in the 1960s, opportunities for philanthropic activity became heavily curtailed; most charitable aid went to orphanages and hospitals run by US missionaries. In the late 1960s Oxfam took a different direction, channelling aid through Buddhist organisations. The Buddhists' anti-war sentiments became famous in the West when monks began to burn themselves to death; but in social welfare they were 'silent workers, unknown and neglected'. Not only did their simplicity keep them close to the people, but their activities were integral to people's beliefs and culture, and would, Oxfam believed, endure when the long years of war and madness ended.

Oxfam's earliest connection was in 1966 with the Buddhist School of Youth for Social Service in Saigon, the only school of its kind in the country. Students went on village secondment to run literacy classes, health centres, sports clubs, and festivals. Oxfam regarded this work as important because of the disruption in the countryside caused by the war; but after the Tet offensive in 1968 this disruption consumed the programme itself, whose students were drafted into the army.

From 1970 onwards, an important ally was Dr. Thich Minh Chau, Rector of Vanhanh University, described by Don Shields, Oxfam's Field Director in the Far East, as 'the best of our co-operators in Vietnam'. With the help of two Buddhist nuns, Dr. Chau ran a Social Action Centre (SAC) which set out to 'acquaint Vanhanh students with the misery of the lower classes, to inspire them with a spirit of responsibility and dedication to the poor'. Students worked voluntarily in day care centres, orphanages, refugee camps, and hospitals. From 1971, Oxfam funded annual courses for the volunteers in sociology, health, and administration, and helped the SAC in other ways with the mounting casualties of military havoc.

When the US forces withdrew from South Vietnam in 1973, Oxfam posted Andrew Clark to work with the Buddhist groups in Saigon in the expectation that peace would pave the way for rural development. Clark, an enthusiast for participatory approaches, tried to nudge the Buddhists in this direction. He hoped that day care centres in communities served by nuns and monks might be the launch pad for something less paternalistic than typical Buddhist social work. This turned out to be a non-starter, partly because the delicate and subtle Buddhist world was not susceptible to egalitarian dialectics; and partly because continuing hostilities destroyed all hopes of anything bar yet more relief.

By April 1975, Oxfam had spent £250,000 in Vietnam; Clark left when Saigon fell; North and South were unified in one communist-led Vietnam which had little use for philanthropy inspired by any religious system. The SAC closed down and Buddhist social work became strictly circumscribed.

At the beginning of December 1978, Brian Walker undertook a 10-day visit to Vietnam. This was prompted by a request from UN Secretary-General Kurt Waldheim that NGOs consider giving aid to Vietnam. The boat people exodus was already exacerbating Vietnam's pariah status in the West; but Walker was impressed by the scenes he witnessed in town and countryside. 'What made this tour the most thrilling I have ever made for Oxfam was to see in practice almost everything we are trying to bring about elsewhere in the world. Self-reliance, village co-operation, the sharing of resources, discipline, energy and ingenuity on a widespread and convincing scale, especially in terms of basic needs, was the order of the day. Nor was this grim, Marxist, bureaucratic collectivisation. Quite the opposite.'

A sympathetic attitude towards Vietnam was to colour Oxfam's response to the gathering crisis in Kampuchea.

Within days the Vietnamese army had invaded Kampuchea ,reaching Phnom Penh after a hard-fought campaign on 7 January 1979. This invasion liberated 'Democratic Kampuchea' from Khmer Rouge domination, the nature of which was not then known except to a very few observers. The invasion was widely condemned in the West as an act of aggression against a neighbouring country, and the Vietnamese client government set up in Phnom Penh was not recognised except by the USSR and the Eastern bloc. The rulers of 'Democratic Kampuchea' had maintained a closed society; the new rulers of the 'People's Republic of Kampuchea' did the same. Meanwhile, attention shifted to the plight of the boat people.

Since 1975, the outpouring of refugees from Indo-China had reached close to one million. Increasing numbers were taking passage from Vietnam on crowded, leaking, ramshackle boats across the South China Sea. Faced with their own problems of poverty and overcrowdedness, the countries they were heading for – Malaysia, Singapore, Hong Kong, and Indonesia – were strenuously resisting their entry. The International Red Cross Committee (ICRC) issued a statement in mid-1979 about Indo-Chinese misery they were powerless to help, which included that of 15,000 boat people then at sea for whom all permission to land had been refused.

Boat people who landed on the Malaysian coast were removed and dumped on the tiny offshore island of Bidong. By July 1979, Bidong was threatening to become a boat people graveyard. Normally uninhabited, the island was a steep-sided granite cone with a small strip of barren land. On this strip 42,000 men, women, and children were huddled under the flimsiest of bamboo and plastic shelters. All food and all water had to be brought 14 kilometres across the straits by barge; there was no storage and bad weather could hold up supplies for days.

The Malaysian authorities seemed unable to cope with basic public health, and the United Nations High Commissioner for Refugees (UNHCR) asked Oxfam to send a technical person to make an assessment. That person had to be Jim Howard. For some years Howard

– whose background was in engineering – had been functioning as a technical extension of Oxfam's disasters office. Among other emergency aids he had developed a 'fly it in and put it up in hours' sanitation unit to use where influxes of disaster victims were crowded into makeshift camps.

On Bidong, Howard found a settlement of unbelievable squalor. There were no sanitation facilities; rubbish and excreta lapped the shore; the topsoil was so shallow that it was not even possible to bury the dead properly. Epidemic and fire threatened. Howard recommended the construction of water tanks, both fresh and sea, and latrines serviced by a simple sea water sewage pipe. A programme costing £500,000 was set in motion, towards which Oxfam offered UNHCR £125,000, and helped recruit instant engineering assistance.

A few days after his return, Howard went to Geneva to the International Conference on the Boat People. Even as he attended, the agonies of Kampuchea were beginning to emerge from the shadows. Since the Vietnamese had invaded in January, the natural vanguard of the international humanitarian community, ICRC and UNICEF, had been jointly trying to provide help inside the country without success. But by mid-1979, theVietnamese authorities had become alarmed about the food situation. In early 1979, the collective agricultural camps set up by the Khmer Rouge had been disbanded and people had set off for their villages and to find lost family members. The Khmer Rouge, meanwhile, retreated towards the Thai border with the Vietnamese army in pursuit. The end-result of all this social and military disruption was that rural and agricultural life was thrown out of joint and little planting was done when it should have been. In July, the Vietnamese sought 129,000 tons of food aid from the UN's World Food Programme on the basis that 2.2 million Kampucheans faced starvation.

This crude estimate of need was the only one available, then and for many months to come.

To prepare the way for the vast and urgent relief operation the Vietnamese had requested, representatives from UNICEF and ICRC were finally granted visas and flew into Phnom Penh on 17 July. But they were only allowed the briefest of stays and were able to make very little progress in verifying the scale of need or setting up the programme. Because the situation was sensitive, the two organisations imposed a total press and information blackout about the mission. Thus, very few people even on their own staff, let alone in the NGO community, had any knowledge of their efforts.

The secrecy surrounding the mission and its activities from July onwards was to give the impression, once Kampuchea hit the headlines, that the international agencies were dragging their feet and doing little for suffering Kampuchea. The failure to take the NGOs into their confidence, justified or otherwise, set the scene for many of the actions subsequently taken by Oxfam. These were to cause a nearly disastrous rift in the international machinery of compassion.

In the late summer in Oxford, a Frenchwoman with long-time Cambodian connections, Louise du Plaud, was badgering Michael Harris. Two French doctors had visited Phnom Penh from Vietnam and returned with a horrendous story of medical breakdown. They were putting together a planeload of food and medicines. Would Oxfam help? Harris' proviso was that an Oxfam person accompany the plane. In Paris, through du Plaud's connections in the Vietnamese exile community, Jim Howard was given a visa for Kampuchea. The plane took on its cargo in Luxembourg and left for Phnom Penh on 24 August 1979.

Thus began Oxfam's engagement with a small and unfamiliar Asian country gradually emerging from a holocaust.

Jim Howard was overwhelmed by his encounter with the devastation wreaked upon a beautiful land. A passionate and big-hearted man, he found the evidence of physical and social pain beyond comprehension. It began at the airport. Apart from one decrepit mobile staircase there was no equipment of any kind. Everything had to be unloaded by hand, and those who manhandled the sacks of food down the steps were so weak that he opened up some packages to feed them on the spot.

The Khmer Rouge had plunged Cambodian society back into the Dark Ages. During the four years of their revolution, every institution belonging to the old way of life had been vandalised. They had emptied the cities at gunpoint; dismantled the country's administrative and intellectual structure; killed or driven into hiding all professionals including doctors and teachers; abolished money; banned religious worship and learning; disallowed anything tainted by Western influence. Every man, woman, and child was compelled to live under a system of rigid collective farming. The most trivial infringement of the rules – wearing spectacles, eating at the wrong time of day – was subject to fearful punishment, even death. Since the Vietnamese invasion had ended these horrors, the evidence of the 'killing fields' had been unearthed in mass graves. The torture chambers with their fastidious documentation had been left untouched, opened as a museum lest anyone doubt that the Vietnamese invasion had been necessary.

Amidst the upheavals of 1979, millions of acres of ricefields in what was a naturally fertile terrain had been left unplanted. Thus two huge problems compounded one another: a severe shortage of food, coupled with a lack of seed and agricultural inputs; and the almost complete disintegration of the country's infrastructure – roads, vehicles, energy supplies, equipment, surveys, maps, communications, paper on which to write instructions, pens to write them with, and qualified people to carry them out – on which any rescue operation would have to depend.

The only significant organisational channel was the Vietnamese army; no relief operation based on the generosity of Western donors, governmental or private, could allow its supplies to pass into their hands. The hospitals, on which casualties of sickness and hunger were descending, were in a state of disrepair and lacked staff, drugs, and medical supplies. In Phnom Penh, a handful of Kampuchean officials were trying to reintroduce a semblance of administrative normality. Their experience was negligible, their dependence on the Vietnamese all but complete, their distrust of outsiders acute, their understanding of the principles governing Western aid non-existent, their needs vast.

All of this came across to Jim Howard in an accumulation of heart-rending incidents over the ten-day period he spent in and outside Phnom Penh. The conditions in hospitals, orphanages and clinics were universally awful: 'Children in bed in filthy rags dying of starvation; no drugs, no food, 550 beds with 600 patients. A high school next door used as a TB hospital with 250 dying people, depressing and hopeless. In one ward a boy of 13 tied down to the bed because he was going insane ...' Howard was convinced that what he was seeing was the tip of massive distress. He was also sure that the Kampucheans would deeply appreciate help: one woman doctor broke down when she understood that this was what he was promising: 'Her lips and hands quivered and we were shattered by the tragedy of it all.' What she asked for was not bandages or penicillin, but coloured cloth for clothes so that her dying patients could dress and feel human again.

Unlike the representatives from ICRC and UNICEF still trying to negotiate terms – staff, distribution channels, monitoring – for a massive input of international aid, Howard went around making lists. Drugs, medical supplies, and nutritional supplements for children, obviously; what else was lacking that Oxfam could supply? What was broken that Oxfam could mend? He took down the specifications of broken plant, in the city waterworks and the power station; he went to the textile mill and found them running out of yarn. He developed friendly relations with officials at the Ministry of Health; he discussed transport with ICRC/UNICEF with whom he committed Oxfam to full co-operation in the face of such disaster. But he did not much care about a formal agreement. Action was what mattered. He would take back his lists and his story and Oxfam would go urgently about its business.

It happened that when Howard arrived in Phnom Penh, John Pilger of the *Daily Mirror* was there making a television documentary, courtesy of Vietnamese confidence in Pilger. Their encounter and the powerful impression Howard made on Pilger were to have an important influence on the public tumult soon to surround Kampuchean aid. From Pilger, Howard also took over the Kampuchean woman interpreter – Sopheak – who was to make an important contribution to Oxfam's operation in Phnom Penh over the months to come. Not only did she have her own story of family tragedy under Pol Pot, but she was extremely committed to helping her people and invaluable in smoothing Oxfam's path with prickly or obstructive officials.

Howard returned to Oxford on 7 September. A few days later, Oxfam held a press conference at which he described the Kampucheans' suffering as 'beyond tears'. They needed '100,000 tons of rice, 15,000 tons of sugar, 7,000 tons of vegetable oil'. Oxfam was planning to spend £250,000 on food supplies immediately; but this was a fraction of what was required which only governments could provide.

On 12 September, coincidentally with Howard's report, the *Daily Mirror* devoted many pages to John Pilger's account of 'The Death of a Nation'. Oxfam was described as the one agency trying to do anything for a Kampuchea now in a state of terminal collapse thanks to Pol Pot, Western antipathy to the Vietnamese, and the woeful inadequacies of the international humanitarian machinery. Pilger was not in the least sympathetic to the difficulties presented by the Phnom Penh authorities to ICRC and UNICEF in their efforts to secure reasonable safeguards for the programme of full-scale relief.

The public response to the powerful *Mirror* coverage was stunning. Attention from other media began to build; Kampuchea's tragedy was suddenly in the limelight, triggering a huge cash response to Oxfam, and giving its efforts maximum publicity coverage. On 16 September, there was a Disasters Emergency Committee television appeal for South-East Asia in which Jim Howard appeared. But the publicity – Oxfam's oxygen, the international agencies' anathema – had its negative side: it began to drive the whole operation.

For four and a half years a country at the periphery of the Indo-Chinese drama had been a black hole in the world's consciousness. Suddenly an empty picture was being filled in, predominantly with description from a well-known popular journalist with undisguised leftist sympathies, and a deeply concerned Oxfam official. Their canvas was lurid, full of atrocity and death. A holocaust had occurred; concentration camp imagery was evoked. The legacy was imminent famine; another one to two million people out of an already decimated population of five million, including most of the children, would be dead by Christmas unless a vast tonnage of food was sent in. The basis for this scenario was largely impressionistic, backed by the original

Vietnamese request stating that 2.2 million Kampucheans faced starvation. Not just Howard and Pilger but all visitors to Kampuchea were convinced of this reality by the ruined state of the country, the stories of Khmer Rouge brutality, and the evident hardship they had witnessed.

Inevitably, the public response included an outcry against those allowing such a thing to happen. The candidates for this role boiled down to two: the uncaring West for allowing a genocidal Pol Pot to come to power and then washing their hands of the result; and the Vietnamese for occupying a weakened neighbouring country by military force and then obstructing efforts to bring its people help. The already fraught international climate in which aid for Kampuchea had to be mounted began to hum with recriminations. As in the case of the Nigerian civil war, passionate sympathy with the plight of the victims made it extremely difficult for those trying to bring relief to maintain a spirit of impartiality.

The new regime in Phnom Penh was desperate for international respectability, as had been the Biafran leaders. But the US, China, and the non-communist countries of South-East Asia continued to condemn what they saw as Vietnamese aggression and illegal occupation. Thus, Vietnam's self-presentation as the liberators of Kampuchea from Pol Pot, and their desire for Western aid to help repair its destruction and consolidate the new regime's position, had connotations other than simple empathy for the Kampuchean people. Any Western-backed relief effort was inevitably a weapon to be deployed in the propaganda war, as well as in the continuing civil war raging in the north-west where the Khmer Rouge were still in control. Indeed, the idea of neutral humanitarian aid was incomprehensible to officials in Phnom Penh.

In such a context, all statements about the country's predicament were grist to the East-West propaganda mill. Oxfam, which by mid-September had become increasingly fired up about the fate of the Kampuchean people, aligned itself with the view that the chief obstacle to the relief of suffering was foot-dragging on the part of the Western-backed international establishment and its antipathy towards the Vietnam-installed Phnom Penh regime. Adopting the role of saviour of the Kampuchean people, Oxfam set itself the task of breaking the logjam in which international relief was grounded.

This role, however inspirational and well-intentioned, was much more operationally and politically complex than most in Oxfam realised.

Jim Howard's Kampuchean report had not only fired up the Oxfam publicity people; it sent the overseas programme into top gear. On 21

September, a second charter flight took off for Phnom Penh, with a cargo of food and medical supplies and two Oxfam staff members besides Howard: Marcus Thompson, an ex-Field Director in India, and Dr. Tim Lusty. Lusty, who was also an agriculturalist, had begun his Oxfam career in emergency relief in Nigeria just after the civil war, and had worked in famine nutrition for Oxfam during the Ethiopian emergencies of the 1970s. Since 1976 he had been head of its health unit; with his particular range of experience and qualifications, Lusty was a special Oxfam asset.

On 18 September, three days before, Guy Stringer had left for Bangkok. Brian Walker had sent his Deputy Director to pursue the idea of buying food in South-East Asia and landing it at the Kampuchean port of Kompong Som. Sea-going routes, obviously, were the most apt for the huge tonnages regarded as necessary by all the relief organisations. Stringer later wrote up the story of his exploits in a report entitled: 'A slow boat to Indo-China, or the most expensive cruise in the world'. His undertaking must rank as one of the all-time exotic humanitarian adventures, an illustration of Oxfam's unique blend of flair, courage, and innocence, underpinned by British leadership and common sense.

The rounds of agencies and officialdom in Bangkok taught Stringer that the attitude of the Thai authorities towards their Vietnamese-backed neighbours in Phnom Penh made it impossible to clear a ship from Bangkok into a Kampuchean port of entry; or indeed a plane, unless assigned to ICRC/UNICEF. He therefore went on to Singapore. 'I was a man with a briefcase, $50,000 and one introduction to a shipping man.' He pondered ruefully whether any other organisation in the world 'despatched its servants on enterprises like this with such an air of nonchalance'.

The introduction was to an Irishman, David Moody of Asiatic Navigation Ltd., the tug and barge operation which had supplied the island of Bidong, and whom Jim Howard had encountered in July. Moody proved an invaluable ally. Everything known about Kompong Som – which no Western shipping had entered in years, was heavily guarded by the Vietnamese and thus unvisited by anyone in Phnom Penh – was negative. There were no cranes; the labour force was unskilled; unloading might take days, clocking up huge demurrage rates; there might be no tugs to manoeuvre a large vessel alongside. Stringer therefore decided to charter from Moody a sturdy tug and a large barge. The cargo, for ease of unloading, would sit on the deck of the barge sheltered by tarpaulins against unfortunate encounters with the monsoon.

Having chosen his boat, Stringer set out to fill it. Navigating his way through Singaporean markets turned out to be more hazardous than a typhoon in the South China Sea. The vexing question was whether to buy rice, the staple Kampuchean food. Rice, a strategic product, required an export license from the Singaporean authorities. As a member of the Association of South-East Asian Nations (ASEAN), Singapore was a hardline opponent of the installation by Vietnam of a government in Phnom Penh; this ASEAN was currently protesting about vociferously in New York where the UN General Assembly was meeting. Stringer feared that an application for an export licence might draw down a Singaporean embargo on his whole operation. In the event, a meeting at the Ministry of Foreign Affairs gave him cause for optimism that his 'cruise' would be allowed to proceed; but a frosty British High Commission made it clear that Oxfam was treading on political eggshells.

When Stringer had nearly completed his purchases of rice, maize, wheat, sugar, and oil, Jim Howard arrived from Phnom Penh and added seeds and hoes to the manifest: getting a good crop sown was essential to Kampuchean food recovery. Howard's presence and his eye-witness accounts helped confer authority on what seemed at moments even to Stringer a hare-brained do-gooding adventure. Asked by UNICEF to complete his load – 200 out of 1,500 tonnes altogether – in their name and at their cost, he did so. The total value of the cargo was £250,000; the insurance he obtained covered piracy and not much else.

Sack trolleys, wood, and carpenter's tools were purchased to make gangways for unloading; 200 foot of powered roller conveyor was ordered, but failed to show. Cooking utensils, firewood, and rations were laid on to feed the Kompong Som dockers. On 5 October, the specially fitted barge was towed round to the wharf; before loading could begin, Stringer had to give a personal assurance to the stevedores that the food would not reach Vietnamese soldiers. Prompted by Oxford, an army of journalists besieged the dock. The port and immigration authorities became distinctly nervous. To the last, Stringer feared his ship might not be allowed to sail.

On 9 October 1979, the 250-ton tug 'Asiatic Success' pushed the Oxfam barge out into the waterway and Stringer's bizarre voyage began. Oxford had sent out another staff member – Chris Jackson, ex-merchant navy – to accompany Stringer. The captain was Irish, the crew Filipino and Indonesian. They travelled at six knots towards the Gulf of Siam with the barge – 'the size of a football field' – 200 yards behind. It took four and a half days to cover the 640 nautical miles; weather and pirates were kind. Jackson, nonetheless, was constantly sick. Stringer, eating breakfast boiled eggs on the bridge, listened to the BBC World Service 'and heard our little expedition reported as the lead item among all the major world affairs. It was strange to be part of something of that consequence, and to know that we now would almost certainly be the first Western input of a sizeable quantity of food into Kampuchea.'

Instead, he nearly landed his entire cargo and crew on the sea floor. On arrival outside Kompong Som on 13 October, he ran up from courtesy a Kampuchean flag purchased in Singapore, overlooking the fact that Singapore recognised the Pol Pot regime and that the flag they were flying was therefore that of the enemy. Fortunately the expedition was expected and the Vietnamese navy took no action. The only tug in port drew up next morning and 12 young officials, their jobs designated by cardboard tags pinned to their chests, inspected the manifest and wrote studiously in penny notebooks. Marcus Thompson and Tim Lusty were on the quay; so were three Ministers, of Economy and Reconstruction, Health, and Agriculture. After speeches, beer, and a ceremonial burning of the Pol Pot flag, unloading began.

This was a true moment of Oxfam triumph. Oxfam had pioneered a sea-going route with a large consignment of food; another barge was already loading in Singapore, and others were to follow up the Mekong River. The authorities had done more than welcome the Oxfam contribution. In fact, the level of the reception appalled Stringer. 'It gives some idea of the immense problems which Kampuchea faces in management if it needs the third most important Minister in the government [Ros Samay, Minister of Economy and Reconstruction] to arrange the detailed reception of a 1,500 ton barge.' Every truck in the country plus 50 extra from Vietnam – his crew demanded another assurance about Vietnamese intentions towards the cargo – had been sent down from Phnom Penh. The sacks were manhandled ashore by a motley gang of young men and women. The unloading took five days. There was no way, Stringer concluded, that major tonnages could be imported through Kompong Som. Logistics, not supply, were going to be the problem.

The following day, in a ruined villa of Prince Sihanouk, he talked with Ros Samay. The Minister gave him a personal assurance that 'the food will be used for the most needy masses of the civilian population.' There was no undertaking about when or how. Logistics were indeed to prove a problem; one of no mean dimensions.

While Stringer had been buying food in Singapore, events had taken several dramatic turns in Phnom Penh. These went some way to explain the grandeur of his barge's reception.

On 21 September, the propaganda war over the legitimisation of the government in Phnom Penh between Vietnam and the USSR on one side, and China, the US, and their Asian allies on the other, reached a climax. To the fury of the former and the incomprehension of the humanitarian world, the partisans of China won a critical victory: a majority of UN member states voted that the Kampuchean seat in the UN General Assembly be retained by the monstrous Pol Pot regime. By this act, the UN was seen in the outside world as having forfeited all claim to morality. The reaction in Phnom Penh was outrage. ICRC and UNICEF, still struggling to obtain agreement for their plans, took the brunt of Vietnamese and Kampuchean disfavour with a hostile international world. Their difficulties took a definite turn for the worse.

A pre-condition of any international relief effort supported by major government donors to the tune of hundreds of millions of dollars was an adequate presence in the country to facilitate distribution and allow proper monitoring. This would apply anywhere, but especially in a country under military occupation whose regime was unrecognised in the West. The Phnom Penh authorities, on their side, were now more than ever unwilling to allow more than a handful of 'unfriendly' Western foreigners into Kampuchea or agree to country-wide monitoring. But these were not the major stumbling blocks.

The Kampucheans wanted ICRC and UNICEF to give an undertaking that they would not give any aid 'to the other side', to people under the control of the Khmer Rouge in the west of the country or in camps along the Thai border. This, neither agency would concede. The principle of humanitarian neutrality – aid above the political divide – was at the core of their organisational mandates. They had undertaken to Thailand to help Kampuchean refugees at the border, also a condition of Thailand's use as a staging-post for aid into Kampuchea. At the time, the Thai army were operating a closed door policy and keeping all but a trickle of refugees at bay. Thus, although an important principle was seen by ICRC/UNICEF to be at stake, to all concerned the main practical problem was regarded as that of starvation inside Kampuchea itself.

At the end of September, now under great pressure as a result of the hue and cry raised all over the world, the ICRC and UNICEF negotiations were reaching a climax. On 28 September, Brian Walker, Oxfam's Director, landed in Phnom Penh.

Up to this time, Howard and the other Oxfam people had been doing their best to work closely with their international colleagues, even though their inclination was for doing things first and sorting out the bureaucratic details later; they felt that ICRC/UNICEF's obsession with 'agreement' was a wrong ordering of priorities. But Walker had another vision. Fired up by 'two million dead by Christmas' and the outpouring of public compassion at home, he had developed the idea of Oxfam at the head of a consortium of voluntary agencies rescuing the stricken nation. Shortly before he left for Phnom Penh, he obtained the support in principle of several key European NGO partners. He now offered Phnom Penh a £25 million programme, to be overseen by a team of seven 'NGO Consortium' staff.

When it was put to him that: 'Our people would prefer to eat grass or die than share aid with Pol Pot', and that ICRC and UNICEF were in disgrace for 'helping Pol Pot by passing aid across the Thai border', he agreed to the demand that Oxfam would give no aid to those under Khmer Rouge control. He was under great pressure, keen to 'break the logjam', confident that other NGOs would deliver aid at the border and that it was therefore unnecessary for Oxfam to do so. Nevertheless, this agreement to drop the humanitarian principle UNICEF and ICRC were insisting upon cut the ground from under their negotiating position. It was also in breach of Oxfam's own principles and its policy towards victims of conflict, a policy articulated only months before.

Walker also agreed that co-operation between Oxfam and the UN and Red Cross programme should end forthwith; ICRC/UNICEF were under threat of eviction from the country and he hoped to spare Oxfam the same fate. Walker believed that he had private encouragement from the international organisations to do whatever was necessary to enable Oxfam to stay in Phnom Penh. He was unquestionably faced with an acute dilemma; one unprecedented in Oxfam's experience.

Inexperienced as the Kampuchean officials were, and desperate for signs of legitimacy from the West, they on their side did not properly understand the nature of a 'voluntary agency': they talked to Walker about signing a 'treaty', as if they were talking to a representative of a government or international authority. Oxfam was seen as a pawn to bring the other agencies to heel. Nor did they fully understand the relative scale of operations of which the different organisations were capable. Walker saw in the discomfited position of the internationals a gap that needed filling. But to imagine that an NGO consortium, no matter how many agencies joined it, could ever substitute for the combined weight of UN and ICRC donors and agencies was unrealistic. More immediately problematic to the Oxfam team in Phnom Penh, however, was the split in humanitarian ranks which a separate aid agreement created. Relations between the agencies, whose personnel were all obliged to live and work at the same hotel in what amounted to a foreigner ghetto, plummeted.

Walker's agreement with the authorities conferred on Oxfam a favoured status. Alone among representatives of the distrusted and distrustful imperialist West, Oxfam was an ally and a symbol of genuine friendship, as well as a channel through which something of a Kampuchean case might be put. For the next weeks, Oxfam was to enjoy a honeymoon period of relations with the authorities. This certainly eased the path of the Consortium Team in obtaining permission to travel around and carry out their work.

In between Walker's negotiations at the Ministry of Foreign Affairs he toured hospitals and orphanages and visited two provincial headquarters. Tim Lusty, Oxfam's emergency health and nutrition expert, accompanied him. Like others, Walker was bowled over by the Pol Pot destruction, the grotesque evidence in Tuol Sleng prison, and the atrocities recounted by Khmer Rouge victims. Everywhere, he heard of ration shortages; one provincial Governor claimed that '50 per cent of my people are starving', another that '260,000 of my people are hungry'. However, outside hospitals and other crisis centres there was little evidence of this. Lusty was by now beginning seriously to question emotive interpretations and anecdotal estimates of need.

The shocking nature of so much that Walker saw and heard, together with his feeling for the people, reinforced his augmented sense of the Oxfam mission. At this stage, the fact that he and Tim Lusty, his famine relief advisor, had seen no evidence of massive starvation did not deflect him from the conviction that there was widespread and urgent need, both for food and other inputs. Walker put what might well be only a temporary 'lift' in people's condition down to the distribution of Vietnamese food aid.

Walker flew back to Britain on 10 October. Relations with UNICEF and ICRC reached their nadir when he was reported in the Bangkok press as confirming that the two organisations were about to be thrown out of the country. On his return to Oxford, Walker pressed ahead with his plans for the NGO Consortium. In Brussels on 19 October, he put before representatives of 31 agencies a proposal for a six-month programme of aid for Kampuchea on the basis of the agreement reached in Phnom Penh. His presentation of this – that pragmatic action had won the day and 'broken the logjam' – was accepted. Among the key Consortium partners were Dutch and German CARITAS, the Lutheran World Federation, and other Oxfams: US, Belgique, and Community Aid Abroad.

The initiative Walker proposed was daring. Every month, on an operation for one country, Oxfam was to organise expenditure to the tune of £2 million, more than one-fifth of its annual income. Its experience with huge supplies operations was nil; its Indo-China expertise, negligible; it was unused to working through government channels, especially in a centralised communist country; the Consortium framework was unfamiliar and untried. Nothing daunted, Walker's case and Kampuchea's plight won the day. It was a brilliant achievement.

In Phnom Penh, meanwhile, ICRC and UNICEF had finally managed to reverse their fortunes and reach agreement with the authorities on mutually acceptable – if antagonistic – terms. On 13 October, a daily relief shuttle began from Bangkok and cargoes set off from various South-East Asian ports. Guy Stringer, arriving in Phnom Penh on 16 October in a convoy of 23 battered trucks full of rice, met the delegates and was told that their $104 million programme had been accepted. He wrote later: 'Obviously their success, which is very much in the interests of the people of Kampuchea, meant that we had to re-jig our plans from the massive food delivery and distribution programme which Brian Walker had foreseen under totally different circumstances, to a supportive programme of the more traditional Oxfam kind.' Having confirmed with the Ministry of Foreign Affairs that there was no longer any problem over co-operation with ICRC and UNICEF, fences were mended. The possibility of two competitive and overlapping humanitarian programmes was ended.

The programme of the 'more traditional' kind Stringer meant was one that filled in gaps in, or supplemented in special ways, the efforts of the international heavyweights. However, in few other ways could it be described as 'traditional'. Lusty was setting up feeding programmes in Phnom Penh hospitals and orphanages according to the emergency format; this might be typical but nothing else was. But then nothing about Kampuchea could be done in a typical way because the circumstances were altogether extraordinary. In meetings at various Ministries it was settled that a textile mill and a fishing-net factory would be put back in order; hundreds of pumpsets and diesel fuel for irrigation would be sent; 1,000 orphanage 'kits' would be made up; large tonnages of seed and agricultural supplies would also come in on barges sent up from Singapore. UNICEF was bringing in a fleet of vehicles; Oxfam ordered another 50 trucks, to be air-freighted from Turkey.

The speed and the scale of the Kampuchean relief operation were in a different league from anything done by Oxfam in the past. The impact on the organisational psyche was similar to that of 20 years ago when the Congo famine was at its height; those then at Oxfam had felt as though they were playing leading parts in an international crusade. The effort for Kampuchea was similarly gaining a heroic and folkloric stature.

At the end of October, the already high rev counter of Kampuchean relief wound up to a level which put Oxfam under a degree of pressure close to breaking-point.

On 10 October, the Vietnamese army had launched a new offensive against the Khmer Rouge in the north-west of the country. By 27

October, 130,000 Kampucheans trapped by the fighting had fled across the border into Thailand, and another 120,000 were right behind. They were sick, starving, and in a lamentable condition. The Thai government finally declared an 'open door' policy provided the UN would accept responsibility for their food and shelter. The principle of 'aid on both sides' suddenly took on a new significance. The flow of refugees did not slacken for many weeks, reaching around 650,000 in early December. Unlike in Kampuchea, where access and information were extremely limited, the Thai border began to swarm with journalists, aid people, and prestigious visitors.

On 30 October, John Pilger's documentary about Kampuchea, 'Year Zero', made back in August, was shown on ITV – transmission had been held up by a television strike. For the first time, the British public – and later others all over the world – saw in spellbinding and awful detail the horrors perpetrated by the Pol Pot regime. They learned about the threat of famine, a threat apparently confirmed by the state of the refugees flooding across the Thai border, now daily in the news. They saw Jim Howard interviewed in Phnom Penh; and at the end, Oxfam's address and telephone number.

The next day, the BBC's *Blue Peter* programme launched an appeal for Kampuchea focused on Oxfam shops. The identification with a named charity was an unprecedented step, as it had been for Pilger's film. From 7.30am the following morning and for weeks to come, the telephones at Oxfam in Oxford and in offices and shops throughout the country were never silent.

The Pilger documentary alone raised £500,000, half of which was spent on the contents of Barge No. 4, departing 24 November. *Blue Peter*, which had hoped to raise £100,000, reached that amount in four days; the money was spent on trucks and a ferry. The appeal finally closed in December having brought in over £3 million.

The need to save Kampuchea from the jaws of death had now become ·a *cause célèbre* all over the Western world. Barges and trucks plying sea and air, rushing to the rescue thanks to the public's heartfelt generosity, were the subject of daily media exposure. What was not subject to exposure, however, was the actual situation inside Kampuchea itself. In the two months which had passed since John Pilger had taken his footage, much had changed.

The authorities in Phnom Penh were not enjoying the fanfare of attention and scrutiny unleashed by their request for food to relieve a famine. They particularly disliked the spectacle of aid being given to people under the control of the various opposition groups up on the Thai border. They began to accuse the West of inventing the famine as a cover for resupplying the Khmer Rouge – whose legitimacy the Western nations still formally recognised – and enabling the opposition to fight on. They also began to impose tighter restrictions on the movements of the limited number of Westerners present, and were less than free with information in spite of promises they had made about regular reports. All agency officials tried for months to organise a proper system for monitoring the use of their relief goods. None succeeded.

This was not surprising, given the lack of skilled people in every department of government and the damaged state of the entire administrative infrastructure. The agencies did their best to compromise with deficiencies, towards which – given what the country had endured – they were naturally sympathetic. Oxfam was especially so; they prided themselves on their close relations with many ministry officials, including the senior Vietnamese advisor in the Ministry of Foreign Affairs, who regularly visited for tea. They developed these contacts much as an Oxfam Field Director would normally build up relations with local project partners expecting, perhaps naively, to enjoy a similar influence over the way things were done.

Nothing was easy. Understaffed, overstretched, often emotionally overwrought, confined to a curious hot-house life in the Hotel Samaki, teams of relief workers were trying in chaotic circumstances to see to the safe landing of their supplies and delivery to the storage facilities of the Ministries supposed to get them to their respective destinations. Even this proved taxing. Oxfam's primary concern, like that of the other agencies, was to develop a semblance of order in their programme. What was actually happening out in the villages was largely a matter of speculation. Few were in a position to make a sound judgement about whether or not, as the Vietnamese now claimed, the threat of famine was exaggerated.

Tim Lusty left Kampuchea in late October and, back in Oxford, wrote up his report on the nutritional and medical situation in early November. Lusty was inclined from professional experience to apply epidemiological techniques in famine situations rather than rely on his eyes and emotions. There was little hard data available, as he freely admitted. But the limited nutritional and agricultural assessments he had been able to undertake had convinced him that there was no serious threat of famine. He described the nutritional status in the areas he had visited as 'fair to good'; in one of the orphanages where children had been described as 'starving to death', he had taken arm circumference measurements and found that 'the general state of nutrition of this vulnerable group is very good, certainly better than in an average village in Wollo, Ethiopia, in non-famine times.'

There were certainly still great needs and 'no room for complacency'; but he believed – although he did not recommend this as a basis for planning – that the rural population could scrape through without food aid. He based this on Kampuchea's fertility, the ingenuity of the people, and evidence of agricultural revival; he believed that the provision of Vietnamese or Soviet food aid had had at best a marginal effect. This was mostly being distributed in the towns and to government officials. Rice, in the absence of money, was still the medium of exchange and thus food aid had been used to pay wages and re-start market life in the towns.

With the crescendo mounting in Britain in the wake of 'Year Zero' and the *Blue Peter* appeal, Lusty's report was not well-received in Oxford. The NGO Consortium was at a critical stage of formation; Oxfam was riding the wind. In New York, a special UN conference had been called for government donors to pledge funds for a re-estimated $250 million relief programme over the next 12 months. The statements of delegates were strongly influenced by the reports of journalists and embassy officials in Bangkok. They had all drawn the same conclusion: that the misery of refugees reaching the Thai border was typical of millions more inside Kampuchea. In Oxford, Lusty's view that there was no serious threat of famine was disbelieved. A speaking tour to Oxfam supporter groups was cancelled; he was asked not to speak to the media.

Other Oxfam observers later confirmed his view. In mid-November, Malcolm Harper, the Oxfam Consortium Team Leader in Phnom Penh, and Hans Page, an FAO agriculturalist, were given permission to make the first extensive tour of the provinces undertaken by any Western aid official. They saw and heard of food shortages; but nowhere was there outright famine. Harper's view was that 'things could easily slip back very quickly', but fishing and farming were reviving, and there was a roaring market in goods coming across the border from Thailand. Robert Mister, Oxfam's Disasters Officer, made a similar trip in December, and reported: 'I saw no evidence of famine, starvation or serious hunger. In fact, I found it hard to believe that there ever had been famine or starvation on a massive scale in the parts of the country I visited. It is, however, clear that there are serious food shortages.'

What had happened to the famine so confidently predicted? In the first place, the people of the Kampuchean countryside, however dislocated by events, had not abandoned farming life on the suicidal scale imagined. The tropical climate and natural productivity of the soil were allies of long familiarity. They had cultivated maize, cassava, bananas in garden plots; they harvested fish from rivers and lakes; and they did manage to bring in a rice crop in November amounting to around one-third of the required 900,000 tonnes, much more than the one-fifth anticipated. The authorities in Phnom Penh also cancelled the grain tax which would have normally been exacted from the farmers to feed the towns and government officials. Whatever they produced, they kept.

Meanwhile, those in the war-stricken north-west still under the control of the Khmer Rouge were in a very different situation. It was these people, whose care Oxfam had decided to leave to others, who genuinely faced starvation. Their only source of aid was from across the border with Thailand via an informal land-bridge: tens of thousands of Kampucheans who trekked there by foot, bicycle, and cart, were issued with 20 kilos of food and 10 kilos of rice-seed per person. Because of such unpredictabilities, the principle of 'aid above the political divide' turned out to be not only philosophically, but practically, vital. Although Oxfam never reneged on its agreement not to help those on the Kampuchean side of the Thai border under Khmer Rouge control, it did provide a grant of £250,000 to UNHCR for child feeding in refugee camps inside Thailand in late December 1979.

Oxfam's public commitment to the prediction of famine and the questionable way in which the subsequent hue and cry drove many of its actions was a lesson it absorbed in time. Without 'two million dead by Christmas', there might not have been such a compelling sense of the 'need to break the logjam', the need to compromise the principle of humanitarian neutrality might not have seemed so pressing, and the programme might have been more carefully and more economically planned. Much later, after Lusty's view was redeemed, it became accepted practice in Oxfam that no such famine clamour again be mounted without the full sanction of its own professional emergency health staff.

By mid-December 1979, the question of what had happened to the famine was exercising those in Phnom Penh less than the question of what had happened to their aid.

In the docks at Kompong Som, much of the relief sent on the first two Oxfam barges and UNICEF/ICRC ships was still languishing undistributed. Vehicles were arriving, flown in at considerable expense in Oxfam's case; but there were not enough signs of their deployment on delivery of food and medical supplies around the country. When reports began to appear in the press accusing the Vietnamese of wilful maldistribution and diversion, Western inclination to give the liberators of Kampuchea the benefit of the doubt about their intentions towards the Kampuchean people swiftly evaporated. They had declared a famine and asked the West for help; help had been sent and it was sitting in warehouses.

Worst affected were the international programme's shiploads of food, piling up at the rate of 30,000 tons a month in congested Kompong Som: Stringer's observations about port handling capacity in October had proved sadly accurate. The Consortium's barges, despatched from Singapore by Oxfam's Geoff Busby, were now travelling up the Mekong River and off-loading at the better-run port of Phnom Penh. But the international hue and cry again put all the agencies under great stress. The continued belief in the famine made the outside world doubly incensed; but to suggest that the famine had gone away was not only to suffer loss of credibility, but also to risk cutting off the flow of aid. Whatever the precise degree of immediate crisis, aid in quantity was sorely needed.

Food distribution was still the priority, as well as seed and irrigation equipment to promote agricultural recovery. To those in Phnom Penh, the dwindling threat of famine did not detract from the crying need for rehabilitation of every conceivable variety. Bad roads, poor logistics, continuing shortages of trucks, boats, and all the administrative confusion went a long way to explain shortcomings. But the reality was difficult to explain even to their own headquarters, let alone to an outside world whose understanding of complex relief programmes is not sophisticated and whose commitment is fickle at best. Oxfam, trying to reassure the British public that the aid they had given was not being abused, was inclined to downplay the authorities' failures.

During the early months of 1980, the Consortium's emphasis was on seed, for rice, maize and vegetables; over 100,000 hoe heads had already arrived, as had 200 irrigation pumps and 36,000 handsprayers. Rat poison and 500 tons of fertiliser arrived in January on the seventh barge. The agricultural consignments were dealt with by a Consortium Team member assigned by the Lutheran World Federation; an engineer was sent by Bread for the World. In February, Dr. Nick Maurice, a nutritionist, joined the team from Oxford.

By this time, relations with the government were growing considerably cooler. Gradually, the degree of like-mindedness between the authorities and Oxfam was dwindling. In April, a nutritional surveillance survey carried out by Maurice showed that one-quarter of children were malnourished. When this was brought to the attention of the authorities with a statement regarding the need for better food distribution, they took the gravest exception. Maurice's attempt to carry out nutritional survey training for health workers in the provinces was obstructed, and he returned to Oxford in some frustration. At this point Oxfam believed that the government was no longer meeting the terms agreed for monitoring the Consortium programme. Relations were restored following a threatened rupture and a visit by Walker in June; but it had become clear that the agencies worked in Kampuchea on sufferance, and on terms which suited the centralised and socialist political agenda, or not at all.

In June 1980, when Jim Howard visited Kampuchea with John Pilger to follow up 'Year Zero' with an anniversary television documentary, he was amazed by the improvements they found. 'The changes were quite breath-taking and show the incredible tenacity of human beings to survive and recover when given even modest opportunities and assistance.' Everyone had begun to feel that the crisis in the country was essentially over, or at least that it was on a secure hold. After this, the programme settled down and became less highly-charged. The crusade was over; but not before a few scales had fallen from certain eyes, nor before Oxfam had entered into a lasting love affair with the Kampuchean people.

By the end of 1980, the Oxfam-led Consortium programme for Kampuchean relief had brought into the country supplies worth £12-13 million, and 43 barges had shipped out of Singapore. The largest component was agricultural goods, including £4 million worth of seed for the 1980 planting. The second largest was 190 trucks and other transport items worth £2.25 million. £2 million had been spent on food; £1.3 million on industrial items. Freight had added around £3 million.

The Consortium wound up its operations in mid-1981. Oxfam set up a country office of its own and continued to support the long process of Kampuchean recovery. In the strange circumstances of that politically isolated land, it was always far from 'a traditional Oxfam programme'. Instead of projects carefully targeted towards the poor – employing OXWORP-type 'community contact persons' or sending Mistry to advise villagers about forming co-operative societies – the major emphasis was on infrastructural repair. There were large grants for Phnom Penh's waterworks, industrial plant, rural water supplies, irrigation equipment, and spare parts. This is not Oxfam's chosen type of programme. But while the Vietnamese occupation continued, and while the parties to the continuing civil war failed to reach a settlement, no support for Kampuchea from the international economic community was forthcoming. If humanitarian agencies like Oxfam had not been willing to help, no-one else would have done.

In 1983, Oxfam's Asia Committee commissioned an evaluation of the 1979-81 Kampuchea Oxfam-NGO Consortium relief operation. It was undertaken by Tigger Stack, connected to Oxfam since the Bihar famine in 1966 and a participant in the maelstrom of activity which took over the organisation at the height of the Kampuchea pandemonium. The task proved virtually impossible. By the standards of accountability normally applied in Oxfam – whose standards for regular project funding are high – much of the programme and its style of management was subject to criticism.

There were over-expenditures; there was operational confusion; there was political naivety; expectations of Oxfam's partnership with government were misplaced; above all there was a failure to recognise what pressures such a vast, unprecedented programme would place on Oxfam and expand administrative capacity fast enough to meet them. There had been great strains within Oxfam during much of the emergency period. Now they were re-evoked. Stack's report was too painful; it was not widely circulated.

In time, Oxfam undertook a reappraisal of emergency procedures, and changes were introduced. But as Stack herself suggested, an attempt to extract 'lessons learnt' from many of the judgements in her report was almost an irrelevant exercise. In every way, Kampuchea was an exception. Many rules in the regular book had gone out of the window because it had been necessary to react creatively once the Kampuchean engagement was joined; therefore, the rules normally governing evaluation could not be applied. If Oxfam functioned according to the careful planning and administrative routines which would allow such an operation to run on rails, it would not be the organisation that it is. If a day comes on which the reports of a Jim Howard and a John Pilger could not set the Oxfam torch aflame, part of its soul will have died. Oxfam is ultimately a vehicle of British compassion towards suffering people overseas; in that capacity it performed heroically for the people of Kampuchea in 1979.

The Kampuchea crisis brought Oxfam a new visibility, high prestige, and a vastly greater income; some people on the international scene – who did not previously take such organisations very seriously – regarded the crisis as the time at which 'the NGOs came of age'. Walker's vision had propelled Oxfam into a stage of growth more dramatic than even he could have envisaged.

For people from the top to the bottom of the organisation and in partner organisations overseas; people in Britain, Singapore, and Phnom Penh; for people who had given their all for stricken Kampuchea, who had brought off incredible coups, who had done their best in chaotic and préssurised circumstances, who had felt great pride in the way Oxfam had risen to the challenge of a late 1970s holocaust, this was its finest hour.

11

BLACK MAN'S BURDEN REVISITED

By the late 1970s, the euphoria which had blown through Africa in the aftermath of independence had faded. The excitement of nation-building, of *ujamaa* and the other new doctrines of the freedom era, had slowly evaporated as their promise remained unfulfilled.

Disillusion came earliest in the political sphere. The crisis in the Congo and the Nigerian civil war – the events which first familiarised a mass audience in the West with the shocking face of famine and placed Oxfam's name prominently before the British public – turned out to be the foretaste of a contagion of wars, coups and secessionist movements. The 1970s witnessed bloody internal conflicts in Burundi, Chad, Sudan, Ethiopia, and Uganda, many prompting clashes with neighbouring states. They caused terrible hardship and human dislocation. For Oxfam these crises frequently provoked emergency response, particularly where people were forced onto the move and fetched up, empty-handed, in relief camps.

Away in the south, the political struggle ground on in the pre-independence format. Rhodesian UDI in 1965 and Portuguese intransigence until 1975 blocked the onward rush of African freedom. During the 1970s, armed liberation struggle, first in Mozambique and Angola, then in Zimbabwe and Namibia, was a main regional pre-occupation. After 1975, South Africa's reaction to the advent of black socialistic regimes in countries on her borders, and the pressures building up inside her own society, was external destabilisation and internal clampdown. Social and economic progress in the 'Frontline States' was inhibited, in some places destroyed. As time went by, Oxfam found itself increasingly drawn into the human ramifications of apartheid's last stand in the one remaining minority-dominated white redoubt.

In the rest of the continent, Africa's patchwork of peoples faced a longer journey than those in other developing regions to become card-carrying members of the industrialised world. Development thinking was long dominated by the idea that what was required to make Africa 'catch up' was a transplant of Western technology and the instant construction of institutions which mirrored those of the colonial *alma mater*. There was neither time nor need for the paraphernalia of the modern economic state to grow organically; it could be parachuted in courtesy of aid and earnings from African minerals and agricultural commodities.

In the West, countries like Britain saw aid largely as a form of subsidised exports and long-term investment on concessionary terms. Africa's leaders were receptive. They had fought for independence to run the economic machinery set up by the colonisers – plantations, mines, mills, office blocks, governors' palaces – in the interests of Africans, not to dismantle it. The fact that its design connected it to international markets and financial systems instead of to the primeval ways of the African plains was seen as a blessing, not as a curse.

Thus, while the inherited political clothing was being cast off or patched beyond recognition, the economic clothing remained essentially intact. Until the mid-1970s, rapid rates of industrialisation and economic growth – some as high as 15 per cent a year – obscured the fact that the economic clothing was as poorly-tailored for its developmental role. Only after the shock of the 1974 oil crisis, along with the gradual realisation that terms of trade were never going to move significantly in Africa's favour, did it become obvious to those who examined these matters that you could not deposit modernisation, Western-style, onto an economic foundation as fragile as that in most of sub-Saharan Africa and expect it to flourish.

Gradually, the purveyors of official aid began to decry 'our failures in Africa'. Their almost exclusive focus on a small, modern, economic plateau, marooned above an ocean of semi-subsistence living, came under fire from all those who took part in the reappraisals of the 1970s and debunked the myth that the benefits of growth automatically 'trickled down' to the poor. A handful of Africans had managed to adopt the automobile-and-verandah lifestyle of the old colonial masters while most of the rest were still making do with huts and headloads. Power stations, showpiece hospitals, cement factories towering like cathedrals over the bush: nowhere in the world were such infrastructural totems more conspicuously irrelevant to most people's lives.

There was no connection between the economy of the jumbo-jet, and that of two hectares of maize and one of sorghum. Indeed, the planners had behaved as if the economy of Africa's subsistence producers did not exist. Traces of it might fleetingly be seen, in the interstices of crop production or cattle sales. Only in a handful of countries – Tanzania was the chief example – was the condition of the majority of people living in the rural hinterland the chosen focus of public policy. The fact that the dynamics of the thatched hut economy, especially the contribution of its women members, had not been taken into account was one reason why many development ventures had proved so ill-conceived. In time, this realisation led the official aid community to look more carefully at projects funded by the voluntary agencies. Their activities were by their nature concerned with those living at or close to subsistence, and interacted with the economy the least well-off were living in rather than the one described in the national plan. Aid from charitable organisations, by definition, was designed to be poverty-focused.

Through the 1970s Oxfam's grants to Africa mostly consisted of the good old traditional kind to clinics, flying doctors, school gardens, leprosaria, vocational workshops, and the occasional VSO-type technical team (notably in Zaire and Zambia). Projects were typically run by expatriates, most belonging to Christian missions. There were almost no indigenous organisations to work with: one or two enterprising village councils in West Africa; women's self-help networks in Kenya; Tanzania's Community Development Trust Fund; white-led welfare groups in Rhodesia and South Africa. Signals of a new direction came from Tanzania, and from parts of West Africa where 'animation rurale' drew its inspiration from a similar spring as conscientisation.

Some mistakes of the white elephant variety were made at the Oxfam level: broken pumps with nobody to mend them, high grade bulls stewing in the cooking pot, maize-shellers run by bicycle power which no-one would use because only women shelled maize and only men rode bicycles. The Africa hands did their best to correct the errors, setting off by Landrover for the bush where they tinkered with breeds and seeds and water-lifting devices copied from 19th century manuals.

Like counterparts elsewhere, Oxfam Field Directors in Africa began to use terms such as 'technologically appropriate', 'cost-benefit', and 'self-sufficiency'. But their perspective, fixed in the semi-subsistence world of the African farmer, was mostly dislocated from the national development scene and the national balance sheet. By the same token, the national planners as yet took little account of what the humanitarians were up to. In the micro-project vineyard, life went on virtually untouched by rumblings in the political and economic firmament. Gradually, this was to change.

The first influence was the massive demand of emergencies. In 1973, six years of poor rains in the countries of the Sahel, the southern fringe of the Sahara, climaxed in a pasturage crisis which decimated livestock herds and brought starvation to 250,000 people. In the same year, drought in the northern Ethiopian provinces of Wollo and Tigray triggered a famine which cost 200,000 lives and, because of a television documentary by Jonathan Dimbleby, horrified the world. For Oxfam, these two 'natural' calamities opened a new, more intense, chapter in Africa.

One aspect was the scale and type of disaster response: in Ethiopia's famine camps, Oxfam medical people – notably Tim Lusty and Susan Peel – were closely involved in improving the methodology of emergency feeding for malnourished children, building upon the experience of Biafra and Bengal. This was repeated and enlarged upon in the refugee camps set up for nomadic ethnic Somalis from Ethiopia's Ogaden region, dislodged first by Somalia's disastrous Ethiopian military adventure in 1978, later by prolonged drought. When famine struck the Karamajong people of northern Uganda in 1980, Oxfam again fielded a team operation, running supplementary feeding centres in conjunction with SCF and UNICEF.

The close involvement in African emergencies led to the realisation that not only in a war did a famine have to be 'man-made', or at least 'man-influenced'. The tragedies in Ethiopia, the Sahel, Somalia and Uganda were blamed not only on the weather, but on national and international neglect of peoples whose fate was marginal to the political and economic interests of those manipulating the levers of power. A closer look showed up something even more fundamental: the iniquitous impact of the forces of modernity – or 'development' – on ancient environmental equilibrium.

The crisis in the Sahelian countries was so severe that few governments survived it; in Ethiopia, famine cost Emperor Haile Selassie's ruling dynasty its 2,000-year-old throne, and set in train years of strife and social breakdown. Population pressure on land becoming over-grazed and over-cropped, unaccompanied by any organised form of input into family agriculture, was beginning to overwhelm the farming base. Agricultural investment – what little there was – went into large-scale farms and plantations, mainly for non-food crops. Even when the rains returned to the Saharan fringe, the Ethiopian highlands, the Ogaden plains and other climatically vulnerable places, life limped along within steadily eroding margins.

Throughout the 1970s, although food production per head failed to keep pace with population growth and terms of trade worsened, some African countries still kept their economic chins up. The living standards of many people continued to improve, modestly. Housing, education, health, and social services managed – just – to expand. An upcoming generation of well-educated Africans waited in the wings. Talk of 'basic needs' and 'poverty-relieving strategies' prodded some investment into drains and schools instead of flyovers and factories. Gradually, it seemed, the dislocated development worlds were moving closer together. In Tanzania and Malawi, for example, Oxfam Field Directors began to examine how to support the spread of primary health care within the national plan. The British Overseas Development Administration (ODA) began to support, through co-funding with Oxfam, simple training courses for Zairean cultivators in such arts as mulching, ridging, and rotation of crops. The poor, in their own right, were finally becoming a focus of wider attention.

In the early 1980s, the economic storm clouds began to build more ominously than before. As world recession struck, the house of cards against which Africa borrowed and Western institutions invested collapsed. The airports and highways, the showpiece hospitals and convention centres, could not be paid for, could not be maintained. Compromising its development prospects still further, Africa slid deeply into debt; and the Structural Adjustment Programmes (SAPs) which have since been supposed to pull countries out of it have undermined social services, raised the cost of imports, sent prices soaring. Even the traditional economy began to buckle. 'We are SAPped,' say the women in a West African market town.

For women, above all, the burden of development failure in Africa has been heavy. At times of upheaval, those who fetch up in the camp destinations of last resort are the weakest: the elderly and disabled; above all, the women and children. The menfolk stay with the cattle, or with the rustlers, or with the rebel army. When the family plot or the ancestral grazing grounds can no longer yield enough to fill the family larder, the men go off to the mines or the towns, leaving the women to farm the plot and manage the household on their own. In spite of women's central role in family food production, many projects with an economic or agricultural focus – improved seed, training, fertiliser, credit – have been heavily biased in favour of men. Meanwhile, it is women who feel most strongly the impact of environmental degradation as they are obliged to walk further to fetch fuel and water. In the 1980s, Oxfam began to address the role of women in projects and programming more carefully; a Gender and Development Unit was set up in 1985, and since then not only have women recipients' needs been addressed more systematically, but more women project staff have been taken on.

Africa's poverty statistics have always been searing. Here are to be found 29 of the world's 36 poorest countries; the highest average rates of infant mortality, the commonest incidence of child undernutrition, the lowest life expectancy, the worst illiteracy rates. Yet as any traveller in Africa knows, however basic the village lifestyle might be, however narrow its margins, and however empty its pockets of the usual means of exchange, the word 'poverty' with all its Dickensian overtones can seem pejorative and misapplied.

There is self-respect and independent-mindedness, still, in much of traditional Africa of a type unusual in the brutal squalor of urban poverty, the rural slum of a plantation settlement, or the beggary of landlessness. These qualities do not show up in the economic and social statistics; yet they have borne the thatched hut economy on their shoulders and seen its members through bad times even as the jumbo-jet economy was begging for loans and mortgaging its future. In the past, the balance between humankind and nature maintained a rural lifestyle which might be desperately poor by Western material standards but at least was self-sufficient, self-contained.

The problem is now that the reverberations from a political economy inimical to the interests of these 'poor' have disrupted that balance. Not wealth but poverty – in the form of pauperisation, especially of women – is what has trickled down. Africa's ultimate safety-net, the relationship between land and people, is collapsing. Nowhere in the world is the unskilled, undereducated, and underemployed population of urban squatter settlements expanding so fast as in Africa. More than 10 million Africans, two-thirds of the world's toll of refugees, have been uprooted. Most camp in mud and wattle shanties along borders and in wastelands, living precariously on innate resourcefulness and hand-outs.

In the course of this heartbreaking chapter of African history, Oxfam and fellow agencies have found themselves groping after a new development role in Africa. During the 1980s, with more resources at its disposal and a wider set of horizons, Oxfam outgrew the 'project-by-project on its merits' approach which simply addressed small, unconnected oases of need. It looked for ways in which positive experiences in the intricate workings of the semi-subsistence world could be transferred into other locations or onto plans grander in dimension than its own: what it described as 'scaling up'. It borrowed from experience elsewhere, helping local organisational capacity to emerge. It worked with the international big league in an effort to find ideas which worked for people, especially for women, as well as for national balance sheets.

Above all, Oxfam sought out partners trying to build new networks of mutual support based on adaptations of ancient survival skills so that the old indomitable spirit of Africa could yet win through.

A striking example of effective Oxfam aid is to be found in Burkina Faso, the country which used to be Upper Volta, in the dryland zone of the Sahel.

Twenty years ago, the Yatenga plateau, home of the Mossi people, was covered with woods and vegetation. Today much of the landscape is bare: denuded of trees, soil baked hard or turned to dust. The change is partly due to declining rainfall, which reached an all-time low in the drought of 1983-84. But population and economic pressures have encouraged creeping desertification.

The Mossi have always cultivated on a shifting basis, clearing a stretch of grass and woodland to grow crops and moving on after a year or two to let the land recover. Fallow periods used to last for up to 20 years. But as the human and animal population grew, these became shorter and the demands of livestock on pasture more severe. The plant cover shielding the soil was destroyed, and the torrential downpours of the rainy season washed exposed topsoil away. Farming ways which used to be in league with the landscape suddenly became its despoiler. Patches of hard earth with a clay skim began to appear, spreading across the Yatenga like an infection.

After the drought of 1973-74, the Mossi farmers of Yatenga began to notice that their land was dying. Some resorted to an old technique of containing soil by piling stones in lines across eroded fields and gullies. Outsiders who came to help focused on the fate of the trees. Not only was their loss contributing to desertification, but was presenting the women with a serious domestic fuel problem.

In 1979, Bill Hereford, Oxfam's Field Director in the Sahel, hired a forester, Arlene Blade. At first she encouraged farmers to grow trees, using a technique she had studied in the Negev Desert. Species of many kinds – shade, nuts, fruit, fodder, and especially fuel – were planted within semi-circles of stones positioned along field boundaries and designed to trap water around their roots. But it gradually became clear that the farmers were more interested in harvesting water for food production; it could not be spared for trees.

A new project director, Peter Wright, turned his attention to the traditional lines-of-stones across the ground. If these were built more solidly and aligned with the contours of the land, they dammed up rainwater for up to ten yards behind, enabling it to soak in even where the soil had formed a crust. The problem was the contour alignment. The terrain's undulations were so gentle that they were hardly visible to the eye. Without surveying instruments, the Mossi could not position their stone lines efficiently. Wright concocted a supremely simple landscape spirit-level: a clear hosepipe filled with water. The hosepipe was attached at each end to a stake, and the stakes moved about until the water level equalised; the stones were laid from stake to stake. This instrument cost all of £3.50.

This stone dyke, or *diguette*, technique first emerged in 1981. By the following year, 15 villages were dyking their fields. In the disastrous drought years of 1983 and 1984, treated land produced crops when adjoining fields grew nothing. There could be no better advertisement:

snaking lines of stones had managed to draw crops from land otherwise lost to cultivation. The *diguettes* retained soil particles and organic matter to nourish the soil, as well as precious water. Millet crops improved by 50 per cent.

Oxfam spread the technique by running two- to three-day training courses for farmers in contouring and the use of the hosepipe level. In 1984-5, Peter Wright and a Bourkinabe colleague, Mathieu Ouedraogo (subsequently manager of the programme), trained 600 farmers from 30 villages. The courses were in great demand; the technique began to spread. The Naam movement, Burkina Faso's largest voluntary association, has since proselytised the idea among its 1,400 member groups. Oxfam itself held seminars and organised visits from farmers in other parts of the country. It has caught on as far away as Mali and Northern Ghana. This example of widespread consumer-driven development cost Oxfam a total of £350,000.

Some of the Yatenga farmers have now begun to grow trees in the *diguettes*. A decade after the project was launched as a tree and desert-reclaiming exercise, the people themselves have reached the point where its original idea is now embraced as their own next stage of agro-conservation.

Another similarly successful enterprise, also launched in the Yatenga plateau, was a scheme for village cereal banks. The banks consist of village storerooms, constructed with the help of loans from Oxfam. But the buildings are not the critical part. The point of the programme was to enable farmers to retain control over their economic lifeblood – their food crop, which also served as their main means of exchange; to trade and speculate in such a way that they did not become the victims of other people's market and pricing arrangements.

Immediately after the annual harvest when prices are at their seasonal lowest, African farmers normally sell part of their crop to the grain merchants in order to pay off their inputs. This means that, months later in the hungry season, they are obliged to buy back food grains from him at scarcity prices. The cereal banks that Oxfam supported, not only in Burkina but subsequently elsewhere, enabled the villagers to cut out the middleman. In the Burkina scheme, each village received an initial loan of 250,000 CFA (£466) to buy grain, mainly from farmers in their own community. If they did well enough in the first year to pay back a part of the loan, a second instalment materialised, and a grant to construct a simple cereal store: no building before an indication of sound financial management.

Five village cereal banks were launched tentatively in 1983, a year in which the harvest proved a disaster. An even worse season in 1984 underlined the need to enter into purchasing agreements with farmers in food-surplus areas elsewhere. The villagers, or rather the men since the banks are so far entirely male-dominated, swiftly caught on to the novel idea of travelling outside their vicinity to deal in foodstuffs. All the banks succeeded. 'The main reason', reported the Oxfam Field Director in 1986, 'is that their revolving fund really does revolve. They continually buy and sell cereals, profiting from the change in prices.'

Here was another case where people's own abilities had been given rein on the basis of small, manageable inputs which enabled them to develop confidence and organisational capacity. The results in terms of village numbers might be modest, but the model was viable and could be repeated. In 1987 Oxfam provided £7,556 for another five banks. The scale seems tiny, the sums absurdly low; but they illustrate the value of small beginnings, and how important it is for the economic worlds of donor and receiver to connect. Most official aid agencies cannot afford to spend time and trouble dispensing such small sums of money to a handful of communities. This is where, at their best, voluntary agencies such as Oxfam can trailblaze approaches which allow those locked into the shrinking traditional economy to cross the modernity divide.

Up until the 1980s the search for 'alternatives' within Oxfam's Africa programme was fairly restricted. One notable exception was in the field of savings and credit, where Oxfam identified a need to teach people newly initiated to the cash economy – especially women – how to deploy money for family investment and security. Another area in which Oxfam was up among the pioneers was in its support to primary health care – simple preventive health for the many – within medical mission programmes, initially in Malawi, later in Tanzania, Ethiopia, and Zambia. But for various reasons, some internal and some to do with the business of Africa being 'different', Oxfam came to the challenge of structural poverty and working with non-expatriate partners – as well as employing indigenous staff – later in Africa than elsewhere.

The turning point came when, as the new decade arrived, white domination in the southern part of the continent suffered an important reversal. In April 1980, Zimbabwe became the latest independent nation to 'emerge' on the continent. From this event stemmed an important evolution in Oxfam's southern African policy and a move towards a new style of African programme generally.

Up until Zimbabwean independence, Oxfam's attitude towards the southern African liberation movements had been one of resolute Quakerish fence-sitting. Grants had been given both in Rhodesia and the Republic of South Africa for school-based feeding and agricultural training since the 1950s, and for people directly hurt by apartheid such as families of those killed at Sharpeville in 1960. But the liberation movements were another matter. With the rarest of exceptions, involvement with the humanitarian activities of those who had taken up arms against white rule was scrupulously avoided on political grounds.

As the guerrilla war inside Rhodesia intensified in the late 1970s, and many rural people were herded into 'protected villages' or fled across the borders into camps run by the liberation movements ZANU and ZAPU, the question of whether Oxfam should help the refugees became pressing.

In parts of the world remote to British interests, it seemed possible to distinguish between the humanitarian and the political strands enmeshing aid for victims of conflict – at least in the eyes of British supporters. In Central America and Cambodia (where crisis erupted simultaneously with the final stage of the Zimbabwean struggle), keeping the strands separate could be extremely tricky; but if they did become tangled in the view of certain groups on the ground, and Oxfam-associated people or projects found themselves accused of being partisan, at least there was no echoing resonance of controversy at home. In Britain, Oxfam did not feature its work in Central America in fundraising literature, and until the late 1980s, at home the programme went unchallenged.

In parts of the world tied by history to British hearts and pockets, it was another story altogether. In all those countries of white-ruled southern Africa not previously run by the Portuguese there were close British business, professional, and family connections, and major British foreign policy considerations. In such circumstances, uncoupling 'the relief of suffering' from its underlying political dimensions in the eyes both of those on the ground and their allies back home, was almost impossible. As the demands for majority rule in southern Africa intensified, it became progressively more so.

For those in the countries affected, fence-sitting was untenable. The question, simply put, was: 'Whose side are you on?' In 1978, Mozambique made it clear to Oxfam that its aid was unwelcome because, from its perspective, Oxfam was tarnished by its links to projects run by Rhodesian and South African whites. Early in 1979, the question of whether it was a political act to give humanitarian support to refugees from the internal Rhodesian conflict caused echoing conflict within Oxfam's Africa Committee. It was eventually agreed that the principle of neutrality – aid on either or both sides solely on the basis of need, conditional on access for inspection of use – should be applied, as was consistent with Oxfam's charitable objects and basic philosophy of non-discrimination. This decision turned out to be the prelude for others.

In July 1976, Brian Walker had sought the trustees' approval for an expanded Oxfam programme in South Africa. At this time there had been riots by students in Soweto against the imposition of Afrikaans as the language of instruction in school, followed by the rise of the Black Consciousness Movement. Walker, with his background of bridge-building amidst the troubles in Northern Ireland, was determined that Oxfam would not duck the increasing problems of operating a programme in the Republic. He won the trustees' approval for the appointment of a Field Director for South Africa, Joe Parsons, based in Lesotho (as had been Jimmy Betts many years before). The following year a black South African field worker, Alex Mbatha, was also taken on although he was formally employed by the South African Catholic Bishops' Conference.

Parsons consolidated links with those organisations whose work included welfare and education alongside their human rights and political activities. To protect those involved, most of his work and contacts were kept confidential. However, not everything was 'under wraps'. For example, Oxfam gave help for women and children dumped in the impoverished homelands, eking out existence on remittances from migrant-worker husbands. Oxfam also supported projects for women domestic servants, a category of workers with no legal rights or protection, miserable levels of pay, no family life of their own, and no educational or social opportunities. In time, SADWU (the South African Domestic Workers' Union) was to attract a membership of nearly one million; Oxfam paid salaries and costs for social workers.

After the murder of Steve Biko in 1977, Oxfam came under considerable pressure from anti-apartheid campaigners to cut off its South African grants and pull out with a loud public fanfare. That Walker insisted that Oxfam stay on and work inside an increasingly repressive South Africa, whatever the problems, was greatly to his credit, indicating a commitment to helping the disadvantaged in South Africa no matter how unacceptable the ideology of the regime under which they suffered. In mid-1979, he decided to articulate an Oxfam policy towards victims of conflict and political oppression.

Not only in southern Africa but in Central America, armed conflict was increasingly disrupting the Oxfam programme. Sandanista forces were on the point of overthrowing President Somoza, and the fall-out from the Nicaraguan revolution was polarising reformist and reactionary groups all over the region. The long nightmare of death squads and disappearances of individuals who championed the interests of the poor was descending on El Salvador and Guatemala.

In some parts of the world, educators and health workers working for church or voluntary groups could be routinely harassed, even

JIM HOWARD/OXFAM

64 *The island of Bidong, Malaysia, home to 42,000 Vietnamese boat people in 1979. Uncollected rubbish and human waste created a public health nightmare, which Oxfam helped to solve.*

TIM LUSTY/OXFAM

65 *Phnom Penh, Kampuchea (now Cambodia), late 1979: a ghost town.*

66 *Roads and bridges in the Kampuchean countryside were wrecked or damaged, increasing the extreme difficulties of relief distribution.*

PETE DAVIS/OXFAM

67 *Oxfam's intrepid Deputy Director Guy Stringer landed in Kampuchea in October 1979, having captained a barge full of relief supplies across the South China Seas. With interpreter Sopheak and Kampuchean officials.*

68 *The first Oxfam barge, the 'Asiatic Success', with the first sizeable relief cargo into Kampuchea, unloading at Kompong Som, a port closed to the world for five years.*

69 *M.D. Mistry*, left, *joined Oxfam's India staff in 1979. He set a new pattern in programme style and content among poor villagers, emphasising local organisation.*

70 *Oxfam's 'Wastesaver' centre in Huddersfield, set up in 1975, was an effort to alchemise household waste into development aid. Sorting rag for industrial use.*

71 *Africa, a continent in crisis. An Ethiopian child receiving special foods in a supplementary nutrition programme, 1974. And wearing an Oxfam jumper.*

72 *Nomadic refugees from Somalia arrive in Derwenagi camp in Ethiopia, 1991. In the foreground, an Oxfam 'fly it in and put it up in hours' emergency water tank.*

73

73 Yatenga plateau, Burkina Faso, 1984. An Oxfam invention: a landscape spirit level, a clear hosepipe filled with water, is used to measure elevation for contour bunds.

WILL CRITCHLEY/OXFAM

The independence of Zimbabwe, 1980, opened a new Oxfam chapter in southern Africa. 74 Sithembiso Nyoni (right), consultant on rural community development, with colleagues.
75 Tea break in a training session for women run by ORAP, Nyoni's non-governmental network for rural progress in Matabeleland.

74

OXFAM

75

CHRIS JOHNSON/OXFAM

76 *'The Campaign for Rational Health' was based on an Oxfam study into the supply and use of pharmaceutical products in the Third World. Dianna Melrose,* centre left, *presents signatures to the 'Rational Health Declaration' to Minister of Health Kenneth Clarke,* centre right, *1984.*

77 *The launch of Oxfam's new campaign in 1984. Among the letter-holders,* left to right: *(G) Jonathan Dimbleby, (R) Roy Hattersley, (Y) John Pilger, (O) Guy Stringer, (R) David Owen, (N) Edward Heath, (G) Geraldine James, (E) Joanna Lumley.*

78

78 *Chico Mendes, chairman of the Rural Workers' Union in Xapuri, Amazonia. His organisational work to defend the living of the rubber-tappers of the Brazilian forests was supported by Oxfam in the 1980s, but Mendes was murdered in 1988.*

79

79 *22 October 1985, 20,000 people lined up outside the House of Commons, Westminster. The largest-ever lobby of the British Parliament was on the subject of Britain's poor aid and development record.*

ROBERT M DAVIS/OXFAM

81

ROBERT M DAVIS/OXFAM

80 *The campaign for greater international recognition and response to the plight of the Cambodian people was the subject of Charity Commission criticism in their 1991 report on Oxfam. Protesting: Sir Russell Johnston MP* left *Jim Lester MP third from left, Mary Cherry, Oxfam Chair* third from right, *and Ann Clwyd MP far right, with supporters.*

81 *Julie Christie lights a candle for Cambodia at a vigil in St. Martin-in-the-Fields, November 1988.*

82

82 *In the aftermath of the Gulf War: suffering among the civilian population, and humanitarian relief on a tight rein. Frank Judd visits Kurdish areas in northern Iraq on his last field trip as Oxfam Director, November 1991.*

83

83 *India has always been in the vanguard of Oxfam's development learning and programme experience. In conference with Indian project partners and staff: David Bryer, Oxfam's fifth Director.*

persecuted; the people they helped, forced to flee, even killed. In such places the forces supporting the *status quo* were upholding it with violence, usually without the formal backing of the law although with the complicity of law enforcement agents; uniquely in the case of South Africa, with legal backing. Where this was the case, the Oxfam mission to tackle, where practical, both the causes and effects of human suffering could not wholly escape the overlap between removing obstacles to people's development, and protecting their human rights.

Drawing upon 'Oxfam, An Interpretation', Walker attempted to set up a conceptual and practical framework in which Oxfam could pursue solidarity with the poor in situations where their interests were being violently opposed, and yet remain within the charity law. He tried to steer an acceptable course with the Charity Commissioners, while recognising that poverty and rights issues were often inextricably interlinked and that this conundrum was very vexing from the point of view of charity law. With modifications, the paper was accepted by the Oxfam trustees in July 1979. This was the policy statement that articulated Oxfam's notion of humanitarian neutrality – need above the political divide; in the case of Latin America, it was thought of as an effort to carve out 'humanitarian space' in which to work, without being ideologically labelled. Such labelling tended to arise from the fact that, in certain circumstances, Oxfam might only be able to provide help for people in need via an organisation – such as a union branch or local political association – whose primary function was not philanthropic.

In the autumn, a settlement to the 15-year long Rhodesian crisis was brokered at the Lancaster House conference in London. In January 1980, Michael Behr, the most senior member of Oxfam's Africa staff, went to what was soon to become Zimbabwe to explore the possibilities of an Oxfam programme. He began by employing several expatriate doctors to restart medical services in rural areas whose mission hospitals had been closed because of war, and by supporting rehabilitation for the many thousands of people disabled by injury.

With formative West African experience behind him, Behr wanted to avoid in Zimbabwe simply responding to requests and letting the Oxfam 'programme' grow into a string of disconnected projects scattered about the countryside. He also wanted to avoid the usual state of friendly anarchy developing within the donor NGO community, whereby each vied to show off 'their' projects, all applying different rules about how much money to give, what it was supposed to achieve, and how the recipients should answer for their use of it. Thus, in the third area he selected for Oxfam involvement – rural development – he took time trying to find the way to assist.

Behr, who had a strong presence and tended to be outspoken, made it clear to Oxford that he did not find it easy to establish links with Zimbabwean allies. He felt, in retrospect, that Oxfam had failed to grasp the depth of feeling with which the rural population had supported the independence movement, and the suffering experienced by those forced into protected villages or exile. The fence-sitting sustained almost until the very end provoked distrust of Oxfam's motivation among people now courted but previously ignored.

Zimbabwe's biggest problem was the vast wealth disparity between whites – and a few blacks – operating in the modern economy, and the rural poor relegated to impoverished and over-crowded 'tribal trustlands'. Oxfam's pet project of the past – the promotion of savings clubs – had appeared to condone the availability of credit and agricultural services for wealthy white farmers while expecting black farmers to make do with only their own meagre resources to pay for modern inputs.

Behr's perspective was strongly influenced by the Zimbabweans whom he brought into the Oxfam fold early on. One of these was Peter Nyoni, who later became Oxfam's first African Field Director; another was Sithembiso Nyoni. As a consultant to Oxfam, Sithembiso Nyoni developed a 'new strategy' for rural development in Zimbabwe. This was of great significance for the different type of role in Africa Oxfam was seeking. Her approach, forged in the fire of the independence struggle, centred on helping poor people understand and overcome their powerlessness in the face of the forces controlling their lives. 'Participation' was Nyoni's word, but she meant something close to conscientisation.

In 1981, Nyoni set up a Zimbabwean non-governmental development network called ORAP, the Organisation of Rural Associations for Progress, with headquarters in Bulawayo. ORAP's field workers helped village associations develop themselves; they did not merely reward communities – as NGOs had in the past – with a package of inputs (seed, fertiliser) if they agreed to co-operate by digging contour ridges and building feeder roads. Many associations grew out of committees which had been active during the war, when they had helped solve village problems as well as shelter guerrillas. They already had experience in running their own affairs. And they did not want the old paternalistic ways. As Nyoni put it: 'They do not want the kind of development that trains them to be good beggars and imitators of other people's way of life.'

Although Michael Behr was closely involved in ORAP, Oxfam wanted to avoid being 'in charge' and the initial funding came from War on Want. In 1982, however, Oxfam provided £59,000 for an office, field staff, and funds for group projects. By the following year, 220 villages were in the ORAP network.

ORAP's operational area was in Matabeleland, the old ZAPU stronghold. Many village groups endured terrible times during the period in 1982-83 when 'dissident' activity became the target of heavy security crackdown. The Zimbabwean government took Oxfam to task for favouring the Matabele people with the majority of its aid, to which Oxfam's response was that in the selection of recipients, poverty was the criterion, not tribal affiliation. Behr and a group of concerned agency representatives, including Walt Johnson of Oxfam America, went to see President Mugabe in an effort to protect ORAP's people. They protested that although ORAP was a popular grassroots movement it was in no sense political. Behr told the Africa Committee in April 1983: 'It is vital at this difficult time that organisations such as Oxfam do not waver.' Oxfam did not do so, committing around £210,000 to ORAP over the next few years.

In 1985, Sithembiso Nyoni addressed an Oxfam staff conference in Britain, and made a powerful impression. She described how ORAP attempted to express the vision of rural people themselves, the way they and their ideas, not 'projects' designed and deposited from outside, must be the starting point. 'Organisations like Oxfam have got to be clear about what exactly we are doing. Are we helping people to participate in their own oppression and to live in the ghettos; are we entrenching that which they have been and the confusion in which they find themselves? Or are we helping people to liberate themselves?'

Liberation: in southern Africa, the word and the issue were never far away.

In the early 1980s, following Behr's appointment in Zimbabwe, there was a gradual changing of the Oxfam guard in southern African. A new generation of Field Directors, and an intake of African field staff, began to make the country programmes more coherent and address wider policy issues. They also demanded that Oxfam take a clearer stance on aid to victims and casualties of the liberation struggle.

Zimbabwean independence had acted as a stimulus to the fight for freedom in Namibia and South Africa. But most of the programme in both countries had been kept under careful wraps. Its lessons, therefore, could not be incorporated into any view of the main problem in the region: the impact on the poor, directly in South Africa and Namibia, indirectly in the Frontline States, of the machinery upholding racist domination. Oxfam was also still prevaricating on aid to refugees and exiles under the protection of the South African and Namibian liberation movements, ANC and SWAPO. These two issues were interwoven and their sensitivities were acute, both because of the easy confusion in the eye of the British or South African beholder of 'humanitarian' with 'politically motivated' aid, and because open support to projects run by those associated with the liberation struggle might place both projects and people in jeopardy.

In September 1981, the southern Africa Field Directors and the top decision-makers from Oxford met for a 'summit' in Harare. The stage was set for a dramatic shift in Oxfam policy. Zambia, Tanzania, and Zimbabwe were all hosting large camp populations of ANC and SWAPO refugees, and the relevant Field Directors were keen to respond to outstanding requests to provide assistance. Behr, the most senior, was determined that Oxfam's past record of fence-sitting in the Zimbabwean freedom struggle should not be carried over into the work inside Namibia and South Africa. This must be seen as a foundation for the day when freedom dawned and real progress towards a better society for the poor began. Over a fraught few days, the issues were thoroughly thrashed out and a new policy framework developed.

Very soon afterwards, an event took place which shocked Oxfam deeply and harnessed support for the anticipated stronger line. Before dawn on 22 October 1981, Alex Mbatha (who had attended the Harare meeting) and his wife Khosi were violently arrested in their home and taken into police custody, she with their small baby. Months later, no charges had been laid – they never were – and a wall of silence surrounded their detention. That one of their own should be brutally imprisoned had the effect of an electric shock on the Oxfam community, bringing home to supporters the realities of humanitarian work in South Africa more powerfully than anything else could have done.

In mid-1982, the new Oxfam policy towards southern Africa was presented to the trustees. Peter Wiles, the Desk Officer in headquarters, was its architect. His paper described the worsening situation and increasing outflow of refugees from South Africa and Namibia. 'In both countries, institutionalised violence against individuals, families and communities in the form of population removals, detentions, [and] bannings has increased.' The liberation movements had called upon the world to retaliate against South Africa with economic disinvestment and boycotts, calls which had been endorsed at the UN. These events obliged Oxfam to re-examine its position.

Whatever repugnance Oxfam felt against the evils of apartheid, it had never given direct support to the fight against the system *per se* and was not now proposing to do so. The target of Oxfam aid had always been the relief of suffering and poverty. But the apartheid system and poverty were two sides of one coin. In South Africa, the legal enforcement of human rights violations amounted to a structural enforcement of poverty. And this poverty was not the absence of modern goods and services characterising the poverty of traditional African rural life, but pauperisation: poverty created by turning people into units of cut-price labour in a society over whose workings they had absolutely no say at all. As the liberation struggle gathered force, Oxfam had come not only to accept that apartheid was the main cause of suffering in South Africa, but to feel a moral obligation to bear witness to this reality in the effort to help change it.

Intense behind-the-scenes efforts were made by Harris and others to persuade Oxfam trustees with residual doubts that the motivation for policy change was humanitarian, not political. In June 1982, the policy was accepted by the Oxfam Council. In future, all grants must harmonise with the view that the ultimate obstacle to relieving poverty in South Africa and Namibia was the existence of apartheid. Preference should be given to those people who 'as a consequence of the struggle for change, suffer most'. Aid would no longer be denied to refugees and exiles because they were in the charge of ANC or SWAPO. Oxfam would also begin to talk more openly to supporters and the general public about the evidence concerning the links between apartheid and poverty that its programme in South Africa brought to light. The special ties between Britain and South Africa might mean that some supporters would be affronted by Oxfam's unequivocal line; equally, because of those ties, there was a possibility that greater awareness in Britain might contribute to international pressure for change.

In 1983, a new South African constitution was introduced which continued to exclude the country's 24 million black people from political representation. This triggered a new phase in the struggle against apartheid within the Republic. As the campaign for international pressure intensified, Oxfam felt obliged to examine its own 'disinvestment' position. Since the Oxford Committee's earliest days, Barclays Bank had been an invaluable and trusty ally. But its involvement in the South African economy had become a strong focus of anti-apartheid campaigning in Britain. A special committee was set up by Oxfam in 1984 to examine the implications of withdrawing its accounts from Barclays. The issue was felt to be so sensitive that Lesley Kirkley, ex-Director of Oxfam, was invited to chair the committee.

After long deliberation and painstaking legal consultation, Oxfam announced in late 1985 that it had reluctantly decided to change its bankers. By this time, Barclays had lost accounts in Britain worth an annual turnover of at least £6 billion a year. A few months later it announced its own South African disengagement.

Meanwhile, a new spate of bannings and detentions had followed the imposition in South Africa of a State of Emergency in July 1985. Advice Offices for black township families in distress became a frequent destination of Oxfam aid. One reported: 'We have had a constant stream of police-connected cases, between 500 and 600 people in the last two months. Of course, we have had the usual number of welfare cases as well, and a considerable increase in poverty cases. The unemployment figure in Port Elizabeth now is 56 per cent.' In 1986, Oxfam stepped up the level of its informational activity about township and homelands misery, about detentions of programme allies, and the mounting sense of crisis in southern Africa generally. In May 1986, a strong focus was put on conditions in Namibia, 'the last colony in Africa', with the publication of a report called: 'Namibia: A Violation of Trust'.

Later that year, Oxfam's trustees discussed their position towards the key instrument for exerting international pressure on South Africa: economic sanctions. The paper before them stated: 'The changing climate of public debate in Britain, following the government's own acceptance of the need for sanctions, means that we can now advocate sanctions with greater confidence within the constraints of Charity Law.' The decision that Oxfam should adopt a position advocating sanctions was not taken until March 1987, after further deliberation. But the view that it could do so and remain within the charity law was to prove sadly mistaken.

By the mid-1980s, the notion of 'campaigning' had become familiar among Oxfam's local staff and supporter networks. This activity began in the late 1970s. The drive for the 'educated pound', such a strong theme of the 1960s, had in recent years given way to a drive for the pound pure and simple via gifts, donations or Oxfam Trading profits. Oxfam shops, with their emphasis on merchandising, had become the almost exclusive volunteer activity.

In 1978, a new fund-raising campaign was launched called 'Move Against Poverty'. This was mainly directed at young people interested in Third World poverty as an issue, who would happily fast, collect signatures, or stage a 'happening' outside the Town Hall, but did not want to support Oxfam by selling goods in a shop. MAP was masterminded by the energetic Bill Yates, newly returned from Brazil, and it was a success: in the first year, 1,500 supporter groups were formed or reformed, and £220,000 raised. These funds went to specific MAP projects: slum colonies in Bolivia, meals for children of working mothers in Dominican Republic, wells in Ethiopia, destitute working women in Bangladesh.

By 1980, a strong push to take up specific issues on behalf of the Third World was emerging. The situation was quite different from that of a decade ago when Nicolas Stacey's proposals for a large Oxfam role in public education had been rebuffed. In those days, frustration with the small size of voluntary agency projects and their 'drops in the ocean' impact had prompted demands that governments devote far more money to 'aid'. Although not uncritical, the lobbyists had talked as if official aid was more or less the same as voluntary aid, only delivered in much bigger amounts. In the intervening years, a sharper distinction had emerged between the type of development normally promoted by official aid and Western investment, and the type of development promoted by humanitarian NGOs. The new impulse for public education arose from perspectives gathered by Oxfam as a result of the evolution in its programme philosophy, and was part of an attempt to bring these to bear on governments giving and receiving 'aid'.

Oxfam's overseas staff frequently found themselves confronting issues which demanded not only better programming skills, but required special advocacy inside the country and internationally. For example, a policy switch into primary health care, stressing simple preventive care for the many instead of high-tech curative care for the few, needed not only to be adopted in a handful of mission projects, but supported by a country's health-care establishment. The lock-in of Western economic interests to those of the small minority living a Western-style existence frequently resulted in the poor being deprived of any real share of new opportunities or services. All the voluntary agencies in the world could not compensate for such discrimination via their projects and programmes, whose sum impact was minute on any national or international scale.

One classic illustration of the dilemma was presented by the vigorous promotion in Third World countries of breastmilk substitutes by Western babyfood manufacturers and their subsidiaries. In the hands of a mother who could read instructions, understood their importance, and whose kitchen contained fridges, cookers, and a sterilising gadget, infant formula was a nutritionally adequate babyfood. In the hands of a semi-literate and poverty-stricken woman, a tin of formula eked out in weak dilutions with impure water not only starved the child but could easily cause fatal diarrhoeal infection. Many babymilks were being promoted without taking into account how hazardous they could be in such an environment, and often by highly dubious methods: giveaways in maternity wards, salesgirls in nursing uniforms, incentives to doctors.

The first shot across the bows of the babyfood manufacturers came from *New Internationalist* magazine with a cover story in 1973. The issue was taken up by War on Want, and by a number of American and European NGOs during the 1970s, the most prominent of which was the US Infant Formula Action Group (INFACT). In 1979, action within the international health community moved towards a climax. Although the babyfood manufacturers were beginning to self-regulate their more outrageous marketing techniques, their own 'code of conduct' did not go far enough in the view of WHO, UNICEF, and NGO activists.

A much stiffer 'international code for the marketing of breastmilk substitutes' was drafted to go before the World Health Assembly in 1981. This would place a ban on all infant formula advertising to the general public, and place its distribution in health facilities in the exclusive hands of health personnel for medically-approved purposes. If the Code was agreed by the WHA, it would become incumbent on governments to promote breastfeeding and control the marketing of infant formula by means of legislation. This offended the school of ideological thought which saw restraint on commercial marketing practice as restraint on natural liberty. Fears were expressed (especially in the US) that, if enacted, the Code would set a precedent – for example, for control of the marketing of pharmaceutical products by major international companies.

In the months before the World Health Assembly, Oxfam and War on Want ran a public information campaign about the Code, hoping that the British government – which initially seemed reluctant – would give it backing. This issue, a hungry child issue if ever there was one, was taken up by thousands of Oxfam supporters and shop volunteers. Jack Ashley MP led the case for British support to the Code in a debate in the House of Commons on 26 February 1981. A deputation visited Patrick Jenkin, Secretary of State for Health. Esther Rantzen, the popular TV campaigner, was recruited. Over 220 MPs signed a parliamentary motion. At the World Health Assembly, Britain voted in the Code's favour; only the US voted against.

The babymilk campaign was the first time Oxfam systematically mobilised its own network behind a cause close to its heart. The second occasion was in January 1982, when after weeks of silence from the South African authorities concerning the fate of Alex and Khosi Mbatha, a mass protest was mounted with CAFOD (the Catholic Fund for Overseas Development) and the British Council of Churches. At 4am on 22 January 1982, three months to the hour since the Mbathas' arrest, John Clark, Campaigns Manager, knocked on the door of South Africa House. The letter he delivered announced a vigil to draw attention to the Mbathas' plight. In the next 16 hours, MPs, peers, churchmen and celebrities took part and 2,512 signatures were collected.

After the Mbathas were released three months later, Alex described how, to his bewilderment, prison officers had asked him why he was so important in the eyes of people abroad. He thanked the campaigners for their letters, vigils, and protests. 'People saw for the first time the amount of goodwill that existed in other parts of the world for people in my country smashed by the apartheid machine,' he wrote from exile in Zimbabwe. 'I wish to put on record that your efforts were not in vain.'

During the early 1980s, Oxfam also began to hone its machinery for taking up issues of specialist as opposed to popular concern. The lead came from the Public Affairs Unit, which had evolved into a research and information arm of the overseas programme. A number of useful reports and publications had emerged from the PAU over the years, but new ground was broken with the publication of *Bitter Pills* by Dianna Melrose in 1982. This study of the use and supply of medicines in the Third World was the cornerstone of 'The Campaign for Rational Health'. Melrose's work was instrumental in making the PAU an important Oxfam force; as was that of David Bull, author of *A Growing Problem*, which highlighted the dangers in misuse and overuse of pesticides marketed in the Third World by international companies. These two studies established an important principle of all subsequent Oxfam campaigns: thorough research before action.

These campaigns were not tub-thumping affairs but careful efforts to place solid information on a subject of Oxfam programme concern, based on experience in the field, strategically before those who mattered. The information in question might be quite technical; it was directed less at the public than at members of the professional, governmental and business community who were in a position to exert a beneficial influence on international marketing or export policies. The medicines issue in many ways resembled babyfoods; it also concerned the potentially pernicious entry of modern marketing techniques into a world of consumers whose poverty, illiteracy, and ill-health made them highly vulnerable, and whose interests were ignored not only by exporters but by many leaders in their own societies. As with babyfoods, wrong use could lead to suffering, even death.

This was also an issue which, as part of 'primary health care', was high on the international health agenda. WHO was elaborating a policy on 'Essential Drugs', matching the real health needs in poor countries with a priority list of 220 medicines and extolling the virtues of low-cost generic products. With the pharmaceutical industry set against another Code and the US on its side, powerful vested interests were keen to protect their activities in the South from the kind of scrutiny they could expect in the more regulated, consumer-conscious North. Meanwhile, millions of Third World parents were selling their possessions to buy brightly coloured antibiotics, tonics, and multivitamins, when a child dying of diarrhoeal dehydration could be saved by a salt and sugar drink, and did not need a medicine at all.

Over the next years Oxfam, a founding member of Health Action International, helped to put the weight of knowledge drawn from the voluntary sector and information from the field behind national and international activity. Not only was 'rational health' promoted at home, but it was supported with funds in the field. In 1982, amidst a furore from drug exporters, Bangladesh imposed a ban on 1,700 wasteful and potentially harmful medical products. This happened largely at the instigation of Dr. Zafrullah Chowdhury, a national primary health care pioneer consistently supported by Oxfam, which then helped support the local manufacture of essential drugs. In the Philippines, Oxfam helped Dr. Michael Tan's Health Action Information Network (HAIN) off the ground to monitor the government's National Drugs Policy.

In Britain, action reached a crescendo in 1984, in the run-up to a WHO Conference designed to overcome residual opposition to WHO's Essential Drugs programme. Oxfam collected 2,000 signatures, mainly from medical professionals, to a 'Rational Health Declaration', and presented them to Kenneth Clarke, Minister of Health. Clarke subsequently wrote: 'May I thank you for your patience in pursuing a constructive response from this Department and congratulate you on the creditable manner in which you have sought to highlight the problem of drugs for the Third World.' In May 1986 the World Health Assembly finally passed the crucial resolution giving a green light to widespread WHO activity concerning the equitable and safe use of drugs worldwide.

In the 1982-83 Annual Report, Oxfam's overseas and home activity were described as twin fronts of 'the Oxfam Campaign'. The 'determination to represent the poor who have no voice of their own in the decisions and councils of the rich nations' was becoming integral to Oxfam thinking. In 1983, with income at the record level of £19.7 million, an increase in educational and campaigning staff was set in motion as part of a major reorganisation of Oxfam's fundraising network throughout the country. To ensure that these ingredients of the overall programme remained within the range of activity permitted under Charity Law, Oxfam set in motion a revision of its charitable objects. The new clause was eventually accepted by trustees and the Charity Commissioners in 1985. To Oxfam's mandate was added: '... to educate the public concerning the nature, causes, and effects of poverty, distress and suffering as aforesaid, to conduct and procure research concerning these and to publish or otherwise make the results thereof available to the public.'

Towards the end of 1983, Brian Walker departed after ten years at the helm, handing over to his deputy, Guy Stringer. In the autumn of that year, Oxfam launched a new campaign: 'Weather Alert'. There had been a spate of freak weather all over the globe, causing an exceptional number of droughts, floods, and cyclones. 'Weather Alert' pointed out that, for the really poor, freak weather patterns were not the cause of their problems but the straw which broke the camel's back. In one of BBC TV's *Blue Peter* programme's many associations with Oxfam, a 'Weather Beater' appeal raised £1.25 million.

In the case of drought, where farming people gradually sold their reserves – cattle, land, pots, jewellery – hoping for the rains to improve, a delay of up to a year could be expected before disaster became acute. Paddy Coulter, Oxfam's Communications Co-ordinator, did the rounds of television news producers to encourage coverage of crises in the making. Visiting Oxfam's South African programme, he called on Michael Buerk, the BBC's Africa correspondent, to discuss – among other things – the drought in Ethiopia.

In mid-1984, Oxfam put out three special 'Behind the Weather' reports. 'This year', the blurb read: 'the consequences [of bad weather] are causing widespread suffering. Some of the worst-hit places are going to be in the news. One of them, almost certainly, will be Ethiopia.' The failure to follow up more strongly on that conviction haunts some Oxfam consciences to this day.

On the evening of 23 October 1984, BBC television news carried a report from the northern Ethiopian province of Wollo. Its impact worldwide was explosive. 'Dawn, and as the sun breaks through the piercing chill of night on the plain outside Korem, it lights up a biblical famine, now, in the 20th century. This place, say workers here, is the closest thing to hell on earth.' With the agonising images accompanying these words, reporter Michael Buerk and cameraman Mohammed Amin succeeded in bringing to global attention famine of an intensity unimaginable in contemporary times. Western audiences watched in glazed disbelief as children with ravaged faces and stick-like limbs died before their eyes.

The impact of this seven-minute report, subsequently shown by 425 TV stations all over the world, is a supreme illustration of how powerful a role the media has come to play in international humanitarian affairs.

The numbers of those who died of hunger and disease from the long accumulation of crop failure, social breakdown, and inadequate relief in Ethiopia during 1983-85 are thought to be between 500,000 and one million. The international relief operation, which geared up properly only after the television footage and public outcry shamed Western governments into providing adequate quantities of aid to a country whose Marxist regime they abhorred, kept alive around seven million. But all the accomplishments of this effort, in which Oxfam played a small but significant part, failed to wash from the humanitarian conscience the stain of having let this apocalypse occur. In Oxfam's case, it led in time to a radical overhaul of its whole approach to disasters and disaster relief.

Eleven years before, identical faltering, emaciated figures had thronged the main road of Wollo province and crowded helplessly in identical camp locations. After the 1973-74 famine, the government set up an early warning system to forecast food shortage in the parts of the country where agriculture was precarious. Life was hardest amidst the wild topographical extravaganza of the north where rugged escarpments, deep gorges, table-top mountains, and mighty rivers presented a farming landscape over-burdened and eroded to its margins. That the Emperor Haile Selassie had lost his throne because he had let his northern subjects starve was a political lesson not lost on the new revolutionary regime. The task of monitoring scarcity and seeking international food aid was assigned to the powerful Relief and Rehabilitation Commission (RRC). During the late 1970s and early 1980s, reports of impending crisis succeeded each other with numbing monotony; but the RRC's effectiveness on the ground and regular supplies of foodstuffs from the international aid community managed to maintain farming families on their precipice of need, preventing any widespread plunge into the abyss.

During the 1975-76 drought in the south-eastern Ogaden, Oxfam was actively involved with the RRC in supplementary medical and feeding programmes; but in the late 1970s as the regime became committed to Soviet-style socialism and more xenophobic towards the West, Oxfam wound down its programme until it only supported a handful of well-tried Christian missionary health and nutrition projects. In 1982, with organisational resources and vision in their post-Cambodia flood, Hugh Goyder, a Field Director previously based in India, was posted to Ethiopia to try and foster the kind of self-generative grassroots structures by now regarded by Oxfam as the mandatory prescription for genuine rural development. This, with mixed success, was what he was busy doing as catastrophe crept up.

During 1983, reports from various parts of Ethiopia began to indicate alarming pockets of food scarcity. But only after widespread failure of the November harvest was it possible to predict something in an altogether different league from typical endemic hunger. To complicate matters, parts of the north were under the control of rebel insurgents. At Korem, a camp close to the edge of government-secured territory, early 1984 saw a sudden rapid rise in the numbers of malnourished children registered for supplementary feeding by Save the Children Fund (SCF), and an increase in the numbers of those already reduced to matchstick fragility.

At a fateful meeting on 30 March 1984, Commissioner Dawit Wolde Giorgis, head of the RRC, informed the representatives of UN agencies and donor governments in Addis Ababa that a situation of the utmost gravity was developing. He presented a detailed request for 450,000 tonnes of food aid. This was only half the 900,000 tonnes the RRC believed was needed, but it represented the amount it thought it could distribute. Five months later, only 95,000 tonnes had been pledged in response, and none had yet reached RRC food stores. The reason for the lacklustre response was partly that the donors were almost inured to hearing prophecies of doom from a regime they distrusted; and partly because the UN estimate of need, compiled by a World Food Programme mission, implied that the RRC was guilty of exaggeration. The UN appeal was for 125,000 tonnes. By July, the RRC had run out of grain to distribute and widespread deaths were being reported in Wollo.

On 19 July, a documentary film called 'Seeds of Despair', made by Peter Gill, about famine in the south of the country was shown in Britain. In the wake of the film, a Disasters Emergency Committee TV appeal for Africa raised a record £8.5 million, of which Oxfam's share was £1.8 million. Having so far resisted a major Ethiopian emergency involvement, Oxfam now found itself under pressure less from demand of distress from the field, where the magnitude of requirements was way beyond the charitable remit, than from supply of compassion from the British public.

In August, Marcus Thompson, Oxfam's Disasters Officer, went to Ethiopia to see how the relief programme might be expanded. Because the government had imposed a ban on all travel to the north in the run-up to celebrations of the tenth anniversary of the Ethiopian revolution, Thompson was unable to visit Wollo. But every office he went into, every person he talked to, repeated the same story. There was serious famine, and no food. He therefore made a devastatingly simple proposal to Oxford: charter a ship, fill it with grain, and send it to the port of Assab. That the procurement and export of foodgrains in thousands of tonnes was way outside Oxfam's normal or desirable operational range – or indeed its immediate financial resources – seemed irrelevant. Something exceptional needed doing not only because of the crying need for food but as a spur to get the laggard international food aid machinery whirring.

In Oxford, the idea was immediately acted upon. Oxfam first ascertained that, in spite of a European bumper harvest, few major donors were planning to ship large amounts of food aid via the normal UN World Food Programme or EEC channels. Nor were they receptive to the notion. The decision that Oxfam should ship food was taken with trustee approval. Guy Stringer, Oxfam's Director, signed the necessary grant for upwards of £3 million in faith that Oxfam would manage to find other partners to help offset the extraordinary expense. This marked the transition for Oxfam into an unprecedented league of disaster response – and not just for Ethiopia but for any major emergency. By the time Michael Buerk's report and the subsequent barrage of media attention burst upon the world, the MV *Elpis* was on the high seas with a cargo of 14,000 tonnes of grain.

When Oxfam announced the shipment on 10 September, it pulled no punches in pointing out that it was undertaking this extraordinary action because major donors, including Britain and the EEC, were not making the deliveries of staple foods normally provided by the international community in a famine emergency. As anticipated, the response of voluntary agency friends and partners was positive. Most of the costs of the food ship, which left Hull on 10 October, were jointly met by a consortium including Norwegian Church Service, Norwegian Save the Children, and Dutch NOVIB. The EEC gave £400,000, and at the request of its own representative in Addis, the British government contributed 4,000 tonnes of grain to the cargo. The cost to Oxfam was £500,000.

In Addis Ababa, the RRC was grateful, not only for the food but also for the pressure exerted on other donors by the publicity, which also enhanced Oxfam's profile. By 31 October when the ship docked at Assab, philanthropic air cargoes were being mounted from Britain. But these amounts were negligible against the necessary 60,000 tonnes a month. Not until after a UN donors' meeting in New York in December was food aid on the scale required committed in earnest. The new estimate of need, 1.3 million tonnes over 12 months, was drawn up by Kurt Jansson, the UN Secretary-General's Special Representative in Addis Ababa, on the basis of RRC and WFP figures.

Jansson had been appointed in early November in the wake of the media and public uproar. This was another indication of the world's seeming inability to act without the goad of a real life television horror show of human tragedy, which only occurred – seemingly could only occur – at a point when, for many of its victims, the situation was already past redemption. The shortage of food in the relief pipeline remained a serious problem for those running food distribution and supplementary child-feeding programmes for many months to come. However, Jansson's appointment as UN relief co-ordinator brought a coherence to the overall operation which was welcomed by everyone, including the voluntary agencies. Unlike at the time of the Cambodian crisis five years before, the UN agencies engaged in a proper dialogue with the NGOs from the moment a full-scale relief emergency was declared.

In November, the British Government reacted to Ethiopia's plight by lending RAF aircraft for the airlift of food to camps and inaccessible mountain-top areas. The scale of the compassionate response in Britain was overwhelming, and the government's actions reflected this concern. Many groups of citizens launched their own initiatives. The *Daily Mirror* sent its own mercy flight, with Robert Maxwell on board. Bob Geldof, the Irish pop singer, galvanised the popular music and entertainment world behind Band Aid, and raised an extraordinary £50 million over the next year. Band Aid deployed a small fleet of mercy ships and, over the coming months, took on Oxfam and other agency cargoes for free.

In Newcastle, the Oxfam office under the energetic leadership of Karen Schofield became the nerve centre of a city-wide drive to send a 'People's Plane' from Britain's North-East. So successful was this campaign that a Christmas appeal on local TV raised half the costs of a £3.9 million shipload on the *Link Target*; the 'People's Boat' departed Newcastle on 11 January 1985.

Rarely had Britain witnessed such an outpouring of concern, particularly among the young, for the world's dispossessed. Through its local networks of shops and fundraisers, media contacts and celebrities, the staff and volunteers of Oxfam and many other charitable agencies worked around the clock to transform people's compassion into support. Ethiopia and its problems became a part of many people's daily pre-occupation. In the four months following Michael Buerk's report from Wollo, Oxfam received £12.5 million in donations. Supreme efforts were also made in other parts of the world. Oxfam Hong Kong raised over £1 million for Ethiopia and Sudan, and a fund-raising drive in Bermuda produced £110,000 from an island of only 55,000 people.

The crescendo of concern for Ethiopia happened to occur just at the time when Oxfam was launching a major new popular campaign called 'Hungry for Change'. This was a bigger, bolder successor to MAP, an attempt to attract people into a network of Oxfam support groups whose fund-raising would dovetail with self-education and the presentation of issues to the public. The theme of the campaign – the unfairness of a world that produced more than enough food to feed the global population but managed to let 500 million people go hungry – could not have been more timely.

On 10 October, the line-up for the national launch included David Owen, Ted Heath, and Roy Hattersley from the political parties, as well as leading churchmen, journalists, and showbusiness stars. At the Press Conference, David Owen summed up the campaign's purpose: 'A million people combining together under the guidance of Oxfam committed to doing something about hunger could have a major effect on this country, and through this country, the world. The people of this country can make this, once more, a political live issue.' Not only in London, but in cities all over the country, events were staged in which celebrities held up billboard letters spelling 'Hungry for Change'. The publicity was immense and much of it reflected a new willingness to address the underlying causes of Third World hunger on the part of both the media and the public.

Within a few weeks, over 200 'Hungry for Change' groups were formed, with back-up from a new network of campaigning staff based in Oxfam's local offices throughout the country. Thousands of people took part in locally-organised fasts on a week-end in late November. The images from Ethiopia gave the campaign both a heartening boost and a sickening poignancy. One channel to which the response was directed was pressure on the British government to increase its own aid for Ethiopia and to urge other governments to do the same. MPs, MEPs and government offices were deluged by letters and calls from members of the public angry about the months of international inertia in the face of impending catastrophe.

On 21 November, Oxfam published the results of an opinion poll which showed that three-quarters of people in Britain thought that official aid should be increased or maintained, and that its main purpose should be for long-term development to prevent famine. In the face of this kind of public sentiment, a government proposal to make further cuts in the aid budget was threatened by a parliamentary revolt from within its own ranks. The planned cut was dropped. Even under the Wilson government, when aid had enjoyed a heyday of post-colonial popularity, the Third World lobby had never achieved such a victory.

At the same time, Oxfam stepped up its programme in Ethiopia. A team of health and nutritional workers were sent to Wollo to establish a feeding programme 'off the road', in the countryside, to avoid the descent of hunger-stricken families into the crowded and disease-ridden camps. Large tonnages of a high energy 'Oxfam biscuit', developed by Oxford Polytechnic and manufactured by a British firm, Fox's of Batley, proved invaluable as an easy-to-eat child-feeding ingredient. Oxfam water engineers Paul Sherlock and Ben Fawcett were despatched with Oxfam kits for setting up instant water supplies – pumps, tanks, pipelines, taps – and worked with the Ethiopian Water Authority to deploy these in 40 camps. In December, Oxfam joined with SCF in setting up a trucking fleet for shifting food and relief supplies from main depots to points deep in the rural hinterland. In Addis Ababa, Hugh Goyder successfully lobbied the main relief operation to have sufficient basic foodstuffs sent up for off-the-road distribution.

Oxfam also worked through the rebel movements in Tigray and Eritrea to take supplies through to places which convoys under government and UN auspices could not reach. In one unconventional operation, an Oxfam Field Officer, Karen Twining, was sent in from Sudan with a convoy of lorries and a pillowcase of currency to an area in the northern Ethiopian highlands. She hired 3,400 donkeys and a camel caravan to distribute 366 tons of grain and tools for soil conservation works in mountain villages.

By the turn of the year the famine crisis had spread to Sudan. Here too, after some of the same initial delays which had dogged the international response to the growing disaster in Ethiopia, Oxfam contributed to the overall relief operation with special feeding and water teams, both in the west of the country and in eastern camps where 300,000 drought refugees from Tigray province had congregated. The emergency programmes in Ethiopia and Sudan absorbed £21.7 million in the 12 months between late 1984 and late 1985: a scale of activity completely unprecedented in Oxfam's history, even in Cambodia.

In November 1984, Oxfam's long-standing Overseas Director, Michael Harris, retired. The combination of the change in senior personnel with profound organisational self-criticism over its failure to detect in time the depth of the Ethiopian and Sudanese famine crises led to an overhaul of Oxfam's disaster response mechanisms. The new Overseas Director, David Bryer, requested a full *post mortem* on what had gone wrong; and the lessons of the evaluation were accepted and institutionally acted upon.

For many years, Oxfam had wrestled with the conflicting claims of disaster relief and development work on its time and resources. Although in the public mind Oxfam's paramount role had always been to spirit instant succour across the world to victims of emergency, there had long been an ideological resistance within the organisation to elevating its 'curative' work in disaster relief to a level of importance near that of 'preventive' development. In Ethiopia up to 1984, for example, Hugh Goyder had been told to concentrate on creating rural self-help networks like ORAP in Zimbabwe, and not to allow Oxfam's resources to be frittered away in the perennial saga of emergency relief. This, it was thought, was best left to the international donors.

Valuable work had been done by the health and technical units in developing Oxfam disaster 'packages' – water supply kits, including a suitcase laboratory for testing water quality in the field; feeding kits, including the new Oxfam biscuit – which made sure that whatever the relatively small size of Oxfam's input in any disaster relief effort, that input was maximally efficient and effective. But the overall organisational response to disasters, even of the slowly-building kind, was typically reactive. It often depended on requests from the Field Director or other field agencies. In a major emergency, it also depended on the kick start of television exposure, the pressure of British generosity, Oxfam's reputation as an emergency relief agency, and its highly responsive fundraising apparatus.

Oxfam's allocation of aid for 1984-85 described one reality, however much the organisation might prefer another: 69 per cent of its aid went on emergency assistance; social development absorbed 17 per cent, and health and agriculture, 14 per cent combined. This was exceptional; but in the previous year emergencies had accounted for one-third of aid – the second largest category – and in the following year (1985-86) they would account for nearly half. In terms of income, there was no question that Oxfam's major spurts of growth were disaster-related. Just as Cambodia jumped Oxfam into an entirely different financial league, so did Ethiopia; from £23.9 million in 1983-84, income rose to £51.1 million in 1984-85. Although there tended to be a drop-off in subsequent years, most of the growth was retained as donors brought in by the emergency maintained their support.

The reality was that Oxfam's role as an agency for disaster relief was neither negotiable nor decreasing. Historically, this was the context in which Oxfam had become a household word in Britain, and because disasters make news, this was the context in which it was most visible and well-known. Given the parlous state of environmental, economic, and political affairs in Africa, as well as in the turmoil-stricken Middle East and Central America, disasters and emergency relief were bound to be a continuing preoccupation.

From 1985 onwards, Oxfam no longer struggled with the disasters versus development dichotomy. It set up an expanded disasters unit under Marcus Thompson and began to monitor upcoming emergencies from headquarters. Both programmatically and in terms of advocacy with governments, international agencies, and the media, it adopted a pre-emptive approach. It maintained on staff a handful of experienced water engineers and emergency health and nutrition workers ready to go wherever needed; seldom have they since been underemployed.

As the 1980s gave way to the 1990s, as Liberia erupted, Somalia imploded, Sudan disintegrated, as war clouds gathered over the Persian Gulf, as Bangladesh was inundated by cyclonic floods, the agony of millions of disaster victims had never been more compelling. The recognition that disasters must be taken fully and systematically on board has meant that there has not since been a case when Oxfam was caught unprepared.

12

CAMPAIGN FOR A FAIRER WORLD

On 22 October 1985, a crowd of 20,000 people lined up outside the House of Commons to take part in the largest-ever lobby of the British Parliament. Their unlikely cause of complaint: Britain's record on overseas aid. In a year when the British people had given over £100 million from their own pockets for famine in Africa, they had come to express dismay that such a small proportion of the official aid budget was similarly spent on measures to prevent hunger and starvation.

The lobby was co-ordinated by the World Development Movement (WDM) and supported by the aid agencies and churches. Around 15,000 people filed through to the central lobby in the Palace of Westminster to speak personally to their MPs. The leaders of the three opposition parties – Neil Kinnock, David Owen, and David Steel – pledged dramatic increases in aid towards the UN target of 0.7 per cent GNP should they ever be in a position to deliver them. The Conservatives, the party in power, actually felt obliged to make an increase in aid of £57 million for 1986-87 as a result. In a budget of £1,100 million this was not financially impressive, but it represented an important psychological victory.

The reaction to tragedy in Ethiopia had ushered in a mood of concern about world hunger in Britain not seen for 20 years. Much credit was due to Bob Geldof and the 'Aid' craze with which he fired up a new generation of young people: Band Aid, Live Aid, School Aid, Sport Aid. Although British generosity tended to peak in emergency-generated spasms, yet it seemed to be more sustainable, and to be underpinned by a more positive popular attitude, than for many years. The long years of agency-promoted development education in the classroom and the cultivation of interest in the media seemed at last to be paying dividends. Princess Anne's work for Save the Children was also important in lifting a long-standing cause out of its rut. Suddenly disc jockeys, actors, and all kinds of celebrities wanted to be identified with it. MPs of all parties began to respond to the popular mood on a subject usually seen as of negligible political importance. The government, having treated aid with disdain since 1979, began to change its tune.

This was marked by the appointment of the highflying Chris Patten as Minister of Overseas Development during 1986.

With appropriate symmetry, it was at this time of renewed political interest in aid that upon Guy Stringer's retirement Frank Judd, an ex-politician, took over the Directorship of Oxfam. Judd came from an 'internationalist' family; his father worked at the League of Nations Union (precursor of UNA) from the 1920s through to the war-time days when its leading lights, including Gilbert Murray, were protesting the rights of the hungry in enemy-occupied Europe. After six years as Secretary-General of International Voluntary Service (IVS), Judd was elected Labour MP for Portsmouth West in 1966. He served in government from 1974-79, first at the Ministry of Defence, latterly as a Minister of State at the Foreign Office; for a few months in 1976-77 he was Minister for Overseas Development. After losing his Parliamentary seat in 1979, he became Director of VSO (Voluntary Service Overseas).

Thus Judd was not only the most prominent figure to be employed by Oxfam since Nicolas Stacey, but his career had embraced overseas aid in both the official and the voluntary spheres. He had been instrumental in establishing a government fund for development education in the late 1970s, and had done much both in and out of Parliament to promote the cause of British aid. At 50, he brought to Oxfam his Westminster contacts and populist instincts; also passion, energy, and respect for an organisation whose concentrated calibre and commitment he initially found quite daunting. Judd was very much cast in the non-patrician, let's-get-on-with-it, tradition of Oxfam leadership. But, although carefully non-partisan, he tended to adopt a more political line than previous Directors, slipping effortlessly into the role of a peripatetic 'alternative' Minister of Foreign Affairs with a mandate from the Compassionate Party.

Judd had strong views about where he wanted to take Oxfam. From a charitable organisation which had gained its reputation helping the poor he wanted to shift its profile to that of an organisation speaking out for the poor. Oxfam's size and presence in the developing world had grown considerably in the early 1980s in the wake of the Cambodian and Ethiopian crises, and now he hoped to use this enhanced capacity to create a role for Oxfam in the wider task of building international understanding around the ideals of peace and justice in one interdependent world. In his view, Oxfam's programme experience permitted – even required – it to champion humanitarian values in the international political arena.

Judd's earliest field trip as Director of Oxfam was to Central America. In El Salvador, he was much affected by witnessing the damage of conflict to human lives. He also visited Nicaragua, and on his return spoke out strongly against the US government's desire to provide military aid to the Contras. He justified his stand on the suffering endured by the poor as a result of the fighting, and on the fact that the war forced Oxfam to shift its funding emphasis from long-term development to short-term relief.

Such a statement, made as publicly as possible, showed that under its new Director, Oxfam was not afraid to sail close to the charitable wind regarding legitimate lobbying activity. Sincerely believing in the morality of the case, Judd and his advisers hoped that the official weathercock was pointing in a favourable direction.

In the mid-1980s, the slate of contemporary Oxfam campaigning concerns was not primarily connected to political hotspots and civil wars but to the parlous state of many African countries. A few weeks after the October 1985 Parliamentary lobby against famine, Oxfam's second annual 'Hungry for Change' fast took place, involving 50,000 people and raising over £300,000.

Although the overt theme of this campaigning activity was the same 'hungry millions' concern of the 1960s, the subtext was the tangled skein of much more complex Third World issues: debt, aid, and trade and how they interacted with conditions of hunger overseas. By a careful dissemination of briefing notes, reports, and literature of various degrees of sophistication, Oxfam was helping its own supporters to bone up on these subjects enough to mount fundraising and attention-seeking events around them. The fine print of its presentations was quite technical; Oxfam's specialists, employee or volunteer, were equipped to discuss campaigning issues cogently with policy- and decision-makers. But the popularisation of the issues was the key dimension.

The incorporation of aid and trade into campaigning activity had begun with the 'Campaign for Real Aid', in which Oxfam was a leading partner alongside Christian Aid and WDM. In 1981, the publication of the Brandt Commission report on North–South relationships had helped rekindle the dormant debate on development assistance and led to the setting up of the 'Independent Group on British Aid' (IGBA). IGBA's own report entitled 'Real Aid: A Strategy for Britain' was published in 1982. This marked the maturity of the voluntary agencies in demystifying 'aid' – the use of public funds in countries overseas – and distinguishing between the use of 'aid' for investment purposes, and its use for the kind of development that helped the poor.

By this time, the voluntary agencies no longer thought of themselves, as they had in the early 1970s, as mere suppliers of pennies from heaven, calling for governments to 'give more aid' in self-confessed frustration with the puny dimensions of their own impact on world poverty. A decade of 'alternatives' had given them a new sense of self-worth, a body of experience on which to erect their own aid and development philosophy and to evolve a less emotional, more objective and scientifically-based critique of others'. The IGBA report set the agenda for challenging the nature and content of British overseas development assistance over the next decade.

The cornerstone of the critique was that a far greater proportion of government aid should be spent in the poorest countries or on schemes directed at the poor. Not only was this what the public expected of 'aid', but – the agencies argued – it was ultimately the most effective way of investing in famine prevention as well as in international social, economic, and environmental stability. An Oxfam briefing paper of mid-1985 took up this theme. A special target of criticism was the volume of aid used to promote the subsidisation of British exports. Investments in large-scale infrastructural schemes – major dams instead of small irrigation works, for example – were also attacked because their effects were often damaging both to the poor and to the environment.

It was time, the voluntary agencies suggested, that government took on board that modern sector investment of a type suited to industrial-ised economies, while it might apparently coincide with the short-term interests of investors and exporters, was not necessarily developmental as far as poor countries and poor people were concerned. The growing burden of Third World debt, much of which had its roots in slaphappy investment in economically dubious ventures, showed that they had a point, and that even assumptions about the interests of investors were illusory. Change in the way British aid was deployed could not alone alter the pattern of disastrous Third World investment and its negative impact on the poor; but it could make some difference, it did represent some form of leverage with both recipients and other donors.

The following year, 1986, Oxfam focused on the debt crisis in Africa as the theme for the annual 'Hungry for Change' fast. John Clark, Campaigns Manager, prepared a short book: *For Richer For Poorer: An Oxfam Report on Western Connections with World Hunger*. This described in comprehensible layman's terms how the poor were affected by international policies on debt, aid, trade, arms, and agriculture, and how such policies might be reoriented to reduce their negative impact on the poor. The analysis coincided with the call by UNICEF and others in the international sphere for adjustment programmes to take their human consequences into account. In the case of African debt, Clark cited Oxfam's own experience in countries such as Zambia, where the austerity imposed by the government's attempts to meet creditors' demands had forced dramatic food price rises and reductions in health care and social service provision. President Julius Nyerere of Tanzania put things in a nutshell: 'Should we really let our people starve so that we can pay our debts? ... If African governments are really representing their people, they cannot accept conditions that would lead to more hunger, to social chaos, to civil war.'

It was the combination of well-researched positions with the involvement of a nationwide supporter network which gave Oxfam campaigning its edge. To hold Oxfam's intellectual head up with bankers and bureaucrats, and at the same time enable volunteers to engage with confidence in a drive on an issue such as debt, required extraordinary flair. John Clark's ability to render arcane material into popularese was exceptional. The African debt theme was reduced to a neat and compelling formula: 'For every £1 the world contributed to famine relief in Africa in 1985, the West took back £2 in debt repayments.' Although some feared that the message would provoke the public to feel that there was no point in giving at all, the injustice of the equation worked in its favour. In 1987, Nigel Lawson, Chancellor of the Exchequer, put forward to the Group of Seven a set of proposals for reducing the debt burden of the poorest African countries. The debt campaigners claim a share of the credit for Britain's forward attitude on debt relief, then and subsequently.

In 1987, 'Hungry for Change' turned its attention back to aid, with the help of an Oxfam 'White Paper'. The focus was still on the high degree of linkage between aid and exports and the primacy of British commercial interests; in 1986, according to Oxfam estimates, as much as 79 per cent of the UK aid budget been spent on UK goods and services. Although Chris Patten, now Minister of Overseas Development, defended the linkages, the atmosphere around government policy had definitely thawed. The aid budget was rising at a rate ahead of inflation; and the amount of government money available for 'Joint Funding' of projects with voluntary agencies rose from £6 million to £9 million in 1988-89. (Oxfam was one of the four main charitable recipients of grants under this programme, receiving nearly £2 million in 1987-88.)

Their critique might sometimes be publicly brushed aside, but the dialogue between government and voluntary agencies, and their willingness to seek common ground, was steadily increasing. Gradually, the particular merits of NGO programmes, especially their greater capacity than government schemes to promote equitable and sustainable development among the poor, was beginning to command wide recognition. But in the high noon of Thatcherism, this sudden rush of official enthusiasm for the voluntary sector was to bring less welcome attentions: a greater degree of official scrutiny and an incipient desire to contain.

Oxfam's campaigns on aid and debt raised no question of propriety from the Charity Commissioners. As in the case of babyfoods and rational health, the clear intent was to pursue its charitable purposes by a change in public policy; but the self-evidently political as well as informational content of the campaigns went unchallenged.

However, questions did arise over Oxfam's identification with disarmament, which had re-emerged after a long spell in the wilderness during the late 1970s and early 1980s. The disarmament campaigners, canvassing a 'bread not bombs' position, linked their cause with that of world poverty and looked for endorsement to the aid agencies. Brian Walker, a convinced anti-militarist, responded positively. In 1980 and 1981, he gave two £10,000 grants to the World Disarmament Campaign run by the veteran Brigadier Michael Harbottle. The Charity Commission, alerted by an angry Oxfam supporter, found these grants legitimate only so long as they promoted the elimination of poverty in the Third World.

Although this response hardly amounted to a ringing endorsement, Walker read it as support for the thesis for which he gained the approval of Oxfam's trustees. This maintained that excessive world expenditures on armaments negatively affected the lives of millions of poor people by consuming resources which might otherwise have been spent on social and humanitarian activity. In 1985, Oxfam gave wide circulation to a leaflet supporting the Campaign Against the Arms Trade (CAAT), which extrapolated this idea into the slogan: 'The arms trade kills.' In the view of the Charity Commissioners this was a leaflet too far.

At a meeting with Oxfam trustees, the Charity Commissioners suggested that there was no provable direct relationship between purchases of arms and the lack of development in a country since there was no guarantee that money not expended on weapons would be spent for the benefit of the poor. Oxfam could cite field experience to back legitimate protest about the effects of armed conflict on people and projects; but opposition to the arms trade itself was a different matter. However, the Commissioners did not deliver an actual reprimand; merely expressed their reservations. The position they adopted, not only with Oxfam but with other charities associated with CAAT, was that any cause for which a charity campaigned must be directly covered by its main charitable objects.

In September 1986, the Commissioners issued new guidelines to charities about how far they might engage in 'political' activity, elaborating this line. A charity concerned with the elderly, for example, could present reasoned arguments to government about defects in the social security system as it affected the elderly; it could publish material based on reasoned research and direct experience. 'But it would not be proper for such a charity to advocate a particular line of policy or legislative change unless this is justifiable as entirely subsidiary to the achievement of its charitable purpose, and the manner and content of that advocacy is appropriate to that end. And it would not be open to a charity for the relief of the elderly to campaign on some completely different cause like apartheid or defence policy.'

A number of impulses had put the perennially vexed question of the dividing line between permissible and impermissible political activities by charities up for public airing. One was the government's new interest in the voluntary sector; another was the scrutiny to which the official watchdog body on charities was itself being subjected. A 1986 National Audit Report criticised the Charity Commission as lacking in teeth, both in the instruments it applied and the administrative zeal with which it used them. A 1987 public inquiry under Sir Philip Woodfield revealed that British charitable activity was in need of tighter regulation, and the recommendations were made for toughening the law and revitalising the Charity Commission.

In 1989 came a Home Office White Paper. With possible legislation in the offing, the question of a statutory definition of charitable activity (not attempted since 1601 and avoided in the 1960 Charities Act) might again be raised. A case was likely to be made by those who thought that certain charities made too much of their role as analysts and opponents of social policy. Hardly anyone close to the charitable world, including the Commission, wished for such a definition to be placed on the statute book. Its effect would almost certainly be to restrict the flexibility with which legal precedents could be interpreted and reinterpreted in the light of changing social and political attitudes when cases came to court; also, it must be said, in the light of the views of those occupying the offices of the Charity Commission at any given moment. These views were usually kindly disposed towards the charities' tendency to push interpretation outward, but not inevitably.

In 1988, a new Chief Charity Commissioner was appointed. Robin Guthrie, previously head of the Joseph Rowntree Memorial Trust, was welcomed by the charities as 'one of us'. Guthrie took what he called 'a robust view' of matters concerning the overlaps of charitable with political activity. In the 1988 Goodman lecture, delivered at the invitation of the Charities Aid Foundation, he said: 'Charity is a part of the life of the nation. It cannot avoid influencing or being influenced by the politics of the day, whether it be 1601 or 1991.' But while he essentially repeated the position established in the 1986 guidelines, he added a caution: 'If [charities] are working in circumstances adverse to their objects, they should seek to influence and encourage change in those circumstances if they can. But how far should they persist ...? Not very far in my view.'

When they sought guidance from the Commission, the charities were used to being told: 'Much depends on style'; hence the emphasis in the 1986 guidelines on *reasoned* argument, *reasoned* research. Now Guthrie was adding persistence. How far was the 'not very far' he thought they should go? Oxfam was the charity fated to find out.

During the late 1980s, a new tendency emerged in Oxfam campaigning. From debt, aid, trade, from babyfoods and health, Oxfam moved further into geopolitical issues. Such campaigns – as in the case of South Africa – were perceived as extensions of Oxfam's overseas programmes currently obstructed by conflict or repression; hindrances which might be susceptible to pressure from Britain or an international grouping in which Britain played a part, such as the European Community. To begin with, activity was limited to careful research and its dissemination in Public Affairs Unit publications. The first case history was a 1983 pamphlet by David Bull: *The Poverty of Diplomacy; Kampuchea and the Outside World*. This was followed in 1985 by *Nicaragua: The Threat of a Good Example* by Dianna Melrose, and in 1986 by *Namibia: A Violation of Trust* by Susanna Smith. Although the two latter publications generated a few complaints to the Charity Commissioners (who take up issues on a reactive basis), the Commissioners examined the publications closely and took no exception to what they contained.

With the benefit of hindsight, however, these were portents of what was to come. Once geopolitical issues were moved out of the rarefied air of targeted work with decision-makers into the popular arena, and thereby became much more visible, the volume of such complaints was almost bound to increase. For it is very hard to find a place in the world about which any given presentation of facts will not seem politically partisan to one or another ideological, strategic, or 'kith and kin' interest group.

In 1988, a right-wing group called Western Goals UK, with close links to the anti-Communist, pro-Contra lobby in the US, began an orchestrated effort to portray Oxfam, Christian Aid, and War on Want as dominated by extreme left-wingers. They complained to the Charity Commission about the charities' involvement in 'Central America Week 1988', an educational programme, and called in question their charitable status. Given its ideological derivation and agenda, this initiative was not a cause of serious concern either to the charities or the Commissioners, however upsetting.

The following year came another series of complaints to the Commission. After making grants on and off for 40 years to projects on the West Bank of the Jordan, and Gaza, Oxfam had decided to put out more information to staff and supporters about the situation of people and projects as a consequence of Israeli occupation. Central America was not a part of the world which had a strong constituency in Britain, and statements about the situation in that region could pass unchallenged except by fringe extremists. Statements about the Arab-Israeli conflict in the Middle East were quite another matter.

The refugee problems stemming from the creation of Israel in 1948 had been the earliest concern of the then Oxford Committee for Famine Relief beyond the continent of Europe. Over the next decades many grants had been made for the displaced people of Palestine, especially for clothing and vocational training to UNRWA (the UN Relief and Works Agency). There had also been support for agricultural, health, and educational projects in various countries, mostly under church and mission auspices. But as a sphere of importance to Oxfam, the Middle East had increasingly taken a back seat to Africa, Asia, and Latin America.

In 1975, in the wake of the changes wrought in the Arab world by the explosion of oil wealth, Oxfam began to reconsider its role. The expectation was that Arab money would soon take over the role of Western aid: 'The prospects for the poor in the Middle East are a great deal better than in most countries where Oxfam operates,' suggested a contemporary report. 'We should increasingly face south to less developed areas such as Yemen. Otherwise we should only respond to exceptional situations as in Lebanon and the Occupied Territories, and be prepared for emergencies.' This recommendation became the basis of future activity.

At this point Oxfam appointed David Bryer, a specialist in the region, as its Director for the Middle East. Bryer's background was academic, and his inclination was for systematic programming for targeted populations rather than project-delineated, philanthropic pot-pourri. Initially he confronted a familiar constraint: a lack of suitable local partners, especially within the Moslem community. Two key initiatives were a primary health care training programme in Yemen, carried out with CIIR (Catholic Institute of International Relations); and support through the Egyptian Coptic Church to improve the living and working conditions of the Zabbaleen, Cairo's traditional garbage-collectors. The only group in Israel in future to receive support – Israel could not be regarded as a third world country – were Palestinian bedouin in the Negev.

Earlier, Oxfam had virtually phased out its work in Lebanon, also on the grounds that this was no longer an underdeveloped country. But the civil war which erupted in 1975 led to increasing involvement in emergency relief and reconstruction. Many grants were made to UNRWA, church organisations, and the Palestinian Red Crescent, and links built with local community groups. After the Israeli army invaded in 1978 and 170,000 people had fled to Beirut and Sidon, the situation in southern Lebanon became increasingly violent and unstable. The absence of central control meant disruption of health and social services; people were in great distress, yet few aid agencies were prepared to help rebuild camps or undertake rural reconstruction in such a volatile environment. In 1979, Chris Dammers, the new Middle East Field Director based in Cairo, argued strongly that Oxfam must maintain its programme. He felt it important psychologically and in other ways not to desert those trying to uphold community cohesion and build a non-sectarian Lebanese society.

In 1982, when the Israelis launched their push for Beirut in an attempt to wipe out the Palestinian liberation forces in Lebanon, Chris Dammers happened to be in the south when the army swept through. Along with many thousands of refugees, he escaped to Beirut. Within days Oxfam launched an appeal for £250,000, and Dammers was able to give money directly to community, student, and first-aid organisations to buy food and drugs, deploy ambulances and set up blood banks during the siege of Western Beirut. A public health programme followed in the devastated refugee camps around Tyre and Sidon, restoring water supplies and sanitation. Blankets and health care were also provided to 60,000 Lebanese and Palestinians who had fled to the Beqa'a Valley. Seedlings were given out to farmers struggling back to their ruined smallholdings.

In the aftermath of the Israeli occupation, Oxfam attempted to raise international consciousness about the lawlessness in southern Lebanon and the threat to civilian and camp populations. But its most important contribution was still to support those community groups providing health and education services, clearing rubble from camps with unexploded ordinance, running women's income-generating projects, helping disabled people and abandoned children. Between 1982 and 1984, Oxfam committed over £1 million to Lebanon, of which more than half was spent on emergency relief. The Israelis began to withdraw in early 1985. Over the next years, with the state disintegrating and internecine violence increasing, Oxfam maintained an office in Beirut and kept up support. But efforts to move away from damage control into development were persistently interrupted by the endless state of crisis.

By 1986, aid agencies were coming under increasing pressure because of a deteriorating security situation. Oxfam's expatriate Field Director had to leave, but local staff were recruited and carried on. In a divided and fragmented Lebanon, the task of networking between groups and building a non-sectarian consensus on however small a scale was seen as important. This belief was to prove its value in an extra and unforeseen dimension.

In March 1988, Oxfam was suddenly plunged into an abduction crisis. Peter Coleridge, the Oxford-based Area Co-ordinator of its Middle East programme, and the Syrian head of Oxfam's Lebanese operation, Omar Traboulsi, were arrested by the extreme revolutionary Abu Nidal group while visiting Palestinian refugees in Sidon. Their release was the result of pressure mounted by Oxfam's 30-strong network of Lebanese and Palestinian partner organisations. The publicity concerning the two men's disappearance was intense. On hearing of the arrests, members of partner groups set off for Sidon from places as far away as Tripoli in the north. A series of escalating protest measures was agreed, including sit-ins and hunger strikes, to put pressure on the abductors. After five days, to everyone's intense relief, Coleridge and Traboulsi were released into the custody of Mustapha Saad, the Sunni Moslem leader in Sidon.

Of all the communities in the Middle East, the Palestinians in the Israeli-occupied Territories of West Bank and Gaza consistently attracted the highest level of non-emergency Oxfam support. The level of poverty, at least in Gaza, is among the most acute in the region; but just as important a subsidiary reason were the specific needs progressively induced by the 25 years of the occupation itself.

The impact of the Israeli presence on projects long associated with Oxfam and on their political, economic, and social environment had a telling effect on the organisational conscience. A 1974 report by a visitor to the Arab Development Society in the Jordan Valley, still presided over by the ageing but indomitable Musa Alami, recorded the following: 'There are still some 100 boys, but the Society is under continuous pressure from the Israelis. They want to take over the property. Owing to the destruction of the '67 war he can only farm one-third of the land; of the six wells, he now has only the third working. As we drove up the avenue the devastation was tragically plain on every side. A good portion of his land is occupied by the Israeli army.'

Musa Alami talked of 'sticking things out'; and a windfall of Swedish technical assistance helped put the Society's desert holding back in bloom. But the overwhelming tenor of Oxfam field reports from the mid-1970s to the early 1980s was pessimistic about development prospects, reflecting the atmosphere of depression and fatalism which the occupation engendered. The end of occupation was seen as the precondition for genuine development; but in spite of the 1978 Camp David agreement that Palestinians in the West Bank would be granted some form of autonomy, its end was nowhere in sight. The programme of Jewish settlement and the full incorporation of the Territories into Israel's economic and political system moved inexorably ahead, and the human environment became so charged with antagonism that peaceful co-existence and development seemed extremely remote.

In the 1970s, with little community or self-help spirit around, Oxfam mainly supported traditional charitable activities – vocational training, child care, aid for people with disabilities. Some more adventurous projects began to run up against restraints familiar elsewhere. An example was a scheme run by the Mennonite Central Committee to introduce drip irrigation for small farmers in the north Jordan Valley to combat growing vulnerability to water shortage.

Much of the land in the Jordan Valley was poor and rocky. By the late 1970s, extensive well-sinking for new Jewish settlements had drawn water away from the traditional wells of the Palestinian farmers. If farmers were forced to give up cultivation, Israeli land regulations meant that after three years their holdings could be confiscated. Thus drip irrigation, which was able to raise vegetable productivity by as much as five times, could make the difference not only between a good crop and a poor crop, but also between a farmer's title to land and its seizure and loss to Jewish settlers.

Oxfam remained committed to the Mennonite programme, but by the early 1980s technical problems and the high overhead costs of drip irrigation encouraged greater emphasis on land reclamation, terracing, rainwater conservation, and other forms of appropriate small-scale investment. Oxfam also helped agricultural groups market their produce for export, another context in which economic fortunes tended to be dictated by Israeli policy. The retention of their land became more and more critical for Palestinians in the face of Jewish settlement, both psychologically and economically. The alternative to farming was a job across the border in Israel; but wages for unskilled workers were low and Palestinians valued their economic and personal independence.

By 1982, over half the land in the West Bank had been taken over for Jewish settlement. The only recourse for a farmer whose land had been seized was to protest his title in the courts. Oxfam provided support to the American Friends' Service Council (AFSC) Legal Aid Centre in Jerusalem to help contest smallholder land cases as well as cases of harassment. In 1979, a local chapter of the International Commission of Jurists was set up: Law in the Service of Man (LSM). In 1982, Oxfam began a long association with LSM, providing support for an investigation into the legal status of co-operatives, voluntary and humanitarian associations.

By the mid-1980s, a new note of optimism had begun to enter Oxfam's reports. The dark side was an increased level of violence and tension, and reports of human rights violations. But its corollary was an upsurge of volunteer committees of all kinds through which people were shaking off their 'blame-the-occupation' attitude and taking action on their own behalf. These committees represent the most promising and constructive approach to the problems of development under indefinite occupation,' commented Peter Coleridge in 1985.

Volunteer Works Committees were providing help to farmers threatened by debt, land seizure, or marketing problems. Doctors and nurses disturbed by the poor health care in refugee camps and villages and at people's lack of basic knowledge of hygiene and nutrition, set up Medical Relief Committees to run mobile clinics and collect health data. Women's Committees ran kindergartens and women's literacy courses. With such action came growing self-awareness and community expression. By 1986, Law in the Service of Man, now called Al Haq, had gained international acclaim and financial support for its legal rights work. Coleridge wrote: 'The momentum for personal and social transformation now so evident in the area is breathtaking. What is happening on the West Bank and to a lesser extent in Gaza is an increasingly clear focus on real development, with more and more people engaged in serious debate about the issues.'

Towards the end of 1987 the Palestinian uprising, or *intifada*, began. In January 1988, Frank Judd visited the West Bank and Gaza, and pronounced himself 'appalled' at some of the events he witnessed or that were described to him at refugee camps in Gaza. He visited the Medical Relief Committees, to which the crisis had brought hundreds of volunteer doctors and health workers and which had become a mainstay of medical services in the Territories. The Committees responded to SOS calls from villages under pressure from the Israeli army, and carried on their regular outreach clinics as well as running first-aid training in how to cope with tear gas, fractures and bullet wounds. The volunteer teams showed great bravery, occasionally suffering arrest by army patrols on their way to villages where clinics were due to be held. Some in the network were detained without charge for several months.

In spring 1988, four fieldworkers of Al Haq were detained in the wave of arrests undertaken by the Israeli authorities attempting to quell the *intifada*. This event fuelled an ongoing discussion in Oxfam about whether it should develop a communications policy stemming from what had become a £400,000 a year programme in the Occupied Territories, Israel and Jordan. The rationale – that a certain exercise of political power was causing human suffering – was the same as that which had inspired its outspokenness concerning Central America, and its decision to underscore publicly the links between poverty and apartheid in South Africa. Coleridge, and other Oxfamers including Judd himself, found it hard to maintain a sense of detachment from the Palestinian cause when so much of the humanitarian activity Oxfam supported stemmed from or was affected by some aspect of Israeli control of certain lands in the region.

In a paper prepared for internal discussion, Coleridge suggested that Oxfam should establish a 'clear position' towards the Israel/Palestine issue. It should educate its supporters, start to introduce more material on the Middle East into its regular newsletters, possibly as a prelude to carefully circumscribed informational activity among a wider public. In September 1988, this policy proposal was put to Oxfam's trustees, and endorsed by 32 votes in favour with six abstentions. In December, a year after the *intifada* began, Oxfam associated itself with a joint statement from a group of organisations including Christian Aid, SCF, and UNA International Service condemning the closure of schools and repression of education in the West Bank and Gaza, measures which were affecting 300,000 school-age children.

The following year another step was taken towards a wider dissemination of information to the Oxfam constituency about policy and projects in the Middle East. *Oxfam News* of autumn 1989 carried an article describing programme priorities in the Middle East – land rights, agriculture, legal aid, health, pre-schools, children with disabilities – as well as the reasons for its decision to raise the profile of its work in the Occupied Territories. This provoked a flurry of complaints to the Charity Commissioners. The issue had already been taken up in the *Jewish Chronicle*, which had earlier printed passages from the internal Oxfam discussion paper. A *Jewish Chronicle* interview with a bullish Judd in November 1989 was followed by a riposte written by an ex-Oxfam trustee, who was extremely put out by what he perceived as Oxfam's engagement in 'contentious political debate', and determined to make his views public.

By this time, conciliatory meetings had taken place between Oxfam and leaders of the Jewish community in Britain. It had become clear that Oxfam could not present information to supporters and the public which implied identification with the Palestinian case against Israeli occupation, and be seen as non-political by those with pro-Israeli convictions.

Since then, the efforts of organisations in the Occupied Territories to promote community development, protect landholdings, secure markets for agricultural produce, and maintain basic health and education services have continued to receive Oxfam support. Meanwhile, attention to humanitarian problems in the region, courtesy of Iraq's President Saddam Hussein, has spread elsewhere.

On 25 April 1990, the Charity Commissioners dropped a bombshell on Oxfam. They had decided: 'to hold an inquiry into whether, in advocating and campaigning for political change whether in this country or abroad, the trustees are acting in accordance with their trusts and the restrictions of charity law in England and Wales'. The announcement came at the moment when Oxfam was about to launch a popular campaign about southern Africa, guaranteeing that the campaign opened in a barrage of media publicity; but hardly of the kind desired.

A formal inquiry of this kind into a charity's activity in the political arena was a highly unusual step for the Charity Commissioners to take, and it was viewed by the Oxfam trustees – whose discharge of their responsibilities was being called in question – with the utmost gravity. Should such an inquiry find against Oxfam, the trustees would be bound to suffer reprimand. On top of this, they might be obliged to refund to the Inland Revenue money spent on the activities deemed non-charitable, plus any related tax for which exemption had previously been given. This could add up to a tidy sum – for which the trustees would be personally liable. At the worst, if the findings of the inquiry were unacceptable to Oxfam, they might feel bound to defend the charity's reputation and their own stewardship of its behaviour in court. Whatever happened, the publicity surrounding the inquiry could easily sully Oxfam's name in the eyes of supporters and the general public.

In the world beyond Oxfam's immediate perimeter, the inquiry had a wider significance. Its effect was likely to be to define more strictly for charities generally the furthest political limits of 'educational and information activity'. The outcome would be pertinent for all charities who considered participation in public debate on government policies connected to their purposes an important part of the contemporary humanitarian role: a role which the Thatcher government was currently subjecting to other extra strains. Given the government's attitude towards the nation's charitable affairs, the prospect of new legislation, and the desire to avoid a statutory definition of 'charitable activity', all interested parties – including the Commissioners – were suffering from raw nerves and public sensitivity. While the inquiry would demonstrate that the Commission was pursuing its regulatory functions with diligence, it could also become itself the subject of controversy which might redound to the Commission's disfavour.

The process which led to the Commissioners' decision to undertake the inquiry had its roots in the geopolitical campaigning themes which Oxfam had begun promoting in the mid-1980s. In concrete terms, it had actually begun the previous autumn, with the unusually large number of complaints to the Commissioners – around 40 – about Oxfam's 'position' *vis à vis* Israeli activities in the West Bank and Gaza; complaints which the Commission had upheld. Following various exchanges, the Oxfam trustees and the Charity Commissioners agreed to meet to discuss 'matters of mutual concern'. The meeting took place on 6

April, and the Oxfam group included Mary Cherry, Chairman of the trustees, Frank Judd, and Bruce Coles, a barrister and senior trustee. Cherry, with Coles' support, was to prove tireless in the energy and care she brought to the defence of Oxfam in its most serious brush with charitable law.

At this meeting, the Chief Charity Commissioner, Robin Guthrie, indicated that he was not willing to take a relaxed view towards the complaints against Oxfam about overly political behaviour, even though Oxfam believed that most of these were unjustly based on public discussion of an internal position paper on the Middle East which did not represent actual policy. However, the occasion was seen by all parties as an opportunity for a useful exchange of views on the acceptable limits of charitable advocacy. Oxfam knew that it was under scrutiny, but did not detect serious alarm signals.

In late April, mindful of the discussions which had so recently occurred, Oxfam decided to take the precaution of showing the Commissioners the materials to be used in its upcoming southern Africa campaign a few days before this was launched. The campaigning theme was: 'Frontline Africa: the Right to a Future', and the full exposition of its rationale was laid out in a book of the same name. This drew upon Oxfam experience in the Frontline States, showing how the fate of peoples in the whole of southern Africa was jeopardised by the existing political economy of South Africa, and argued that Britain and the European Community should exert maximum pressure on the South African authorities to create conditions for peace and development in the region.

Among the prescriptions suggested were extra aid to Frontline States; cancellation of their debts to Western lending institutions; and the maintenance of economic sanctions against South Africa until apartheid had been dismantled. When the campaign literature outlining these prescriptions was shown to the Commissioners, they took the view that for Oxfam to adopt a public stance on sanctions was inconsistent with its charitable status.

Oxfam's position on sanctions had been elaborated in the period following the 1985 declaration of a State of Emergency in South Africa. Until a change of premier in February 1989 opened the door to a new era in South African affairs, the authorities had pursued an intensive crackdown on all organisations opposed to apartheid. Such figures as Archbishop Desmond Tutu and Beyers Naude, Chairman of the South African Council of Churches, had emphasised to audiences in Europe and North America that public support for sanctions was seen as crucial by those desperately trying to maintain the non-violent liberation struggle inside the country.

Oxfam, which had a more extensive programme of aid to grassroots organisations than any other European voluntary agency, felt keenly the need to express the solidarity its partners were calling for. But cognisant of the legal implications, it reached the view that it should back sanctions only after the British government declared its own support for them, and only after lengthy internal discussion and an effort to research the impact of sanctions on South Africa's poor. The trustees agreed the position in 1987; but not until preparations for the 1989 campaign did Oxfam plan to go public with its view. The line on sanctions was not seen as an important element of the campaign, but an issue on which the campaign had to have a view because it was at the top of the anti-apartheid international agenda. If it was going to campaign on southern Africa at all at this particular historical juncture, Oxfam did not see how it could make 'no comment' on the most publicly prominent southern African issue of the day.

The Charity Commissioners took a very straightforward line on Oxfam's stance. No causal connection could be proved between the imposition of sanctions on South Africa and the enhancement of public benefit or the removal of immediate obstacles to the relief of the poor. In the short term, the imposition of sanctions was likely to lead to more hardship, not less. This meant that, by definition, it would be non-charitable to press for the maintenance of sanctions. Therefore, 'in seeking to influence the Government in relation to the retention of sanctions, the trustees would be acting outside their trusts.' In the light of this advice, Oxfam immediately instructed its campaigning staff to drop all comment on the sanctions issue. But the Commissioners did not decide to drop their inquiry.

Although sanctions and southern Africa was the precipitating factor, the volume and, more particularly, the range of recent complaints had finally led the Commissioners to the conclusion that the whole sweep of Oxfam's campaigning needed review. The complaints that concerned them referred to statements made or activities undertaken by Oxfam on issues related to British foreign policy; all went beyond calls for more or better quality overseas aid, or debt relief for destitute countries. Around the same time as the Commission had been alerted to the *Oxfam News* article on projects in the Israeli-occupied West Bank in late 1989, some protests had also been received about Oxfam's campaign on behalf of Cambodia.

Ever since the effort mounted by Oxfam in late 1979 to bring aid to a country devastated by the Khmer Rouge, Oxfam had retained a very special feeling for Cambodia. Here was a country stricken in a very particular way. Victim of inhuman persecution by auto-genocidal leaders, its ultimate misfortune had been to be 'liberated' by Vietnam, the pariah of South-East Asia against whom China, the US, and their regional allies were implacably hostile.

As a result of the continued Vietnamese occupation, the regime in Phnom Penh was boycotted by the entire Western world. Only aid defined as humanitarian could be supplied by the international community. The Khmer Rouge as a military force was sustained by arms from China, and the precarious internal situation meant that it might yet fight or manipulate its way back into power.

Oxfam's campaign on Cambodia, launched in 1988, had been originally proposed by its own Country Office. Those running the programme felt that the lack of external support for rebuilding Cambodia's infrastructure increased its vulnerability and placed extra pressure on the aid provided by non-governmental agencies such as Oxfam. The campaign drew attention to Cambodia's ostracisation by the West, and to the tacit support this implied for China's ally, the horrendous Pol Pot and his murderous Khmer Rouge.

The campaign was coincidentally well-timed. The announcement that Vietnam would shortly withdraw its troops from Cambodia led to a flurry of diplomatic activity to produce a settlement between the opposing parties, without which the country would almost certainly again be convulsed in civil war. Oxfam capitalised on these opportunities to put across the idea that afflicted Cambodia needed international economic assistance and must at all costs be saved from a further chapter of Khmer Rouge control. European and North American NGO members of the original 1979-80 Cambodian aid consortium joined the campaign to give it international strength and cohesion.

Against expectations, the campaign in Britain was a wild success, more effective than any previously undertaken by Oxfam. The tragic story of Cambodia caught the imagination of Oxfam supporters all over the country – not just the 'Hungry for Change' groups but regular volunteers as well. The annual fast in 1988, in which thousands of people – including the actress Julie Christie – lit candles at a vigil at St. Martin-in-the-Fields and made their sympathies for the Cambodian people known to Westminster, produced £300,000. A *Blue Peter* appeal attracted an extraordinary response, raising £1.3 million from children's Bring-and-Buy sales and enticing Prime Minister Margaret Thatcher to appear on the programme. Although it was unrealistic to expect that Britain, a country with no special links with Cambodia, would break ranks with the US and Chinese position, Cambodia did join the UK foreign policy agenda and some additional humanitarian aid was released.

The campaign came to the notice of the Charity Commissioners in November 1989. A television documentary by John Pilger precipitated thousands of enquiries to Oxfam and a deluge of 16,000 letters to the Foreign Office expressing concern. Discontent was targeted on the UN General Assembly, where a coalition of opponents to the existing regime, including the Khmer Rouge, occupied Cambodia's seat. Thus, the Oxfam campaigning agenda could be said to have embraced notions beyond the specific lack of international assistance to Cambodia. In early January 1990, local Oxfam networks in Yorkshire, Humberside, and Kirklees ran a mock referendum asking the public what they thought of the British government's lack of action on behalf of Cambodian peace and reconstruction. The subsequent Charity Commission inquiry found that the wording of the mock referendum questions 'went too far'. Overall, the campaign 'far exceeded the Commissioners' guidelines' on permissible political activity.

The Commissioners' report of its inquiry into Oxfam campaigning was issued on 9 May 1991. They had not been able to accept Oxfam's own rationale for its recent campaigning activity, set out in a lengthy and carefully-argued memorandum. The report found that, in recent years, Oxfam's trustees had exceeded the limitations placed on them by the restrictions of charity law. They appeared not to differentiate 'between stating a possible solution to a problem in reasoned fashion and campaigning to have that solution adopted'. Some Oxfam campaigns were found to have overstepped the line in style, content, and degree, and the Commissioners ruled that the 'unacceptable political activities of the charity must cease'. As a result, certain items of campaigning literature were withdrawn from public distribution. The actual penalties imposed on Oxfam were, however, mild. The trustees were not liable for financial compensation for breach of their trusts since they had acted in good faith; financial penalties would, however, be considered if further cases ensued.

Since the report and its reprimand, Oxfam has been in dialogue with the Charity Commissioners to ensure that all its campaigning and information work remains within the law. Although the inquiry sent shock waves through Oxfam and the charity world – shock waves which continue to reverberate – its impact has not been ultimately harmful, and may even have had some positive effects. Once the dust settled, Oxfam was able to come to terms with the delineation of what is, or is not, deemed permissible in terms of campaigning activity in the public policy arena. Since advocacy has been acknowledged a charitable activity so long as its target is directly connected with an organisation's existing charitable objects, there is still plenty of room for humanitarian practitioners to participate in public policy debate in areas of their concern. No taint of bad faith clings to Oxfam's reputation; in fact, in the financial year during which the results of the inquiry were published

(1990-91), Oxfam's income reached an all-time record of £69 million. This can be interpreted as a resounding vote of public confidence.

The charitable world as a whole – in spite of some alarm that the official spotlight has been cast on areas previously left conveniently grey – has probably profited from a thorough airing of the issue. Sharper definitions may be seen by some as a restriction; but they can as well be interpreted as clarifications. Those clarifications cannot be said to represent a reversal in the historical evolution of British charitable activity. Charitable status is not to be tackled in the Charities Act; the inquiry certainly helped to show that the Charity Commission can regulate effectively, and thus to reinforce the tradition of relying on charitable case law and its interpretation when arbitration is necessary. The main effect on the overseas aid charities has been to inhibit them from becoming an alternative voice in foreign policy on issues beyond those reasonably closely related to aid and humanitarian activity.

Certainly, campaigning has not left the Oxfam agenda. In early 1991, with public attention consumed by the Gulf War and the disintegration of the old order in the USSR and Eastern Europe, Oxfam ran one of its most successful campaigns to date: 'Don't Forget Africa'. No-one suggested that the prospect of severe food shortage and famine affecting 30 million people in that much beleaguered continent was not a fitting subject for Oxfam to raise. Frank Judd's personal lobbying helped to push the fate of Africa's people up the agenda, in Britain, in the European Community, and at the United Nations. Resources on a scale far outstripping those of the voluntary agencies were mobilised as a result.

The voice of the new humanitarians, on behalf of victims of conflict, against famine, speaking up for the poor, is not about to be silenced. And as environmental issues climb higher up the international agenda for the containment of human crisis, their voice will also increasingly be heard in another public debate: how to promote the kind of development that protects and sustains both our fragile world and the lives of its least privileged inhabitants.

In April 1987, the World Commission on Environment and Development, a successor body to those led by Pearson and Brandt, published what was known as the Brundtland Report: 'Our Common Future'.

In recent years the acute pressure of modern technology and consumer demands on the planetary fabric, an issue which had been smouldering away unobtrusively since the early 1970s, had suddenly erupted as a matter of global concern. Like over-expenditure on arms, the plunder of the environment was often linked with world poverty:

instead of 'bread not bombs' the suggestion was 'bread not waste', or pollution, or the over-consumption of resources whereby humankind squandered the planet's natural wealth when it might instead do something helpful for the poor. Brundtland linked the twin concerns in a different way. 'Our Common Future' stated that poverty was both a cause and effect of current environmental degradation. The insensitive kind of technological transfer which pauperised land, people, and natural systems would lead to no common future at all; only 'sustainable' forms of development could blend the fulfilment of human needs with the protection of soils, waters, air, and all forms of life.

Oxfam's focus on the poorest groups in the poorest corners of the world had necessarily led it into some of the most marginal environments: deserts and forests, mountains and dryland plains. Its concern in any environment was to marshal and top up existing resources – physical, technical, managerial, and financial – instead of substituting misguided, if well-intentioned, outsider money and know-how. Thus Oxfam, like others in the voluntary sector, had put its efforts into 'sustainable development' without any conscious deliberation; here was another case where the 'alternative' way of development was, to the humanitarian, not an alternative at all but the only logical – and practicable – way to proceed.

Among some Third World audiences, an approach which tried to exploit the inherent values of traditional ways of doing things was not always appreciated. Why reinforce the backward and second-rate? Why not bring in the modern and mechanised? Why should only the First World be allowed to enjoy the jumbo-jet economy and lifestyle? But the people on the lower rungs of the global society, who cannot afford pro-cessed fuel, chemical fertilisers, exotic breeds of edible plant or creature, flush toilets, or proper shoes, see things rather differently. Where their activities reinforce environmental degradation, as on the eroded hillsides of Nepal or in the dryland scrub of the Sahel, it is because the adaptive capacity of their traditional systems has been overwhelmed by forces outside their control and no-one has helped them to protect or enhance it. If the Mossi of the Yatenga Plateau can save their soil with lines of stones; or their womenfolk save firewood by using a fuel-efficient stove; or the Palestinian farmers of the Jordan Valley save their land by terracing, be sure they will practise 'sustainable development'.

In some parts of the world, efforts to promote 'sustainable development' confronted the same political obstacles as social organisation elsewhere. One of the many witnesses to appear before the Brundtland Commission in 1985 was Jaime da Silva Araujo, President of the Brazilian National Rubber Tappers' Council. Araujo came from Amazonas, a part of the world where the tropical forest was being felled at a phenomenal rate to open up new land to cattle ranchers. The loss of the Amazonian forest was fast becoming an international *cause célèbre* because of its potentially disruptive impact on the global climate. Araujo and his co-*seringueros* – rubber tappers – were more concerned about the effect on people.

'The Amazonian forest is being destroyed by large projects, financed by foreign banks and planned by Brazilian interests, that do not take into account the living beings in the forest,' he said. '... We live from the forest. We insist that it be preserved. We agree with the Indians, who in our view share our struggle, who struggle for the preservation of the forest, as well as their customs, and their culture.' In their enthusiasm for 'development', the government had overlooked existing sustainable extraction of rubber, nuts, and other forest products. The result was unsustainable development; continuous conflict between the rubber-tappers and ranchers, who seized land which had been successfully managed by *seringueros* and Indian peoples for generations; and who quickly ruined it because its arable life was so limited.

In October 1985, the Rural Workers' Union of Xapuri in the state of Acre, whose chairman was Chico Mendes, organised the first national conference of rubber-tappers. Out of this came a proposal for 'extractive reserves', protected forest areas based on the Indian model, managed by the *seringueros*, which would allow them to carry on their rubber-tapping life, with legal protection from invasion by ranchers. In 1988, the government signed a decree to set up the first 'extractive reserve', near Xapuri. This victory was the fruit of hard organisational work by the rubber-tappers over many years.

Oxfam was an enthusiastic supporter of this long struggle to gain recognition for an alternative, sustainable, way of life. It funded both the Xapuri Rural Workers' Union and the National Rubber Tappers' Council, paying for land surveys, conferences, and meetings; and it helped the Xapuri Union to set up schools, health posts, and co-operatives. Between 1981 and 1989, Oxfam spent nearly £100,000 on these projects. Chico Mendes, by then a figure of international renown, was murdered in December 1988 by a rancher; but his work for the forest people is not so easily destroyed.

If the fate of people living off the Amazon forests, and the preservation of the rights of Indian populations in countries such as Peru and Bolivia, were among the more conspicuous of Oxfam's environmental concerns, there were many projects all over the world whose original impulse was economic but whose context was creeping environmental loss. Among the economic victims of the erosion of soils and the depletion of plant life, the most invisible were women. In most African and Asian rural societies, household utilities and much of the family food supply were provided by women's cashless engagement with river and woodland, field and furrow. As the resource base shrank, they were forced to walk further and expend more energy to collect fuel and water; cultivation and livestock tending became more problematic. Yet because these activities were outside the cash economy their importance was disregarded; helplessly, women felt the environmental pincers tightening around them.

In the 1970s, in the villages of the Himalayas, a movement began among women which at first raised eyebrows but in time was taken in deadly earnest. Women of the Chipko Movement began hugging trees to stop their wholesale felling by timber firms. In the 1980s, Oxfam began to fund exchanges of experience between Himalayan women in India and Nepal seeking to control deforestation. In eastern Africa and in the Sahel, where many environments are vulnerable to soil erosion, women have been similarly mobilised around enterprises which support their domestic economic role, establishing fuelwood lots and tree nurseries, providing creches which free up their time and energy for what is now labelled 'primary environmental care'. The economic role of women, even in notoriously conservative societies, has been carefully incorporated into work in arid lands, a special focus since the late 1980s. Women project officers are now employed in many Oxfam overseas offices to try and redress the marginalisation of women which skewed economic development and environmental degradation have combined to foster.

At the other end of the spectrum, among the expanding city slums whose growth is the outcome of declining rural incomes and which present an environmental nightmare of a different kind, women and their children are also the worst affected by low incomes, crowdedness, squalor, debt, and family breakdown. In the mounting clamour of green concern about tropical forests, ozone layers, species depletion, and global warming, Oxfam's concern is that the lot of people impoverished by a crumbling resource base should not be overlooked. 'Sustainable development' and 'primary environmental care' are ideas whose time has come. In the run-up to the 'Earth Summit' to be held in Brazil in June 1992, they have become the latest context in which the voluntary agencies are gaining ground for an 'alternative' development agenda.

On 2 August 1990, the forces of President Saddam Hussein of Iraq invaded Kuwait. This act of war brought into being an international alliance of a scale and unanimity of purpose unseen in the world since the group of Allies then called the 'United Nations' took on the Axis powers during 1942-45. The subsequent Gulf War was similarly waged under the auspices of the 'United Nations', institutionally created in

1945 to promote peace, but ironically recast in the post-Cold War climate of international harmony as a military and political alliance much like that of 50 years ago.

The first action taken by the United Nations in response to the invasion of Kuwait was to impose a total trade embargo on Iraq. When Saddam proved unamenable to non-military methods of persuasion, an air and ground assault was launched in early 1991 to force the eviction of his army from foreign soil. But although Kuwait was liberated, and although Shi'ites in southern Iraq and Kurds in the north both rose in rebellion, the regime of Saddam Hussein survived. In the aftermath of the shooting war, terms of peace were imposed by the United Nations designed to ensure that Iraq's military might was permanently impaired; Saddam's military machine and arsenal – chemical, biological, nuclear – were to be dismantled in the interests of world stability. To impose those terms of peace, the less visible economic war declared the previous August continued unabated. The weapon used to reduce Saddam to a more profound level of impotence than that achieved by bombs and armour was the application of UN sanctions, or – in age-old terminology – blockade. Because of the degree of international unanimity against Saddam, UN sanctions were – for once – rigorously enforced. The dependence of the Iraqi economy on oil exports and imported goods meant that the blockade was highly effective; by mid-1991 it seemed that Iraq's economy and support system was edging towards paralysis.

Here, too, were echoes of the second World War. In its 50th year Oxfam, along with other agents of humanitarianism, was confronted with the same dilemma that brought together that group of citizens called the Oxford Committee for Famine Relief in a church library one evening in October 1942. The problem then discussed – delicately, because it was controversial – was how to persuade the Allied war leaders that the claims of innocent Greek and Belgian civilians to be relieved from famine overrode military considerations.

The humanitarian case, as with Iraq in 1991, was that Greece and Belgium normally imported up to 70 per cent of their food requirements, and that those who bore the brunt of shortage were the vulnerable: the sick, the elderly, women, and especially children. The dilemma was the same: how to bring aid to these victims without helping the perpetrator of their suffering out of the trap specifically set to drain his power and thereby bring their travails to an end.

In the early stages of the Gulf Crisis, it was the refugees and returnee migrant workers from Kuwait and Iraq fleeing through Jordan who commanded humanitarian attention. Iraq's huge oil wealth – without which there would have been no military adventure – disqualified its citizens from serious relief concern in the pre-fighting period. But after the battle for Kuwait was won, the consequences to the Kurdish Iraqis of their uprising against a far from declawed Saddam quickly changed the agencies' theatre of concern.

As the Iraqi army and airforce attacked their towns and villages, over one and a half million villagers fled in terror into the mountains towards the Iranian and Turkish borders. The spectacle of hundreds of thousands of shivering people stranded on snowbound passes in early 1991 brought the world's humanitarian community, including Oxfam, into action inside Iraq itself. From that point onwards, in response to the needs both of the Kurds in the north and the Shias of the south, Oxfam engineers and health workers have been playing a role in relief and rehabilitation programmes operated under the United Nations' humanitarian umbrella.

If the emergency brought the humanitarians into Iraq, it was essentially the UN trade embargo that kept them there. By late 1991, the prices of basic foodstuffs – rice, sugar, milk – had rocketed to 10 or 20 times their pre-war levels. Much of the medical, electrical, and public health infrastructure was either wrecked by the war, or reduced to disrepair by lack of spare parts and materials for reconstruction. In the south, the disruption of power supplies brought irrigated agriculture to a standstill. In many towns, raw sewage lay in the streets and polluted the water supply. Everywhere, members of a once relatively prosperous population were selling their assets and descending into poverty.

Although food and medical supplies were supposed to be exempt from the trade embargo, in effect only a fraction of the country's needs was getting through. By mid-1991 a calamity seemed to be in the making, a perception reinforced by reports from an 87-strong Harvard University team of lawyers and public health specialists. This study into the effects of the war and sanctions on the Iraqi people was commissioned by UNICEF, Oxfam, and other international agencies. The experts reported that deaths of Iraqi children under five from malnutrition and water-borne disease had risen by five times since August 1990 and that at least 100,000 were threatened with starvation. In the interests of humanity, UN and other voices demanded, ways must be found to allow more aid through the blockade.

In September 1991, the UN Security Council passed a resolution which allowed Iraq to sell $1.6 billion worth of oil. This sum would cover the costs of war reparations and of $934 million (£522 million) in aid. But the terms of the deal, which allowed Iraq no control over the oil sales nor of purchases from them, were too humiliating for Saddam to accept. Nor was the amount acceptable, a view in which the UN Secretary-General concurred. The sum was roughly half the $1.73 billion for aid alone recommended to the Security Council on the basis of estimates drawn up by the UN Special Envoy to Iraq, Prince Sadruddin Aga Khan.

As 1991 drew to a close, the situation on humanitarian relief for Iraq remained deadlocked. New diplomatic initiatives were needed to renegotiate the relief deal so that its terms – the value of oil to be sold, methods of purchasing and accounting for aid, monitoring of its distribution – would be acceptable to both sides. In November 1991, Frank Judd, the outgoing Oxfam Director, now Lord Judd of Portsea, went to Iraq on his last overseas tour on Oxfam's behalf. On his return, he spoke out about the human damage inflicted by blockade in an effort to keep the humanitarian issue before policy-makers and the public.

It seemed that, in half a century, Oxfam had come full circle.

On 1 January 1992, David Bryer, Director of the Overseas Division since 1984, took over the reins at Oxfam. The crisis in Iraq was only one of many humanitarian conundrums Oxfam and its local, national, and international partners confronted. Many examples around the world could be found besides Iraq to show how the deeds of their own and other people's leaders still plunge the most vulnerable of the world's people into misery and want; and how lacking, still, is the political will to recognise their rights and dignity as human beings by fixing – or enabling them to fix – a safety-net beneath them.

It is to compensate for such deficiencies in the affairs of humankind that organisations such as Oxfam exist, and from the injustices of such deficiencies that they derive their moral force. But if, after half a century, the principle at the heart of the Oxfam mission appears stillborn, then appearances are deceptive. Because the deficiencies are immense and the struggle against them seems ever more urgent and complex, the vast distance that principle has travelled in 50 years can easily be overlooked.

In today's world a policy of 'total war', which makes no distinction between combatants and civilians, which metes its punishment upon oppressors and oppressed alike, which accepts by implication the concept of 'an enemy child', would be universally condemned at the bar of international opinion. In 1942, the Allied blockade was hermetically sealed not only against relief for the vulnerable in enemy countries, but against relief for those in friendly countries enduring enemy occupation. Starvation of civilians was still regarded as a legitimate weapon of war, as was mass bombing of ordinary people in their homes.

After 1949, when the fourth Geneva Convention was passed, this kind of warfare was outlawed, and rules laid down for the care and protection of civilian populations under foreign occupation. Since that time, even when the world is united against a Saddam Hussein, our leaders no longer insist that the starvation of innocent civilians under the enemy's control is his responsibility alone and that we – members of the 'United Nations', fellow creatures in the human family – may do nothing to prevent it.

The existence of international instruments by no means guarantees their application, even by those who have sworn to uphold them. There are those who say that the opponents of Saddam Hussein are in breach of articles of the Geneva Convention governing food supplies and medical relief. That they are permitted to say such things without accusation of disloyalty; that they have access to information which allows them to make such a judgement; that teams of distinguished academic experts and television journalists take the 'adversary's side' and record the agonising drama of 'enemy' human beings with whose country we are to all intents and purposes still at war: all these things denote a world changed beyond recognition.

Public attitudes are very different from the days when Churchill ordered the bombing of Dresden and Victor Gollancz called upon Britons to take pity on starving and defeated Germans in the bitter winter of 1946-47. During the Gulf War, the unintentional bombing of civilians and the deaths of women and children sheltering in an underground bunker provoked shame and outrage. Under the terms of UN sanctions, what Bishop Bell's and Edith Pye's 1942 national Famine Relief Committee described as 'controlled relief' enters Iraq, to be distributed by the Red Cross and the humanitarian agencies of the United Nations system. Whatever the shortcomings of controlled relief in the 1990s, it has helped to stave off epidemic and famine; and it has provided a route whereby agencies such as Oxfam can 'breach the blockade' and thereby contribute to the relief of suffering without having to raise their voice or plead their case with the British War Cabinet of the day.

Throughout Oxfam's history, the principle of humanitarian neutrality – human need above the political divide – is a constantly recurring theme. Most conspicuously it surfaces at times of war, particularly in times of war-induced or war-exacerbated hunger: in the Congo and Biafra in the 1960s, in southern Africa, Central America, and Cambodia in the 1970s, in the West Bank and Ethiopia in the 1980s and 1990s. In the immediate future, it may become the basis of new emergency initiatives in Eastern Europe and the ex-USSR. The same principle also increasingly provides the ground on which 'development' initiatives are launched. Support to a rubber tappers' co-operative in the Amazonian basin, a rural association in tribal Gujerat, and a legal advice centre in a South African township are attempts to uphold the rights of the poor against policies or practices which reinforce their suffering. The principle of humanitarian neutrality is the basis for an advocacy role on their behalf, even if others mistakenly attach to the humanitarian defence of their rights a political label.

The ideals of 'internationalism', first articulated by liberal and humanitarian thinkers in the years between the two World Wars, have come a very long way in subsequent decades. Married to philanthropy, imbued with missionary zeal, co-opted by the egalitarian spirit of the post-colonial era, a new humanitarianism has come into being. It has its own organisational entities, its codes of practice, and its authentic vision of how to invest in a better, fairer, and more user-friendly world. Oxfam is one context in which that evolution of ideas and institutions has found expression.

To have played a part, great or small, in the attempt to etch a new ethic into the collective 20th century conscience is something of which to be immensely proud.

EPILOGUE

This account of Oxfam's history has been somewhat negligent in keeping the reader continuously informed of changes in the organisation's size and structure, and has failed to provide a round-up of contemporary vital statistics. The following information may help to fill the gaps.

Oxfam's size: With an income of £69 million in financial year 1990-91, Oxfam is Britain's largest overseas aid charity, and in recent years has consistently been in the top three of the income league of British charities. It has 12 local offices in the UK and Ireland; and 34 field offices in the developing world, 12 in Asia, 16 in Africa, 4 in Latin America, and 2 in the Middle East. Altogether, Oxfam employs about 1,700 people, and receives help from 30,000 volunteers, who run the 850 Oxfam Shops, belong to 'Oxfam Campaigning Network', and provide other valuable support.

Oxfam's structure: In keeping with the laws governing charitable activity in Britain, the ultimate policy-making body in Oxfam is the Council of up to 50 trustees, which meets three times a year. An Executive Committee of the Council meets 8 times a year to oversee the charity's management and expenditure between Council meetings. The Council delegates to other Committees the watchdog role over the Overseas Programme in different parts of the developing world and over the charity's Educational and Campaigning activity in Britain and Europe. Day-to-day decision-making is delegated to the Director and staff of Oxfam, but senior trustees and officers play a close consultative role.

Oxfam has been fortunate throughout its history in attracting to the membership of its trustee Committees the services of many distinguished scholars and veterans of public office in Britain and overseas. The following have served as Chairmen of Oxfam: 1942-47, Rev. T.R. Milford; 1947-60 Rev. Henry Moxley; 1960-65, Rev. T.R. Milford; 1965-71, Professor Charles Coulson; 1971-77, Michael Rowntree; 1977-82, Sir Geoffrey Wilson; 1983-89, Chris Barber; 1989- Mary Cherry.

The distribution of Oxfam resources: Since 1975, Oxfam has included the expenditure of resources on public education and informational work in the objects of its charity, as well as its grants to projects overseas. In 1990-1991, 79 per cent of income was spent on the overall programme; 13 per cent on fundraising costs; 4 per cent on administration; and 4 per cent on shop development and working capital. Oxfam aims to spend 80 per cent of its income on the programme, and usually manages to come very close to this target, occasionally exceeding it.

Of the £46 million spent overseas during 1990-1991, 18 per cent was spent on social organisation, 4 per cent on productive activities and income generation, 13 per cent on education, 9 per cent on agriculture, 11 per cent on health, and 45 per cent on emergency relief and rehabilitation. In recent years, the pattern of expenditure has been geared to spending more on advisory services to local groups and organisations so as to enhance their own capacity for project development and management, and less on large grants for material inputs. In 1990-1991, the total number of projects and organisations supported was 2,900. The highest proportion went to Africa, 61 per cent; Asia and the Middle East received 21 per cent; Latin America and the Caribbean, 16 per cent; the remaining 2 per cent went to projects of a general nature.

Sources of income: Donations to Oxfam from the public, in response to appeals and through the area network, bring in approximately one-third of income. Oxfam Shops raise a further third, including their sales of handicrafts. In recent years, official aid sources have been an important source of funds, through the co-funding schemes of Britain's ODA and the European Community. A ceiling of 10 per cent towards the regular overseas programme is imposed for governmental contributions so as to maintain Oxfam's independence, although additional funds are accepted in times of emergency. In 1990-91, these two sources provided £11 million; a further £3.4 million was received from other voluntary agencies.

Oxfam Trading: Oxfam's trading company celebrated its 25th anniversary in 1990. Since 1965-66, when Bridge was set up with the principle aim of promoting the interests of poor third world producers, Oxfam's experiment in 'alternative trading' has flourished. By 1985-86, Oxfam Trading's annual turnover had reached £2.5 million, and in 1989-90, sales of £8.5 million were achieved from Bridge products alone. Oxfam now purchases handicrafts for sale in its shops and through the Oxfam Trading Mail Order catalogue from over 295 groups in 43 countries; four overseas Bridge offices in India, Bangladesh, Thailand and Mexico provide producers with the services that enable them to improve their products, their manufacturing methods, their business and marketing skills.

Oxfam international: The cooling of relations between Oxfams in different parts of the world which took place in the 1970s when Oxfams in Canada and the US were asserting a separate identity from the parent body has given way in recent years to a global Oxfam warming. Each Oxfam defines its own programme and employs its own field staff; but in many countries there are close co-operative links between the staff of the various Oxfams. New Oxfams have also come into being. Oxfam Hong Kong began life as a fund-raising support committee for Oxfam UK; in 1984-85, the group raised £2 million (in the wake of the Ethiopian famine), and on the strength of this success, became an independent entity in 1988. The latest member of the movement is Oxfam New Zealand, established in 1991.

Hong Kong is the first country to move through the spectrum of Oxfam recipient to Oxfam benefactor, reflecting its own development over 30 years. In India, a different impulse – that of decolonisation – is prompting discussions on whether the staff of the various Oxfams represented there should form their own 'Oxfam', raise their own funds, and gradually negotiate independence from the parent body. This is the first occasion on which the Oxfam policy of encouraging the growth of indigenous organisations and enabling them to build up capacity has led in this, quite logical, direction. A primarily recipient as opposed to donor Oxfam would be a new creation, and the practicalities have yet to be fully explored.

Oxfam's future: At the end of 1991, Frank Judd – elevated to the House of Lords as Lord Judd of Portsea – left Oxfam, and David Bryer, previously Overseas Director, became the new Director. An extensive management review was in the final stages of completion, and the process of reshaping Oxfam's internal structure continued into 1992.

Apart from the need to pre-empt the hardening of organisational arteries – to which Oxfam is nowadays more prone than when it was a much smaller and leaner outfit, along with other British charities Oxfam has also been confronted by the need to adjust to the recession of the early 1990s. The record-breaking income of 1990-91 was almost certainly the product of a series of calamities during that year, including the Kurdish refugee crisis following the Gulf War, continuing crises in Africa, and massive flooding in Bangladesh, to which the public responded with typical compassion and generosity. This helped to override the impact of the recession on charitable returns, particularly on the High Street, where the foreseeable prospects for regular fund-raising are not regarded as promising. Adjustments to Oxfam's structure include a cutback in the number of Oxfam area offices in the UK, with greater emphasis on centralised fundraising. It is becoming ever harder to keep costs within 20 per cent of income.

The trends in Oxfam's overseas programme, towards more investment in local organisational capacity, networking among project partners, particular attention to the problems of the especially marginalised (the landless, pastoralists, aboriginals (tribals), sufferers of poverty as a consequence of human rights violations, inhabitants of arid lands, and particularly the womenfolk in all these categories), are likely to continue. Greater emphasis may be given in future to advocacy of 'alternative' policy approaches, both in developing countries as a part of programming, and among the international community as a component of campaigning.

However, predicting the future directions to be taken by such a volatile and energetic mass as Oxfam would be a fool's game and is not – fortunately – the task of the historian. Judged by the record of the past, Oxfam will remain up among the risk-takers and trend-setters in voluntary overseas aid, both in the donor countries of the UK and Europe, and in the recipient countries of the South. The first 50 years of Oxfam's life have witnessed a great humanitarian adventure, and the next chapter in the post-Cold War world will undoubtedly do the same.

AN OXFAM CHRONOLOGY

1942   29 May: national Famine Relief Committee formed to spread information about the plight of civilian populations in Europe.
January: 2,000 people a day dying of starvation in Athens/Piraeus.
20 July: Edith Pye, Secretary of NFRC, speaks at Oxford meeting.
5 October: meeting of concerned people at University Church. Oxford Committee for Famine Relief formed under chairmanship of the Rev T R Milford, including in its membership Professor Gilbert Murray OM.

1943   October: 'Greek Week' in Oxford raises £10,700 for the Greek Red Cross, including £2,300 from a temporary gift shop (now Dillons bookshop).
Cecil Jackson-Cole, Honorary Secretary, becomes the driving force behind the Oxford Committee's activities.

1942–44 Committee members, with other famine relief committees, lobby unsuccessfully for lifting of Allied naval blockade to permit cargoes of 'controlled relief' – dried milk and vitamin supplements – into Greece and Belgium.

1945   November: the Oxford Committee pledges support to Victor Gollancz's appeal to 'Save Europe Now' by providing food parcels and clothing for the war-affected in Germany and elsewhere on the continent.

1946   January: European Relief Week in Oxford; £6,000 raised in two months.
11 November: first clothing collection depot opened.

1947   By the end of May, European Relief Appeal had raised £20,000 and 800 sacks of clothing had been collected. Aid sent to Quakers, Salvation Army, Save the Children, and other organisations working in Europe.
November: office acquired at 17 Broad Street, Oxford. Shop opened on ground floor during 1948. Full-time paid manager appointed in November 1949.

1948   Spring: first project grant made: £200 to the Friends' Service Council for the Domestic Training College for girls in Salonica, Greece.
September: due to determination of Cecil Jackson-Cole, Oxford Committee decides to continue in existence, although other war-time and post-war charitable committees had closed down.

1949   September: first grants for Palestinian refugees after creation of State of Israel in 1948.

1951   General Secretary appointed: Leslie Kirkley.
First grants made to Greek villages for water piping.
First grants to India: famine relief in Bihar.
Total aid 1950/51: £83,556 (money £16,711; clothing and supplies £66,845).

1953   August: earthquake in Ionian Islands; Kirkley visits and organises relief.
Grant to Korean war victims.
Gift shop income £10,000.
First roving fundraising organiser appointed: Frank Carter.

1954   First grants to Kenya for relief work during Mau Mau troubles.

1954–56 Grants to Korean orphanages and welfare programmes £60,000.
Grants to Chinese refugees in Hong Kong.

1956   September: first grant for feeding in South Africa.
October/November: Hungarian uprising. Kirkley visits border and refugee camps; £20,000 provided for feeding and medical supplies, plus 125 tons of clothing and bedding during following year.

1957   Grants Sub-committee set up.   .

1957–58 Grants made to 27 countries, including relief for refugees from the Algerian war.

1958   Grants Officer appointed.

1958–59 Income reaches half a million pounds – just over half in cash.

1959   First Schools Organiser appointed.
First three Regional Organisers appointed, in preparation for the June launch of World Refugee Year. Kirkley is made Chairman of Publicity Committee. £755,900 raised for the appeal.

1960   Second gift shop opened, in Guildford.
2 July: Freedom from Hunger Campaign launched in Rome by FAO.
July: Oxfam Annual Conference on subject of freedom from hunger.
Grants to 56 countries. Approximately 30 paid staff.

1961   Famine in Congo. £20,00 arrives in mail in one day in response to press pictures and appeal. By 21 January, £104,000 raised.
First Field Director appointed. Jimmy Betts draws up and oversees new Oxfam programme of development projects in High Commission Territories in Southern Africa.

1962   Regional Organiser for Scotland appointed.

1963   Gift shops opened, Leeds and Cheltenham. Gift shop income £79,000.
Northern Ireland Regional Organiser appointed. Now 200 staff, including 40 Regional Organisers supporting 250 Oxfam groups.
Canadian committee set up in Toronto, precursor of Oxfam Canada.
Disasters Emergency Committee set up for joint agency appeals.

1964   Oxfam Belgique founded.
Second Field Director appointed: Bernard Llewellyn, in Hong Kong.
Education Department in touch with 12,000 schools.
Oxfam Activities set up to import and sell handicrafts and market Christmas cards.
Oxfam and other overseas aid charities under scrutiny by the Charity Commissioners; questions raised about the charitable nature of development, as opposed to relief, projects.

1965   Third Field director appointed: Jim Howard in India.
14 February: Oxfam desides to support family planning projects.
March: Oxfam's trustees approve a new definition of charitable objects which resolves the earlier dispute with the Charity Commissioners.

1966   Famine in Bihar. Oxfam sends volunteers to help with feeding programme. Oxfam spends £345,500 on water supplies and child feeding in Bihar between December 1966 and November 1967.
100 Young Oxfam groups. Sponsored walks bring in £50,000.

1967–68   Income over £3 million.
Now 7 Field Directors, supporting 638 projects in 89 countries.

1967–69   Nigerian civil war. Oxfam provides £500,000 to relief work on both sides, and fields a relief team in part of the Biafran territory recovered by the Federal forces.
Over 200 volunteer-run temporary gift shops by 1970.

1969   First Field Director appointed in Latin America: Peter Oakley, in Brazil.
'Walk '69': biggest ever Young Oxfam walk.

1971   March onwards. Bengal refugees fleeing from civil war in East Pakistan take refuge in India; eventually over nine million. Oxfam recruits 250 young doctors and medical students in India and runs programme for 500,000 people, at a cost of £120,000 a month.

1972   New state of Bangladesh created; Oxfam's largest country programme to date initiated.

1973   Drought in Western India: Oxfam sets up network of feeding schemes.
Famine in Ethiopia and in the Sahel.

1974   Oxfam opens waste recycling plant in Huddersfield.
Leslie Kirkley retires. Brian Walker appointed Director.
Oxfam's Council of Management agrees up to 5 per cent of income should be spent on information and education at home.
'Oxfam: an interpretation' statement redefines Oxfam's philosophy as working in partnership with the poor for social justice.
Public Affairs Unit set up to research relevant topics in depth.

1975   Trading Company turnover of £750,000.
Funds first received from British Government's Co-funding Scheme.

1975–76   Income tops £5 million. 600 shops raise more than £1 million.
16 Field Directors, with nine assistants, support 800 projects.

1976   February. Guatemala Earthquake. Oxfam purchases over £1 million worth of corrugated iron sheeting for self-help rebuilding programme.

1978–79   575 shops raise over £3 million.
End 1970s: Oxfam establishes three specialist advisory units at headquarters (Emergencies, Health and Technical Units) with medical and technical staff, and registers of stand-by personnel (nurses, water engineers, etc.) ready to go overseas at short notice.

1979   Campaigns Department established. Area campaigners recruited in early 1980s.
Boat people refugees: Oxfam helps with water and sanitation on the island of Pilau Bidong.
Cambodia emergency. Oxfam and a consortium of voluntary agencies

finance massive aid and establish joint agency team. 1979-1981 over £20 million of aid sent: food, fertiliser, equipment, and vehicles.

Oxfam income doubles to £23.8 million, including £11.8 million for Cambodia. Blue Peter TV appeal for Cambodia helps to raise £10 million through Oxfam shops.

25 Field Offices working with 1,200 projects.

1982 Oxfam publishes 'Bitter Pills', an analysis of how medicines serve, and do not serve, the poor; one of a growing number of authoritative Oxfam books on key development topics.

1982–83 War in Lebanon. Oxfam assists with rebuilding programmes.
Oxfam staff 480, including 66 in Field Offices.

1983–84 33 per cent of Oxfam aid allocated to disasters: drought in north-east Brazil, war in Lebanon, drought and war in Horn of Africa. 'Weather Alert' campaign.

1983 October: Guy Stringer appointed Director.

1984–85 Famine in Ethiopia.
Total income £51 million. 69 per cent of overseas aid on disasters. General income for development work also up, by 38 per cent.
Launch of new 'Hungry for Change' supporter network. Nearly 300 new groups during following year.

1985 11 March: joint agency lobby of Parliament on overseas aid. Over 1 million signatories call for more aid, especially to Africa.
July: Guy Stringer retires, succeeded by Frank Judd.

1985–86 Oxfam supporting 2,400 projects in 77 countries.
726 staff; 41 overseas and 94 in education/information/campaigning.

1986 Gender and Development Unit (GADU) established to research and encourage women's development.

1987–88 Record income of £52.3 million including £4.8 million from the British government and nearly £3 million from the EC.
Oxfam's Cambodia campaign raises awareness on lack of international economic assistance to Cambodia; most successful campaign to date.
Oxfam participated in Comic Relief in February, which raised a total of £14 million.
Oxfam shops total 830 including 13 second-hand furniture shops.

1989–90 Income £62 million. Over £12 million spend on emergencies; Ethiopia, Sudan, Mozambique and Angola.
Staff 1153, including 128 overseas and 180 in Oxfam Trading.

1990 Charity Commission conducts inquiry into Oxfam's campaigning activity. Reports in 1991.

1991 Gulf war precipitates crisis for Kurdish refugees and others inside Iraq. 'Don't Forget Africa' campaign.

1992 David Bryer appointed Director.

SOURCES AND REFERENCES

Chapter 1
1 First minute book of the Oxford Committee for Famine Relief; Oxfam archives.
2 *Pacifism in Britain 1914-45: the defining of a faith*, Martin Ceadel; Oxford University Press, 1980.
3 *War and Society*, Volume 8, Number 2, October 1990; paper by Joan Beaumont: 'Starving for Democracy: Britain's Blockade of and Relief for Occupied Europe, 1939-45'; Department of History, University of New South Wales, Australian Defence Force Academy. [This is the only authoritative account of the Famine Relief protest movement known to the author.]
4 Parliamentary Debates, Hansard; Vols 364-404, 1940-44; (for Churchill's speech 20 August 1940, and other debates; also ration statistics).
5 *War without Weapons*, Marcel Junod, Jonathan Cape, 1951.
6 *The Children and the Nations*, Maggie Black; UNICEF 1986.
7 *An Uncommon Man: The Triumph of Herbert Hoover*, Richard Norton-Smith; Simon and Schuster, 1984.
8 *Famine over Europe*, Roy Walker, Peace Pledge Union, October 1941.
9 *Food Relief in the Second World War*, Roy Walker, Food Relief Campaign pamphlet, PPU.
10 *The Government's Case*, Roy Walker, PPU pamphlet.
11 *Greece in the 1940s*, ed. John O. Iatrides, chapter on the economic effects of the war by Stavros B. Thomadakis; Modern Greek Studies Association 1981.
12 Report of the *Kurtulus* arriving in Athens: *Daily Telegraph*, 27 October 1941, from Ankara.
13 *One Humanity: A Plea for Our Friends*, Howard E. Kershner, with an introduction by Vera Brittain, England, 1944.
14 *Saving a Nation*, issued by the Greek War Relief Association of America; in Friends House Library archive, London.
15 *The Second World War Diary of Hugh Dalton 1940-45*, ed. B. Pimlot, London, 1986.
16 *The Fateful Years, Memoirs 1931-45*, Hugh Dalton, London 1957.
17 *Manchester Guardian*, letter from Gilbert Murray and Mr. Wickham Steed, 23 September 1942.
18 Death toll in Athens in January: *The Times*, 22 January 1942.
19 *Hunger in Europe*, Famine Relief Committee, October 1942; original source, Inter Allied Information Committee Report, No. 2. Friends House archive, London.
20 Address in Oxford by Greek Ambassador's son, *Oxford Times*, 27 November 1942.
21 *The Occupation of Chios by the Germans*, Philip Argenti, Cambridge University Press, 1966.
22 *Sunday Times*, letter by Dr. Cawadias of the Greek Red Cross in London, 11 January 1942.
23 Total deaths during winter 1941-42: *Manchester Guardian*, 11 April 1942; total deaths 1941-44, Iatrides et. al. [11].
24 Gilbert Murray archive, Bodleian Library; letter from Lord Robert Cecil to Gilbert Murray, describing his visit to Dingle Foot on 12 January 1942.
25 *Testament of Experience, An autobiographical Study of the Years 1925-50*, Vera Brittain, London, 1957.
26 *Humiliation with Honour*, Vera Brittain, PPU, London 1942.
27 *'One of these little ones'*, Vera Brittain, London, 1943.
28 *The Times*, parliamentary report 28 February 1942.
29 *George Bell, Bishop of Chichester*, Ronald C.D. Jasper, OUP 1967.
30 *Quaker Relief*, Roger Wilson; George, Allen and Unwin, 1952.

31 *The Friend*, 31 December 1965; obituary of Edith Pye by Roger Wilson.

32 *Food Conditions in Europe*, pamphlet of the Famine Relief Committee, July 1942.

33 *A Year's Work*, pamphlet by Famine Relief Committee, May 1943.

34 Article by Gilbert Murray in *Rotary Service*, October 1943.

35 Brief memoir on the beginnings of Oxfam, Cecil Jackson-Cole, unpublished, early 1970s; Oxfam archive.

36 Newsletters of the Famine Relief Committee, Friends House library archive, London.

37 *Oxford Times*, reports in November 1942 and February 1943.

38 Recollections about Jackson-Cole and the Oxford Committee for Famine Relief, by Raymond Andrews; correspondence in *The Friend*, March 1989.

39 *So Much More to Do*, Voluntary and Christian Service, (undated, 1980s).

40 Leeds and Oxford Greek Appeal literature, Oxfam archive.

41 *Oxford Times* and *Oxford Mail* for October-November 1943.

42 Report of the delegate conference, Famine Relief Committee, January 1944.

43 *Save the Children of Belgium*, pamphlet by Emile Cammaerts, 1943.

44 Eden's trip to Greece and increases in food relief: *The Times* reports, October 1944 and November 1944.

45 Belgian situation and US action: *Manchester Guardian*, February 1944.

46 Archive of the Manchester and Salford Famine Relief Committee, held by Lionel Cowan.

Chapter 2

1 Contemporary press reports; notably the *News Chronicle*, *The Times*, the *Manchester Guardian*. Also the *Economist* and *New Society* for the period.

2 Parliamentary Debates, Hansard, for the period.

3 *The Hunger winter, Occupied Holland 1944-45*, Henri van der Zee; Jill Norman and Hobhouse, 1982.

4 First minute book, Oxford Committee for Famine Relief, Oxfam archives.

5 *Oxford Mail*, 21 January 1946.

6 *If thine enemy hunger ...;* and *Leaving them to their Fate*, pamphlets by Victor Gollancz; Gollancz, March 1946.

7 *Save Europe Now*, Peggy Duff ; Gollancz, 1948.

8 *Victor Gollancz, a biography*, Ruth Dudley Edwards; Gollancz 1987.

9 National Dictionary of Biography.

10 'Food Facts' notices in the *Oxford Times*.

11 Newsletters of the Famine Relief Committee, also called European Relief Bulletin, 1945-47, Friends' House Library.

12 *In Darkest Germany*, Victor Gollancz; Gollancz Spring 1947; also contains copies of the many letters he wrote to the press in autumn of 1946.

13 *Oxford Times* 18 April 1947.

14 *Clothing News*, issued by FRS in 1946,1947, and 1948.

15 *The history of UNRRA*, George Woodbridge (ed); Columbia University Press, 1950.

16 Raymond Andrews, unpublished recollections about Cecil Jackson-Cole and his work; personal correspondence.

17 Interview with Harold Sumption.

18 Minute books of the Manchester and Salford Famine Relief Committee, lent by Lionel Cowan.

19 *Quaker Relief*, Roger Wilson; George Allen and Unwin, 1952.

20 *Charity*, tribute to HL Kirkley, by Peter Burns, 1989.

21 Transcript of interviews with HL Kirkley by Janet Kirkley in 1988; lent by the Kirkley family.

22 Famine Relief Committee documentation, London; correspondence between

Manchester Committee and Leeds Committee, courtesy Lionel Cowan.

23 Interview with Joe Mitty, and archive materials.

24 Archive materials and scrapbooks, Robert Castle.

25 *The Guardian* and *Oxfam News*, obituaries of HL Kirkley, February/March 1989.

26 *The Oxfam Story*, Pergamon Press, 1964.

Chapter 3

1 *The Times, Picture Post*, and other contemporary newspaper sources.

2 *A future preserved*, Yefime Zarjevski; UNHCR and Pergamon, 1988.

3 *Refugees*, UNHCR magazine, November 1986; article by Yefime Zarjevski.

4 *The Refugee connection: A lifetime of running a lifeline*, James A. Carlin; MacMillan, 1989.

5 Lacey, Janet (196?): (title title); Pelican.

6 Transcript of interviews with HL Kirkley by Janet Kirkley in 1988; lent by the Kirkley family.

7 Contemporary correspondence from Kirkley to his staff in Oxford; report entitled *Hungarian Relief Situation* from 23 November 1956.

8 Oxford Committee for Famine Relief; Minutes of the Committee and the Executive Committee; 1949-1960.

9 *The history of UNRWA*, George Woodbridge (ed);Columbia University Press, 1958.

10 *Refugee World*, Robert Kee; OUP, 1961.

11 Frankie Hamilton: Resumé of social activities of AMF Hamilton among refugees and refugee children in the Refugee Camp 106 Enns in Austria, from April 1955 to February 1962; unpublished, written in 1991 for the author.

12 *The Oxfam Story*, Pergamon Press, 1964.

13 *The Friend*, 2 January 1953; account by Lewis E. Waddilove, a member of the of US-British Quaker Mission to Korea

14 Archive material from Oxfam; notably on projects in Korea, Hong Kong, the Middle East, Algeria; including correspondence between HL Kirkley and Mrs. Donnithorne; also between Frank Carter and Mrs. Donnithorne.

15 Oxford Committee for Famine Relief, Annual Reports; 1954-55 onwards; Bulletins (not a complete set) from Issue 7, September/October 1954 onwards.

16 Contemporary press cuttings, *Oxford Times, The Christian, Daily Telegraph*.

17 *Crossbow*, Spring 1958, 'Wanted: a World Refugee Year', article by C. Chataway, C. Jones and T. Philpott.

18 Oxford Committee for Famine Relief News Releases and press cuttings; World Refugee Year bulletins.

19 Parliamentary Debates, Hansard; 1958 and 1959.

20 Oxford Committee Famine Relief Bulletin, No. 16, January 1959.

21 Grants List for Middle East, Jordan, Europe, Hong Kong, Korea, Algeria, etc.

22 Tour reports of Middle East countries; UNRWA file, Oxfam archive.

23 *Two ears of corn – Oxfam in action*, Mervyn Jones; Hodder and Stoughton, 1965.

24 *The Red Cross and Refugees*, UNHCR, Geneva, 1963.

25 Friends' Service Council bulletins and newsletters.

26 Special report on clothing, Oxford Committee minutes, 1956.

27 Raymond Andrews; memorandum on Cecil Jackson-Cole; personal papers, unpublished, on his experiences as manager for Andrews and Partners; correspondence with the author, 1991.

28 Text of a speech made by Timothy Raison at a ceremony in which he and his three WRY colleagues received the Nansen medal from Auguste Lindt, UNHCR; lent by Raison.

29 Save the Children Fund Annual Reports, newsletters, and other

contemporary literature.

30 *Onslaught*, a special publication brought out for the WRY, British Refugee Year Committee; British Refugee Council archive.

31 *We Strangers and Afraid*, Elfan Rees; Carnegie Endowment for International Peace, published for WRY, 1959.

32 *World Refugee Year Finale Programme*; The Times Publishing Company Ltd, June 1960.

33 *Oxfam and WRY, An Interim Report*, March 1960.

34 *Report of the International Committee for World Refugee Year, 1959-1961*.

Chapter 4

1 Contemporary newspapers, including *The Observer*, *The Times*, *The Sunday Times*, *Manchester Guardian*, and the *Economist*.

2 Oxfam news releases.

3 Transcript of interviews with HL Kirkley, by Janet Kirkley, 1988; lent by the Kirkley family.

4 Interviews with Harold Sumption and Joan Rough.

5 *The Congo disaster*, Colin Legum; Penguin Books, 1961.

6 *Oxfam and the Congo Operation*, article by Oxfam Information Department.

7 *Famine Relief Operations in the Congo*, report by Leslie Kirkley, 16 February 1961.

8 Minutes of Grants Sub-Committee and Oxfam Executive Committee, Oxfam.

9 *Oxfam Bulletin*, 1950s; new series, 1962-.

10 Parliamentary Debates, Hansard, 1960-61.

11 *The Colonial Reckoning*, Margery Perham, Reith Lectures 1961.

12 *The New Africa*, Basil Davidson; Daily Mirror Publications, 1960.

13 *From Three Worlds, Memoirs of William Clark*, Wiliam Clark; Sidgewick and Jackson, 1986.

14 Lectures given by Barbara Ward and William Clark, among others, at Oxfam Conferences, 1961-1964.

15 *White Man's Dilemma*, John Boyd-Orr and David Lubbock; Unwin, 1964.

16 *The Freedom from Hunger Campaign in the United Kingdom*, Donald Tweddle; VCOAD, 1974.

17 *The First Five Years: Freedom from Hunger 1960-65*, FFHC Report issued by the UK FFH Committee.

18 *Oxford Mail* and *Oxford Times*, 31 July and 5 August 1960.

19 Gordon Rudlin, interview with the author.

20 *Oxfam's Grants Policy*, a paper prepared for the Executive Committee of Oxfam, 24 April 1961.

21 *Freedom from Hunger Campaign News*, FAO, Rome; August 1962.

22 *Oxfam's Freedom from Hunger Projects*, address given to 4th Residential Oxfam Conference, St. Hilda's College, Oxford, 1962.

23 Country and project write-ups, Oxfam Information Department.

24 Leaflet put out by Basuto Department of Agriculture, 1962.

25 Project files, Oxfam archives.

26 *Drops in the Ocean*, Peter Gill; Macdonald, 1970.

27 Richard Exley, interview with the author.

28 *New Society*, 'Phenomenal Oxfam', Christopher Driver, 3 October 1963.

29 Reports on publicity policy to Oxfam's Executive Committee, Richard Exley 15 November 1962; Harold Sumption and Philip Barron, 15 January 1963.

30 *Two Ears of Corn – Oxfam in Action*, Mervyn Jones; Hodder and Stoughton, 1965.

31 *The Oxfam Story*, Pergamon Press, 1964.

32 Pat Davidson; correspondence with the author.

33 Scrapbook of contemporary newspaper reports, kept by Henry Fletcher; in particular *Daily Mail*.

Chapter 5

1 Newspaper reports, notably *Oxford Mail* and *Guardian*, early 1964. Many cuttings from Oxfam Information Department archive, undated.

2 Oxfam Executive Committee minutes.

3 Report of the Charity Commissioners for England and Wales 1962; discussion in Oxfam Executive Committee.

4 Correspondence between Oxfam and the Charity Commissioners, 1964.

5 *Nathan on the Charities Act, 1960*; Butterworths, 1962.

6 *The Alms Trade: Charities, past, present and future*, Ian Williams; Unwin Hyman, 1989.

7 *A social and economic history of Britain 1760-1972*, Pauline Gregg; Harrap, 1973.

8 *OXFAM: The 1.8 million contribution to the Freedom from Hunger Campaign*; Booklet published by Oxfam in 1965.

9 Oxfam Africa Committee papers, and files for projects in Basutoland, 1964.

10 Parliamentary Debates, Hansard, House of Lords, May 1964.

11 Report of the Charity Commissioners for England and Wales 1963.

12 Notes on a meeting with the Charity Commissioners, and correspondence with the Charity Commissioners, provided to the Oxfam Executive Committee meeting of 24 September 1964 as Appendix A.

13 *Sunday Times*, 'Insight' column, 19 July 1964.

14 Press reports in *Daily Mail*, *Guardian* in late 1964.

15 *The Children and the Nations*, Maggie Black; UNICEF, 1986.

16 *The State of Food and Agriculture, 1964*; FAO.

17 Bernard Llewellyn's field reports, quoted in Council and Executive minutes.

18 *Oxfam Annual Reports*, 1960/61- ; particularly 1964/65.

19 *Already too many, an Oxfam Special Report on Population, Family Planning and Development*, Bernard Llewellyn, August 1974.

20 *Sunday Times*, 'Insight' column, 14 February 1965.

21 Oxfam Council of Management Minutes, March 1964.

22 *Oxfam Bulletin* No 9, Spring 1965; Special Feature on Hunger and Population; Press release from Oxfam, 14 February 1965.

23 *The Observer*, 14 February 1965.

24 *The Times*, 16 February 1965.

25 Oxfam Asia Committee papers, February 1965 and following.

26 Personal correspondence with Harold Sumption.

27 *New Society*, 'Phenomenal Oxfam', Christopher Driver, 3 October 1963.

28 Scrap-books lent by Henry Fletcher and Mattie Townsend; cuttings lent by Joe Mitty, Harold Sumption, and Bruce Ronaldson.

29 *Daily Mail*, September-December 1964.

30 Interview with Leslie Durham.

31 *Oxfam Bulletin*; *Oxfam broadsheet*, Oxfam Information Department (on shops).

32 *Daily Mail*, 14 December 1965.

33 Gallup Poll findings; Oxfam summary, 8 January 1963.

34 Report to the Executive Committee, January 1964.

35 Interview by Elizabeth Stamp with Elizabeth Wilson.

36 *20 ans*; publication by Oxfam-Belgique on their 20th anniversary.

37 Interview with Raymond Andrews.

38 Account of HLK's visit to North America in the Information Department broadsheet.

39 *The origins of Oxfam Canada*, Henry Fletcher, supplemented by documentary evidence lent by HF.

40 *OXFAM-Canada: origins and early history*, Ormond McKague, February 1991.

41 Supplement to a Special Report to the Executive Committee, 16 January 1964.

42 Interview with Jonathan Stockland.

43 Oxfam promotional leaflet and articles on 'Operation Oasis'.

44 *The Illustrated London News*, 16 April 1966; *Sunday Mirror*, 3 April 1966 (John Knight); *Sunday Telegraph*, 3 April 1966, (Ronald Payne). The two latter reporters went on 'Operation Oasis'.

45 Paper (untitled) lent by Peter Burns; 7 December 1962.

46 *Catholic Herald*, July 29 1966.

47 *The Observer*, article by Colin McGlashan, 25 July 1966.

Chapter 6

1 Film made by Oxfam in 1963 for promotional purposes, which used Richard Dimbleby's 1960 radio appeal as a sound-track; *Who cares wins*.

2 Oxfam Grants Lists, 1966-.

3 Reports of the Charity Commissioners for England and Wales, 1963, 1964, 1966.

4 Debate in the House of Lords, 6 May 1964, on Refugees, Disasters and International Aid; Parliamentary Debates, Hansard.

5 Raymond Andrews; conversations with author in 1991 on views and policies of Cecil Jackson-Cole.

6 *Oxfam News*, 1965-.

7 *Oxfam Bulletins*, Information Department, 1965-67, on the India famine.

8 *The Children and the Nations*, Maggie Black; UNICEF, 1986.

9 Interviews with Jim Howard by Chris Barber and the author, 1990-91.

10 *The Conquest of Famine*, W.R.Ackroyd; Chatto & Windus, 1974; Chapter 15: 'Bihar, 1967'.

11 Interview with Tigger Stack, 1990.

12 *Sunday Times* Colour Supplement, article on Famine, April 1967; other contemporary press reports, including *The Times*.

13 *Beyond the Famine*, George Verghese; Bihar Relief Committee, 1967; quoted in Aykroyd [10].

14 *Sunday Telegraph*, 1 October 1967 (Hugo Charteris); *Daily Mirror*, 6 October 1967 (Malcolm Keogh); *Oxford Mail*, 29 September 1967.

15 *25: Oxfam 1942-67*, Philip Barron (ed); Oxfam, 1967.

16 Appeal letter sent out over David Frost's signature, Oxfam archives.

17 *Oxfam Annual Reports* for the period, notably 1967-68.

18 *Food for Tomorrow*, Oxfam, 1967.

19 The background to the Nigerian civil war comes from contemporary articles and analyses from various sources, notably *The Observer* (Margery Perham, Ruth First, Colin Legum); *The Economist*, April 1968 – January 1970.

20 Oxfam has an organised collection of press coverage of the Nigerian Civil War from daily and weekly newspapers and magazines which the author has drawn upon extensively.

21 Debate in the House of Commons, 12 June 1968 on the Supply of Arms to Nigeria; Hansard Vol. 766 243-300.

22 *The Nigerian Civil War*, John de St. Jorre; Hodder and Stoughton, 1972.

23 Tim Brierly; notes from extensive research into his own archive on the Nigerian crisis; letters from Tim Brierly in Lagos, July 1968, to a close relative.

24 'Grants to Nigeria in connection with war emergency', Oxfam Informatin Department, May 1970.

25 *Sunday Times*, 14 July 1968; *Sunday Telegraph*, 1 September 1968.

26 Day-to-day news log, kept by Elizabeth Stamp, Oxfam Information Officer.

27 *Sunday Telegraph*, 13 October 1968.

28 *The tragic years: Nigeria in crisis, 1966-70*, Ola Balogun; Ethiope Publishing Corporation, Benin City, Nigeria, 1973.

29 *Sunday Times*, 28 June 1969, article by Nicolas Stacey; others articles in *Evening News* and elsewhere.

30 *Sunday Telegraph*, 'The fight behind the fight to help Biafra', 2 February 1968.
31 *The Biafran nightmare; the controversial role of international relief agencies in a war of genocide*, John Okpoko; Enugu, 1985.
32 *The Observer*, 14 July 1968.
33 Transcriptions of taped reports from Bruce Ronaldson to Leslie Kirkley, late July and early August 1968; Oxfam archive.
34 Joint Church Aid International; press information service Nigeria/Biafra, Geneva, April 1970.
35 *Sunday Telegraph*, 15 September 1968 (Colin Legum); *The Observer*, 29 May 1968; *Sunday Telegraph*, 21 July 1968 (Douglas Brown).
36 Letters from Patrick Kemmis, November and December 1968, Oxfam archive.
37 *Oxfam News*, reports by Dr. Bruno Gans.
38 Contemporary press reports about the churches' review of their airlift in late 1969 at a meeting in Stockholm.

Chapter 7
1 Various biographies of Gandhi.
2 *Oxfam News*, 1965-72; article by Alan Davidson, following a visit to Bihar in 1968, and many others on Indian and African projects.
3 *India, A Wounded Civilisation*, V.S.Naipaul; Andre Deutsch, 1977.
4 Oxfam Asia Committee Papers, 1964-1972.
5 Interview with Jim Howard by the author; also by Chris Barber, 1991.
6 *Oxfam Bulletin*;project write-ups on India; Information Department, 1966-
7 Oxfam publication: *Food for Tomorrow*, 1967.
8 Oxfam Annual Reports and Grants Lists, 1964-72.
9 *Two Ears of Corn – Oxfam in Action*, Mervyn Jones; Hodder and Stoughton, 1965.
10 *Drops in the Ocean, the work of Oxfam 1960-1970*, Peter Gill; Macdonald, 1970.
11 Interview with John Staley by Elizabeth Stamp, 1990; correspondence and discussion with John Staley by the author.
12 OGAP project files, Oxfam archive; evaluation reports by Alan Leather, 1972, 1975.
13 Interview with Alan Leather by the author, 1991.
14 *Socialism in Tanzania*, Lionel Cliffe and John S. Saul; East African Publishing House, 1973.
15 CDTF: personal knowledge; Oxfam project files and project write-ups.
16 *New Internationalist*, May 1973; issue on Tanzania.
17 *New Society*, profile of Daudi Ricardo, 27 November 1975.
18 *Report on a visit to Chunya district*, Adrian Moyes, 1975; Oxfam archive.
19 Oxfam Africa Committee papers, 1965-75.
20 Oxfam Information department, Tanzania file.
21 *The Children and the Nations*, Maggie Black; UNICEF, 1986.
22 *Statement on East Bengal Refugee Situation in India*, Alan Leather, 1971; prepared for the US Senate Sub-Committee. on Refugees; tabled with Oxfam Asia Committee Papers.
23 *Relief for Refugees from East Bengal*, Oxfam Information Department, 1971.
24 *The Testimony of Sixty*, Oxfam, 1971
25 Press cuttings from archives, and *Oxfam Bulletins* on Bengal refugees, 1971.
26 *Oxfam News*, special issue on the India-Pakistan situation,November 1971.

Chapter 8
1 *The Three Worlds*, William Clark; Sidgewick and Jackson, 1988.
2 *Oxfam News*; reports on the setting up of the Pearson Commission, and reviews of its findings; articles and correspondence indicating preoccupations of the time (1969-71).

3   *The Children and the Nations*, Maggie Black; UNICEF, 1985.

4   Og Thomas, interview by author; also files lent by E. Stamp on Oxfam's own preparations for a political campaign; most material dated 1968 and 1969.

5   References to the James Report: taken from material described in [4]; 'Manifesto' for AWD included.

6   Haslemere Declaration; discussion with Og Thomas, Derek Walker of VCOAD.

7   Stacey: *Oxfam News* articles; interview with Stacey by author.

8   3W1: conversation with Leslie Adamson; *Oxfam News* reports, press cuttings, interview with Stacey, Executive Committee minutes.

9   VCOAD history, taken from material provided by Derek Walker.

10 Stamp: material provided by E. Stamp; AWD and material from *Oxfam News*.

11 WDM history; note provided by WDM.

12 Kirkley's paper to 1970 Executive Committee on 'The Future of Oxfam'.

13 Stacey's confidential memo: provided by Stacey (not available in Oxfam).

14 Many press articles and cuttings, as well as *Oxfam News* articles and a number of discussions with key Oxfam contemporaries, and the interview with Stacey himself and material lent by him have been used to arrive at the picture presented of the Stacey saga. Article in *Sunday Times*, 4 Jan 1970, 'Dissension at Oxfam' was rebutted by NS, and led to a statement by HLK to the staff.

15 Charity Commissioners' report: press articles of June 1970.

16 WDM: see [11], plus discussion with Derek Walker and Elizabeth Stamp.

17 Reorganisation: Executive Committee minutes; Sackur Wood report and working parties (1973).

18 Stringer: *Oxfam News* articles and interview with author.

19 Shoes: *Oxfam News*, press cuttings, Executive Committee minutes.

20 Shops: Executive Committee minutes, *Oxfam News*, interviews with Joe Mitty and Leslie Durham, press cuttings.

21 Growth and development of shops 1970-79; chart prepared by Leslie Durham.

22 Oxfam Trading: Executive Committee reports, *Oxfam News*, *Bridge News*, discussions with Guy Stringer, Bridge information staff, Edward Millard, Jonathon Stockland.

23 'Unemployment, an Unnatural Disaster' by Peter Adamson; articles in *Oxfam News*.

24 Oxfam project write-ups and profiles of projects in *Bridge News*.

25 History of Oxfam Canada, two papers prepared by Oxfam Canada, one of them by Henry Fletcher.

26 Round-up of Oxfams overseas from *Oxfam News* and annual reports; also their own accounts.

27 Executive Committee papers, prepared by Kirkley (1969, 1971) and discussions in Executive Committee; working party for 1974, ditto.

28 'White Paper on Political Affairs' by Meyer Brownstone, 1972; Executive Committee papers; discussions with Michael Harris and Charles Skinner.

29 *Oxfam News*; announcement of Brian Walker's appointment.

30 Transcript of interviews with HLK by Janet Kirkley; interview with Peter Burns in which he credits Oxfam's success in the way described here; obituaries and *Oxfam News*.

Chapter 9

1   *The Barefoot Revolution*, A Report to the Club of Rome, Bertrain Schneider; IT Publications, 1988.

2   *From Three Worlds*, William Clark, Sidgewick and Jackson, 1986.

3   *The Children and the Nations*, Maggie Black, UNICEF 1986.

4   *Oxfam News*, 1972-76; in particular articles by Michael Harris, Bernard Llewellyn, Adrian Moyes, Reggie Norton; critiques of *Pedagogy of the*

Oppressed by Paulo Freire, and of the work of Ivan Illich.

5   *A Picture of Poverty*, Harford Thomas (ed); Oxfam, 1979.

6   *A theology of liberation*, Gustavo Gutierrez; Orbis NewYork, 1973.

7   'Latin American Liberation Theology', Phillip E. Berryman in *Theological Studies*, Vol 34, No. 3, 1973.

8   *Oxfam Annual Reports*, 1966 (Radio Schools), 1967 (*Oxfam at 25, 1942-67*), 1968-69 (Irma Dulce), 1969-70; *Oxfam Grants Lists*, and research by Elizabeth Stamp.

9   Project write-ups, Oxfam Information Department; on Irma Dulce, FASE, MOC, and others.

10 *Minutes of the Latin American Field Committee*, 1969-80; in particular reports by Peter Oakley, 1969-72.

11 *Reflections from Recife 2*, Bill Yates 1976, and other presentations on conscientisation.

12 Adrian Moyes (with Bill Yates), Reports on the integrated development programme in the Lower Tocantins; Latin America Committee discussions.

13 Executive and Council minutes on the row with Canada, see also Chapter 8; and personal discussion with Michael Harris and others.

14 Project write-ups and *Oxfam News* articles on BRAC.

15 *Oxfam Bulletins* on Maharashtra drought relief programme.

16 *May in December*, a report by John Staley on a tour of drought-affected Maharashtra in December 1972.

17 Project write-ups on feeding and medical programmes, Maharashtra 1973; Jamkhed comprehensive rural health project; *Oxfam News* articles by Eve Hall, Gerald Priestland, Ausma Acworth during 1973; *Oxfam News* reports on the Maharashtra campaign.

18 Interview with John Staley by Elizabeth Stamp, 1991; personal conversation with John Staley.

19 Papers of the Oxfam Policy Group, May to December 1974, including Brian Walker's report on his visit to India.

20 Report of the Fundraising Workshop; Papers of Oxfam Council of Management and Executive Committee, 1974-75.

21 'Disasters and Settlements', Reggie Norton in *Disasters*, Vol 4, No. 3, 1980.

22 Project proposals and verbatim reports to the *Latin America Committee* by Reggie Norton, February and May, 1975; interview with Reggie Norton.

23 *Oxfam project write-ups*, Information Department, Guatemala 1 and 12.

24 *Two Ears of Corn*, Roland Bunch; World Neighbors, 1982.

25 *Oxfam News*, for reports on the post-earthquake programme, and on policies and developments in Latin America.

26 Interview with Richard Mosley-Williams.

27 Annual Reports by Oxfam for *Central America and the Caribbean*, 1975-1981.

28 *Reflections on Puebla*, CIIR, 1980.

29 *Nicaragua: The threat of a good example?*, Dianna Melrose, Oxfam PAU, 1985.

Chapter 10

1   Interview with Brian Walker by the author, 1991. Other interviews with contemporary Oxfam staff.

2   Reports of Brian Walker to the Executive Committee, 1974-1980; report on visit to India, 1974.

3   Executive Committee minutes and papers submitted to the Executive Committee and Council of Management, 1974-81.

4   Annual Reports of Oxfam, usually called *Annual Reviews*; 1974-1983, including the accounts and breakdowns of income and expenditure.

5   Items in *Oxfam News*; monthly and later bi-monthly; 1973 to 1980; reports of Oxfam's Chairman to the AGM.

6 On the *New Internationalist*: Executive Committee reports, 1975 to 1978; personal discussion with Peter Stalker, NI editor during the period.
7 PAU: Executive Committee minutes, 1974 and 1975.
8 European drive: Executive Committee minutes, 1975.
9 Wastesaver: Proposals and reports to the Executive Committee, 1975-79; *Oxfam News*; materials issued by Oxfam's Information department; interview with Guy Stringer 1990.
10 Asia Committee papers, 1975-1983; covering policy ideas, individual field reports, project reports, and Field Director's reports to the Committee.
11 Interviews with Tony Vaux and Marcus Thompson, both Field Directors for Oxfam in India in the 1970s and 1980s.
12 *The San Martin Development Program: Lessons in Rural Development*, evaluation by Peter Shiras, 10 December 1978.
13 *Democratizing Development, The role of Voluntary Organisations*, John Clark; Earthscan, 1991.
14 Search: Asia Committee papers; Oxfam Information Project write-up; interviews as above, and by Elizabeth Stamp with John Staley.
15 OXWORP: Asia Committee papers, including statements of objective, on-going reports and evaluations, to 1982; also Information Department project files; articles in *Oxfam News*; discussions with Peter Wiles and Andrew Clark.
16 M.D. Mistry; Project write-up Gujerat 230; Slide tape show *A Day in the Life of Oxfam*, by John Clark, Oxfam; Asia Committee papers, *A Year with Oxfam* by M.D. Mistry, 1980; interviews with Tony Vaux and Pram Unia.
17 *The Quality of Mercy: Cambodia, Holocaust, and Modern Conscience*, William Shawcross; Simon and Schuster, New York, 1984.
18 Vietnam: *Annual Reports*, *Oxfam News* articles, reports to the Asia Committee; project write-ups; extracts from letters to Oxfam from Andrew Clark.
19 Brian Walker's visit to Vietnam described in Director-General's report to the Executive, 21 December 1978.
20 Boat people: Special spread on Indo-China Refugees in *Oxfam News*, August-September 1979, including an article about the island of Bidong.
21 Interview with Jim Howard by Chris Barber, 1991.
22 *The Children and the Nations*, Maggie Black, UNICEF, 1986; Chapter 16, 'The Crisis in Kampuchea'; this chapter based on UNICEF archive sources and interviews with key UN/UNICEF officers involved.
23 'How Oxfam became involved in Kampuchea' in Tigger Stack's Report on the Kampuchea Emergency Programme, August 1983; commissioned by the Asia Field Committee. Restricted circulation.
24 Report by Jim Howard on a visit to Kampuchea and Vietnam, 24 August – 7 September 1979; Oxfam archives.
25 Kampuchea general information file; daily Press Reports prepared by Oxfam Information Department; September 1979 to January 1980.
26 *The Guardian*, report on Jim Howard's visit to Kampuchea, 12 October 1979.
27 Coverage of the Cambodia emergency in the *Daily Telegraph*, *The Guardian*, and *The Sunday Times* through the period until January 1980.
28 Cambodia/Kampuchea Bulletins no, 1 through 14, 11 Sept 1979 to 9 July 1981, produced by Oxfam's Information Department.
29 'A slow boat to Indo-China, or the most expensive cruise in the world,' report by Guy Stringer, 14 November 1979.
30 'The Year of the Goat', a report by Brian Walker of a tour of Kampuchea from 28 September – 8 October 1979; report dated 13 November 1979.
31 Account of UN General Assembly and UNICEF ICRC negotiations, see Shawcross [17] and Black [22]; also press reports of the time [see 26 and 28].
32 Diary of Oxfam involvement in Kampuchea 1979; report to Executive

Committee, 18 December 1979.

33 Chronology of events in Tigger Stack's 1983 report [see 23].

34 Reports by Marcus Thompson in Phnom Penh, 9 October to 2 December 1979 (9 reports); Oxfam archive.

35 *'Relations with the government of the country of operation'* and *'Relations with other agencies in the country of operation'*; Tigger Stack's 1983 report [see 23].

36 *'Kampuchea: Medical and Nutritional Sitrep'*, T.D. Lusty, 12 November 1979 (this report is not in Oxfam's archive).

37 Reports from Malcolm Harper, Consortium Team Leader, Phnom Penh; 16 November 1979 – 15 December;(8 reports, transcribed from tapes).

38 *'Report on a visit to Kampuchea, [3-13th] December 1979'* by Robert Mister.

39 Correspondence of John Saunders, UNICEF Chief of Mission in Phnom Penh November 1979-May 1980, concerning the international relief operation mounted for Kampuchea; papers held by the UN Career Records Project, St. Anthony's College, Oxford.

40 Reports from various Oxfam and Consortium staff members in Phnom Penh, December 1979 – June 1980, notably by Pete Davies, Malcolm Harper, Nick Maurice, Henny Brown.

41 *An Evaluation of Oxfam's Programme in Kampuchea* (September 1988); Hugh Goyder and Josephine Reynell.

Chapter 11

1 *False Start in Africa*, Rene Dumont; Sphere books, 1964.

2 *Africa in Crisis*, Lloyd Timberlake; IIED/Earthscan, 1985

3 *The Greening of Africa*, Paul Harrison; Penguin, 1985.

4 *Fighting the Famine*, Nigel Twose; Pluto Press, 1985.

5 *Changing Perceptions, Writings on Gender and Development*, Tina Wallace and Candida March (eds); Oxfam 1991.

6 Interviews with Brendan Gormley, Susanna Smith, DavidBryer.

7 *Fragile future*, a Report by Oxfam in association with *The Observer*, written by Paul Harrison, Edited by Geoffrey Lean, 1988.

8 Project write ups, Burkina Faso 93, Water Harvesting in the Yatenga (1989); Burkina Faso 123, Village Grain Banks, Yatenga (1988)

9 *Burkina Faso: New Life for the Sahel?* ,Robin Sharp; Oxfam 1990.

10 *Putting People First, Voluntary organisations and Third World organisations*, Robin Poulton and Michael Harris (eds)(in particular, Chapter 11: *Cereal Banks and Food Supplies* by Nigel Twose); MacMillan, 1988.

11 Oxfam Africa Committee papers; Report on a visit to West Africa by Guy Stringer, 1981.

12 Interviews with Peter Wiles and Susanna Smith.

13 Oxfam Africa Committee papers; 1979, 1980, 1981.

14 Minutes of Oxfam Executive Committee, 1975-1984.

15 *Oxfam News*, issues of 1979-1985.

16 Oxfam Africa Committee papers, *A New Strategy for Rural Development in Zimbabwe*, Sithembiso Nyoni, 1981.

17 Oxfam Zimbabwe Annual Reports, 1980/81, 1982/83, by Michael Behr.

18 Oxfam Africa Committee papers, application for a grant for ORAP, 1982.

19 *Oxfam in South Africa*, information brochure, mid-1980s (undated); *South Africa, Oxfam's Role in a Fragmented Country*, 1989.

20 *Frontline Africa: The right to a future*, Susanna Smith; Oxfam, 1990.

21 Talk by Sithembiso Nyoni to Oxfam Supporters Conference, April 1985.

22 Annual Reports for South Africa, 1982, 1983, Peter Wiles.

23 Oxfam's Policy in Southern Africa, paper to Oxfam's Council, 1982.

24 *Oxfam News*, Winter 1985/86.

25 Oxfam Press Release, 'Oxfam Announces Decision to withdraw account from Barclays Bank', November 1985.

26 *Daily Telegraph*15 April 1985, on the annual Barclays Shadow Report.

27 MAP: *Oxfam News*, 1979 seq.

28 Babyfoods campaign; *Oxfam News*, 1980 seq.

29 Interview with John Clark by Chris Barber, 1991.

30 *The Children and the Nations*, Maggie Black; UNICEF 1986.

31 Mbathas: *Oxfam News* and *Oxfam 2000 Newsletter*.

32 *The Rational Health Campaign*, review by Philippa Saunders, 1987.

33 *Oxfam 2000 Newsletters*, 1983, 1985, seq.

34 Project write-up, Philippines 72, Information Department, 1989.

35 *Bitter Pills, Medicines and the Third World Poor*, Dianna Melrose, Oxfam, 1982.

36 Oxfam Annual Reviews, 1980s.

37 *Weather Alert*: special supplement in *Oxfam News*, October 1983.

38 Interview with Paddy Coulter.

39 *'Behind the Weather'* Reports, Oxfam 1984.

40 *A Year in the Death of Africa, Politics, Bureaucracy and the Famine*, Peter Gill; Paladin 1986.

41 *The Ethiopian Famine*, Kurt Jansson, Introduction by Michael Harris; Zed Books, 1987.

42 *Ethiopia, The Challenge of Hunger*, Graham Hancock; Gollancz, 1985.

43 *Oxfam News*, 1984, 1985; Annual Review 1984/85.

44 *Oxfam's Response to Disasters in Ethiopia and the Sudan, 1984-85*, Internal evaluation, Robert Dodd, 1986.

45 Interviews with Hugh Goyder, Marcus Thompson.

46 Executive committee papers, 1984 and 1985.

Chapter 12

1 *Oxfam News*, issues of autumn and winter 1985.

2 *'Oxfam Youth and Education Programme; a General Review 1974-1991'*; Oxfam Education Department Report, October 1991.

3 *Oxfam News*, Autumn 1985, interview with Frank Judd; Gilbert Murray archive, Bodleian Library; Who's Who.

4 Frank Judd, notes on visit to Central America, Jan-Feb 1986; *Oxfam News*, Spring 1986.

5 *Annual Reviews*, Oxfam; 1985/86 and seq.

6 *Oxfam News* Special Report: *'To what extent is British Aid Real Aid?'* February/March 1983.

7 Reports by the Independent Group on British Aid, 1982, 1984, 1986, 1989.

8 Papers of the Oxfam Executive Committee, 1983- ; briefing note for MPs taking part in an H of C debate on famine and debt prepared by John Clark, included in Director's Report to the Executive, June 1985.

9 *For Richer, For Poorer, an Oxfam Report on Western connections with World Hunger*, John Clark; Oxfam 1986.

10 Newsletter of *Oxfam 2000*; issues from 1984-1991.

11 *White Paper on Aid*, Oxfam, October 1987.

12 Oxfam Policy on Arms and Poverty; paper prepared by Brian Walker for Oxfam Council of Management, November 1981.

13 Correspondence with the Charity Commissioners concerning Oxfam and the arms trade; Oxfam statement for the Charity Commissioner concerning the leaflet 'The Arms Race Kills', submitted to Executive Committee September 1985; other pertinent internal notes and minutes.

14 *Political Activities by Charities*, Paper CC9 issued by the Charity Commissioners for England and Wales, HMSO, 1985.

15 *Charity and the Nation,* the Goodman Lecture 1988 by Robin Guthrie, Chief Charity Commissioner.

16 Correspondence with the Charity Commissioners concerning *The Threat of a Good Example* (1985); concerning the activities of Western Goals UK (1988).

17 Grants Lists; Tour reports from the Middle East, 1975- ; *Annual Reviews;* Reports of the Middle Eastern Field Directors and Area Co-ordinators, 1976-.

18 *Oxfam News,* reports on the war situation in Lebanon and Oxfam emergency activity, 1976, 1978, 1982, 1985- ; also on projects in Yemen.

19 Reports on the kidnapping of Peter Coleridge and Omar Traboulsi, contemporary press coverage and *Oxfam News.*

20 West Bank/Occupied Territories: extracts from tour reports, and other Middle East materials, as [17].

21 *Oxfam News* and *Oxfam 2000 Newsletter* for reports on projects in the West Bank, 1988- ; and detentions of project partners; article in *Oxfam News* spring 1989 on health committees.

22 Tour notes by Frank Judd, January 1988; also *Oxfam News* Spring 1988.

23 Oxfam Position Paper on Israel/Palestine, prepared by Peter Coleridge for Oxfam Executive Council, July 1988.

24 Minutes of Oxfam Executive Council, June 1989.

25 Interview with Mary Cherry and Bruce Coles, Oxfam trustees, 1992.

26 Articles in the *Jewish Chronicle,* 10 November and 8 December 1989.

27 Press releases and correspondence with the Charity Commissioners, April 1990; notes on a meeting between Charity Commissioners, Oxfam trustees and senior staff, 6 April 1990.

28 *Cambodia Campaign Evaluation,* Report by Maggie Black, commissioned by Oxfam's Campaign Unit, on the 1988-89 Oxfam campaign on Cambodia.

29 *Oxfam's Public Education and Campaigning Programme,* a memorandum prepared by Oxfam's trustees in response to an inquiry initiated by the Charity Commissioners, October 1990.

30 *Oxfam, Report of an Inquiry submitted to the Charity Commissioners,* 8 April 1991.

31 Press coverage and correspondence about the inquiry, including the trustees' response to the Report of the Charity Commissioners, November 1991.

32 *Our Common Future,* Report of the Brundtland Commission; *A Reader's Guide, the Brundtland Report explained,* IIED/Earthscan, 1987.

33 *Amazonia, Oxfam's work in the Amazon Basin,* Oxfam 1986.

34 *Oxfam and the environment; Oxfam poverty and the environment;* Oxfam papers on the environment; *People and the Environment,* on Oxfam-supported projects.

35 Project write-ups: Brazil: Rubber-tappers in the Amazonian Basin (BRZ 326, 425, 561); Accomplish, Paravet programmes (Sudan 038, 040); *Oxfam in Kenya, Oxfam in Sudan;* also *Trees, a dwindling resource.*

36 *Primary Environmental Care,* a brochure produced jointly by Oxfam and other agencies in preparation for the 1992 UNCED Conference.

37 *Oxfam News,* article on Chico Mendes, spring 1989.

38 *Annual Review,* Oxfam, 1990-1991.

39 Humanitarian Crisis in Iraq, Oxfam Updates, issued regularly during 1991.

40 *The Other War,* TV documentary for Channel 4 in The Critical Eye series, by Tessa Shaw, transmitted September 1991.

41 *The Guardian* (Victoria Brittain, August 1991-November 1991); *The Independent* (Sarah Helm); *Observer* (including article by David Bryer, 15 September 1991).

42 Oxfam Monthly Emergencies Report, issues for 1991.

43 Report on Frank Judd's visit to Iraq, November 1991, prepared by Mark Turpin, Oxfam PAU.

INDEX